M000290580

Law Librarianship in the Twenty-First Century

Second Edition

Edited by Roy Balleste, Sonia Luna-Lamas,
and
Lisa Smith-Butler

THE SCARECROW PRESS, INC.
Lanham • Toronto • Plymouth, UK
2014

Published by Scarecrow Press, Inc.
A wholly owned subsidiary of The Rowman & Littlefield Publishing Group, Inc.
4501 Forbes Boulevard, Suite 200, Lanham, Maryland 20706
http://www.scarecrowpress.com

Estover Road, Plymouth PL6 7PY, United Kingdom

British Library Cataloguing in Publication Information Available

Library of Congress Cataloging-in-Publication Data

Law librarianship in the twenty-first century / edited by Roy Balleste, Sonia Luna-Lamas, Lisa Smith-Butler. -- Second edition.
pages cm
Includes bibliographical references and index.
ISBN 978-0-8108-9232-3 (cloth : alk. paper) -- ISBN 978-0-8108-9255-2 (pbk. : alk. paper) -- ISBN 978-0-8108-9233-0 (ebook) 1. Law libraries. 2. Law libraries--United States. I. Balleste, Roy, editor of compilation. II. Luna-Lamas, Sonia, editor of compilation. III. Smith-Butler, Lisa, editor of compilation.
Z675.L2L38375 2013
026.34--dc23
2013019163

™
The paper used in this publication meets the minimum requirements of American National Standard for Information Sciences Permanence of Paper for Printed Library Materials, ANSI/NISO Z39.48-1992.

Printed in the United States of America

For my mom, Ana, my wife, Melisande, my colleague, Cecile Dykas, and my mentor, Billie Jo Kaufman— I cannot begin to describe the profound impact you have had on all aspects of my profession. I am a better person for the wisdom you shared with me.

R.B.

For Tony and Christopher, who selflessly allow me to spend an enormous amount of time away from them on professional activities. Thanks to all of you who have supported and encouraged me to do more than I thought I could ever do, especially St. Thomas University School of Law, which made it possible for me to contribute to my profession; Roy Balleste, for asking me once again to be part of the great ideas behind this book; and to Gordon Russell, associate dean, professor of law, and director of the Law Library at Duncan School of Law, for always believing in me, feeding me unbelievable ideas, and pushing me to never be afraid of trying new things. And last but not least, immeasurable gratitude to my technical services librarian extraordinaire, Iraida Garcia, who makes sure that technical services runs smoothly so that I can focus my time and attention on professional activities and library administration.

S. L. L.

Many thanks to all who have mentored, encouraged, supported, and helped me throughout my career in law and law librarianship. I have been blessed with wonderful family, supportive colleagues, marvelous mentors, and fabulous staff. I want to say a special thanks to my mother, Martha McDonald Smith, and my brother, Lee Smith. As always, for Victoria and Frank—you make everything possible.

L. S. B.

Contents

Foreword   vii

Preface   xi

Acknowledgments   xiii

Introduction   xv

1 A Brief History of Law Librarianship   1
Robert C. Berring

2 Working at the Law Library: A Practical Guide   15
Karl T. Gruben

3 The Administration of the Academic Law Library: The Glue That Binds   45
Lisa Smith-Butler

4 Public Services   71
Anne Klinefelter and Sara Sampson

5 State Law Libraries in the Twenty-First Century   89
Steven P. Anderson

6 The Curious Case of County Law Libraries   105
Robert Riger

7 Law Firm Librarianship: Money, Dashboards, Strategic Planning, and a Dash of Patience Are What It Is All About   117
Abigail E. Ross

8 Collection Development, Acquisitions, and Licensing   133
Frederick W. Dingledy, Benjamin J. Keele, and Jennifer E. Sekula

9 Foreign, Comparative, and International Law Librarianship   165
Mary Rumsey

10 Technical Services   181
Sonia Luna-Lamas

11 The Evolution of Government Documents: Federal Documents—A Brief Historical Overview   195
Jennifer Bryan Morgan

12 The Future of Law Libraries: Technology in the Age of Information   235
Roy Balleste and Billie Jo Kaufman

13 The Law Library of Congress   255
Christine Sellers

14 Library Consortia in the New Economy: Collaboration to Scale   267
Tracy L. Thompson-Przylucki

Core Competencies of Law Librarianship   283
Top-10 List for New Depository Staff   287
Bibliography   293
Index   313
About the Contributors   325

Foreword

Law librarianship integrates information professionals into the legal field, where they are expected to be interdisciplinary collaborators. Law librarians, perhaps more so than any of their colleagues in other subject-intensive areas of library and information science (LIS), are enmeshed in the legal educations and law practices of the students, professors, and attorneys with whom they work. As such, it is challenging to educate and prepare law librarians for the roles that they will occupy. This requires LIS educators to trust that the foundations of information work will be effectively combined with the knowledge of legal research and the practice of law. LIS educators must recognize the impact that the dramatic changes in technology have had on the practice of law. These changes in turn impact law librarians and alter how they perform their jobs and interact with the public, students, and other legal professionals.

We are living in a time of rapid change that offers unprecedented challenges and opportunities. These opportunities result from an increasingly complex and technologically advanced information society. While this description sounds like a cliché, LIS professionals in all subject areas know this to be true. They encounter and handle the change on a daily basis in their interactions with patrons. In the context of law librarianship, the evolving complexities of the information society come from both rapid advances in information and communication technologies, and enormous changes in how law is now practiced. Information technologies have created new legal issues in areas such as intellectual property, compliance, e-discovery, Internet governance, and privacy rights. Legal professionals, academics, and government entities expect to have access to legal information, as does the general public. The general public now has similar expectations regarding access to legal information, which is perhaps nurtured by Internet sites, such as Findlaw or Washlaw. It is the unique understanding that a professional librarian brings to patron interactions that will be crucial in navigating these new challenges. Law librarians not only have subject expertise, they also understand the structure of information systems, the technology behind these systems, and how to effectively interact with people to help them satisfy their information needs.

LIS education has struggled with how to best prepare specialized librarians in law, medicine, and other subject areas. In usual cases, we take in individuals with varying educational and professional backgrounds

and attempt to instill in them both the theoretical and practical knowledge of LIS. LIS subject-specific courses attempt to resolve the educational issues, but have fallen short of expectations. In contrast to other specialized areas of librarianship, there is a tradition of law librarianship
being more or less a branch of the legal profession. Up to a third of law
librarians will hold the JD degree, usually directors or heads of reference
services, coupled with the MLS, in order to act as both a subject expert
and an information professional. This is not nearly as common in other
areas, such as medical librarianship. Medical librarianship has very few
librarians with an MD or other advanced health profession credential,
although there are a number of medical librarians with nursing backgrounds or equivalent training. In law, the work of the information professional and legal professional is often very integrated; law librarians,
along with their patrons, tend to inhabit and evolve in the same environment, providing law librarians with a better understanding of the changing needs of their patrons.

Despite the numerous and much-heralded technological advances,
there remain many complexities related to the use and preservation of
print materials. This may in fact be compounded in today's digital age.
Many legal enterprises, public or private, generate or require access to a
vast amount of print material. Law librarianship requires archival and
other skills necessary to maintain access to important legal documents,
even if these documents were originally created digitally. The upshot is
that the projected evolution of the law library does not mean traditional
functions will be eclipsed any time soon; rather, the law library will likely
be an environment in which heterogeneous users, needs, materials, and
services will continue to shift. The legal profession and academy will
continue to value the new information professional's judgments and
understanding of the structure of these sources, their relative usefulness
to a given environment, and how best to cull and add value to information retrieved. The research role of the law librarian is likely to expand,
both as generator of new knowledge on the theory and practice of this
information field, and as collaborator on legal research projects.

Roy Balleste, Sonia Luna-Lumas, and Lisa Smith-Butler are each particularly well suited to serve as editors of this text, given the range of
their respective experiences and knowledge, which reflects the complexity and depth of the field. The new edition is helpful to faculty seeking an
in-depth survey of the field to share with students in LIS programs, and it
also provides plenty of updated information for those already working in
the field. In addition to extensive coverage of each of the core functions in
law librarianship, there is ample discussion of how the field has evolved
over time. The varying contexts of law libraries are discussed throughout,
and important updates have been provided in the core areas of the field.
The additional chapters contain essential information for incoming law
librarians. For instance, the chapter on the Law Library of Congress and

the one on state and county libraries provide greater depth and practical insights into the field.

The true future of law librarianship depends upon the readiness of high-quality information professionals to be leaders. It is very clear that not only will information and communication technologies expand our ability to provide value-added services to users, but they will usher in new sociocultural changes that, in turn, will mean new challenges to the legal profession at a global level. The expectation is that librarians will be even more integrated with the work of legal professionals and scholars. Law librarians will serve as collaborators, instructors, and leaders, helping patrons navigate the maze of information and technology.

James E. Andrews, PhD
Director
University of South Florida, School of Information

Preface

The title of this textbook reflects a new age in law librarianship. A hundred years ago, little had been written about the management of law libraries and their contributions to the legal profession. Since then, there has been a gradual but rapid growth of articles and books on various aspects of law librarianship. Today, law libraries exist at an important time in history. It is a time of great challenges, uncertainty, and rapid evolution. The introduction of the Internet and the continuous development of other technologies have created enormous tension in the library community. The world community has acknowledged the challenges that lie ahead in the information-delivery arena. The United Nations World Summit on the Information Society, which was held in two phases, first in Geneva (2003) and later in Tunis (2005), expressed a desire and commitment "to build a people-centred, inclusive and development-oriented Information Society, where everyone can create, access, utilize and share information and knowledge." This is a tremendous challenge, and it is an important goal that promotes access to and delivery of information throughout the world. This book is a small part of that all-encompassing effort.

The chapters set forth here are indicative of the universal role that law libraries continue to play in the legal profession. The book is intended to serve students in programs of library and information science. As in many other areas of library science, law librarianship continues to evolve. Since the publication of the first law librarianship book, libraries and legal information centers have changed dramatically. Law librarians today must master legal materials while balancing them with an understanding of the latest technologies. Topics such as Internet governance and the Law Library of Congress will be addressed, along with administration, consortia, collection development, and others, as we consider their future impact on the profession. The world of law librarianship is entering an exciting time, and one that offers us an opportunity to shape the profession for the next century.

Roy Balleste
Sonia Luna-Lamas
Lisa Smith-Butler

Acknowledgments

This book would not have been possible without the generous support of great human beings and institutions that understand the importance of law libraries and their contributions to society. First, we would like to thank the editorial and production staff at Scarecrow Press. In particular, we want to thank Martin Dillon, senior consulting acquisitions editor, for all his help and guidance during the entire process. We also want to thank Andrew Yoder, production editor, for his valuable assistance during the editorial process.

We are indebted to the following individuals for their support and/or permission to reprint excerpts of their material: Roy Tennant, senior program officer, OCLC Programs and Research; Rosemary Bunnage, estate of Roy M. Mersky, Introduction to *Law Librarianship in the 21st Century*, first edition; Steve Anderson, director of the Maryland State Law Library; James E. Andrews, director and associate professor of the University of South Florida School of Information; Robert C. Berring Jr., professor of law at the University of California, Berkeley, School of Law (Boalt Hall); Lisa Smith-Butler, associate dean and director and a professor of law at the Charleston School of Law, Sol Blatt Jr. Law Library; Frederick W. Dingledy, reference librarian at the College of William & Mary Law School; Karl T. Gruben, associate dean for library and information services, director of the Legal Research Center, and professor of law at the University of San Diego School of Law; Benjamin J. Keele, reference librarian at the College of William & Mary Law School; Anne Klinefelter, director of the law library and associate professor of law at the University of North Carolina at Chapel Hill; Sonia Luna-Lamas, associate director and head of technical services at St. Thomas University School of Law, Miami Gardens, Florida; Jennifer Bryan Morgan, documents librarian at the Maurer School of Law at Indiana University; Tracy L. Thompson-Przylucki, executive director of the New England Law Library Consortium (NELLCO), in Albany, New York; Robert E. Riger, director of research for pushDC.com and author of the blog techbytes4lawyers; Abigail F. Ellsworth Ross, library manager at the law firm of Keller and Heckman LLP in Washington, D.C.; Mary Rumsey, foreign, comparative, and international law librarian at the University of Minnesota Law Library; Sara Sampson, deputy director of the library and clinical assistant professor of law at the University of North Carolina at Chapel Hill; Jennifer E. Sekula, head of access services, and foreign and international law specialist at the College of William & Mary Law School; and Christine Sellers, a research specialist at Nelson Mullins in Columbia, South Carolina. We owe a great debt of gratitude to our contributors.

Many thanks to the law library and technology staffs at our institutions, the Charleston School of Law and St. Thomas University School of Law, who have read, suggested, and assisted in numerous ways in the creation of this book.

Finally, we express our gratitude to all others who have helped in any way during the drafting of this text.

Roy Balleste
Sonia Luna-Lamas
Lisa Smith-Butler

Introduction

This introduction was drafted by Professor Roy Mersky in 2007 for the first edition of Law Librarianship in the Twenty-First Century. *We want to thank his estate for allowing us to reprint it here. Although Professor Mersky is no longer with us, many of his comments and ideas in this introduction continue to be timely and helpful. Shortly before his death in 2008, he completed an oral history for the University of Texas at Austin and said this: "Technology is changing everything and the librarians aren't librarians anymore. They're information specialists. We concentrate on empirical skills and empirical research, statistics, math. Those are the kinds of people that are going to be working in the future. And they are going to be the gatekeepers to all this online stuff for the faculty and they're going to be knowledgeable in that."*

(IN MEMORIAM)

Recently I addressed two librarian groups, the American Association of Law Libraries (AALL) Computer Services Interest Section (CIS) and attendees of the summer Center for Computer-Assisted Legal Instruction (CALI) conference.[1] At both of these gatherings, I talked about the future of law librarianship. The title of my presentation at the CIS gathering was "The Future of Law Librarianship: There Is None," and at CALI, "Look, Ma, No Books!" Both presentations were meant to sound controversial in order to encourage discussion and thought beyond the everyday issues facing the profession.

In this introduction, I am excited about the opportunity to provide some insight into opportunities for a career in law librarianship. To me, there is nothing controversial about the future of law librarianship. The profession is increasingly important and interesting, but there are matters that need to be considered when one enters the field. In 1980 Virginia Wise of Harvard Law School and I contributed a chapter titled "Law Librarianship," for the publication *Special Librarianship: A New Reader.*[2] We wrote that law occupies a unique position in American society, and that the complexity of and the rapid changes in the legal profession have generated a new specialization of experts on legal information sources. When the first meeting of the American Association of Law Libraries was held in 1906, there were twenty-six members. There were 2,000 in 1980, and now there is a membership of over 5,000. The stated purpose of our article was to provide an introduction and an invitation to the profession of law librarianship.

We attempted to answer the questions: Why become a law librarian? What does a law librarian do? What are the qualifications needed to be a law librarian? What are the opportunities for professional growth? To answer these questions, we considered the importance of law in contemporary society.

Law is a method of peaceful revolution that affects everyone on a daily basis. It determines what time you get up (statutorily imposed by daylight savings time), what you eat (Food and Drug Administration regulations), and whether your sleep will be undisturbed by a burglar (sanctions of the common law of crime). Whether a law librarian is doing research for an attorney involved in a products liability suit that ultimately results in a defective item being removed from the market, is helping to draft a statute that requires seat belts, or is finding a piece of information that tips the vote in an important Supreme Court case, law librarians can affect the quality of our society in a tangible way. These are exciting opportunities. Since September 11, 2001, important principles have been at stake, including the right of law enforcement officials to use the Patriot Act to demand library records in counterterrorist investigations.[3]

The legal and law librarianship professions are constantly changing. Intelligent and well-educated persons are needed to keep up with the volume of legal material being generated, the increased access to information resources, the complexity of the digital information age, and the impact of information technology on library services and activities. Thinking back on my career, I remember that when I entered the profession in the 1950s, "chip" meant a piece of wood, "hardware" was found in a general store, and "software" was not even a word. Reading library literature, I am reminded that currently there is a new library vocabulary, suggesting new intellectual opportunities for law librarians: podcasting, licensing contracts, copyright clearance centers, and open URL link resolvers. Additionally, there are evolving collection-management strategies: consortia, resource sharing, preservation, conservation, document-delivery services, and e-books. Law librarians must know how to integrate bibliographic knowledge with technical, reference, and instructional proficiency.

Law libraries of the future will look very different from our prototypical law library today. I foresee a time when a large percentage of academic law libraries will maintain a basic collection of primary materials and will contribute to funding a regional collection for secondary resources and for regional jurisdictions. Some libraries may be bookless. One of the main libraries on the University of Texas campus has been converted to a multidepartment information center.[4] At the same time that that university is creating the bookless information commons, it is entering into consortium arrangements with other public and private universities within the state of Texas to develop a digital library of the institutions' work products.[5] Google announced in December 2004 that it was indexing all or part of the book collections of several major research libraries, and indicated that the company hoped to create a virtual card catalog of all books in all languages.[6]

If, as I predict, the law library of the future will, in the majority of situations, contain only a core collection of hard volumes, librarians and IT professionals will continue to be expected to enable access to an increasingly wide variety of interdisciplinary and international materials. The role of the law librarian as an instructor will be more demanding, and the roles of the librarian and computer specialist as creators of resources that serve the particular and very specialized needs of their institution's user group will expand as well.

What are the problems within the profession? Newly appointed academic law library directors are less likely to have tenure status. The title of assistant or associate dean of information or technology places law librarians in the same category as career services administrators or admissions directors. Library budgets are shrinking; salaries are often lower than in secular organizations. Law library professionals are more frequently put in the position of fighting for every dollar. An American Library Association (ALA) task force in 2002 collected data and reported its findings, and among the important issues facing academic law libraries were topics similar to those in law librarianship: recruitment, education, and retention of librarians; impact of information technology on library services; creation, control, and preservation of digital resources; chaos in scholarly communication; and funding.[7]

Issues in scholarly and legal publishing are creating concern about publisher mergers, increasing the concentration of legal journals in the hands of a few publishers and the effects of price escalation on law library budgets. Privatization of information troubles law librarians.[8] The Government Printing Office and the Federal Library Depository Program proposed a budget for fiscal year 2006 that provides for electronic dissemination of 95 percent of the documents currently distributed to depository libraries, but as Victoria Trotter, the outgoing president of AALL reported,[9] the budget does not provide funding requests for authentication, permanent public access, or preservations mechanisms so important to the successful adoption of an electronic government information model. The guidance and input of the library community is increasingly important in assisting these government agencies to make these documents available to the public through documentary libraries.

So, is there a future in law librarianship? To rebut my own statement that "there is no future in law librarianship," the profession is increasingly important, and the future is bright with tremendous prospects for those with degrees in library science, law, computer science, language, management, and other specialized credentials. The challenge to emerging and veteran law librarians is to take a hard look at what we are doing and how we are doing it. There is a need to educate new law librarians and to reeducate existing librarians with skills and knowledge to meet the challenges of the profession and to ensure a proactive approach to services.

As you read the articles in this publication, *Law Librarianship in the Twenty-First Century*, I am confident that you will be struck—as I was— by the extraordinary changes and advances in our profession. There are magnificent opportunities for a new generation of law librarians. The work of a law librarian is indispensable in our legal and educational system. And perhaps the best incentive to be a law librarian is the satisfaction of knowing that one's work is stimulating, exciting, and challenging.

An added incentive is in earning the gratitude of one's constituencies. My friend the Honorable Justice Michael Kirby, justice of the High Court of Australia, expressed his appreciation for the profession in his welcome to participants in the High Court Symposium:

> I take this occasion to say thank you to all librarians who have been such special friends, colleagues and guides in my professional life: a warm appreciation. We should say it loud and say it often. Through you, I express the gratitude of generations of judges. Your work is indispensable. In the complexities of life it will become more so. It will change in delivery. It will be enhanced by technology. But it will always be there and essential to the idea that human beings can attain the noble goal of equal justice under the law for all. [10]

Roy M. Mersky, professor
Harry M. Reasoner Regents Chair in Law and director of research
Jamail Center for Legal Research
The University of Texas at Austin School of Law
(1925–2008)

NOTES

1. American Association of Law Libraries annual conference, San Antonio, Texas, July 18, 2005, and CALI annual conference, Chicago, Illinois, June 10, 2005.

2. Roy M. Mersky and Virginia Wise, "Law Librarianship," in *Special Librarianship: A New Reader* (Metuchen, NJ: Scarecrow Press, 1980), 306–14.

3. Alison Leigh Cowan, "At Stake in the Court: The Use of the Patriot Act to Get Library Records," *New York Times*, September 1, 2005.

4. "Packing Up the Books," *Chronicle of Higher Education*, July 1, 2005.

5. "At Year's End, Facts at Your Fingertips," *Austin American Statesman*, July 13, 2005.

6. "Libraries Concerned about What Next Chapter Will Be," *Austin American Statesman*, July 24, 2005.

7. "Top Issues Facing Academic Libraries: A Report of the Focus on the Future Task Force," *College and Research News* 63, no. 10 (November 2002).

8. Lee C. Van Orsdel, "Antitrust Issues in Scholarly and Legal Publishing: Report on an Invitational Symposium in Washington, D.C.," *College and Research Libraries News* (May 2005): 374–77.

9. Victoria Trotter, "Marching On . . .," *AALL Spectrum* (March 2005).

10. "A Law Librarian's Love Affair," *Australian Law Librarian* 4 (Summer 2004): 7–11.

ONE

A Brief History of Law Librarianship

Robert C. Berring

INTRODUCTION

Sketching out the history of law librarianship is no simple task.[1] First, one must confront the inevitable hurdle of defining just what law librarianship is. Does it refer to anyone who works with legal materials? Does one have to work in a law school library? Are law firm and court librarians a separate group or part of the same professional cadre? Does one have to have a degree from a library school to qualify? Must one have a law degree? Are law librarians different from other librarians? Form follows function in pursuing these questions. There is no definition of law librarianship that cannot be disputed or contested. Given the nature of the law, perhaps this is as it should be. Still, we need to find some way of finding the heart of the profession of law librarianship so that we can answer the questions posed above.

One could follow any of a number of pathways to locate the heart and soul of law librarianship. The American Association of Law Libraries (AALL) provides an institutional framework for studying the profession. Biographical glimpses of the men and women who played crucial roles in its development could be equally enlightening. Probing the line that separates law librarianship from the more general profession of librarianship could also be fruitful; in the alternative, one could also study the institutions for which law librarians worked. Tracing the development of law schools, courts, law firms, and membership libraries could provide another avenue for examination. As with so much in life, the question of how to organize the discussion proves crucial to the dimensions of the discussion itself.

In the end I chose an organizational principle that touches upon all of the factors above, yet reaches beyond them. I will mix in each of the factors enumerated above, but will approach the profession of law librarianship with special focus on the way that the content, format, and research practices of legal information have shaped the profession. Instead of following the money, we will follow the legal information.

Law librarianship has always been closely tied to the nature of legal information. The form in which legal authority is published and the way in which it is used have dictated the dimensions of the profession from the start. No matter in what setting a law librarian worked, her duties were formed by the information that she was manipulating. The special nature of legal information and legal authority brings this home with emphasis. Legal researchers search for statements of the positive law. This is different than most social science disciplines, in which one searches for guidance or opinion. Legal researchers believe that they can find the truth.[2] When one combines this with the fact that the law has a profound impact on American society, the importance of legal information is undeniable. Further, legal information sources are arcane and highly specialized. Using legal information as the touchstone, we can center our discussion around five eras of legal information: the classic period, the setting of the stage, the field as it matures through the growth of law school libraries, its depth and expansion into law firm libraries, the growth of law firm libraries, and the current questions facing legal librarians, questions that we still encounter today.

Caveat

Before beginning, I issue this caveat: what follows is no more than an overview of the history of law librarianship, and a brief and highly subjective one at that. Fortunately for the reader who wishes to delve deeper into the questions at hand, 2006 was the centennial anniversary of the American Association of Law Libraries (AALL). In conjunction with this celebration, the 2006 annual convention of the AALL focused on the history of the association. And throughout that year, the *Law Library Journal* (LLJ) ran articles outlining AALL history, the reminiscences of past leaders, and biographical sketches of historical figures. This material provides a mother lode of source material for anyone who wants to explore further.

Even before the centennial celebrations began, a great deal of scholarly work had been done on the history of law librarianship. Professor Frank Houdek of the Law School at Southern Illinois Law School is both past editor of LLJ and the coordinator of many of the historical projects.

Professor Houdek also edits a loose-leaf publication titled *AALL Reference Book: A Compendium of Facts, Figures, and Historical Information about the American Association of Law Libraries*. This publication began in 1994 and is updated regularly. It contains a plethora of sources on the progress of law librarianship, complete with a timeline and a truly comprehensive bibliography. Anyone who wishes to dig deeply into the history of law librarianship should start there, and indeed should be in contact with Professor Houdek. The best research advice is to go to someone who knows and cares about the subject, and no one surpasses Professor Houdek on either count.[3]

THE CLASSIC ERA: FROM JANITORS TO SCHOLAR LIBRARIANS

Law libraries began as rather modest enterprises. The United States is a common law jurisdiction. In common law jurisdictions, judges write opinions that resolve disputes between parties. In theory, these opinions do not represent the judge's personal decision based on equitable grounds. Instead, they represent the judge's written statement of the existing law as applied to the facts of the particular case. The distinctive feature of common law systems is that these judicial decisions are viewed not as interpretations of the law but as the law itself.[4] They become legal precedent and are called *primary authority*. Just how these judicial opinions rise above the status of representing the personal opinions of the judge and reach to the level of articulated legal principles is a thorny question that has been debated for decades by the best legal theorists, with no answer yet in sight. But the debate aside, the fact remains that judicial opinions are the foundation of the common law. Once they are issued, such opinions can be cited as statements of the law. Lawyers spend many hours in law school mastering the skill of using such precedent via analogy and logic.[5]

From the earliest days of the American republic, the publication of judicial opinions was at the core of legal research. Indeed, well into the twentieth century, legal researchers believed that one only needed to read cases to understand the law. From the early days, there were treatises to explain the common law and books to explain foreign law, especially that of Great Britain, but the heart of any law library was its collections of judicial decisions.

At this stage, the legal researcher's problem lay in getting copies of the judicial decisions. The number of decisions was small enough that a practitioner could read each case in his jurisdiction, plus most federal cases and perhaps English cases as well. Most of his interpretation was done inside his head or in his notebooks. A good law library consisted of a collection of judicial reports and little more. Obtaining copies of the opinions was the challenge. While a handful of practitioners assembled more extensive libraries, the finest repositories were in law school libraries and in the libraries of private subscription societies. Even these collections did not call for the skill set being developed by the nascent profession of librarianship. Judicial opinions are issued in series and came with their own indexing and abstracting systems that precluded the need for cataloging and classification. These libraries needed simple maintenance, not professional attention. Indeed, one of the earliest references that I have found to a law librarian comes from a history of the Harvard Law School Library, which explains that in the middle of the nineteenth century, the librarian was usually a student, assisted by a janitor.[6] Their tasks were minimal. Indeed some professors preferred to buy materials themselves and keep them in their offices. These small law libraries did not produce a profession. Such collections need a caretaker, not an information professional.

By the end of the nineteenth century, the great libraries at law schools like Harvard, Yale, and Columbia, and the great subscription law libraries like the Social Law Library in Boston, the Jenkins Library in Philadelphia, and the Library of the Association of the Bar of the City of New York were preparing book catalogs and growing, but law librarianship was not yet needed.[7]

SETTING THE STAGE: THE EXPANSION OF LEGAL INFORMATION

As the twentieth century progressed, the world of law was swept by a number of powerful forces. The Brandeis Brief serves as a famous marker of one important change. The Brandeis Brief is considered by many in the legal community to be a turning point in the use of nondoctrinal authority in legal argumentation. Louis D. Brandeis represented the state of Oregon in *Muller v. Oregon*, 208 U.S. 412 (1908), a case involving the constitutionality of state restrictions on women's working hours. The court reached a unanimous decision in this landmark case upholding the statute, justified on the basis of the state's special interest in protecting women's maternal functions. Rather than the traditional format, Brandeis instead wrote his brief using only a few pages on the doctrinal test of the law's constitutionality, spending the remainder on data supporting the law as a "reasonable" regulation. In his 113-page brief, Brandeis compiled empirical data from hundreds of medical, economic, and sociological journals to illustrate the impact on women of working long hours. Not only was the brief persuasive in *Muller*, it became a landmark of its own, as a frequently used model for nonlegal arguments in presentations to the courts. This type of brief became commonly known as a *Brandeis Brief*.

The success of the Brandeis Brief led legal researchers to look outside the world of judicial decisions and into the world of social science. The Brandeis Brief is only the most famous marker of this change, but the pressure to look to sources outside of traditional judicial reports came from a variety of sources. The change resulted in the need for law libraries to hold new types of material. Selecting and acquiring books and serial publications became important, as did the cataloging and classification skills of librarianship. Reference services became more than just directing researchers to the right case reporter or digest. The whole world began to open up.

In addition, due to the growing number of materials found in libraries, the amount of available legal information reached a critical mass. There is a point at which any information system is inundated by the data that it holds. No longer can most researchers hold in memory the information that they need. At this point, the primitive organizational schemes that worked in a smaller information universe break down. Only an informational idiot savant can remember where everything is. Systems are needed. A profession has a role. The stage was set for a broadly based profession of law librarianship to emerge.

THE PROFESSION MATURES: ACADEMIC LAW LIBRARIES TO THE FORE

Great law libraries grew in the middle of the twentieth century. Elite law schools like Harvard, Yale, Columbia, and Michigan built huge collections of materials. More importantly, the profession of law librarianship grew beyond the small band that founded the AALL into a much larger group. It is worth noting that the AALL was founded by A. J. Small, who was curator of the Iowa State Law Library.[8] Those early days, well recounted in numerous articles cited by Professor Houdek in his bibliography, were characterized by small numbers and a variety of nascent law libraries. State and court libraries were central players. Great collections could be found at libraries maintained through cooperative societies of lawyers, such as the Law Library of the Association of the Bar of the City of New York and the Social Law Library in Boston. The Los Angeles County Law Library, supported by filing fees from court cases in California, was a leader as well. Many such libraries have histories that start well before this time period, but it was at this point that they too had to expand their collections dramatically. Indeed, at one point these subscription law libraries were at the very forefront of the law library world. But inevitably these libraries, supported by membership dues or filing fees, could not keep up with the ambitions of the law schools. They would carry on, but they would no longer lead the way. That mantle would fall to academic law libraries. Academic institutions began investing in their legal libraries.

The law library had long been held to be crucial to a law school. Dean Christopher Columbus Langdell, the man who founded the modern version of the Harvard Law School, is the progenitor of it all. Langdell is credited with designing the law school curriculum that is still used today, introducing both the Socratic method and the case approach to legal education. Langdell also believed in the primacy of the law library. Since Langdell believed that judicial opinions were the soul of the law, he felt that the law library was the laboratory of the law. Legal researchers reading judicial opinions were like scientists conducting experiments. Of course, Langdell conceived these ideas at a time when the law library consisted mostly of sets of judicial reports, but his influence ran deep, and it paved the way for the modern academic law library to hold pride of place at the heart of the law school that it served.

Law schools began to compare the size of their law libraries as indicators of institutional quality. Bigger was best. An arms race of acquisitions began. Law school faculty and deans would watch for the results of the annual American Bar Association (ABA) survey to see which law schools had the highest volume count. (Remember, this is long before *U.S. News and World Report* came up with its cash cow rankings.) While the elite schools competed to have the largest collection of books, the ABA and the American Association of Law Schools (AALS), the agencies that accredited law schools, promulgated standards of the minimum collection that a law school must maintain. Eventually the ABA and the AALS would require that the director of the law library be made a member of the law school faculty, a rule that states a principle, though it was never truly enforced.

The middle of the century also saw great figures emerge to guide law librarianship. Naming a few influential figures is a chancy enterprise, as the list is never complete, but several names from the middle of the twentieth century demand mention. Each of these individuals represents a great body of work and a large number of people. If you are to understand the nature of law librarianship, they are names that you must know.

Miles Price[9] (1890–1968) at Columbia Law Library trained several generations of law librarians and helped guide the profession into its adulthood. With his protégé Harry Bitner (1916–2001), he authored a text on legal bibliography that served as the bible for law librarians for decades.[10] At Yale Law School Frederick Hicks (1875–1956) brought a scholarly heft to law librarianship. Hicks published books on legal research as well as on substantive topics. His ideas on legal research are relevant even in the days of the Internet.[11] Rosamond Parma (1884–1946), the longtime director of the law library at Berkeley's Boalt Hall School of Law, was a pioneering woman who was the first female president of the AALL. Indeed she is one of the few individuals who served two years in the office. William Roalfe (1896–1979), director of the law library at the University of Southern California, conceived of the Roalfe Plan, a roadmap for making the AALL a true professional organization. This crucial step made all that followed possible. Arthur Beardsley (1889–1950) at the University of Washington School of Law began a program to train lawyers to become law librarians, inventing the Masters of Law Librarianship (MLL) in the process. The program was subsequently taken over by the amazing Marian Gould Gallagher (1914–1989), who trained more law librarians than anyone else and established a great network of professionals. Her program, carried on today by Penny Hazelton, continues as a vital source of new law librarians. Mike Jacobstein (1920–2005), who spent the bulk of his career at Stanford, and Roy Mersky (1925–2008), who became famous as the long-tenured director of the law library at the University of Texas, were both influential in many ways. Jacobstein trained under Miles Price, and Mersky spent his first years working at Yale. Together they produced a book on legal bibliography that was the main text for legal researchers for many years.[12] These two men collaborated on more than two dozen titles, and their influence reached far beyond their own libraries. For several decades, Professor Mersky turned the University of Texas Law Library into a training ground for law librarians that, while smaller than the University of Washington program, produced many high-profile law librarians. At one time he could point to the fact that the law library directors at Harvard, Stanford, Berkeley, and more than two dozen other law schools were all trained in his apprentice system. Morris Cohen (1927–2010), who had the rare distinction of serving as director of first the Harvard Law Library and then the Yale Law Library, picked up the intellectual mantle of Frederick Hicks and produced scholarship of the first order. Professor Cohen's writings were hugely influential.[13] In 1961 Elizabeth Finley (1898–1980) was the first law firm librarian to be elected president of the AALL, demonstrating that law firm librarians were ready to move into leadership. William Murphy (1916–1996), longtime librarian of the law firm Kirkland and Ellis in Chicago, served as patron saint to the AALL executive offices in Chicago. Antoinette (Babe) Russo (1919–1994) served as the executive director of the AALL during its period of growth. Everyone knew Babe. Julius Marke (1913–2003), longtime director of the New York University Law Library, wrote widely on both substantive law and law librarianship. He was also a pioneer in understanding the importance of copyright law in legal information. Each of these individuals was crucial to the growth of law librarianship in the mid to late twentieth century.[14]

All but one of the figures mentioned above had law degrees. As law libraries grew and as legal education expanded, it became common for the director of the law library to hold a JD degree. Eventually it would become a requirement for accreditation. This development followed the recognition that legal materials were so specialized that the normal skill set of a librarian would not be sufficient, at least in public contact positions. To function as the director of an academic law library, and as time passed, to serve as a reference librarian in such an institution, one needed the kind of subject expertise that could be gained only through experience or by being a law school graduate. This skewed the profession toward a more scholarly bent. A quick glance at the *Law Library Journal*, the official publication of the AALL, shows that it resembles an academic law review. Law librarians at law schools identified with legal information and with the legal institutions that they served.

Academic libraries served as the model and set the tone for law librarianship deep into the twentieth century.

LAW FIRM LIBRARIES AND THE AGE OF THE PRIVATE SECTOR

During the last third of the twentieth century, legal culture in the United States underwent profound changes. Law firms became larger and larger, and the practice of law became more and more like a corporate enterprise.[15] Where once a law firm of thirty was thought to be large, and all but a few law firms were limited to practicing in one city, during this time law firms might boast dozens of offices and might employ more than a thousand lawyers. This shift occurred alongside a dramatic change in the world of information.

Legal information had benefited from highly sophisticated research tools in the world of print. This is not the place to rehearse the pioneering work of the West Publishing Company or the Shepards Company. Suffice it to say that law had the most advanced print systems of information tracking and delivery known to humanity. One company, the West Publishing Company, dominated this world. Staffed by a cadre of lawyers and devoted both to serving the legal profession and making money, the West Company brought experience and deep expertise to its business. The many smaller legal publishers shared the same characteristics. Each was run by people who were lawyers, law librarians, or men (and they were all men) who had grown up in and around legal literature.

The sophisticated print systems were built around the primacy of judicial opinions and were closely integrated with the work of law schools, leading to one seamless information universe. However, law firms often maintained impressive libraries of these print sources. Though law firms largely confined themselves to collecting judicial reports and statutes, leaving the gathering of the burgeoning social science works regarding law to the law schools, law firm collections could be substantial. Large law firms prided themselves on architecturally striking law libraries, sometimes building the entire office around a showpiece collection of books. The book collection was not just a gathering of legal information; it was a statement about the quality of the law firm. It was a rare PR photo of a partner that did not have him (and it was usually a him) posed in front of ranks of law books. When printed books ruled the world, a showplace library spoke to the intellectual heft of the law firm. Larger law firms might employ a law librarian to oversee such a collection, but in all but the grandest firms, the librarian was often little more than a secretary assigned to watch over things.

This too began to change. Just as law school librarians sprang from a root system of janitors and student librarians, law firm libraries grew from collections of books stewarded by legal secretaries. As the practice of law saw the development of ever-larger law firms, the information needs of these firms grew. No longer just collections of judicial decisions, statutes, and a few form books, law firm libraries became sophisticated collections. Law firm librarians very early developed interlibrary loan capabilities that allowed them to combine the power of their collections. The increasingly sophisticated research needs of lawyers in these large firms demanded increasingly sophisticated law librarians to assist them. Expensive sources that served the narrow needs of highly specialized practice areas like tax and securities blossomed. Academic law librarians had no use for them, even if they could have afforded them. The explosive growth in the number of lawyers and law firms made law firm librarianship a growth industry. While some law firm librarians had law degrees, most did not. Law firms needed professionals who could work with information and find them what they needed.

In the early 1980s, a law firm librarian, still living in the pre-Internet world of paper, came to speak to my Advanced Legal Research class at Berkeley. When a student asked for an example of a piece of information that she could not find, the librarian replied, "There is no piece of information that I cannot find. You might not be able to pay for it, but if you can, I can find a way to get it." Her bravado stunned the students, but I saw it as a simple truth. Academic law libraries had the bigger collections, but law firm libraries were more nimble and service oriented. Because the lawyers who employed them were part of profit-making enterprises and responded to clients, they demanded fast turnaround times and accurate performance. When a professor asks a reference librarian in a law school to locate an obscure article, there is normally no immediate deadline staring the professor in the face. As an academic, she might understand that it would take a few days to obtain what she needed. By contrast, when a partner in a law firm demands a piece of similarly obscure information, the law firm librarian goes on red alert. A client who is paying by the hour cannot be kept waiting, nor can a court or agency be asked to be patient. The information may be needed now, no excuses accepted. That sort of incentive leads to a different level of performance.

The pressure of the private sector and the demands imposed by market forces compelled law firm librarians to hone research skills and to become skilled managers of information emergencies. Before long, the law firm libraries were leaders in innovation. Many academic law librarians can share harrowing tales of new professors hired out of positions in law firms, who arrive at the law school expecting the same level of service the law firm librarians provided and who have a hard time adjusting to the slower pace. When the budget for searching for information is not provided by a paying client, but instead is funded out of a fixed academic

budget, priorities change. Where once the law school libraries could put
the budgets of county and court libraries to shame, now law firms were
ready to invest in information in ways that the law schools could only
dream about.

THE NEW WORLD

Since law librarians had always been wedded to legal information, they
had to follow it into the digital world. The digital revolution came to law
librarianship in the last two decades of the twentieth century. Lexis and
Westlaw, each a full-text database of judicial opinions, statutory material,
administrative sources, and secondary materials, changed the face of legal information. Both Lexis and Westlaw (LW) were pioneers in automated searching. Each invested massive amounts of resources in training law
students to use their systems by providing deeply subsidized access, in-
person training and support, and innovative marketing. LW forced law
librarians to become computer literate.[16] In a shadow play of the paper
world, LW first took root in the law schools, as a generation of students
came to rely on digital information. But it flowered in the law firm environment. LW knew that the money to be made was in the private sector,
so they trained law students to use the systems, but then focused on
working with researchers in law firms.

Law firm librarians were ready. As ever, they followed the needs and
requests of the lawyers who employed them. When the Internet came on
the scene and LW migrated to more sophisticated platforms, law firm
librarians were there to meet it. Because LW had worked to create a base
of users who would use Boolean searching and digital systems instead of
the old book-based tools, the Internet opened up whole new worlds.
Suddenly law librarianship was turned on its head. Where academic law
libraries with their large collections of books and highly trained staffs
had once been the gravitational center of the profession, now law firm
libraries, which could innovate and had the resources to buy newer and
more sophisticated databases, took over. The students arriving at law
school at the end of the twentieth century were computer-savvy search-
ers who cared little for the giant collections of paper materials in the
library. They wanted access to databases and sophisticated search engines. In other words, they arrived at law school expecting the resources
of the law firm environment.

By the end of the twentieth century, law firm librarians were the heart
of the profession in many ways. By developing intranets, running their
law firms' information and systems operations, and implementing
knowledge-management systems, law firm librarians were moving the
ball forward. This is not to say that academic law libraries stagnated.
They too responded and changed, but the real energy was in the private

sector. Once again, if one follows the money, one finds the leading edge of development.

It is fortunate that the law firm librarians continued to see themselves as members of the same profession as the academic law librarians. There were several points at which the AALL almost sundered over this issue. For decades, AALL had been dominated by those from the academic side, and some law firm librarians felt that they should break away. But the moments of crisis always passed.[17] In 1977 the AALL formed Special Interest Sections (SIS), which allowed the different groups of stakeholders to each have an autonomous entity and yet still remain united under an umbrella organization. The dream was that law librarianship could remain united if groups like the private law librarians and those who worked in state, county, and court libraries had form within the association. In the AALL of the twenty-first century, law firm librarians play a central role both in leadership positions and in numbers of members.

CURRENT QUESTIONS

Where does law librarianship stand in 2012, and where does it go from here? In recent decades, some law firm librarians have gravitated toward the Special Library Association, feeling that they have more in common with librarians who work in other private sector and specialized environments than they do with their academic counterparts. The Private Law Librarians SIS has taken on a life of its own. Some academic law librarians feel that their interests now differ so much from those of their colleagues in the private sector that they should put energy into working with the American Association of Law Schools, the professional association that serves law schools. The AALL's solution of creating SISs can only provide so much glue to the diverging interest groups. Add to these disquieting trends the possibility that law librarianship might simply be absorbed whole by the larger field of librarianship, or absorbed into the organizational chart under the direction of the IT department.

Some feel that the term *librarian* itself should be abandoned in favor of a term that is more reflective of a professional who manages knowledge by working with information, systems, and databases. The entire profession of librarianship has struggled to find its identity and its place at the table in the information economy. Will the term *librarian* become synonymous with a middle-management position in which one reports to a manager to whose job one cannot aspire?

Additionally, the consolidation of the legal publishing industry could have potentially significant consequences for the field of law librarianship. The traditional legal publishers were once conservative bastions of highly specialized information, managed by individuals with significant subject expertise, who knew and understood not just the books that they sold but what was in them. Today, these publishers are part of large international information corporations. The West Publishing Company, which had always been owned entirely by certain employees, went public and became part of the Thomson Publishing empire. Thomson has now joined with the British firm Reuters. When West was a closely held corporation, it could make decisions based on the long-term view of what was best and upon its understanding of legal information. A publicly traded company owes responsibility to its shareholders and must keep its eyes fixed on the bottom line. Most of the small legal publishers have been absorbed into either the Thomson/West camp or that of Lexis, which is owned by Reed, Elsevier, the English–Dutch information conglomerate. Reed, Elsevier also looks to its bottom line and sees legal information as one of its products. Will legal information soon be indistinguishable from the other commodified information that inundates all of us? The entry of Bloomberg into the legal information world may shake up things even more. What about Google Scholar? The possibilities boggle the mind.

These new entities thrive by designing simpler yet more powerful search engines. They bypass the librarian and work directly with the researcher. Law librarians worry about the legitimacy and stability of information; publicly held information vendors worry about the bottom line.

It is important that the field of law librarianship holds together. Law librarians, no matter what the specifics of their situation, have a great deal in common, enough to overcome the centrifugal trends set out in the previous paragraph. Law librarians have fought to protect the integrity of information, to keep it available to the public. The Washington office of the AALL, pioneered by Professor Robert Oakley (1945–2007), has a seat at the table of national information policy. Battles over copyright issues, privacy concerns, and access to information have made AALL savvier on policy. By combining the intellectual power and contacts of academic law librarians with the financial power of law firm librarians and the influential position of court and county law librarians, law librarians can continue to occupy a unique position. In the information wars, the law librarians wear the white hats. We have to make sure that they know it.

Can the profession survive and prosper? The answer to that question lies in the future. For the sake of legal information and those who use it, I hope so.

NOTES

1. My thanks to Roxanne Livingston for her assistance with the manuscript.
2. Legal information in the form of positive statements of the law represents a special kind of cognitive authority. The late Patrick Wilson's *Second-Hand Knowledge: An Inquiry into Cognitive Authority* (1983) provides an excellent discussion of this issue.

3. The AALL Publication Series, now past seventy volumes in length, includes numerous titles that can offer perspectives on law librarianship as well as guides to its practice. Of special interest is *Law Librarianship: Historical Perspectives*, edited by Gasaway and Chiorazzi (1996). This volume contains perspectives from all points of view on the profession and its roots, and its editors are two of the leaders in contemporary law librarianship. For a glimpse of personal perspectives on law librarianship from a variety of viewpoints, presented in the form of oral histories, see Garson et al., eds., *Reflections on Law Librarianship*(1988). Frank Houdek's *The First Century: One Hundred Years of AALL History, 1906–2005* (2008) is a good source of institutional history.

4. Common law systems all have roots in the legal system of the United Kingdom.

5. See *Hart v. Massanari*, 266 F.3d 1155 (9th Cir. 2001). Judge Kozinski lays out the history of precedent in his own inimitable style.

6. See *The Centennial History of the Harvard Law School: 1817–1917* (Harvard Law School Association, 1918) at page 98. "The librarian had generally been a member of the School, who occupied a room in Dane Hall, and received a trifling compensation in addition to his room rent and tuition. It is not any part of his duty to spend any of his time in the library; still less to exercise any authority or supervision over those who used it. The janitor had certain duties to perform in reference to the library but it was not his business to exercise authority."

7. For a fascinating history of the development of library catalogs, which is a more exciting saga than one might think, see Battles, *Library: An Unquiet History* (2003).

8. Small, "Reflections," *Law Library Journal* 24, no. 12 (1931) gives a short first-person view of the AALL's early days. It took almost twenty years before an academic law librarian was elected president (Frederick Hicks) and more than fifty years before a law firm librarian (Elizabeth Finley) would be so chosen.

9. Each figure mentioned here is the subject of scholarly analysis. I will not belabor the text or footnotes with citations about each of them. They are easy enough to find.

10. Price and Bitner, *Effective Legal Research* (1953). There were many subsequent editions.

11. Hicks, *Men and Books Famous in the Law*, is one of my favorite titles in legal literature. Professor Hicks discussed the great books of the law with descriptions of the book, its author, and why it is important.

12. Jacobstein and Mersky, *Fundamentals of Legal Research*. This text, which was taken over from Professor Erwin Pollack, was for a time known as *Pollack's Fundamentals of Legal Research*, edited by Jacobstein and Mersky. It has gone through many editions, added junior authors, and spun off a paperback abridgement, *Legal Research Illustrated*. Both continue under the authorship of Barkan, Mersky, and Dunn.

13. Cohen, *How to Find the Law*, remains a masterwork of legal bibliography. It has seen numerous editions and junior authors. Professor Cohen's massive *Bibliography of Early American Law* (1998) is perhaps the greatest single achievement of modern legal bibliography.

14. "The American Association of Law Libraries: A Selective Bibliography," contained in the AALL Reference Book cited above, lists articles and tributes to all librarians mentioned here. Rather than pepper the page with multiple citations, I refer to the existing source.

15. The discussion of a publicly held law firm, with shareholders driving business decisions, is underway.

16. As one who started in the profession in 1975, I experienced the changes taking place.

17. When I retired as president of AALL in 1986, I wrote, "Dyspeptic Ramblings of a Retiring Past President" about these issues. Twenty-five years later they are still being discussed by the AALL executive board.

TWO

Working at the Law Library: A Practical Guide

Karl T. Gruben

INTRODUCTION

There are three types of law libraries: state, court, and county; firm or private; and academic. While each is unique, all are similar. They are differently named because of the clientele they serve. The state, court, and county law libraries serve courts of all varieties, as well as federal, state, or municipal agencies, such as the federal Department of Justice, a state's attorney general, or a city attorney's office. The firm or private law libraries serve law firms or corporate legal departments, while the academic law libraries are associated with a law school.[1] Some libraries fulfill multiple functions,[2] but most fill only one role and serve the main clientele of that particular law library. The differences that arise among these law libraries are because of the different clienteles. Each group has a different aim and use for legal materials.

Academic law libraries have a mission to preserve the law and the legal materials associated with it. Because of this mission, academic law libraries contain collections that are generally larger than those of other types of law libraries. They must also fulfill their academic mission, often purchasing ephemeral law school materials that the other types of law libraries do not purchase. These would include such materials as casebooks and study aids. Academic law libraries also are "collecting for the ages." As such, they retain superseded materials, such as older editions of treatises, superseded pocket parts from treatises and statutory materials, and long runs of periodicals.

All academic law libraries have collection-development policies that spell out what is to be purchased. Financial considerations and the advent of electronic serials and books have caused many academic law libraries to review their collection policies. Because of this, the academic law library might purchase a serial title once in one format, rather than in the multiple film, fiche, paper, and electronic versions that exist.[3] Additionally, academic law libraries often purchase materials that appear to be outside their mission but that are purchased for the research needs of the faculty.[4] This results from the interdisciplinary nature of legal scholarship that has come about in the past twenty years. Law professors incorporate many works from outside of mainstream law sources, delving into history, sociology, and, lately, statistical research.[5] It is also important to recognize the American Bar Association's requirements for the academic law library, pursuant to chapter 6 of the Library Resource Section of the Accreditation Guidelines, standard 606. This standard requires a "core collection of essential materials." Standards 604 and 605 require a staff of law librarians "sufficient in number to provide appropriate library and informational resource services," as well as an "appropriate range and depth of reference, instructional, bibliographic, and other services to meet the needs of the law school's teaching, scholarship, research and service programs."

State, court, and county law libraries and law firm law libraries do not usually purchase case books and study aids, because their clientele neither requires nor requests it. These libraries have smaller collections, known as *working collections.*[6] Firm libraries usually do not maintain large back runs of periodicals;[7] instead they keep only the current editions of treatises, and they retain pocket parts for limited materials, such as the local statutes. State, court, and county law libraries fall between the academic and firm libraries in their retention policies, depending on their locale and mission.

Firm and state, court, and county law libraries collect numerous quantities of "practice" materials that the academic law library usually does not.[8] Some practice materials that the smaller state, court, and county or law firm libraries often acquire are defined for such small local jurisdictions and practice specialties that huge law libraries, such as Harvard and Yale, are unlikely to purchase them. Such materials include form books, specialty treatises penned by experts in the specialty, and checklists. Practicing attorneys like checklists that provide information to help prepare depositions and cross-examinations. Smaller firm or county law libraries purchase materials based on demand from their clientele. This is in contrast to the collection-development policies of academic law libraries.[9]

Collection development depends on the clientele served and the funding available. Academics purchase materials that would seldom appear in a state, court, and county or law firm library and vice versa. All libraries have materials in common; however, academic law libraries have collections that are historical in nature and aimed more at the academic study of the law. State, court, and county and firm libraries are aimed at the actual practice of law, and their collections reflect this mission.

Where does the new law librarian fit into this picture? It depends. It is highly unlikely that a novice librarian will enter an academic law library anywhere other than at an entry-level professional or paraprofessional position.[10] Academic law libraries usually do not have an employment track. Advancement in academic law libraries tends to occur by sheer happenstance. Why? Typically academic libraries have been established for many years and have loyal and dedicated staff members. State, court, and county law libraries often have the same types of employees: loyal, dedicated, and long term. To advance, librarians will need to move, changing jobs and sometimes changing cities and states. Because law firms do expand based on attorney and client needs, law firm libraries often decide to create a law librarian position, or they sometimes lose a librarian.[11] There is more movement in the firm librarian job market.

THE DUAL DEGREE

Possession of both an MLS and a JD allows librarians to begin work in the public services area of an academic law library. Public services positions deal with the public. In an academic law library, the public consists primarily of faculty and students, although academic law librarians in the public services arena do sometimes encounter *pro se* patrons or practicing attorneys. While it is not required that reference librarians in an academic law library setting possess a JD to work in public services or reference, most reference librarians do have dual degrees. The majority of job listings for such positions stipulate a JD as either highly desirable or required. In academic law libraries, public service jobs that do not require a dual degree include collection maintenance, circulation, and audiovisual services (AV). Some law libraries place an electronic services librarian in public services, while others locate the position in technical services. Providing audiovisual services is often a function of the law library in a university setting; performing or managing AV services does not require a dual degree. Jobs in collection maintenance, circulation, and AV services often provide experience in personnel supervision that other public services jobs, such as an entry-level reference job, do not. Supervisory experience is often the best stepping stone to midlevel management jobs with their attendant higher salaries.

Public service positions at firm libraries and in some state, court, and county libraries often do not require a dual degree. Sometimes very small county or law firm libraries may not even require a master's degree in library science. Advancement will require the degree equivalent to an

MLS. Years ago, it was unusual to find a dual-degreed librarian in a county or firm library. Why? Many believed that the dual-degreed individual's ultimate goal was to obtain a job as an attorney. As the number of dual-degreed law librarians increased in the profession, this perception changed. Now county and firm law libraries often require librarians to possess both degrees.

MOVING AROUND IN THE LAW LIBRARY

The best introduction to a law library is a tour through all departments. Some law libraries start new employees in this manner, believing that a tour enables the new professional to learn the requisites of law librarianship. A stint of duty in each department helps the new employee understand how all departments within a library fit and work together. Many large academic law libraries require new staff members to work in the various jobs in the library. This allows the new employee to become acquainted with how things work before settling entirely into the new position.

A new public services librarian might work a few hours a week in circulation to see the types of problems and questions that arise at what is often the main point of contact between the law library and the students. The next stop might be AV, which also provides services to faculty and students. Organization skills are essential in AV services, as there are often conflicting demands during peak class periods. Stack and collection maintenance is a high priority in a law library,[12] but it is routine and dull. Shelf reading is tedious. Shelving and shelf reading, however, can lead to the discovery of treasures and to a knowledge of the collection that cannot be matched. The shelver must be alert, notice how materials relate to each other through the call number system,[13] and find out what materials appear to be used. Knowledge of materials can lead to better reference service and can assist in the acquisition of new materials.

This chapter will take the tour, beginning in the back offices known as *technical services* and ending with the front offices referred to as *public services*. Starting in technical services provides the basic knowledge needed to understand how the law library is put together, as one sees all the materials that come in: the books, the loose leafs, and the supplements. One learns when and why those pieces arrive, and how the works to which they belong are arranged. Next, the tour will continue through the public services areas. Assume that this is a midsized law library containing many units that may not be present as standalone units in many smaller law libraries but that may be present in larger libraries and therefore require some introduction.

MOVING AROUND IN TECHNICAL SERVICES

The Mail

Sorting and distributing the mail, each piece of which must be handled and directed to the appropriate staff member, and observing the vast array of materials that flow into the law library can be a mammoth job. Large manuals can, and have, been written about the handling of the day-to-day mail. Each institution has its own procedures for handling the mail, but most include some form of opening, stamping a date on the envelope or the cover of whatever piece was received, and distributing the pieces to the appropriate person or workstation. Box mail (i.e., that mail received mainly from publishers and shipped inside some form of corrugated container) will need to be opened. Many institutions retain shipping boxes for reuse with other items, such as interlibrary loan shipping, or to return unwanted items to the publisher. Know institutional policies before recycling boxes.

Processing

After receiving the mail, the next step is processing what was delivered in the mail. Processing involves checking the pieces into a receiving system and dealing with any anomalies that arise, such as missed issues, odd issues, and pieces received out of sequence.[14] When items are not received after a specified amount of time, claiming must then occur. Claiming is an art, because it will vary from one publisher to another and consists of telling the publisher or producer that a particular piece of some subscription has not been received and is needed immediately. While some publishers are very quick to respond to claims, others are not. The art lies in knowing how and when to make a claim with individual publishers. Claim too quickly, and the publisher advises that the item is "in the mail"; claim too late, and the piece will no longer be available. Many academic libraries use a *jobber*. A jobber serves as a middleman between the library and a vendor to claim missing serial pieces.[15] It is here that the novice librarian will learn the quirks of publishers. What are some of these quirks? Some publishers send supplementation for items that have been long discontinued, send items that are claimed to be "on standing order" or "related to such and so" publication, and include items that have never been ordered but are shipped and billed along with a large number of other items. These will all need to be checked against the library's integrated system, and those items that are suspect will then need to be looked at by someone with the authority to decide whether to retain the item or to return it. These missent items will be returned to the publisher for credit against the bill, a process that often takes a long time to be resolved. Sometimes the reviewer will be intrigued by a title and allow it to be purchased. This illustrates one of the reasons why publishers will send out such items.[16] Remember two things: (1) do not stamp an item unless intending to purchase it; and (2) maintain paperwork in good order to settle billing problems. Acquisitions personnel must be organized.

Once checked in, the pieces received in the mail are processed for the shelf with stamping, tagging, labeling, and security stripping. New monographs might arrive preprocessed from a jobber such as Yankee Book Peddler, Ebsco, or Blackwells, already bearing a label with a call number, having been stamped in the appropriate places with a property stamp, and with the security strip already inserted. The only thing left is to have the cataloging data reviewed, the quality of the preprocessing checked, and the item placed on the shelf. This, of course, is the highest level of preprocessing. An institution may find their standards higher than those of the jobber and prefer to do the labeling, stamping, and stripping in house.

Acquisitions

Acquisitions require that materials be selected or acquired for the library. Most libraries deal with either a blanket book plan or a slips plan. Large law libraries do not want or have time to select each item that falls into a subject area. Rather, large law libraries know they will want everything published in a particular subject area. Blanket plans take care of this and are available through large monographic jobbers such as Yankee Book Peddler, Midwest Library Service, or Blackwell. In addition to these plans, the jobbers offer something for the smaller law libraries called a *slips program*. Using a slips program, the library will set up a profile with the jobber of Library of Congress (LC) classification numbers. The jobber has relationships with many publishers and receives a prepublication notice that something is published. The jobber then prepares a slip of paper with basic bibliographic data and the LC classification number. It then sends the participating libraries the slips corresponding to the profiles previously developed by each receiving library. Public service librarians cull through these slips and select those book titles they want to purchase. This selection process on the part of the librarians requires a thorough knowledge of the collection and of the collection-development policy. While these items were initially paper slips, publishers now tend to publish slips in electronic format, allowing libraries to sort and choose materials electronically.

Once selections have been made, the acquisitions staff processes those selections for presentation to the jobber for purchase. The jobber often has an automated system for handling this process, so there is no passing to and fro of paper pieces but, rather, the simple flow of electrons between the jobber's system and an integrated library system. Purchase through a jobber eliminates multiple bank checks to different publishers and streamlines the work.[17] Because jobbers are often purchasing many copies of the same item, jobbers frequently receive and pass along a discount off the list price of the books ordered.

Once the items are ordered, an acquisitions staff member puts some form of notice into the integrated library system. This alerts the acquisitions processor that an item has been ordered, who requested it, and how it should be handled. Failure to follow this procedure usually results in the loss of productivity and sometimes the purchase of unwanted material. The system in place might be as simple as a card file, or if an automated system is available, an abbreviated record might be placed therein, indicating the placement of the order.[18]

Most law libraries also purchase materials outside the jobber programs, since no jobber can handle everything published. This purchasing process is particularly difficult when dealing with foreign publishers. Often the publishers do not speak English, and if they do, their command of English is often limited, as is the librarian's understanding of the foreign publisher's language. In addition, it may be necessary to find some alternative methods of payment for the foreign publisher. While a credit card often takes care of the method of payment, it is sometimes difficult to prove that a payment has been made when the foreign seller claims nonpayment. All of these issues fall into the hands of the acquisitions personnel and demonstrate valuable lessons to the novice librarian (i.e., that ordering a book does not necessarily mean that the book will arrive on time, or that payment might be made without ever receiving the desired end product of that payment).

Publishers have shortened their press runs and sometimes underestimate the number of copies that will be needed. A latecomer might have to wait for republication, which can take a long time or may never occur. Some publishers try to gauge the need for their items by sending out prepublication notices and soliciting prepaid orders.[19] This can cause problems for both the publisher and the purchaser when the author does not follow through in a timely fashion.[20] Many pages have been written about the acquisitions process, so suffice it to say that the novice librarian must grasp the procedure of processing and the attendant problems.[21] One will need these details only if planning to work full time in acquisitions.[22]

Cataloging

Catalogers are usually precise. A great deal of the tedium of cataloging and classification has been removed by the use of bibliographic utilities such as OCLC, formerly the Online Computer Library Center, and SkyRiver, a company founded by former members of the Innovative Interfaces company. Both provide uniform cataloging data from cooperating libraries as well as from the Library of Congress.[23] There is still room for flair by the cataloger, however, in that many collections require the insertion of individualized materials into a classification scheme, or wish to put certain materials in a place that the Library of Congress would not place them. Beginning catalogers, with training at the graduate school level and no practical experience, will not be given the ability to insert data, other than under the strict supervision of an experienced librarian. Watching a cataloger can be very instructive to a public services librarian. Why? The public services librarian learns the various fields of the machine-readable cataloging (MARC) record and how those fields can be searched in the library's online public access catalog (OPAC). Note in particular the policies that the library follows for different types of materials and which MARC fields are used and which are not. This gives a librarian an idea of what is searchable by the general public. Often there is a paraprofessional who does base-level cataloging, such as the insertion of MARC records into the local database, which is then later checked by a librarian. This process frees the professional librarian to do more technical processes, such as the addition of subject headings or additional tracings. Each library has its own rules. Know what the library's policy is with regard to additional subject headings and tracings.

What about upgrades to an integrated system? Upgrades entail their own special problems for technical services, since an upgrade sometimes has unanticipated results, such as eliminating the customizations made for the institution. Learn what the problems inherent in an upgrade are, as this allows one to spot problems that need correction while using the systems in the future.

This book has a chapter on technical services. The level of description there is much more inclusive of what happens in the technical services department of a major law library, and I would advise the beginning librarian to read that chapter several times if planning to work in public services. Read the technical services chapter *twice* if intending to work in public services. That enables the librarian to understand the vital processes that take place "in the back office" of the law library. What goes on out front is hectic, sometimes loud, and often confusing. What goes on in the back makes what goes on in the front much easier.

MOVING AROUND IN PUBLIC SERVICES

After rotating through technical services, librarians being trained should move to public services. When entering public services, it is logical to start at circulation. In circulation, staff members check resources in and out, which is also known as charging and discharging items. Circulation is often operated by student employees, both law and undergraduate, under the supervision of a circulation manager or supervisor, who is usually not a librarian.[24] Circulation is usually the primary focal point of the law library, as almost every student and faculty member will come into contact with a circulation employee. These employees, then, need to be highly trained in the policies and procedures of the law library; they also need to know what to do when their knowledge of those policies and procedures does not cover a circumstance. It is crucial that they learn when to refer a problem to a higher authority.

The job is one of using the circulation system, often automated, to charge an item out to a library user and to discharge items back into the law library. There are usually a number of different types of materials, each with its own period of available circulation, as well as different types of users, who may have different charging rights. For example, items from the general collection might circulate for two weeks to students, a semester to faculty, and one week to outside members of the bar. Those items from the general collection that are volumes from a multiple-volume set, however, might not be allowed to circulate at all, perhaps not even to faculty members.[25] The items from the reserve collection typically circulate for twenty-four hours, while those from the course reserve collection only circulate for four hours. Those from the reference collection do not circulate at all, though, again, it is possible they might circulate for short periods of time to faculty.

While this sounds complicated, it generally isn't, because of an automated circulation system. The automated circulation system is set up to include all of these multiple variations of material and user types. When the final record for the item is inserted into the integrated library system, the period of circulation is set. When users are entered into the integrated library system, their rights to charge materials are set. When the item is *wanded* or the bar code is read, as long as the items and users are noted in the system in the correct category, their charge period is not a discernible problem to the circulation staff. To them, the material is charged out and the receipt bearing the appropriate date is printed and inserted into the material for removal by the user. It is the good circulation staff member, however, who recognizes that the return date is peculiar and that a particular item or user has not been properly categorized. Those instances are then drawn to the attention of a supervisor or superior.

Circulation staff are often asked to check the shelves and pull items for faculty and students and to perform what is usually called *stack maintenance*. *Stack maintenance* is the catchall phrase used for three functions carried out by circulation staff: shelf reading, cleaning, and reshelving. Shelf reading is a highly tedious but a necessary part of working in a library of any kind. Mistakes are often made when items are reshelved. Materials are sometimes deliberately misshelved. Generally, the circulation supervisor divides the library into areas of equal amounts of shelving. Each staff member in circulation, and sometimes other staff members in the law library, is responsible for examining each piece on the shelves and determining whether it is in the right location, particularly with regard to the call number order of the other items on the shelf. If an item is misshelved, it is lost in the general mass of the collection. Deliberate, concerted shelf reading does not solve the problem of misshelved materials. People do make mistakes, but as problems occur they can be corrected on a regular basis. Tiny areas of chaos are brought back into order.

Cleaning the shelves is often a part of stack maintenance. While it might not seem like it, libraries are often dirty. Thousands of individuals come and go daily, bringing in dirt, dust, and particles, which then spread across the library, settling on the carpet, the shelves, and the furniture. The circulation supervisor should assign cleaning areas to each employee; these areas might correspond to the shelf-reading areas. The employee may find that the monotony of shelf reading can be eased by alternating it with shelf cleaning. The use of disposable paper products, along with a good dusting agent moistener, allows an employee to place the dirt on the paper and place it in a waste receptacle, rather than merely move it around. It is, however, a never-ending battle, particularly if the library has high foot traffic, which is a good thing, and an aging carpet, which is not a good thing.

Finally, the circulation staff is often responsible for keeping the law library open late into the evening. This is one reason why such positions are usually held by student workers. Generally, students are thrilled to sit at a desk in the evenings, earning money while often reading homework, chatting with classmates, or working on a paper. Good employees understand that all stack-maintenance tasks assigned must be accomplished first, but a good supervisor will usually not assign more than a couple of hours of stack maintenance per shift; too much more than this and errors will be made. There will also be rush times when students pile up at the desk, wanting to remove materials for classes or overnight, so all desk personnel will be busy serving patrons. Many times in the evening, however, there is little more to do than find staples for an empty stapler, replace paper in a printer, and make sure someone is not trying to sneak something out past the security system. It is during these slow times that decent studying can be accomplished; good supervisors realize this and allow it to happen, but only after the maintenance work has been accomplished.

Interlibrary Loan

Interlibrary loan is often a part of public services. Interlibrary loan (ILL) is divided into two parts: borrowing and lending. Most academic and state, court, and county law libraries and a few firm libraries use the OCLC interlibrary loan system,[26] which allows a search of the OCLC catalog records system and the placement of a request to borrow into the OCLC electronic system. OCLC uses the WorldCat system as the basis for

ILL, with two requirements for participating in loaning: the requirements are the contribution of the holdings of the library to WorldCat, and a subscription to the WorldCat database through the FirstSearch reference service. A library willing to lend will respond to the system and mark the request to prevent multiple libraries from responding. This speeds the interlibrary loan process up, and it is now much faster than in the past, when paper forms were used and the U.S. Postal Service delivered both the forms and the borrowed and returned items. The system is highly sophisticated and allows the borrower to request that items be filled from certain categories of lenders first, before the request is placed with other lenders. Such prioritization allows the borrower to take advantage of cooperative and network relationships that provide lower costs to the borrowing library if the item is filled "within the network" of cooperating libraries.[27] Outside such a cooperating network, there is often a fee for borrowing from non-network libraries. Such fees are usually reasonable, costing between $15 and $25. If that fee can be avoided, however, it makes ILL more desirable. Borrowers may set an upper limit of cost, such as $50, and ask for notification if the cost of borrowing would exceed that cost.

Lending is easy. The employee checks the OCLC system several times a day for requests placed to the library. Since the OCLC system has cataloging records of what the potential lending library owns, the request will seldom be for an item that the library has never held. If, upon checking the shelves, the item is found, the lending library enters a system response that the request will be filled. If another library has responded in the interim while the shelf is being checked, the ILL employee will be unable to respond, and the item will have to be returned to the shelf. If the librarian decides to loan it, the item is checked out to the borrowing library using the library circulation system, packed for shipping along with any documentation the library uses to identify the item as an ILL piece, labeled, and shipped out to the borrower.[28] The entire system is fairly efficient and usually has only a modest cost.[29]

Novice librarians will most likely not be allowed to do any unsupervised record keeping in any ILL system used by the library until thoroughly trained. Observing the process can be highly instructive. Inquire about *good* lending libraries and *bad* lending libraries. Some libraries are understaffed and take a long time to respond to requests; as a result, those libraries receive fewer requests than they would otherwise. Others do their best to respond as quickly as possible and, consequently, do more volume.[30] Responsible libraries usually have a fairly balanced ratio of borrowed items to lent items. It is better to be a net lender rather than a net borrower, as net borrowing indicates a need to improve and increase the collection. ILL statistics can also give acquisitions librarians an idea of where their collection needs additions.

Audiovisual

In some law libraries, the staff is sometimes responsible for providing AV services to the library clientele. This will be more likely in an academic environment, but state, court, and county libraries often provide such services. It is not beyond the realm of possibility that a firm library will do the same. AV services can be demanding. It will often be the case that multiple events occur simultaneously, and staff will not be sufficient to cover everything. The smart staff will endeavor to make the plug-in and switch-on connections for equipment in the rooms, LCD projectors, VHS and DVD players, and sound systems, as uniform as possible. Uniform equipment connections make it more likely that, with a little user education, the end user will be able to make the connections to any needed equipment, thus freeing the AV staff for more technical work. Adequate signage also assists the end user with simple details for starting and using equipment. Finally, some form of training program for end users will lessen the need for AV staff to attend to such minor tasks as turning on a computer or lowering a screen. For other services, such as recording services, both audio and video, individual personnel will be needed on site to handle the equipment. If multiple services are required at the same time, often the camera or recording equipment can be started and left running while the staff member goes on to the next event. AV services require an organized person with a good technical knowledge of equipment to direct and run such an operation. Moreover, the superior AV person knows enough to read the manuals and how to troubleshoot problems with malfunctioning equipment. Typical services include connecting computers to LCD display projectors, connecting audio equipment to record or reproduce sound, connecting video equipment to display video, or using video cameras to record sessions. Because there will generally need to be more than one person making connections, assisting end users, and troubleshooting problems, AV is a good place to learn management and personnel supervisory skills.

Electronic Services

The electronic services librarian (ESL) position does not exist in every library. Someone, however, does the work. If an individual is not assigned to the position, the work will be divided among several people. In the modern law library, many of the products and services are offered to patrons as electronic versions. A serial title may be available in several formats: print, microform, or electronic. No matter the format, someone must make that product available to the end user. Paper formats are easy to use, usually grouped by title or subject or arranged by call number, and their location may be found through the online public catalog. Users are familiar with paper products and, once directed to the location or call number, can find what they need with ease. Microform formats are a bit more difficult, mainly because the equipment to view and print them is difficult to use. Nonetheless, the concepts are familiar: there is a physical location, something identifying the physical item such as a fiche header, a specific method for using the item, and specific equipment to view and print it.

The location of the electronic item being sought, though, is not "physical" in the normal sense of the word, since it cannot be seen with the naked eye, though it is physical in the sense that it exists as electrons in time and space. The location of the product can only be *seen* by using a personal computer and high-speed access to a network. Someone must construct something that allows the user a *place* to go to see electronic products. That is the job of the electronic services librarian.

Typically, many of the electronic products are accessible several ways: through hyperlinks in the online public access catalog or through a custom-built Web page with similar hyperlinks. The ESL will usually work on the second access method, while the first method is produced by the technical services staff catalogers. The Web page must be built to certain rules, sometimes dictated by a larger entity in the organization, such as an IT department or a main library, but the ESL must use those rules to standardize access to numerous products that are not always easily categorized and arranged. Luckily, electronic products allow the links to then appear in many areas at once, thus placing materials with multiple subjects in several subject areas at the same time. A quick click on the link, and the user is on the way to the material.

The ESL may also provide, or work with IT in providing, a proxy server. Institutional subscriptions to electronic products have two usual methods of authenticating who may use the services: either by having a specific username and password for each user or through an IP authentication process. The former requires a great deal of administrative time, requiring a staff person to keep up with current users, delete users who have departed, and locate lost usernames and passwords for current users. A system of individual passwords works well for use away from the institutional IP range.[31] IP range authentication allows anyone within the institutional network (IP range) access to the products made available in that manner, as long as the user is authenticated into the institution's network. Issues arise when users want to make use of the electronic products when away from the institutional network (i.e., working from home). The proxy server provides links to electronic products that mimic the IP range once users have authenticated themselves to the proxy server as a member of the institution. A similar arrangement could be achieved through the use of a virtual private network (VPN), but that usually requires an active personal computer inside the network. The proxy server is a reliable server inside the institution's network and will typically run almost all the time, save for maintenance. The ESL would maintain the currency of the institutional IP addresses in the proxy server, as well as the proxy server links to the electronic products.

Electronic serial products produce additional work for the ESL, as the institution may have multiple electronic points of access to the product, all with different pricing. For instance, a periodical title may be available through Lexis or Westlaw,[32] through two or three different repackagers, and through a subscription to the hard copy that allows the institution access to the product electronically as part of the subscription.[33] The job of the ESL is to produce the links in such a manner that the cheapest item appears first to the user. The cost will vary for every institution, depending on the contracts with the electronic providers. Tools are available to provide a price-differentiated list, such as the combination of a federated search engine and a link resolver. Federated search engines should allow a user to run one search across multiple full-text databases. The results are presented to the user in the form of multiple links, through a link resolver, to products available within the institution. The order in which these products are shown is dependent on an algorithm developed by the ESL, which should show the link with the lowest cost to the institution first in the list.

For example, a law firm library will probably not want to direct users to Lexis or Westlaw for serials that are available on HeinOnline,[34] as using Lexis or Westlaw will incur a charge for each use, which can be substantial charges for firms, while the HeinOnline service is a flat-fee product. Every use drops the overall per-item cost. Lexis and Westlaw, however, are more likely to have the current issues of periodicals first, as HeinOnline takes longer to make them available. The way to use the tools to present items in a cost-efficient manner is an intellectual problem for the ESL. This issue may be solved in a multitude of ways, all of which are highly dependent on factors present in the institution's contracts and cost schedules.

Reference

Many educated laypersons and even librarians think of public services as consisting solely of reference. As such, reference librarians are not on the reference desk eight hours a day, five days a week. In a typical week, a reference librarian works only three to four hours of each day providing reference services. The balance of the time is spent working on other law library services, such as the selection of materials, creating pathfinders, creating and editing Web sites, creating bibliographies on special subjects, and interacting with other library staff members concerning the location of materials, services, and cataloging records. The current academic model, and one that translates to the law firm, also has librarians teaching classes in legal research, new developments in legal research, and legal research in foreign or international material. The advent of electronic research has left at least one generation of lawyers wondering which resource is the most efficient: electronic or paper. The interconnectedness of the legal world makes at least some knowledge of treaties and the law of foreign countries a must for current practitioners. Librarians can assist practitioners by learning the best tools and then teaching them.

Because of their professional status, most librarians have offices. The modern office, however, has changed from the traditional one person, one office model with a closable door. Offices in academic law libraries vary, but many times a *cube farm* has been developed for the junior staff members—one large room is shared by several reference staff members, using modular furniture to create a personal space. The individual office is often the exception, rather than the rule. Those having managerial or supervisory roles, though, often require a private space for counseling the supervised staff.

Reference positions, when advertised for in an academic law library, generally require a dual degree: the possession of a master's in library science, the MLS or its equivalent, and the juris doctorate, the JD. One does not have to have an MLS and a JD to do reference. Much of the reference currently done in a law library is not necessarily legal in nature; a great deal is directional and nonlegal.[35] Legal reference often requires the interpretation of citations,[36] location of cases using the sparsest of information, and, occasionally, some interpretation of what a case or statute means.[37] While the JD will introduce the student to the language of the law and some of its peculiarities, a good student can learn the basics on his or her own. More complicated questions are aided, however, by the depth of knowledge in a subject area that can only be obtained through intensive study, such as is required for the law degree. Mediation, arbitration, and negotiation are also good skills to have, as the law library reference desk is often the place for settlement of grammar disputes between faculty members.[38]

MOVING UP IN YOUR LAW LIBRARY AND OUT OF IT

Almost everyone wants to advance. There are some who are perfectly happy to take a reference job, a cataloging job, or an acquisitions job, and stay in it for years. There is nothing wrong with that. Such employees develop skills, such as a "sense of reference," far beyond the skills of those who move from job to job. However, there is usually a limit beyond which a law library will not go in the pay for a specific position. That is, salaries get capped at a certain level. To make more money, it is often necessary to move up.

Large law libraries have some sort of track for advancement. Thus, an entry-level reference librarian might have the opportunity to move to one or even two higher levels of reference service, often dependent on time in grade or some form of performance evaluation and recommendation, totally within the institution. It might be that there are different midlevel management positions to which one can aspire. These often require some supervisory experience, as noted previously.

A glance at some statistics about law libraries reveals that on average, there are 8.69 librarians in academic law libraries, 5.22 librarians in private/firm law libraries, and 3.57 librarians in government libraries.[39] These are exceedingly low numbers upon which to develop a career track. This is a good news/bad news situation. There is a very limited career track. However, it is also likely that a librarian can locate a director position. Directors and institutions need a fit in order to work effectively together. Putting the two together is usually the test.[40]

If hired into one of the largest of the academic, private, or government law libraries, one will be able to advance from position to position, gaining skills that will serve in the next position. A typical progression in public services is from reference librarian to head of reference to head of public services to associate director to director. It is unlikely that a librarian will be able to accomplish these moves within the same institution.

In order to advance, a librarian will probably have to move from institution to institution, perhaps moving up a notch in one institution before moving to another. It is merely the nature of a specialized profession that there is not always an ideal career path inside a single institution. As the librarian moves up, she or he will have to contend with family issues, location issues (some areas are prohibitively expensive to live in for married, single-income families), and job-satisfaction issues. A work life in which one deals day in and day out with attorneys or law students can be stressful.

The Road to Management

Reference is not the best job in which to obtain required skills in supervision and management. As stated above, often the non-reference public services and the technical services jobs have a better *track to management* than do the reference jobs. The American Bar Association requires the director of an academic law library to hold both law and library science degrees. In the past, because this was also a requirement for reference positions, the reference job became the stepping-stone to a directorship. Today, the number of technical services librarians and non-reference public services librarians who are moving toward directorships is increasing. It is my contention that the *all-around* librarian who knows all the facets of both public services and technical services is the better director.[41] The better a director understands the workings of the machine that is the modern law library, the better the machine will be maintained and will work for library patrons.

Entire courses are devoted to management and management skills. There are probably courses offered in library management in library school. Take all of them. If that proves impossible, take courses that emphasize personnel management and budgeting. Managing people is a skill required of every librarian. It is only through the direction of the efforts of others that all the jobs in the law library are accomplished efficiently, thoughtfully, and professionally. The delegation of tasks to properly motivated and skilled staff members will result in necessary tasks being accomplished more easily than if one person tried to do every task himself or herself.

Some of the hardest issues with which librarians will deal in a law librarianship career will involve personal interactions with people. These may be coworkers or library patrons and even institutional support staff from outside the law library. The ability to handle the situations that arise from these relationships is crucial to the perception of how a director is doing the job. If a director is adept at handling people, that perception will be positive. If a director is unable to handle people or tries to do so but fails, chances of promotion or advancement are lowered. As a manager, it is best to start slowly, locate boundaries, and, seek guidance from someone with higher authority or more experience.

A position that involves supervising students is an excellent place to learn supervisory skills. Students are usually tractable and interesting; generally they know less than a new librarian does. Supervision is best done lightly. Supervision can be analogized to riding a horse. Recall that, when riding a horse, the reins are not pulled tight, as the horse will come to a complete halt. Rather, hold them lightly, allowing the horse to think he is going his own way and deigning to carry the rider along for the ride, while the rider nudges the horse in the correct directions.

Unfortunately, much of the clerical work done in libraries is boring and repetitive, but very necessary. Consistency is the watchword in a library. Failure to be consistent is the general cause for misinformation and dissatisfaction. If at all possible, vary the tasks given to clerical staff so that they do not burn out on one task and start to make errors due to inattention. Shelf reading, for instance, requires a great deal of concentration but does not engage the intellect. In addition, because the majority of items will be in the correct order, the worker will start to think that everything is in order and begin to skip over segments of the assigned shelving, missing misshelved material and then losing the consistency of the call number order. Shelf reading is best done in small segments of an hour or less. This means that the supervisor needs to have other tasks to assign to clerical workers so they may keep busy; thus the supervisor has to be organized and have tasks ready to assign. When doing so, be fair. Don't overload one student with dusting all the time, while others frolic at the circulation desk; remember that no one is able to focus and work diligently all the time. Some slack must be given. Successful supervision of small groups of students will result in recognition by your superiors and the addition of newer, and hopefully more interesting, tasks to supervise.

Budgeting is the anathema that will follow a librarian all of his or her professional life. The need to make choices about how to spend money drives all law libraries in whichever directions they move. Do we spend more on personnel? Do we buy more books? Do we stop buying so many paper books and invest in electronic books? What databases do we buy? Do we buy electronic serials and recycle all our bound volumes? These are all questions a librarian will face as he or she moves into the professional world. They are not easy questions, and the answers are often vague and uncertain. They require some answer, or the law library comes to a halt.

Beginning librarians have a very limited, if any, connection to the budgeting process of the law library. Since it should not be a secret process, find out as much as possible. Advancement may offer a librarian a small piece of the budget to control, such as purchasing reference materials, and the opportunity to learn how to handle money in small steps. Learn skills while there is time to do so and when the sums are small.

In addition to knowing about supervision and budgets, a good librarian exercises self-discipline and is a self-starter.[42] Both of these qualities lead to good evaluations and better work. Procrastination is a curse. The ability to start an assigned task and see it through to an on-time completion is highly regarded. Even more highly regarded is the ability to see a task that needs to be done, start it without someone assigning it, and then follow it through to completion. However, exercise some caution before starting a task. Sometimes what a new librarian sees as "needs doing" will be a task that is being left for a purpose. Suppose one is doing some shelf reading to get ready for an ABA accreditation inspection,[43] and comes across a large section of casebooks that have never been processed but are taking up an inordinate amount of room. The new librarian boxes the materials up and takes them to technical services for cataloging and processing. But the materials may have been serving as a "placeholder" to hold empty shelving. In academic libraries, the perception of nonlibrary deans and faculty is that empty shelving is an indicator that a library has too much space.[44] Such space may be taken from the library and used for other purposes, such as offices and classrooms. Actually, properly run libraries will have a great deal of unused shelf space, mainly because they are planned to last for many years.[45] Deans, partners, and library board members, however, have a much shorter viewpoint than do librarians.[46]

PRIVATE OR FIRM LAW LIBRARIES

Most law librarians in law firms work in small operations. Some law firms might be huge, such as the firms represented in the *American Lawyer* 100, and their library systems will be international in scope, but the size of the library staff may not equal that of a small to midsize academic law library. There are also a great many smaller firms whose library operations are not large at all, tending more to the "one-person library" model, rather than a heavily staffed one. In these libraries, the librarian does it all: ordering the books, checking in and routing the mail, learning to program in HTML, and also providing reference services. There is a lot of room for growth in firm law libraries, and there are many potential opportunities to show the attorneys working in the firm or the corporate legal department one's skills. It is, however, a great deal of work and the individual doing that work must be able to multitask, handling several operations at the same time, or at least carry the state of several tasks in his or her mind, because the need to work on those tasks will arrive at the least expected moment. A short *day in the life* of the firm law librarian is described below.

- 8:00 am—Arrive at work and clear off the tables of materials left out by the attorneys working during the preceding evening. Since it is the twenty-first century and they do not use many books, this might not take fifteen minutes.[47]
- 8:15–8:30—Go to your desk, which might be a desk in the open area of the library or a desk in a small, enclosed area with a door. Turn on your computer to check your e-mail. You probably checked your e-mail on a handheld device before you left home, but attachments and lists of things are difficult to view on that device, so you will actually review them once in the office with a larger screen. There are several queries from the younger attorneys about what materials the library owns as well as requests from them for materials not owned. You respond to those queries for material you own in a physical or electronic format, with some description of where to locate the material. Most of the periodical literature and some of the treatise material you do not own will be available from HeinOnline, Lexis, or Westlaw, but some will require you to borrow from other law libraries. You find one question from a senior partner requiring you to do some research. You respond to the quick answers and start work on the others. It is sometimes easier to complete the small projects first, unless there is a request that requires a great deal of effort in a short time frame. Discerning this is an acquired skill. Assume that everything is urgent in a law firm.[48]
- 8:30–9:30—Work on the little "document delivery" projects that came in late e-mails of the day before. Printing from Lexis, West-

law, and/or HeinOnline should satisfy some requests. If you don't
have HeinOnline, you queue those queries up to print off at the
local county law library or the local university with HeinOnline
access. Others will have to be obtained from one of the same local
public law libraries or elsewhere. You check your local union lists
of periodicals or go to the online catalogs of the institutions where
you do your business and organize your afternoon trip to the local
libraries.

- 9:30–11:30—The mail arrives, allowing you to obtain ILL materials,
  newly ordered books and reprinted articles, bills, and such. Spend
  an hour sorting, checking in, and routing the mail, and an hour on
  the new arrivals, checking them against your files to be sure you
  ordered them,[49] then stamping and processing them, and putting
  them into the interoffice mail to be delivered to the appropriate
  attorney or putting them on the shelves in the library. It is often
  good public relations to physically take a volume to its intended
  recipient, as face time with lawyers is important. You also spend
  some of this time parsing and routing electronic serials to different
  groups. Additionally, some of the Westlaw or Lexis overnight
  watches have been delivered and need to be routed to the appropriate persons.[50]
- 11:30–12:30—Eat lunch, preferably out of the office. You will be
  tempted and sometimes required to eat lunch at your desk while
  you are performing various tasks. At all possible times, eat away
  from your office. This does not mean you can't bring food from
  home, just eat it away from the office. This will keep you fresher for
  your job later on.
- 12:30–1:00—Office raids. You will generally need to seek permission from your managing partner for this type of search and sei-
  zure, but they are usually willing to grant it, particularly if they
  have not been able to look at something because it's missing. Once
  permission is obtained, office searches make the firm librarian's job
  smoother. Notify your attorneys in advance that you are going to
  go through offices looking for materials that have been removed
  from the library but not checked out. The mere notification will
  result in a number of items being returned in the office mail.
- 1:00–2:30—After lunch, head to the local library. You might want to
  vary your lunch schedule to go to libraries when they are not on a
  lunch schedule, eating later and going out afterwards. Why? Do
  this so that you are not competing with every other employee in the
  area for valuable library services over the lunch period. This might
  be moved to one of the first things done during the morning or the
  last things done in the afternoon, arriving a bit late or leaving a bit
  early to do work outside of the office.[51]

- 2:30–3:00—Read e-mails that came in over lunch and during your trip to the library. Respond to those and provide the services necessary, such as computer-aided legal research (CALR) searches and document provision.
- 3:00–5:00—Work on long-term research projects, starting competitive intelligence reviews or digging for company information for business development, and finish up the daily requests that come in.

What's missing from the timeline above? Reading journal literature, attending continuing legal education (CLE) or law library association meetings,[52] working on presentations to make to attorneys in the firm or to other librarians, talking on the telephone with clients and other librarians, attending firm meetings regarding human relations policies and precedent, budgeting, and reading numerous e-mails, both client related and informational.[53] Many law librarians subscribe to listservs such as lawlib or acq-1, which carry e-mail traffic concerning issues relating to your job, or receive e-mail based on membership in one or more of the thirteen AALL special interest sections. Many use Twitter feeds as well. Finally, you may also have a listserv for your local law library network. These listservs, interest sections, and specialty groups are excellent for bouncing odd reference questions off a host of experienced law librarians.

STATE, COURT, AND COUNTY LAW LIBRARIES

Many of the day-to-day tasks noted above apply to the law librarian in the state, court, or county law library, as well. They have a slightly different clientele than do the firm and academic law libraries. Their patrons are the *pro se* patron, the practicing attorney, the public prosecutor and defender, and the judge. Yet the provision of basic legal research services remains the same. The state, court, and county law librarians often have an outreach mission to the general public. They educate the public about the law, lawyers, and the legal process. To this end the state, court, and county law librarians prepare tours of historic legal buildings and exhibits of bits of legal history, such as photographs and materials relating to famous cases. Finally, the state, court, and county law librarians prepare research aids to assist the "do-it-yourself" *pro se* patron in accomplishing specific legal tasks, often working in tandem with a local court clerk's office to do so.[54] Such works assist *pro se* patrons who do not have the means to hire legal assistance. Many times the assistance needed is how to fill out forms or how to file legal papers. Sometimes the *pro se* patron needs to find the correct forms to accomplish something as simple as a name change, or sometimes it is something more complex, such as a divorce. The state, court, and county librarians can assist in this process, and reduce their workload, by preparing comprehensive help pieces, though always keeping in mind the difference between legal reference and practicing law.

In addition, the state, court, and county librarians also have a potential client not shared with the other types of law libraries: the prisoner. Because state, court, and county law libraries are public law libraries, they often provide legal research assistance for the incarcerated, but usually only research of a general nature and often only copies, if the prisoner is able to provide specific citations. Many of the state's highest appellate court law libraries also receive requests from prisoners for copies of the transcripts from the lower court trial of the imprisoned. The transcripts are pored over by the prisoners, looking for any irregularity that might be used to set them free. Unfortunately, many of the requests for service are futile and often incomprehensible because, in general, the prisoners may not know what they are looking for or how to ask for it.

Rather than be besieged by a hail of requests, the library providing this sort of service should institute a payment plan whereby the prisoner will send funds to the law library to pay for copying. The law library should also inform prisoners of the following: that it will only fill requests for specific citations or very easy reference questions,[55] that the prisoner must let the law library know the prison institution's regulations relating to prisoners receiving copies, that the library will copy only as staff time allows, and that they must have cash up front or a prepaid prisoner account before the law library will provide copies. Provision of copies of legal materials to prisoners can be personally rewarding, but it can also cause disruption in the primary mission of the state, court, and county law library, unless strictly controlled.

SPECIALIZED SERVICES OF THE LAW LIBRARIAN

"The librarian performs miracles." "How did you do that?" "Where do you find this stuff? This is great!" "Thanks, thanks, thanks." These are things I have heard said about law librarians from their patron base, their clients. The clients say these things because the law librarian has developed specialized skills at manipulating databases or other information sources to provide what seems like magic to the layperson. The magic is not as specialized today, since many people can get into databases. Most people are too busy doing what they do best to truly learn the ins and outs of the use of information technology. Specialized services include things like:

- Smart Current Index to Legal Periodicals (CILP), which is a current-awareness service for law reviews, providing a subject-customizable listing of the tables of contents of new law review articles. It is modestly priced for law firms and very modestly priced for academic law libraries.

- Dialog databases are a ProQuest company. This database aggregator provides access to a host of databases that allow the librarian to produce lists of publications written by expert witnesses, the market share of an industry to show anticompetitive tendencies, and journal articles in scientific and business areas for attorney education in a field outside the law.
- People finders help the librarian locate experts, witnesses, and others essential to a case. Lexis and Westlaw have their own aggregators of such information, but there are many others to choose from that are not quite as expensive as the legal research providers.
- People information allows you to find information about the assets people own, including property and moving vehicles such as cars, boats, and airplanes.
- Company information shows who and what companies are, whether they have good credit ratings, and, very importantly, whether it is likely that they will be able to pay the fee if they engage the services of your firm.
- Geographic information shows just how far an address is from the courthouse, allowing the attorney to subpoena someone.
- Ephemeral information assists you in determining whether the moon was actually shining that night and can thus corroborate or disprove a witness's testimony.
- Client development may be done by the librarian or attorneys. Large law firms have many people who scan the news and search databases to cull information relevant to landing new clients for the firm. Smaller firms do not, and this work is often done by the attorneys themselves. Unfortunately, these attorneys have neither the expertise nor the time to do such work. If a partner is going to go pitch the firm to a potential client, you can truly impress if you put together a company dossier with pertinent information about the company or individual in question, what they do, and whether they are a good credit risk. Lexis and Westlaw have client-development products that are very useful although costly, so you might trade some of your time and skill to provide a similar product at a lower price.[56]
- Conflict checking is sometimes handled by law firm librarians. Conflicts are a term of art indicating a relationship of your firm with another party, such that you cannot be hired as counsel. *Conflicts* is a shorthand term for pointing out the ramifications of such "conflicts of interest" when a law firm begins to take on the representation of a new client. In highly simplified terms, let us say your firm wants to be hired to do some work for Company A but also represents Company B, which has a pending law suit against Com-

pany A. Legal ethics rules would usually prevent your firm from representing Company A, and if your firm started representing Company A in error, serious repercussions could result, including the loss of income and your firm's good name. Librarians are often able to ferret out complex company relationships that would baffle others by using a variety of paper and online resources. Often, the conflicts in a small firm are handled by one person, who also has other duties. In large firms there are many individuals devoted to keeping the firm out of a conflicting-interest situation. This is usually done before a new client engages the firm.

CONCLUSION

A tour through the various jobs in the law library allows a new librarian or library employee to learn about the new institution, meet coworkers, and learn about law libraries in general. Once each part or department is viewed, the whole (i.e., the library) makes more sense. A brief description of most of the professional jobs in the modern law library gives a novice librarian an opinion as to whether she or he wants to work in a law library. A sense of *a day in the life* at an academic, county, and firm library has been offered. Finally, there is a list of what makes a law librarian special—the various specialized services that can be given to faculty, judges, and practicing attorneys that will make the value of the law librarian worth his or her salary.[57]

NOTES

1. There are three types of law schools: state supported, private or affiliated with a private college or university, and standalone. Typically all are run along the same lines.

2. One prime example would be the joint governance structure existing between the Duquesne University Law Library and the Allegheny County Law Library.

3. In my own institution, for example, we made the decision to drop microform copies of legal serials if we held that serial in hard copy and it was also available to us electronically. In some cases, we found that we had access to as many as five different forms of some serial titles.

4. It has been said that the academic law library truly exists for the research needs of the law faculty, and the students are merely the funding mechanism, but that may be a bit of an overstatement.

5. Witness the title of the 2006 American Association of Law Schools annual meeting: "Empirical Scholarship: What Should We Study and How Should We Study It?" See the 2006 *Proceedings of the American Association of Law Schools.*

6. There are notable exceptions, such as the Los Angeles County Law Library. LA County, as it is known, is one of the largest law libraries in the United States and is well known for its collection of foreign legal materials, which is unusual for a county law library, but necessary in the high-stakes legal world of Southern California.

7. In the law firm environment, space is money. Although a few firms own their own buildings, most rent space that can run into the hundreds of dollars per square

foot per month in the denser metropolitan areas such as New York City and San Francisco. While it is generally cheaper in the less dense areas, it can still run into the mid-double digits. It is prohibitively expensive to retain materials on site when they can be obtained elsewhere or stored off-site.

8. That is, they will not unless they are of a caliber such that the collection-development plan calls for access to nearly everything published in the legal field that comes on the market. This would include law libraries on the magnitude of Harvard, Yale, Georgetown, and the University of Texas. Notice, though, that the call is for access, because even these law libraries cannot have everything, and interlibrary loan is used quite extensively between law libraries. See the Collection Development Policy of the Harvard Law School Library and their Collection Development Matrix, http://etseq.law.harvard.edu/2010/02/harvard_law_library_collection_development_policy_and_collection_developmen/ (last viewed September 2, 2012).

9. This is not to say that law firm libraries and state, court, and county law libraries do not have collection policies. Many will use a collection-development policy to justify what they purchase and to control costs by not purchasing things that are not necessary. See Jennifer Adams, "Digital Divide: Tips for Developing a Digital Collection Development Policy," *AALL Spectrum* 15 (September–October 2010): 36–37; James S. Heller, "Collection Development and Weeding à la Versace: Fashioning a Policy for Your Library," *AALL Spectrum* 6 (February 2002): 12–14; Karen Silber, "Every Library Is Special and So Is Its Collection Development Policy," *AALL Spectrum* 4 (December 1999): 10–11; Jonathan A. Franklin, "One Piece of the Collection Development Puzzle: Issues in Drafting Format Selection Guidelines," *Law Library Journal* 86 (Fall 1994): 753–80. For a different perspective, see also Cindy Hirsch, "The Rise and Fall of Academic Law Library Collection Standards," *Legal Reference Services Quarterly* 58 (2012): 65–103. This article describes the evolution of the academic collection-development plan, its relation to the ABA standards, and the tension arising between the desire to collect appropriately and the lack of funding to do so.

10. My first job out of library school was as a documents receiving clerk in the federal Government Documents Collection at the Texas State Library. That clerical job gave me the entrée to my first professional job eight months later, as a cataloger, reference librarian, and government documents specialist at the Texas State Law Library. A librarian can hone his or her skills while working at a clerical job by having an alert mind and open eyes. This enables the librarian to understand how things are done and to think about how things could be handled better. It allows for the examination of how all the systems that make up the institution relate to each other. Systems analysis can be used at any point in any job, but only if you know the details.

11. Firm library openings are usually caused by someone leaving for retirement. This position is then filled by someone from a smaller firm. An entry-level job then opens in one of the smaller firms.

12. Some very competitive law school students "hide" materials from one another. Students, after examining a class syllabus, will head to the collection to remove materials that might be of assistance to fellow classmates and move them to another location, out of call-number sequence, as a personal library. An active stack-maintenance program can foil this behavior.

13. Technical services staff can make mistakes. Shelvers find those mistakes when they shelve materials, such as mislabeled items and incorrect call numbers, where the call number does not match the item or the area. These can only be caught if the shelver is paying attention.

14. Most modern libraries have an integrated library system (ILS) that integrates a serials system and online public catalog into one seamless whole. Serial items arriving in the mail are generally checked into the serials system. The check-in is usually based on a prediction pattern and is useful if an issue is missed. Missing issues must be claimed as soon as noticed because they quickly become unavailable as time progresses.

15. For instance, some publishers refuse to deal with jobbers. Commerce Clearing House, a subsidiary of Wolters Kluwer, is a large tax, business, and law loose-leaf publisher that does not sell its serials to jobbers for redistribution. Thomson/West, a large legal publisher, has the same policy.

16. Publishers will often tell libraries to keep an unsolicited piece of material if the library requests a postage-paid label to return an unsolicited item.

17. Issuing a check costs the institution money. That cost will vary depending on the bank involved, the types of retention policies, the cost of the staff issuing the check, and other factors such as storage, retrieval, and accounting services. I have found costs varying from $1.50 to $10.00 per check, and have had comptrollers at places where I work quote me figures as high as $20.00 per check over the life of the check. It stands to reason that if you can reduce the number of checks issued, you will reduce your costs of doing business and save money for the place where you work. Some institutions are very high tech and will also engage in electronic data interchange (EDI, which is a standardized data exchange of information that eliminates a great deal of paperwork) and wire transfers (transfers of funds between banks, such that the purchasing institution does not have to write a check at all). More sophisticated EDI systems can also be developed to insert items received in a shipment directly into the ILS, only needing staff verification but without requiring the staff to keyboard the data.

18. Many times these records in the public access catalog are suppressed for the general public.

19. An initial problem for most academic and state-owned institutions is that pre-payment is usually prohibited; payment can only be made for items in hand.

20. When I was working at a firm library, we once prepaid a book order that took two years to be filled. We really did want the publication but were at the mercy of an overcommitted author.

21. See Jesse Holden, *Acquisitions in the New Information Universe* (New York: Neal-Schuman, 2010), or Liz Chapman, *Managing Acquisitions in Library and Information Services*, rev. ed. (New York: Neal-Schuman, 2008). For the acquisition of electronic resources, see Diane K. Kovacs, *The Kovacs Guide to Electronic Library Collection Development: Essential Core Subject Collections, Selection Criteria, and Guidelines*, 2nd ed. (New York: Neal-Schuman, 2009).

22. Public services librarians should learn to use the institution's catalog to ascertain whether or not the library already owns something. Depending on the institution, acquisitions staff may act as the secondary checker, not the primary checker, of whether an institution already owns something.

23. SkyRiver Technology Solutions (SkyRiver) is a fairly recent addition to the universe of bibliographic utilities. Formerly there were two utilities, OCLC and the Research Libraries Group (RLG). OCLC and RLG merged on July 1, 2006. SkyRiver started business in late 2009 as a direct competitor with OCLC in the provision of bibliographic utilities services.

24. As with most rules, this one is proved by the exceptions. Count the number of law libraries in the United States, and you will have some idea of the number of different ways a law library can be staffed. Certainly, in some law libraries, circulation services can be supervised by a librarian. It is not necessarily a "librarian" type of function, however, since a great deal of what is included in this area is clerical by its very nature: cleaning, reshelving, and charging and discharging books. It is a "management" area, since there are a number of staff members working there, so a librarian might be in a managing position.

25. Why? Because these are typically loose-leaf volumes in nature, sometimes very difficult to replace if lost, and the set is often less valuable if a volume is missing from the set for upwards of two weeks. Nothing can be more frustrating to the researcher than finding in the index to a set the citation to a specific part of the set and then discovering that that "piece" is missing. One thing is equally frustrating: finding that the volume with the index is missing.

26. OCLC allows the use of interlibrary loan management software that has been developed by a third party. One software program in common use is called Clio. Clio is produced independently of any integrated library system, but it has reached an agreement with Endeavor to allow some customizations with Endeavor's Voyager ILS. OCLC's basic version is its WorldCat Resource Sharing, which uses their First Search system as a combination of federated search tool and interlibrary loan tool. OCLC also has a more complete software system called Illiad, which integrates the power of the enormous database of library holdings with a management system of high complexity. For instance, Illiad can be set up to allow the placement and receipt of electronic requests by the end user, with intermediation by a library staff member only when there are problems or when a physical object is to be delivered, rather than an electronic object. Finally, OCLC has a new system based on the WorldCat resource, OCLC World Share Interlibrary Loan, which is slated to replace WorldCat Resource Sharing in 2013.

27. As an example, see the South Florida area or the South East Florida Library and Information Network (SEFLIN) networks. Those groups have agreed not to charge each other fees for lending. There is also a courier who makes the rounds among the SEFLIN member libraries, delivering loans and returning borrowed items. While there is a fee for SEFLIN membership, the value of this feature, among others, makes it highly desirable to participate. For example, if a library borrows fifty items per month at an average cost of $15 handling per item, the library will spend $9,000 per year on fees alone, not counting postage charges. Cutting this number in half is highly desirous. Other networks of non-fee lending agreements abound, such as the Southern California Circuit in San Diego, and the Association of Jesuit Colleges and Universities. The former is composed of five moderate to exceedingly large academic collections, the San Diego County Library System, and, in the near future, the San Diego Public Library System. As with the SEFLIN network, there is a fee for membership and a continuing maintenance agreement for supporting a common innovative database. The latter is an association of Jesuit and Catholic universities and their associated law school libraries that have an agreement not to charge each other fees for borrowing. There is no common database, other than the OCLC network, but there is a common desire to cooperate.

28. Some libraries continue to use Infotrieve's Ariel, originally developed by the Research Libraries Group, to send materials. Ariel is a software program that, when used along with a scanner, PC, and high-speed data line, allows the user to scan a document or portion from a book into an image file, and send that scanned document to a requestor who is also an Ariel user. This eliminates the need to pack, label, and ship materials and the resulting time delay, as well as any postal charges. This is very useful for journal articles, since journals are usually not circulated. Previously, if Ariel was not used, then the journals were usually photocopied and mailed. The ubiquity of e-mail and the ability to easily scan and shrink the resulting scanned document size by using an image software program such as Adobe Pro, such that the resulting file does not violate the size restrictions of normal e-mail systems, have reduced the need to rely on the Ariel system. Because scanning requires about the same amount of time as photocopying, there is no savings in staff time for the reproduction of a loaned item, but significant cost savings are achieved in the reduction of packaging, labor for packaging, and mailing costs.

29. The cost of interlibrary lending, of course, varies from library to library. The Association of Research Libraries (ARL) has conducted studies of the costs associated with interlibrary loan, giving libraries a benchmark of average costs. Such benchmarks allow libraries to compare their costs to averages to see if they are in line. One study, performed in 1998, indicated that the total average cost of a mediated interlibrary loan transaction was $27.83 for a research library and $19.33 for a college library. See Mary E. Jackson, "Measuring the Performance of Interlibrary Loan and Document Delivery Services," *ARL: A Bimonthly Newsletter of Research Library Issues and Actions*, no. 195 (December 1997), available at http://www.arl.org/resources/pubs/br/index.shtml. ARL

conducted a follow-up study in 2004. In the intervening years, the ILL systems developed unmediated interfaces, user-based systems, rather than those mediated by staff. The 2004 ARL study by Mary E. Jackson, *Assessing ILL/DD Services: New Cost-Effective Alternatives* (Washington, DC: Association of Research Libraries, 2004), indicates that the unmediated costs have decreased substantially, to a range from $2.39 to $14.00, with the mediated costs decreasing to an average of $17.50. The 2004 study is summarized in "Assessing ILL/DD Services: New Cost-Effective Alternatives," *ARL Bimonthly Report*, no. 236 (October 2004), available at http://www.arl.org/resources/pubs/br/index.shtml.

30. This example illustrates the adage that no good deed goes unpunished, no bad deed unrewarded.

31. When an institution creates its network and connects it to the Internet, the institution will be assigned a range of Internet Protocol (IP) addresses. These are unique to the institution. Some institutions may have multiple ranges as they grow out of their original assigned addresses. Conversely, the institution may want to segregate itself by IP range, such that different parts of the institution have different ranges. For example, a computing lab may have its own range that is different from that of the law school library, which is different from that of the university library. More information about the domain name system and assigning IP addresses can be found at the Web site of the group that does this work, the Internet Corporation of Assigned Names and Numbers, www.icann.org/en.

32. Lexis and Westlaw are two computer-assisted legal research databases that are quite comprehensive in nature. They are competing services owned, respectively, by Elsevier and Thomson, two foreign public companies. Both contain a host of primary legal materials, as well as secondary materials published by their own companies, plus other secondary materials licensed from other providers. There is a great deal of overlap in the primary materials and in the journals, but very little overlap in the nonjournal secondary sources.

33. A good example is the Haworth journals; they are available through repackagers and through direct links for subscription to the hard copy.

34. HeinOnline is a product produced by William S. Hein & Co., commonly referred to as *Hein*. Hein started as a reprint house, providing reprints of legal serials. It also publishes a large quantity of legislative history compilations and individual monographs in the legal field. It produces the "green slips" service for acquisitions of legal materials. Before 2006 it also jobbed the materials represented in its "slips." This service is no longer provided. HeinOnline is a ten-year-old venture that reproduces law review and other serial titles as PDF files via online access. Additionally, HeinOnline mounts reproduced versions of public domain titles such as the U.S. Reports and various state session laws, and some leased content from other providers. The genius of HeinOnline is that, in general, it goes back to the initial volume of the serial, while its competition, Lexis and Westlaw, do not. In addition, HeinOnline has made the *Federal Register* and the *Congressional Record* available back to volume 1, issue 1 — mammoth undertakings, but both long overdue in the legal information industry.

35. Directional reference is directing people to where *things* are, such as facilities within the library (Where is the media department? Where is the bathroom?), as well as the location of materials (Where are the state reporters and the state statutes?). General nonlegal reference consists of queries such as would arrive at the reference desk of any library (What is the capital of . . . ?; Who is the president of . . . ?; What is the address and how should I address the ambassador to Burkina Faso?). Business nonlegal, though, is one of the fastest-growing segments of reference, particularly in law firm libraries. Business nonlegal reference would include things like market share and competitive intelligence questions.

36. This usually involves extremely old citations; only the newest of law students will inquire as to the meaning of a citation to the National Reporter System. For immediate access to Bieber's work, see Mary Miles Prince, *Prince's Bieber Dictionary of Legal Abbreviations: A Reference Guide for Attorneys, Legal Secretaries, Paralegals and Law*

Students, 6th ed. (Buffalo, NY: Hein, 2009), which is exceedingly useful for interpreting very old citations.

37. Great care must be taken in interpretation not to run afoul of the unauthorized practice of law statutes, particularly with the *pro se* or general lay patron. A great bibliography of articles about unauthorized practice is Paul D. Healey, "Pro Se Users, Reference Liability, and the Unauthorized Practice of Law: Twenty-Five Selected Readings," *Law Library Journal* 94, no. 1 (Winter 2002): 133–39.

38. For more information on writing, see Strunk and White; Bryan Garner, *Garner's Dictionary of Legal Usage*, 3rd ed. (New York: Oxford, 2011); or Bryan Garner, *The Elements of Legal Style*, 2nd ed. (New York: Oxford, 2002).

39. Table 8, "Average Number of Professionals per Library (FTE)" in *AALL Biennial Salary Survey & Organization Characteristics* (2011); and Item 18, "Full Time Equivalent Professional Librarians" in the American Bar Association's *Comprehensive Law Library Statistical Table Data from the Annual Questionnaire*, which gives the specific numbers of professional law librarians in each academic institution.

40. As Groucho Marx opined, "Please accept my resignation. I don't want to belong to any club that will accept me as a member." Elizabeth Knowles, ed., *Oxford Dictionary of Quotations*, 7th ed. (New York: Oxford Univeristy Press, 2009), 527, quoting from *Groucho and Me* (1959), ch. 26.

41. It is, of course, by happenstance that the purveyor of this advice has worked in both technical services and public services, as well as all three types of law libraries.

42. When you supervise personnel, you will be able to use them either to the advantage or detriment of the supervised employee when you complete his or her performance evaluation.

43. The annual meeting of the American Association of Law Libraries in 2000 had a program titled "The ABA Reaccreditation Visit: Process and Preparation," July 16, 2000. Two presentations at that meeting resulted in documents posted to the Internet site of the association's Academic Law Libraries SIS. The first is Donald J. Dunn, "What to Expect When the ABA Site Evaluator Arrives—and Perhaps a Bit Before . . ." and the second is a bibliography compiled by Leslie M. Campbell and Ellen Platt, "The ABA Reaccreditation Inspection Visit: Process and Preparation." Both were available on the AALL Special Interest Section Academic Law Libraries (ALL) Web site but, illustrating the problem with citations to information held on a Web site, are no longer. At the time of this writing, they are held as part of the Internet Archive WayBack-Machine at http://web.archive.org/web/20060214093707/http://www.aallnet.org/sis/allsis/abavisit/index.html and in the author's files. The second article can also be found in *Gateways to Leadership AALL Educational Program Handout Materials 93rd Annual Meeting* (2000), 91.

44. And this would be true for firm partners and court judges, as well.

45. It is wasteful to move and remove and move volumes yet again, because not enough space has been left for the growth of a collection. In general, when a library has only 15 percent of growth space remaining, it is time to plan to weed the collection heavily or add more shelving.

46. While it will vary from institution to institution, members of library governing boards are usually elected or appointed for a fixed term of years. Deans, by nature of their contentious jobs, generally serve as dean for approximately four years.

47. There are a multitude of costs appended to an employee besides pay, including unemployment taxes, Social Security taxes, and health care (if lucky). Such ancillary benefits can rise to as much as one-third of the straight salary.

48. Law partners expect results.

49. Some publishers, through inadvertence, sloppiness, or malice, try to get a library to purchase materials that were not ordered. Thus, be careful when stamping new materials. Once stamped, consider it bought. Check the "on order" files to be sure the books and materials received are the books and materials that were ordered.

50. Both of the major computer-assisted legal research vendors, Lexis and Westlaw, allow the creation of profiles of search words, generally called "watches," to be run on

a regular basis against specific databases. These profiles will be run to produce current awareness on specific topics. To save attorney's time, it might be best if the librarian scans the watches first before forwarding them to the attorney because word searches can be tricky and produce null results, or "false drops" in the terms used in database searching.

51. Be careful leaving early or arriving late. Office politics come into play. Perception matters.

52. Join organizations that will aid in professional development. Join the local law librarian group, if one exists, and the regional chapter of AALL. If no local group exists, join whatever local librarian group is available. Join the national association, the American Association of Law Libraries, as this is the premier tool for education and networking for law librarians.

53. E-mail and RSS feeds are good delivery mechanisms for keeping up with Internet-related topics, as well as current happenings in the law library world. AALL used to maintain listservs for its unit organizations, such as special interest sections and caucuses, but changed to a social network form of communication. In the new format there are "Member Communities" representing the various units of the national association. Communication within the community is accomplished by using each community's discussion center. Members may choose, instead, to have e-mails sent to an address of record, or a digest of the community traffic, or even an RSS feed of the message traffic. In addition to the member communities officially sponsored by the American Association of Law Library units is law-lib. Law-lib is the oldest law library listserv. To subscribe to law-lib, send an e-mail to listproc@ucdavis.edu. In the body of the e-mail, write "subscribe law-lib first name last name" without the quotes. This is fairly old technology, so service from the listserv is driven through commands inside e-mails addressed to the listproc. An FAQ for the listserv is held here: http://home.olemiss.edu/~noe/llfaq.html.

54. The clerk's office has a vested interest in helping the law librarian, as the time needed to assist the *pro se* patron in filing court cases can be reduced.

55. Otherwise, the law library will receive long nonsensical recitations of facts, real and fanciful, requesting in-depth research services.

56. The price is really not lower; time has been traded in place of paying someone else (like Lexis or Westlaw) to provide a product.

57. As for your value, see LaJean Humphries and Denise Pagh, "What Makes a Librarian Worth a Million Bucks? Valuing Staff, Resources and Services when Dollars are Scarce," program J-4 from the 105th Annual Meeting and Conference of the American Association of Law Libraries, Boston, Massachusetts (July 21–24, 2012). This program was video recorded and is available with a PDF of the handout, a video of the presentation, and an MP3, from the AALL2go series of Annual Meeting recordings.

THREE

The Administration of the Academic Law Library: The Glue That Binds

Lisa Smith-Butler

INTRODUCTION[1]

Christopher Langdell elevated the academic law library to the center of the law school enterprise in the 1880s.[2] How did he accomplish this? Langdell studied law as a student at Harvard Law School and worked in the library.[3] While studying and working in the law library, he came to believe that the essence of legal study involved the examination of cases. This meant that law could and should be learned as a science.[4] In his preface to his casebook on contracts, which was published in 1871, Langdell stated: "Law, considered as a science, consists of certain principles or doctrines."[5] Since Langdell articulated the theory that cases were the center of the study of law, it was reasonable to believe that the law library, with its access to cases, was the center of the law school.[6]

Since then, academic law librarians have worked hard to maintain that status, ensuring that the law library remains at the heart of the academic endeavor, as well as being the glue that binds the various law school constituencies together.[7] How does the law library accomplish this? The law library director and the library staff manage relationships, personnel, facilities, a collection, and a budget, as well as providing and managing services to various groups.[8] The library staff engages in strategic planning, anticipating future needs and trends, and articulating a vision that mirrors the law school's mission.[9] The director and staff ensure compliance with American Bar Association (ABA) standards,

45

IPEDS,[10] and other accreditation requirements.[11] These individuals also provide documentation to demonstrate compliance.[12]

The law library belongs to everyone: students, faculty, staff, alumni, and the local practicing bench and bar. It is the meeting place where these various groups come together to collaborate. All of this enables the library to remain at the center of the law school. As part of this process, the law library director, while responsible for the management of the library's collection and physical space, is the steward of the library for what will amount to a brief period of time in an enterprise.

As libraries moved from the twentieth into the twenty-first century, academic law libraries began to move away from the focus on the acquisition of large collections.[13] Instead of emphasizing the size of collections, libraries began to concentrate on the availability and delivery of services to students and faculty.[14]

This chapter explores the administration of an academic law library and examines how the academic law library administration can help facilitate this change, enabling the law library to continue to exist as the hub of the law school by managing key relationships, personnel, facilities, collections, budgets, and services. It reviews and discusses how the academic law library director oversees the law library's administration, while also fulfilling the faculty roles of teaching, writing, and serving on committees.[15] To successfully run a law library, the law library director wears many hats and helps dispense the glue that binds faculty, staff, and students together.[16]

To paraphrase Dickens, academic law libraries today encounter both "the best of times and the worst of times."[17] The format of and method of access to legal information have been transformed in the last fifteen years. Computer Assisted Legal Research (CALR) tools, such as Lexis and Westlaw, moved from software-based applications tied to a specific computer,[18] to "cloud"-based Internet systems that could be accessed 24/7 from anywhere a user was able to access a computer and obtain an Internet connection.[19] With 24/7 access to Lexis and Westlaw from anywhere in the world, the attorney, law student, faculty member, or legal researcher could immediately obtain access to the full text of American primary sources of law: cases, statutes, and regulations.[20] Today, Westlaw and Lexis, both expensive resources, face competition from new CALR systems, such as Bloomberg Law,[21] Casemaker,[22] FastCase,[23] LoisLaw Connect,[24] or VersusLaw.[25] Because the individual is no longer tied to a time or physical place in order to retrieve legal data, the twenty-first-century legal researcher has access to a sometimes-overwhelming amount of information. In addition to competition from fee-based legal research sites, reputable, free Internet sites, such as Cornell's Legal Information Institute,[26] Findlaw,[27] Justicia,[28] Google Scholar,[29] and Washlaw,[30] provide free access to reliable information.[31] Today's legal researcher is drowning in information resources that are easily reachable from anywhere at any time. The introductions of proxy server authentication and electronic resources are changes that make a librarian's job easier. One of the librarian's primary tasks today is to help legal researchers successfully and cost-effectively navigate the maze of information that researchers now encounter.[32]

Yet increased competition for space from other law school constituents[33] and declining law school enrollments[34] mean that this is also the worst of times for academic law libraries. Since everything is now online,[35] and big collections are no longer needed, the library's space, perceived as belonging to no one, is often "up for grabs" and is parceled out to satisfy other law school constituency needs, such as those of clinics or career development offices. Declining law school enrollments mean declining revenues.[36] Declining revenues require budget cuts. The obvious large budget that does not appear to belong to anyone is the library's acquisitions budget.[37] This allows schools to make cuts without sacrificing personnel.[38]

This chapter examines how academic law libraries are coping with these changes. Relationships are crucial to any endeavor, so the chapter begins by studying the library's management of people, relationships, and personnel.

MANAGING RELATIONSHIPS: COLLEAGUES, PERSONNEL, STAFF, AND THE BOSS

A law library director interacts with virtually every group within the law school setting and with others outside of the law school as well. In addition to law faculty, students, and staff, directors interact with university faculty, staff, and students, as well as the local bar and law school alumni. Relationships with these constituents are crucial; if managed well, they enable the law library to succeed.[39]

One of the most crucial relationships is the law library director's relationship with the individual who is typically the law school boss: the dean. What does the dean need and expect from a law library director?[40] A library director needs to understand the school's mission and the dean's vision. This will differ among schools, but it is essential that a law librarian understand the dean's mission for the school and then ensure that the law library mirrors it. Deans are also like any boss: they do not like unnecessary unpleasantness or surprises.[41] Library directors often manage large staffs and large budgets. Both should be handled efficiently and wisely.

At a recent Association of American Law Schools (AALS) workshop, library directors and deans spent the day together, reviewing the similarities and differences between their jobs.[42] According to workshop panelists, which included deans and library directors, the job of the dean and the job of the law library director share many similarities.[43] Both deal extensively with personnel, budgets, and multiple constituencies inside and outside of the law school. Their decisions have ramifications that extend far beyond their own departments. Each must then deal with the inevitable issues: the management of people and money. Why does it matter? Both topics often involve or generate conflict, disagreement, and envy.[44] How can these emotions best be managed by the law library director? Try to involve and include everyone. Act on the assumption that the law library belongs to all. Encourage this perception among law school faculty, staff, and students. When making decisions that will have wide-ranging impact, seek input from all stakeholders. While this will not eradicate conflict, disagreement, or envy, it may help contain it.

In spite of all of the library director's efforts, he or she should realize that someone will ask: "What do all of those people in the library do? Why do libraries need so much space and money?" Be prepared to respond to and thoroughly answer those questions. Libraries do occupy a significant amount of space within the law school facility. Libraries also require a great deal of money to build and sustain collections. They must have a staff of sufficient size to organize, classify, and help patrons retrieve information from library collections. How can library directors respond to these concerns? Do not answer defensively when asked these questions. Stay calm, smile, and answer the questions. Share this information by submitting a written annual report to the faculty and dean.[45] Make a brief presentation at the year-end faculty meeting. In short, know what all of those people in the library do and be prepared to explain it to others.

It is crucial that the library director interact with faculty. Why? In addition to being colleagues, faculty members are the library director's patrons. Library directors serve on committees with faculty, attend programs and other events to support faculty, share teaching and scholarship ideas, and also respond to faculty requests for information. Faculty support for the library makes many things possible.[46]

Relationships with other departments are also important. How can a director assist Career Services, Student Services, or Academic Affairs? Monitor and share information that pertains to these departments. Prepare career resources or job-hunting bibliographies to share with Career Services. If this department offers to provide students with mock interviews, volunteer to be an interviewer. Supply Student Services and Admissions with the numerous articles that detail the changes in the legal education market. Distribute alumni articles to Student Services. Set up alerts or readers for all departments.[47] Walk the floors, and talk to individuals within the departments. Use that time not only to discuss the library's services, but also to find out what a department's information needs are.

Despite best intentions and efforts, there will be encounters that prove to be painful, and there will be difficult people with whom a library director must cope. How? Step back and try to view the situation as an outsider might. Examine the other person's perspective and try to understand it. Disagree respectfully. Conflict and tension are inherent in relationships and organizations.[48] Establish boundaries, be clear about them, and then communicate those boundaries to others. Ultimately, each person must decide what behaviors are tolerable or intolerable.

The law library director's relationship with the library staff is crucial. Bookstores, libraries, Kindles, and Nooks are full of books on management style. A glance at titles often indicates that many of the books appear to contradict each other. What is a director to do?

Read widely in order to learn about managing people and ascertain your management style. Useful books, articles, and videos include *Quiet*,[49] "Servant Leadership,"[50] *Managing from the Heart*,[51] and *Fish*.[52] *Managing from the Heart* provides new managers with behavioral suggestions to sometimes do what is painful but necessary for the good of the organization.[53] The Seattle Pike Place Market produced a video, *Fish*, in the early 1990s that has become nationally known. It is a pleasure to watch, and it is also an excellent motivation tool. The *Fish* philosophy of "Play, Make Their Day, Be There, and Choose Your Attitude" is energizing and exciting.[54] "Servant Leadership" speaks of a different kind of leadership. In it, Filippa Anzalone challenges a leader to listen with empathy while committing to the growth of employees and ultimately to building a community.[55] Instead of focusing on outer-directed goals, such as the attainment of status and power, Anzalone, exploring the concepts of Robert Greenleaf and Larry Spears,[56] discusses qualities and behaviors that will allow leaders to listen and help others grow and develop. Susan Cain's discussion in *Quiet* of the attributes of introverts and their ability to be effective as leaders, despite the American culture of extroversion, is also a very helpful read.[57] All of these titles illuminate the path of leadership that the library director must tread.

Ultimately, the law library director's job is to get results. Getting results means classifying and organizing information so that patrons can effectively and efficiently retrieve it. In English, this means that materials, both print and electronic, are catalogued, and that books get out on the shelves with the appropriate call numbers on the spine label so that patrons can find needed information. Supplements and pocket parts are discarded as new materials arrive. IP access is correctly entered on the library's Web page so that patrons can access electronic material from both on campus and off campus. Guides, presentations, and programs are held to help patrons learn how to retrieve information. Who accomplishes these tasks? Staff.

What is expected from staff members? Tell them. Be specific and tell staff exactly what behavior is desired and required. Acknowledge their accomplishments, and praise them publicly. Reprimand personally and privately. The goal is to have a contented staff that works well together, while recognizing that conflict is inevitable.[58] Developing a staff and building a community take time and work.[59]

What happens when a discontented employee continually creates problems? Unfortunately, reprimands and counseling ensue, while termination is sometimes necessary. While never pleasant, it is sometimes necessary for the good of the library. It is not fair to ask other staff to continually cover for and handle the tasks and responsibilities left incomplete or undone by another coworker. How does a director know when termination is necessary? Give the employee the opportunity and time to make the requested changes in behavior. Be specific about what changes are required and then step back, taking the attitude that the employee will make the necessary changes. If repeated attempts fail, termination may be the only option.[60]

Students are another important group of people with whom law library directors must establish relationships. Students are the law library's raison d'être. They are why the library requires so much space, money, and staff. For many law students, the library becomes their second home, as they spend hours there on a daily basis, studying, researching, and collaborating with classmates. Not only is the library a collection that meets their information needs, it is also a student meeting space, individual study space, and often the socialization space among students. What do students want? Are their wants reasonable? Even if reasonable, can the library meet them? How does a library ascertain what the students' needs are and whether it is meeting those needs? How do the library staff and the library director handle disagreements with students? These are questions that the director and his or her staff must grapple with and be able to answer.[61]

In short, people are important. Library directors will need to be able to work effectively with a wide array of people. Interactions and relationships with others will determine one's success as a director.

FACILITIES

The library as space assumes a very large role in the law school setting today. Not only does it house a collection of materials, in both print and digital formats, it provides students with individual study space, as well as collaborative space to study together and interact with faculty.[62] Thus, the design of the library's space;[63] its furnishings; the creation of quiet, cell, and social zones; the establishment and enforcement of a food and drink policy; maintenance and construction are described in this section.

A circulation desk is necessary in an academic law library.[64] It is the focal point for patrons as they enter the library. Circulation staff can answer directional questions, point patrons in the appropriate direction, and check out class reserve materials and study rooms.[65] While study rooms and other materials can be checked out from the desk,[66] some academic law libraries are becoming creative and circulating not only books and rooms, but also therapy dogs, iPads, umbrellas, Kindles, bikes, power cords, and games. Class reserve materials and other heavily circulated items, such as study aids, bar prep materials, reference items, or CLE materials can be located in a closed reserve stacks section that is either behind or surrounding the circulation desk, slowing the loss of these types of materials.

Not only does the desk serve as a directional desk for patrons, it also serves as a reception desk for the library. This is typically the first place that patrons arrive and are greeted by staff. In addition to welcoming them, circulation staff can then direct patrons to the appropriate office, study room, or individual. The circulation desk can also serve as the reception or focal point for the law school. How? Libraries tend to be open longer hours than any other place on campus, so individuals who are lost on campus end up at the law library seeking guidance.

Besides welcoming patrons, answering directional questions, and checking out materials, circulation staff may also be able to multitask and accomplish a variety of law library chores. Stacks maintenance, shelf reading, and the processing of interlibrary loans are some examples of tasks that can be accomplished at the circulation desk by circulation staff. Circulation staff can also maintain statistics about item and patron type data, handle fines, add print money to student printing accounts, check materials in, reshelve, and update the library's circulation calendar.

The reference desk, if there is one, can be located either beside or across from the circulation desk. This is an ideal placement, as it allows circulation staff to direct patrons who have reference needs to an easily identifiable area. Some law libraries are abandoning the idea of a physical reference desk,[67] instead directing patrons to a librarian's office or embedding a librarian in places across the law school campus where faculty and students can be found.[68] The concept of a reference librarian encountering patrons only at a physical reference desk is changing. Librarians are no longer confined to the reference desk. Instead, librarians are embedded within online information portals, via e-mail, telephone, and chat reference, and across the campus.[69]

A help desk offering technology support to students might also be available in the library. It, too, along with the copier/printer room, should be located near the circulation and reference desks near the front of the library. It should be staffed by information technology professionals who can assist students with software and hardware computer issues. Ideally, it should be located near the copiers/printers so that it can provide needed student printer support.

Library offices should also be appropriately aligned. Reference librarian offices should be near the reference desk, while administrative offices should be behind those offices. Technical services, if not outsourced, should be near the loading dock. Under no circumstances should any of these offices be in the middle of the library's stacks or reading room. Why? Because activities in these office areas generate noise and create distractions. Students need to be able to study in a quiet area that is not constantly made noisy by staff members talking, copying, answering telephones, talking to vendors, answering reference questions, answering the doorbell, and opening boxes. These are activities that must occur out of earshot.[70]

Because students will be spending long hours in the library, comfortable furnishings are essential. A mixture of tables and chairs and carrels provide the ideal furnishings. Modular furniture that can be pulled apart and recombined in different ways is now the choice of many law libraries. Students like to be comfortable and arrange the furniture in a way that suits their study habits, instead of using the furniture as intended, as earlier generations did. Food and drink, once absolutely banned in all academic law libraries, now make an appearance. Beverages, nonalcoholic, are generally allowed in spill-proof containers. Food is dicier. Some libraries allow no food, while others permit "non-messy" snacks. At the Charleston School of Law, there is a kitchenette at the rear of the library that has a refrigerator, microwave, and coffee pot. While unorthodox, it does work. Students from the Student Bar Association (SBA) keep the refrigerator, microwave, tables, and chairs clean, and enjoy the ability to be able to eat lunch or dinner while simultaneously studying.

Establishing zones throughout the library facility can also enhance student studying and learning. A quiet zone means quiet, while a cell phone zone allows students to make and accept calls without disturbing classmates. Study rooms allow for talking and collaborative student learning, while a social area allows students to eat, chat casually, and mingle socially.[71]

More libraries are providing students with 24/7 access to the physical law library space via card swipe. Students may be in the library after library staff has gone home; this is something librarians should consider when designing a library facility. It should be possible to shutter and lock off reserve and special collections as well as the reference and circulation desks, so as to limit student access to these areas after staffed library hours.

A good relationship with facilities and maintenance is essential. Managing the library also means managing the facility. Floors must be swept, carpets vacuumed, shelves dusted, lights changed, and bathrooms cleaned. The presence of thousands of students walking daily throughout the building makes cleaning essential. Maintenance is also crucial.

Construction is the last topic to be reviewed. While some library directors never handle a construction project, other directors oversee everything from small annual overhauls to the construction of a new law
school building. Whether a project is large or small, construction is sure
to disrupt the library's schedule and generate complaints.[72] How should
a director handle the disruptions? First, apologize for the inconvenience,
and explain the reason for the construction. Provide faculty and students
with plenty of notice that the library facility will be unavailable for a
specified period of time. Make arrangements for them to use other study
space on campus or within the community. Move the library reference
services to the alternate study space, along with any print materials, typically study aids and textbooks, that students will need. Electronic access
to primary and secondary sources of law will make this process easier
than it would have been a decade ago.

If a director is designing a new law library facility and/or building,[73]
the design suggestions listed below should be useful. Make sure that
there is plenty of appropriate, visible signage throughout the library facility, providing students and faculty with directions. A combined circulation and reference desk with sufficient space for an enclosed reserve/
reference collection should be the first item that patrons encounter as
they enter the library. Offices for reference librarians should be behind or
near the reference desk. Nearby should be restrooms, water fountains, a
printer/copier room, and a technology support/help desk, staffed by technology professionals. Comfortable seating for students should be scat-
tered throughout this area. It should be an area where students can meet,
mingle, and chat quietly. Administrative offices should be located in this
area as well, while technical services offices and processing space should
be at the rear of the library near the school's loading dock, in order to
receive materials without disrupting students' studying.

As patrons leave this entry area, a door to close the area off from the
general stacks area would be ideal. Why? It would help prevent the
spread of noise into the stacks, reading room, and quiet study area. The
reading room area should have plenty of natural light, along with tables
and chairs, power to the tables, and carrels at which students can study.
The type of furniture selected depends on the style of the school and the
library. In the past, beautiful wooden furniture was often the choice of
directors, but there is a movement toward modular, pull-apart furniture
with wheeled task chairs. Students seem to prefer arranging and rear-
ranging their study space.

As print collections are downsizing and electronic materials are increasing, there is a perceived need for fewer shelves. Every law library is
different, but plan on having sufficient shelving to get the library through
twenty-five to thirty years of print-collection growth. Compact shelving,
either manual or electric, is a space saver in terms of shelving, but it does
make it difficult for patrons to use the collection when an aisle is occu-

pied by another patron. If a library's print collection gets extensive use, make sure to shelve infrequently used materials in the compact shelving. If there is more than one floor in the library, make sure that the upper floors are load bearing so that additional compact shelving can be added at a later date if needed.

Study rooms, preferably soundproof, should be plentiful, allowing students the opportunity to collaborate with classmates, as well as interact with faculty members. Students use study rooms for group study, group exercises, moot court or mock trial practices, and occasional meetings with professors. In addition to tables and chairs, some of the study rooms should have LCD projection systems so that students can also use technology to collaborate. There should always be a window in a study room.

A training room that can also double as a seminar room, conference room, study room, and library staff meeting room is also needed. Include a podium in it, and students can then use the room for moot court practices. A computer lab may or may not be needed, depending on the school's mission and whether or not the school has a mandatory laptop requirement. Avoid having regularly scheduled classes take place in the training room. Why? Students make a lot of noise entering and exiting a classroom, forgetting that they are in the *shush* zone.

Stairwells, while necessary, and atriums, while lovely, are both very noisy. Not only do they generate noise, they spread it throughout the library. This results in numerous student complaints about noise. If neither can be avoided, consider installing a white noise machine.[74] A food court or library patio, adjacent to the library, can also make studying more pleasant for students.

Finally, connectivity (wireless access) is crucial. Students today rely on Westlaw, Lexis, Google, and many other electronic resources. They access the school's wireless network in order to study, do research, and print. Since much of a library's collection is now in electronic rather than print format, good connectivity to a wireless network is essential. This then leads to the next section of the chapter: what should the law library's collection contain?

COLLECTIONS

When making decisions about the format and the materials to be contained in an academic law library's collection, some of the factors the library director should consider are:

- user preferences;
- school mission;
- preservation of primary materials for future generations of legal scholars;

- costs of physical and virtual storage space for collections; and
- American Bar Association Standard 606.

The American Bar Association Standard 606 for the accreditation of law schools requires that an academic law library collection:

> Standard 606. COLLECTION
>
> (a) The law library shall provide a core collection of essential materials accessible in the law library.
>
> (b) In addition to the core collection of essential materials, a law library shall also provide a collection that, through ownership or reliable access,
>
> (1) meets the research needs of the law school's students, satisfies the demands of the law school curriculum, and facilitates the education of its students;
>
> (2) supports the teaching, scholarship, research, and service interests of the faculty; and
>
> (3) serves the law school's special teaching, scholarship, research, and service objectives.
>
> (c) A law library shall formulate and periodically update a written plan for development of the collection.
>
> (d) A law library shall provide suitable space and adequate equipment to access and use all information in whatever formats are represented in the collection.[75]

In this standard, the ABA has established a threshold series of requirements for an academic law library's collection. The collection must contain a "core collection of materials" that are deemed essential to legal education. It must also provide materials that satisfy the curricular and educational needs of the students. Lastly, the collection must support the teaching, scholarship, research, and service needs of the faculty. What does this mean?

According to Interpretation 606-2,[76] the format of the library's collection should be determined by user preference, although the interpretation notes that use of a "single format" only may violate the standard. Thus a hybrid mixture,[77] consisting of print, electronic, and possibly microforms,[78] is typically used by law libraries to satisfy the standard. Audiovisual materials, in the form of DVDs, CDs, or cassettes, are also purchased, as are flash cards. The latter formats tend to be study aid items to help students learn doctrinal materials.

As space constraints throughout law schools have increased and electronic access to materials has also increased, there has been a movement away from print to electronic. Why? The perception was that it would save law libraries and law schools money. Does it? It depends. While electronic materials confer benefits such as 24/7 off-campus access to the user, these resources are not necessarily cheaper. A systems or technology librarian is needed to handle electronic materials, and libraries must either acquire the servers or pay companies to host the materials on a server in order to provide patron access to electronic materials. What is the cost of the physical space needed for print storage in comparison with the cost of server space needed to host electronic resources? Is a systems librarian who handles electronic resources more expensive than a library paraprofessional who checks in print materials? Is the school in a suburban location or a downtown location? If downtown, is the school in a major metropolitan area such as New York, San Francisco, or Chicago, or is it in a cheaper metropolitan area such as Atlanta, Miami, or Houston? Answers to these questions will determine the cost per square foot of physical space and help make the choice as to whether print or electronic materials will be cheaper for a particular library.[79]

Does a law school require its students to own laptops? Does it provide its faculty and staff with laptops? If so, it is possible to put more resources in electronic format in patron hands, provided that licensing allows for an unlimited number of simultaneous users, than print would permit. Students and faculty from the millennial generation, as a group, seem to prefer electronic resources.[80] These are user preferences and school missions that may help determine the format of library materials.

Once format has been decided upon, what constitutes a "core collection of essential materials" that a law library must have?[81] Interpretation 606-5 is very specific.[82] A law library must provide, either through ownership or reliable access,[83] the following:

> Interpretation 606-5
> A law library core collection shall include the following:
> (1) all reported federal court decisions and reported decisions of the highest appellate court of each state;
> (2) all federal codes and session laws, and at least one current annotated code for each state;
> (3) all current published treaties and international agreements of the United States;
> (4) all current published regulations (codified and uncodified) of the federal government and the codified regulations of the state in which the law school is located;
> (5) those federal and state administrative decisions appropriate to the programs of the law school;
> (6) U.S. Congressional materials appropriate to the programs of the law school;
> (7) significant secondary works necessary to support the programs of the law school, and
> (8) those tools, such as citators and periodical indexes, necessary to identify primary and secondary legal information and update primary legal information.

Since many of the materials noted above constitute primary sources of American law,[84] it is important that a law library ensure that these primary resources are preserved for future generations. Some organizations that are attempting to digitize and preserve legal and nonlegal materials include the Google Books Project,[85] the HathiTrust,[86] and the Legal Information Preservation Alliance (LIPA).[87] While these projects have been controversial and involved lawsuits, recent events have begun to clear a path forward to permit library book digitization. Google recently settled its lawsuit with publishers,[88] while Cornell and the HathiTrust just won a copyright infringement battle against the Authors Guild.[89] Cornell had begun digitizing its own library collection in a project with Google Books and the HathiTrust when the Authors Guild sued, alleging copyright infringement of over seven million volumes.[90] Publishers sued Georgia State University for copyright violation when Georgia State's University Library placed copyrighted materials, requested by faculty members, on electronic course reserve for student use.[91] On the whole, the publishers have lost their argument at the district court level.[92] While Judge Evans indicated in her order that publisher copyright was infringed, the court held that the fair-use exemption could be claimed in a majority of the infringement issues,[93] while many of the other infringements were de minimis.[94]

If an older library has space concerns and does not want to rid itself of a large print collection, it might consider using off-site storage for selected materials. In some regions, libraries are banding together to arrange for collaborative off-site storage of materials.[95] This will allow them to preserve print materials at a much lower cost. In addition to collaborative off-site storage, some libraries are also engaging in collaborative collection development in order to pool resources and save money. While the ABA requires that each library possess a "core collection," collaborative collections are allowed by Standard 606, Interpretation 606-3.[96] Collaboration is allowed when the agreement is in writing and students and faculty have easy access to the materials.

A discussion of a library's collection would not be complete without discussing library budgets. Because collections are expensive to acquire and maintain, budgeting comprises a large portion of the library director's job. The last few years since the Great Recession have seen a decline in library budgets without a corresponding decline in the cost of materials.[97] Brian Tamanaha, in his new book, *Failing Law Schools*, argues that ". . . (t)he entire set of rules relating to the law library must be deleted. These rules require law schools to maintain unnecessarily expensive library collections and a large support staff; the book-on-the-shelf library is virtually obsolete in the electronic information age."[98] While Mr. Tamanaha's argument is interesting, there is doubt as to whether the book on the shelf is obsolete. While much information is online, not everything is. Much that is online that is reputable and usable is not free either. The assumption that obliterating the "book on the shelf" will eradicate the need for library budgets and librarians appears to be wishful thinking. There is more information than ever to befuddle legal researchers; librarians help researchers sort through this maze of information that technology has helped create.[99]

Most directors will submit an annual budget to their dean, requesting annual allocations for the acquisition of library materials. Directors will also be asked to justify and defend these budget requests. The American Association of Law Libraries' *Annual Price Index for Legal Publications* can be a helpful resource in terms of ascertaining and demonstrating percentage and dollar amount changes from year to year in legal materials.

Libraries use their budgets and their collections to provide services to faculty and students. Their goal is to support the research, scholarly, and teaching needs of faculty, and the curricular and educational needs of the students. What services do libraries offer to accomplish these goals?

FACULTY AND STUDENT SERVICES

ABA Standard 605 says "a law library shall provide the appropriate range and depth of reference, instructional, bibliographic, and other services to meet the needs of the law school's teaching, scholarship, research, and service programs."[100] Interpretation 605-1 further explains the needed services, describing them as "appropriate services include having adequate reference services, providing access (such as indexing, cataloging, and development of search terms and methodologies) to the library's collection and other information resources, offering interlibrary loan and other forms of document delivery, enhancing the research and bibliographic skills of students, producing library publications, and creating other services to further the law school's mission." What services are required? What services should a library offer? According to the standard, cataloging and indexing the library's collection so that patrons can access the collection and use it are essential services. Interlibrary loan (ILL) and document delivery of materials needed by faculty and students to enhance the classroom experience and assist with scholarship are also listed. The library is also directed to produce publications and enhance the "research and bibliographic skills" of its students. Since the above services are named by the interpretation, it seems reasonable to assume that they are required; that is, a law library should demonstrate compliance, and discretion is allowed in "creating other services to further the law school's mission."

What services should a library provide to its faculty?[101] Typically, a library, via a liaison program that matches librarians with faculty members, offers faculty the following services:[102]

Current Awareness

- CILP
- Routing of periodicals
- Jurist's Paper Chase

- Alerts from Google, Lexis, and Westlaw
- Blog

Information and Access

- Catalog
- Newsletter
- List of new acquisitions
- Acquisition recommendations and purchases
- Interlibrary loan and other document delivery
- Class reserves
- Tours
- Programs
- TWEN

Research

- Training research assistants
- Answering research requests
- Preparation of subject bibliographies
- Offering subject research-specific lectures
- Compiling an annual faculty bibliography
- Creating an institutional depository via BePress or SSRN

If the library also oversees technology, it should see that faculty have access to e-mail, classroom technology, classroom recording and other audiovisual assistance, and an intranet to access nonpublic materials.

Current Awareness Services

CILP (Current Index to Legal Periodicals)[103] is an electronic resource that is published biweekly. It allows faculty to view the table of contents of current law reviews and journals. Faculty can choose to view the table of contents either by journal title or subject. There are several ways that a library can provide access to the material, including e-mailing the document to faculty and asking faculty to alert the library liaison if they need copies of any articles.

Periodical items such as newsletters, law reviews, and newspapers, are routed among the faculty. Faculty can ask to be added or removed from routing lists as their interests change. Ideally, the acquisitions staff should handle this function.

Alerts can be created to help faculty remain current with developing legal news. Librarians can create Google, Westclip, or Lexis alerts. Any of these resources will alert faculty when a piece of legislation is enacted, a U.S. Supreme Court decision is handed down, the faculty member's article or book is cited, or the faculty member is mentioned in the news. BNA alerts are also available and will deliver daily or weekly BNA newsletters directly to a faculty mailbox. Create and run searches in *Index to Legal Periodicals* (ILP) and major newspapers databases on all faculty members, so that when the faculty member is quoted, cited, or published, the faculty member will receive, via e-mail, the citation or article.[104] This information should also be shared with the academic dean's office and the publications department. Also provide faculty with access to Jurist's Paper Chase,[105] as it publishes timely current and international legal news.

Blogs have left the trendy stage and are now another current-awareness resource. In order to promote and publicize the library and legal information, a library should create its own blog, writing about important trends in the legal world. Updates should be made several times a week. In addition to using a blog to market the library, librarians should also promote blogs and readers as information resources for faculty. If a faculty member wants to receive headline news from multiple sources, the library liaison can set up an RSS aggregator/reader,[106] with favorite readers being Bloglines,[107] Newsgator,[108] or Feedly.[109] These readers will capture headlines from sites with RSS (Really Simple Syndication) feeds.[110] With these feeds, faculty can maintain current awareness.[111]

Information Services

Keep faculty informed about the services and resources available in the law library.[112] Marketing and promoting the catalog is an excellent way to begin this process. In addition to training faculty, staff, and students to use the catalog to locate library materials, use the catalog to provide an updated monthly list of new books acquired by the library. Write and publish a monthly newsletter to provide the faculty with information about the library. Include faculty publications and presentations.

Publish a faculty manual that includes a directory of library staff. This directory should describe the services for which each staff person listed is responsible. Include the name of the individual to whom acquisition requests should be directed. Provide interlibrary loan services to acquire materials that faculty and students need for their research but that are not appropriate for the library to acquire. Offer document-delivery services, and see that these documents are either delivered to a faculty mailbox or e-mail address.

Maintain textbooks and other study aids on class reserves for students. Enable the library's catalog to search class reserves via professor, course name, or course number. Offer either in-person or online workshops for faculty on various research products or classroom technology choices. Provide assistance with TWEN or Blackboard for faculty using either software program as a course management system. Give library tours to classes, and create library maps. Create a major title locator. Post these items in the stacks and on the library's Web page.

Research Services

Besides offering a liaison program that partners librarians with faculty members, librarians can also help faculty members with research assistance. Librarians can offer a training program for faculty research assistants.[113] They can create subject bibliographies for specific classes. Many law libraries use LibGuides to prepare and post online subject bibliographies.[114] Librarians should volunteer to teach subject-specific research tools and resources for courses.

Librarians often prepare annual faculty bibliographies of faculty publications.[115] A developing trend is the creation of institutional repositories for faculty and school publications that are created and managed by librarians.[116] Over thirty law schools have now used Digital Commons to put faculty and school journals online, making faculty scholarship available to all.[117]

Technology Services

If the law library is responsible for technology services, it should also see that it is providing e-mail access, hardware support, and classroom technology, including learning capture systems, such as MediaSite or Echo 360.[118] An IT help desk that provides support in person, via e-mail, or over the telephone is essential to delivering technology services. An emerging technologies librarian can also help train faculty on Web 2.0 technologies that will allow faculty to engage their students in interactive classroom experiences.[119]

In addition to providing services to faculty, another key patron group needing law library services are law students. Library services to students should include many of the same services provided to the faculty. Student library services should include:

1. Current Awareness

- Jurist Paper Chase
- Law.com
- Google, Lexis, or Westlaw alerts
- Feedly

2. Information Services

- Borrowing materials and realia
- Study rooms
- Interlibrary loans
- Suggestions and recommendations to purchase
- Printing/copying
- Newsletter

- Blog
- Social media

3. Research Services

- Teaching law students to use computer-assisted legal resources, such as Bloomberg Law, Lexis, and Westlaw
- Teaching law students legal bibliography
- Providing reference and research assistance
- Information portal to reputable Internet sources

4. Technology Services

- E-mail
- Help Desk that provides hardware support

Many of the above services are identical or very similar to the services offered to faculty. Regarding current awareness services, librarians should work with students to teach them how to use alerts to create current awareness notices with Google, Lexis, or Westlaw. Resources such as the Paper Chase and Law.com should be shown to students so that they can learn to use these resources.[120] Ultimately the library's goal is to train students to be able to develop and manage their information needs after graduation.

Use social media, such as Facebook, Twitter, or blogs, to keep students apprised of information about the library, including special hours, holiday hours, or other library programming. Establish borrowing guidelines, criteria, and fines for print materials and realia such as cushions, iPads, Nooks, or flash drives. Set up study room criteria, enforce the criteria, and make study room booking available electronically to students. Offer interlibrary loan services and make sure that students are aware of the service and know how to request it. Newsletters, blogs, and programming can inform students about library services, current research topics, and other services. Sponsor a program with Career Services. Show students the library's resources that are available to assist with job hunting. Demonstrate to students how they can create business card CDs with resumes, writing samples, and a video clip of moot court or another law school oral presentation.[121] Printing, seemingly the bane of students and librarians, is, unfortunately, a trigger issue and problem. Find out when first-year memos are due. Make sure the printer has plenty of toner and paper during peak times (1L memos, outlines a month before exams, and exams) and that it works properly.

Librarians, rather than vendors, should provide the training for Westlaw, Lexis, and Bloomberg Law. These are research tools that librarians should train students to use properly and cost effectively. Librarians should also teach legal research skills.[122] They should create online information portals that provide students with access to reputable, free legal and nonlegal Internet sites. Lastly, the library, if it oversees technology, should provide students with e-mail and help desk support where students are trained in the basic computing and computer maintenance skills that they will need throughout their legal careers.

CONCLUSION

Law library directors wear many hats. Typically a director serves as a member of the dean's leadership team. Directors are also faculty members. This means that like other faculty, they teach, write, and serve on committees. Finally, directors are librarians, helping mentor library staff as well as teaching students how to efficiently and cost-effectively conduct legal research. Through these various roles, the law library director helps ensure that the law library remains at the center of the legal academy by managing relationships, building information collections, and providing library services to students and faculty.

NOTES

1. Lisa Smith-Butler is the associate dean for information resources and associate professor of law at the Charleston School of Law, Sol Blatt Jr. Law Library. She would like to thank her current library and IT staff at the Charleston School of Law, Sol Blatt Jr. Law Library and her former library and IT staff at Nova Southeastern University, Shepard Broad Law Center, Law Library and Technology Center, for embarking upon and sharing the leadership journey with her. Thanks also to her two research assistants, Annie Andrews and Cassandra Hutchens, for their research assistance with this project.

2. Robert C. Berring Jr., "A Brief History of Law Librarianship," in *Law Librarianship in the Twenty-First Century*, ed. Roy Balleste, Sonia Luna-Lamas, and Lisa Smith-Butler, 3–5 (Lanham, MD: Scarecrow Press, 2007).

3. Glen-Peter Ahlers Sr., *The History of Law School Libraries in the United States: Defining Moments* (Buffalo, NY: William S. Hein, 2011), 37.

4. Berring, "A Brief History of Law Librarianship," 5.

5. Christopher Columbus Langdell, preface to *Selection of Cases on the Law of Contracts with References and Citations* (Boston: Little, Brown & Co., 1871), reprinted in Alhers, *History of Law School Libraries*, 42.

6. Ibid., 41–43. See Berring, "A Brief History of Law Librarianship," 5–6. See also Glen-Peter Alhers Sr., *The History of Law School Libraries in the United States: From Laboratory to Cyberspace* (Buffalo, NY: William S. Hein, 2002), 8–10.

7. Beatrice Tice, "Academic Law Library in the 21st Century: Still the Heart of the Law School," 1 *U.C. Irvine L. Rev.* 1 (2011): 157.

8. Kris Gilliland, "The Successful Law Library Manager: Training and Skills," in Aspatore Books, *How to Manage a Law School Library: Leading Librarians on Updating Resources, Managing Budgets, and Meeting Expectations* (Boston: Aspatore Books, 2008).

9. Scott B. Pagel, "Changing Libraries and Changing Relationships: Challenges for the Library Director," in Aspatore Books, *How to Manage a Law School Library*.

10. National Center for Education Statistics, *Integrated Post Secondary Data System*, available at http://nces.ed.gov/ipeds/.

11. James S. Heller, "Collection Development, Licensing and Acquisitions," in Roy Balleste et al., eds., *Law Librarianship in the Twenty-First Century* (Lanham, MD: Scarecrow Press, 2007). See also American Bar Association, Standard 600: Library & Information Resources, in *Standards for Legal Education*, available at http://www.americanbar.org/content/dam/aba/publications/misc/legal_education/Standards/chapter_6_2012_2013_aba_standards_and_rules.authcheckdam.pdf.

12. The law library director completes the library portion of the American Bar Association's Annual Questionnaire (AQ). In addition to information about the library's budget, it also provides information about library staffing, facilities, and services. The director also answers a more detailed Site Evaluation Questionnaire shortly before the American Bar Association arrives for its accreditation visit. As long as a school is deemed to satisfy the accreditation standards, the American Bar Association visits a law school every seven years to determine eligibility for reaccreditation. Prior to the arrival of the American Bar Association's site team, the law school, including the library, engages in a strategic plan to move the school forward. The year before the American Bar Association arrives for its reaccreditation inspection, the school, with the library as a part of this process, will engage in a self-study to ascertain what is working and what needs to be tweaked. See the American Bar Association, Accreditation Overview, in *Standards for Legal Education*, available at http://www.americanbar.org/groups/legal_education/resources/accreditation.html. As part of the management of the library and compliance with the accreditation process, the library director will also participate in the strategic planning process and the self-study.

13. Berring, "A Brief History of Law Librarianship," 5–6.

14. Christopher A. Knott, "Libraries as Service Institutions: Meeting Patron Needs in a Changing Environment," in Aspatore Books, *How to Manage a Law School Library*.

15. Penny A. Hazelton, "Law Library Director of the Twenty-First Century," in Aspatore Books, *How to Manage a Law School Library*.

16. Lisa Smith-Butler, Does Your Building Reflect Your Law School? in Program Presentation, American Bar Association, Bricks'nBytes: Continuous Renovations (San Diego, March 2012.)

17. Charles Dickens, A Tale of Two Cities (London: Penguin Classics, 1859), 1.

18. Margaret Krause, "Westlaw and Lexis: The Graphical User Interface," *Trends L. Libr. Mgmt. & Tech.* 1 (1991–93): 7.

19. Diane Murley, "Law Libraries in the Cloud," *L. Libr. J.* 101 (2009): 249.

20. Robert C. Berring and Elizabeth A. Edinger, *Finding the Law*, 12th ed. (St. Paul, MN: West, 2005), 14–20.

21. Bloomberg Law, available at http://about.bloomberglaw.com/.

22. Casemaker, available at http://www.casemaker.com/.

23. Fastcase, available at http://www.fastcase.com/.

24. LoisLaw Connect, available at http://estore.loislaw.com/default.aspx.

25. VersusLaw, available at http://www.versuslaw.com/.

26. Cornell's Legal Information Institute, available at http://www.law.cornell.edu/.

27. Findlaw, available at http://www.findlaw.com.

28. Justicia, available at http://law.justia.com/.

29. Google Scholar, available at http://scholar.google.com/.

30. Washlaw, available at http://washlaw.edu.

31. Greg Lambert, "A Westlaw Product at a Google Scholar Price," *Vermont B.J.* 37 (2011–12): 47, 48–49.

32. Nicholas Carr, "World Wide Computer," ch. 6 in *The Big Switch: Rewiring the World, From Edison to Google*, 107–25 (New York: W. W. Norton, 2008).

33. Lisa Smith-Butler, Throw It Out or Store It? The Digital Future and Unbound Collections, Program Presentation, South Eastern American Association of Law Libraries (SEAALL), Clearwater, Florida, March 2012.

34. Matt Leichter, "Tough Choices Ahead for Some High Ranked Law Schools," *American Law Daily*, July 3, 2012, at http://www.americanlawyer.com/PubArticle-TAL.jsp?id=1202561764452&slreturn=20120901130309.

35. Molly McDonough, "In Google We Trust? Critics Question How Much Judges, Lawyers Should Rely on Internet Search Results," *A.B.A. J.* 90 (2004): 30–31.

36. Richard A. Matasar, "Viability of the Law Degree: Cost, Value and Intrinsic Worth," *Iowa L. Rev.* 96 (2010–11): 1579, 1623.

37. Mark Osler, "Unkind Cuts: Shrinking the Law School Budget," in Law School Innovation Blog, available at http://lsi.typepad.com/lsi/2012/10/unkind-cuts-shrinking-the-law-school-budget.html.

38. Taylor Fitchett, James Hambleton, Penny Hazelton, Anne Klinefelter, and Judith Wright, "Law Library Budgets in Hard Times," *Law Libr. J.* 103 (2011): 91, 92–95.

39. The majority of what I said in the first edition of this book in the chapter on administration regarding relationships continues to be relevant and accurate. See Lisa Smith-Butler, "Administration," in Balleste et al., eds., *Law Librarianship in the Twenty-First Century*, 46–50.

40. Robert H. Smith, "The Librarian's Risk of Irrelevance (In the Eyes of the Law School Dean)," 95 *Law Libr. J.* 95 (2003): 421–23.

41. Janis L. Johnston, "Managing the Boss," *Law Libr. J.* 89 (1997): 21, 22–28.

42. Workshop for Deans and Law Librarians: Reconciling Core Values and the Bottom Line, Program Presentation, Association of American Law Schools Annual Meeting, San Francisco, 2011.

43. Former law librarian and law school dean Donald J. Dunn, agreed with this assessment. Having served in both roles, he wrote about the similarities between the two jobs. See Donald J. Dunn, "From Librarian to Dean to Librarian, or to Hell and Back," *Law Libr. J.* 93 (2001): 391, 393.

44. Alexandra Levit, *Blind Spots: The 10 Business Myths You Can't Afford to Believe on Your New Path to Success* (New York: Berkley Books, 2011), 72–81.

45. Kristin Cheney, "Is An Annual Report in Your Library's Future," *Law Libr. J.* 97 (2005): 493, 494.

46. Michael Whiteman, "Law Library Management in the Twenty-First Century," in Aspatore Books, *How to Manage a Law School Library*, 32.

47. Diane Murley, "The Power of RSS Feeds," *Law Libr. J.* 101 (2009): 127, 133–34.

48. Raquel J. Gabriel, "Managing Conflict," *Law Libr. J .* 103 (2011): 685, 685–87.

49. Susan Cain, *Quiet: The Power of Introverts in a World That Can't Stop Talking* (New York: Crown, 2012), 34–70.

50. Filippa Marullo Anzalone, "Servant Leadership: A New Model for Law Library Leaders," *Law Libr. J .* 99 (2007): 793, 793–812.

51. Hyler Bracey, Jack Rosenblum, Aubrey Sanford, and Roy Trueblood, *Managing from the Heart* (New York: Dell, 1993), 92–101. See also a review of this book by Patrick Brigger, "Leadership Books: *Managing from the Heart*," *Washington Post*, January 20, 2012, at http://www.washingtonpost.com/blogs/leadership-books/post/managing-from-the-heart/2011/03/07/gIQA3rWbDQ_blog.html.

52. Charthouse Learning, *Fish!* Philosophy Video (Media Partners, 2012).

53. Bracey, supra note 51, at 105.

54. *Fish!*, available at http://www.catchthefishphilosophy.com/fish_video.htm?atc=GOG&ctc=FSFV&gclid=CPzlicvK7bICFUui4AodgxEAoQ.

55. Anzalone, "Servant Leadership," 797.

56. Ibid.

57. Cain, *Quiet*, 53–63.

58. Whiteman, "Law Library Management in the Twenty-First Century," 34–37.

59. To help me accomplish my goals, I provide periodic pizza lunches a couple of times a year so that staff can literally sit down and "break bread" together. I always offer an annual holiday luncheon at a nearby restaurant. These activities allow staff to relax and interact together.

60. Bracey et al., *Managing from the Heart*, 104–6.

61. I survey faculty and students on an annual basis, asking about the library's collection, facilities, services, and staff.

62. The law library does serve as a socialization center for law students, as well as a study space. Hillary Rodham and Bill Clinton are said to have met each other one evening in the Yale Law School, Lillian Goldman Law Library. See Carolyn Wyman, "Hillary Clinton at Yale Law School," in *Hillary Clinton Quarterly*, available at http://www.hillaryclintonquarterly.com/hillary_yale.htm.

63. My first directorship was at Nova Southeastern University, Shepard Broad Law Center, Law Library and Technology Center in Fort Lauderdale, Florida. The facility was designed by Roy Merksy, Carol Rohenbeck, and Billie Jo Kaufman. With the exception of stairwell noise and a lack of hurricane windows, a problem in hurricane-prone South Florida, the design of the facility was excellent. I rarely had to consider design, student flow, circulation and reference desks, noise, stacks, or office space. I arrived at the Charleston School of Law in the summer of 2009. Here, the library is located in an 1857 building that was an old railroad depot. It is beautiful, with warm red brick that the students love; however, creating library functionality in it has been challenging at times. The retrofitting of an old building has forced me to think about library design and functionality in a way that I would never have done in the past without the gift of this building.

64. I say this because there was not a circulation desk at the Charleston School of Law when I came in the summer of 2009.

65. The Sol Blatt Jr. Law Library at the Charleston School of Law uses LibCal by Springshare to handle its study room bookings. See Libcal, Springshare, available at http://www.springshare.com/libcal/.

66. It appears that some academic law libraries are increasing items that circulate. While study room keys and books remain typical items to be checked out at the circulation desk, some libraries are now circulating laptops, iPads, Kindles, Nooks, umbrellas, phone chargers, power cords, games, puzzles, bikes, flash drives, and therapy dogs. See "Gadgets that Circulate," Stanford Law School, Robert Crown Law Library, available at http://liblog.law.stanford.edu/gadgets/. See also "What We Have: Non-Book Items," Cornell University School of Law, Cornell Law Library, available at http://www.lawschool.cornell.edu/library/WhatWeHave/Non-Book-Items.cfm. For a discussion about Yale's implementation of its therapy dog program with Monty, as well as Monty's checkout by Yale Law students, see Julian Aiken and Femi Cadmus, "Who Let the Dog Out? Implementing a Successful Therapy Dog Program in an Academic Law Library," Yale Law School Legal Scholarship Repository, available at http://digitalcommons.law.yale.edu/cgi/viewcontent.cgi?article=1008&context=ylss.

67. Mary K. Marzolla, "Facing Reality: The Death of the Reference Desk? Quality Service and Accessibility Are Vital to Reference Services," *Spectrum*, September 2001, 34.

68. Martin A. Kesselman and Sarah Barbara Watsein, "Creating Opportunities: Embedded Librarians," *Journal of Library Administration* 49 (2009): 383, 385–88.

69. Brittany Kolonay and Gail Mathapo, "Experimenting with Embedding: A Law School Embeds Librarians in Clinics and Seminars," *AALL Spectrum* 16 (2012): 18–20.

70. When I arrived at the Charleston School of Law, the technical services area was in the middle of the library's reading room and was a frequent cause of complaint by students regarding noise. In order to establish quiet in the library and quell student revolt, the technical services department was relocated. Technical services staff members were not happy about this relocation, but valued library services and understood the need for it.

71. At the Charleston School of Law, the library has a social area known as the Barrister that is very popular with students. In addition to comfortable and casual seating, it also has bar tables and provides access to food such as sandwiches, salads, fruit, and drinks. This is very much the students' area. Banners from their moot court wins as well as their law review covers adorn the walls.

72. At Nova Southeastern University, I oversaw the installation of hurricane windows over three floors while school was in session since hurricane season and summer coincided. When workers failed to stop hammering at 8:00 a.m. as promised, students were quick to alert me. At the Charleston School of Law, the installation of a new HVAC system in an 1857 building required the closure of the library building and the utilization of a crane to haul disassembled HVAC parts upstairs into the HVAC room. While this closure happened during the summer, it did upset students planning to study for the bar exam. Construction is stressful for all.

73. If plans for a new building or a new library facility are in place, plan to attend the American Bar Association's (ABA) biannual conference, Bricks'nBytes, which addresses facilities and space within the law school. The conference travels to either new law school facilities or recently renovated facilities. Programming focuses specifically on building plans. The March 2012 conference was at the new Thomas Jefferson School of Law in San Diego, California.

74. Check out the Cambridge Sound System, available at http://www.cambridgesoundmanagement.com/?gclid=COqU8u2CibMCFYuY4AodW0kA2g, which is a white sound noise-masking system that can be installed in libraries or other buildings to help reduce noise.

75. American Bar Association, Standard 606, *2012–2013 ABA Standards and Rules of Procedure for Approval of Law Schools* (ABA, 2012), 45–46, also available at http://www.americanbar.org/content/dam/aba/publications/misc/legal_education/Standards/chapter_6_2012_2013_aba_standards_and_rules.authcheckdam.pdf.

76. Ibid., 46.

77. Michelle M. Wu, "Why Print and Electronic Resources Are Essential to the Academic Law Library," *Law Libr. J* . 97 (2005): 233, 235–45.

78. As a new library, started in 2004, the Charleston School of Law, Sol Blatt Jr. Law Library, has no microform materials and has been able to fulfill collection requirements and needs with either print or electronic materials.

79. Wu, "Why Print and Electronic Resources Are Essential," 235–37. As Wu notes, all needed materials are not necessarily online. Legal monographs are plentifully available in print but far less so in electronic formats, in comparison to legal serials, which are extensively available in both electronic and print formats.

80. John Palfrey and Uris Gasser, *Born Digital: Understanding the First Generation of Digital Natives* (New York: Basic Books, 2008), 16–20.

81. American Bar Association, *2012–2013 ABA Standards and Rules of Procedure for Approval of Law Schools*, Standard 606–1, 45.

82. Ibid., 46.

83. Ibid.

84. Nancy P. Johnson, "Best Practices: What First Year Law Students Should Learn in a Legal Research Class," *Legal Reference Services Quarterly* 28 (2009): 77, 80.

85. Google, Google Books Library Project, available at http://www.google.com/googlebooks/library.html.

86. HathiTrust, HathiTrust Digital Library, available at http://www.hathitrust.org/.

87. Legal Information Preservation Alliance, available at http://lipalliance.org/.

88. Jennifer Howard, "Publishers Settle Long-Running Lawsuit Over Google's Book Scanning Project," *The Chronicle*, October 4, 2012, available at http://chronicle.com/article/Publishers-Settle-Long-Running/134854/. See also the statement released by Google and the Association of American Publishers, available at http://www.publishers.org/press/85/.

89. Akane Otani, "Watershed Ruling on Digital Lawsuit Advances Cornell's Digital Library Project," *Cornell Daily Sun*, October 15, 2012, available at http://cornellsun.com/section/news/content/2012/10/15/%E2%80%98watershed%E2%80%99-ruling-lawsuit-advances-cornells-digital-library-project.

90. *Authors Guild v. Hathitrust*, 2012 Westlaw 4808939 (S.D.N.Y. 2012).

91. Steve Kolowich, "Publishers' Fallback Position," *Insider Higher Ed*, available at http://www.insidehighered.com/news/2012/06/04/publishers-seek-injunction-e-re-serve-case.

92. See *Cambridge v. Becker*, 2012 WL 1835696 (N.D. GA 2012).

93. 17 U.S.C. §107 (2006 & Supp.).

94. *Cambridge v. Becker*, 10–41.

95. University of Florida, George A. Smathers Libraries, "Press Release: University of Florida and University of Miami Libraries Collaborate to Establish a Shared Collection," available at http://blogs.uflib.ufl.edu/news/2012/10/05/university-of-florida-and-the-university-of-miami-libraries-collaborate-to-establish-a-shared-collection/. The two libraries signed a memorandum of understanding that will allow them to house a shared collection in Gainesville, Florida, for "long-term preservation" purposes. The materials housed will include both low-use materials and duplicative materials. It seems to me that collaborative off-site storage and collaborative collection development will be important future developments in academic law libraries.

96. American Bar Association, *2012–2013 ABA Standards and Rules of Procedure for Approval of Law Schools*, Standard 606, Interpretation 606-3, 46.

97. Peter N. Ireland, "A New Keynesian Perspective on the Great Recession," *Journal of Money, Credit and Banking* 43 (February 2011): 31–32; Fitchett et al., "Law Library Budgets in Hard Times," 92–94; American Association of Law Libraries Price Index for Legal Publications (AALL, 2011), available at http://www.aallnet.org/main-menu/Publications/products/pub-price.

98. Brian Tamanaha, *Failing Law Schools* (Chicago: University of Chicago Press, 2012), 173. While Mr. Tamanaha is entitled to his opinion, I respectfully disagree with him as to whether the book on the shelf is obsolete.

99. Duncan E. Alford, *The Law Librarian's Role in the Scholarly Enterprise*, 39 J. L. & Educ. 351, 352–54 (2010).

100. American Bar Association, *2012–2013 ABA Standards and Rules of Procedure for Approval of Law Schools*, Standard 605, 45.

101. The Charleston School of Law's Faculty Handbook, Adjunct Faculty Handbook, and Library Student Handbook are published on the law library's Web page at http://www.charlestonlaw.edu/Library.aspy.

102. Carl Yirka, "The Yirka Question and the Yirka Answer: What Should Law Libraries Stop Doing in Order to Address Higher Priority Initiatives," *AALL Spectrum* 12 (2008): 28, 29–30.

103. University of Washington School of Law, Gallagher Law Library, Current Index to Legal Periodicals, available at http://lib.law.washington.edu/cilp/cilp.html.

104. Ebsco, Index to Legal Periodicals, available at http://www.ebscohost.com/academic/index-to-legal-periodicals-books. This resource indexes over 1,025 "legal journals, law reviews, yearbooks, institutes, statutes, bar association publications, university publications, and government publications."

105. Jurist Research News and Services, Paper Chase, available at http://jurist.org/paperchase/.

106. Hugh Calkins, "Really Simple Syndication," *Maine B.J* . 21 (2006): 190.

107. Bloglines, available at http://www.bloglines.com/.

108. Newsgator, available at http://www.newsgator.com/?mkwid=s9pxuMAAO&pcrid=14557693059&gclid=CMTxuPWxl7MCFQWnnQodfEsA6w.

109. Feedly, available at http://www.feedly.com.

110. Lianne Forster Knight, "What About RSS?" *Austrl. L. Libr* . 14 (2006): 7–14.

111. University of Oxford, Bodleian Law Library Current Awareness Services, available at http://www.bodleian.ox.ac.uk/law/e-resources/current-awareness-services-draft.

112. Lisa Smith-Butler, "Public Relations: Overcoming Your Aversion to the M Word," *AALL Spectrum* 14 (2010): 7, 8–9 . It is also available at http://www.aallnet.org/main-menu/Publications/spectrum/Archives/Vol-14/pub_sp1003/pub-sp1003-pr.pdf.

113. Kevin D. Gerson, "Faculty Research Services at the UCLA Library," *Trends in Law Libr. Management & Tech.* 18 (2008): 55, 57–61.

114. Springshare, LibGuides, available at http://springshare.com/libguides/. See also Melanie Cofield and Kasia Salon, "Making the Most of LibGuides in Law Libraries," *AALL Spectrum* 16 (2011): 17–18.

115. Lisa Smith-Butler, comp., and Gail Levin Richmond, ed., Nova Southeastern University, Shepard Broad Law Center, Faculty and Law Library Staff Publications, 1974–2000 (Fort Lauderdale, FL: Nova Southeastern University Publications, 2001).

116. Carol Watson and James Donovan, "Institutional Repositories: A Plethora of Possibilities," *Trends in Law Libr. Management & Tech.* 21 (2011): 19, 20–22.

117. Digital Commons, Law School Institutional Repositories, available at http://digitalcommons.bepress.com/institutional-repository-law/.

118. Echo 360, available at http://echo360.com/. See also Sonic Foundary's Media Site, available at http://www.sonicfoundry.com/mediasite-by-sonicfoundry.

119. Deborah Ginsberg, Meg Kribble, and Bonnie Shucha, "I Want My Web 2.0," *AALL Spectrum* 13 (2009): 28–29.

120. ALM Media, Law.com, available at http://www.law.com.

121. Terrel L. Rhodes, "Making Learning Visible and Meaningful through Electronic Portfolios," *Change: The Magazine of Higher Education*, January 2011, available at http://www.changemag.org/Archives/Back%20Issues/2011/January-February%202011/making-learning-visible-full.html.

122. Judith Welch Wagner, "Teaching Legal Research: Educating Lawyers: Carnegie Report Reveals New Challenges, Fresh Possibilities for Law Librarians," *AALL Spectrum* 13 (2009): 20, 22–23.

FOUR

Public Services

Anne Klinefelter and Sara Sampson

INTRODUCTION

Public services represent the face of the law library. Public service staff connect with library users at both the moment of need and in more anticipatory ways.[1] For many law librarians, public services is the most exhilarating, the most interesting, and sometimes the most frustrating role in the library. Why? The library user drives the work. Although public services includes organizational, instructional, promotional, evaluative, and planning activities to meet anticipated users' needs, much of public services is reactive, and the librarian or library support staff member must be ready to respond to all sorts of questions and requests. Examples include:

"What do you mean I never returned that book?"

"Can I do that research on my tablet? How about my phone?"

"I need a form for service of process in Mexico."

"Are you a lawyer?"

"I need you to get corporate parent institution information on this company, and see what comes up about it on the Web."

"How does the scanner work?"

"How soon can I get the transcript of Senate hearings from this afternoon?"

The background required for law library public services may include specialized knowledge of legal research tools and techniques, or training with library systems that range in complexity from replacing paper in the photocopier to managing multiple online systems. Interpersonal skills are invaluable, and public services staff benefit from a natural enthu-

siasm for interaction and ongoing training. In order to respond effectively to patrons, public services staff need to understand different learning
styles, know how to use the reference interview to fully understand patron requests, handle complaints, and market the library.

The public services umbrella can cover circulation, reference, and
interlibrary loan functions. These areas present several special issues.

Public services are informed by users' needs and shaped by the other
services in the library, such as cataloging, collection development, and
information technology services. In smaller law libraries, one or two library employees may provide the full array of library services. In such a
situation, public services are just one aspect of each library staff member's responsibilities. In larger law libraries, specialization often separates
public services from technical services, information technology services,
and administration.

The type of library and its parent institution dictate the composition
and scope of public services. Law libraries or legal information centers
are present in private environments, such as law firms and corporations,
as well as in governmental institutions. Governmental law libraries include the Law Library of Congress and law libraries at state, court, and
county institutions. Law schools have libraries dedicated to supporting
legal education, while public libraries usually have a law collection. Pris-
ons sometimes have their own libraries, and other law libraries, particularly those serving the public, often provide document-delivery services
to prisoners.

The types of public services can vary, depending on the type of law
library. In a large law firm library or large academic law library, librarians may need specialized law backgrounds to support the research
needs of busy attorneys or professors whose business or interests are
focused on litigation or on highly complex areas such as tax or foreign
and international law. To meet the needs of the parent institution, levels
of service differ among libraries. Law firm librarians may do the research
for the attorney, while academic law librarians may recommend tools
and strategies to the inquiring law student or law professor. In court
libraries, public services staff address needs that include research requests from a judge or providing assistance to the pro se litigant.

In recent years, technology has greatly impacted law libraries. Libraries have responded differently to these changes. Law firm librarians now
identify with electronic resources rather than a central location (i.e., a
library) for materials. This shift in focus has resulted in job title changes,
with firm librarians moving away from the title *librarian* to *information
resources manager* because the latter title more accurately reflects their job
responsibilities. In law firms, the information resources manager may be
involved in checking for conflicts of interest involved in representing
multiple clients, the management of the law firms' internal records, the
creation of a knowledge-management system, and the monitoring of the

continuing legal-education compliance of the attorneys. In court libraries, the public services librarian may see fewer attorneys than in the past because today's legal databases provide reasonably priced access to much legal information. Academic law librarians in public services are teaching introductory and advanced legal research courses that help law students learn to compare and evaluate research options that will change and evolve throughout the students' careers as lawyers.

Whatever the type of law library, librarians and other library employees who perform public services create the public image of the library. Their work is likely to be the source of most of the library's compliments or complaints. Because of the interactive nature of public services, creativity, spontaneity, patience, and judgment can be as important as specialized training and knowledge. Experience, a commitment to service, flexibility, and a genuine interest in working with other people are essential attributes for the librarian performing public services work. While some strategies can be taught, and research skills can be learned, a positive outlook is a powerful tool for overcoming barriers in the research process and diffusing library users' frustration.

CIRCULATION

The circulation function of the law library is generally located at the central service point. This location is where library users come to check out tangible materials in the library's collection. This area, sometimes called *access services*, is the place where all sorts of questions and comments are directed. This public service point is where many library users form their opinions about the library and where they share their opinions about the library and its services. The circulation staff must be adept at using systems, applying policies, and redirecting requests and comments as appropriate. The public relations aspect of circulation work is crucial, as the respect and appreciation users feel for the circulation staff is generally projected onto the entire library.

The Circulation System

In a larger library, an integrated online library system, or ILS, is a standard tool for identifying, locating, and checking out materials from the law library collection. This system may be used for circulation, reserve, and interlibrary loan. Such systems are complex, supporting or thwarting specific services, depending on the system's capabilities and the librarian's expertise in using the system. A thorough understanding of the ILS is extremely useful to access services staff. In a smaller library, the circulation system may be more casual, and the librarian or library staff member may draw on a familiarity with the library users and their research interests to track down missing items. When the user says, "I'm going to take this to my office," the circulation staff member may appropriately either require the user to check out the material or may just thank the user and make a quick note of who and what are leaving together. The differences in behavior are determined by the customs and needs of the institution. Whatever the level of technology, the circulation system is crucial for maintaining order and control over the library collection.

In many law libraries, especially law firm and corporate law libraries, where real estate is expensive, a greater proportion of the library collection may be electronic. In these libraries, the circulation of books is less important than managing access to databases. In such settings, library space is often limited. Accessing centrally managed databases and electronic resources, attorneys then use their own offices or other remote sites to do research from desktop computers or laptops. In these private law libraries, users drive the library's collection and services; if a treatise is in high demand, the librarian is more likely to purchase additional copies than to try to enforce shorter circulation periods. Some academic law libraries accommodate faculty in this way when budgets allow.

Reserves, Stack Maintenance, Special Collections

Some law libraries maintain a reserve collection for highly used items that have limited circulation; this function is often tied to circulation. The reserve collection may be open to users for browsing or limited to access by library staff. Stack maintenance, including loose-leaf filing and shelving, may also be handled by the circulation staff. As electronic resources have replaced loose-leafs and other print materials in law libraries, library staff are spending less time on shelving and circulation and are instead focusing their energies on Web page development, licensing electronic resources, and computer systems management.

The arrangement of the law library collection usually follows local custom, and the isolation of some materials reflects the institution's patron preferences. In academic law libraries, the Library of Congress cataloging scheme tends to direct the arrangement of materials. In other libraries, such a sophisticated system is not as important because primary law publications are identifiable by jurisdiction and a date-related sequential serial format. Areas of specialization, such as tax and foreign and international law, are sometimes shelved separately.

In academic law libraries, rare materials and copies of faculty members' publications may be kept in a special collection space with improved climate control and limited access. In special collection departments, staff members generally provide services at a higher level than in other areas of the library. Staff working with special collections may provide initial research on these unique materials because potential users may not be able to travel to use the collections. Staff may also scan or photocopy materials for patrons because of the items' fragility. Because a number of special collections are older and no longer have copyright restrictions on their use, law libraries are developing projects to digitize these collections, either for ease of local use or for wider access. Public services staff may collaborate with staff in other parts of the law library to identify and produce these special digital collections.

Policies

Policies for circulation and reserve are important guidelines for library users and staff alike. Length of circulation periods, renewal options, and overdue and replacement fines forewarn library users of their obligations and support library staff who interact with users. Consistently applying policies provides predictability and fairness, helping the circulation staff depersonalize the frustrations or complaints of users. However, flexibility in this area can also be important in serving the larger library goals. A law firm librarian who attempts to penalize a productive partner for losing a volume of a treatise is likely to discover that the enforcement of the library's policy is more expensive than the replacement of the lost volume.

Strict adherence to circulation, reserve, and interlibrary loan policies is more common in larger libraries because it is difficult to train a large staff to make such judgments while ensuring fairness. Training programs and manuals are important, but they cannot substitute for experience and a broader perspective on the library's goals. In larger settings, an appeals process to the access services librarian or some other supervisor can be the best solution to a problem at circulation, reserve, or interlibrary loan.

Library Hours/Access

For many law libraries, the circulation department is the area responsible for opening and closing the library. This responsibility reflects the sense that circulation is the most basic and essential function of a library. Some libraries, however, allow particular users or categories of users to gain access to the library after hours. This arrangement serves attorneys working late in the law firm or professors or law students working late in the law school. Such a practice may be constant, or may be a response to limited-time requests. After-hours access presents an added challenge to the circulation staff charged with keeping order and control over the library inventory. Unless systems are available for users to check out materials themselves, the library may lose track of items that after-hours users take from the library. Nevertheless, libraries may find that this loss is worth the expense to meet users' needs and to serve the institution. When the law review student, facing a deadline, asks "Is the library open the Friday after Thanksgiving? May I come in when the library is closed?" a supervising librarian in the law school library might provide a key to this student to use during the holiday.

Of course, electronic resources are generally available around the clock and do not require a physical library to be open to provide access. If the library space itself is limited, library hours become less defining, and public services moves away from a focus on circulation services.

REFERENCE DEPARTMENT

Law library reference services help library users locate legal information and law-related information, both at the moment of need and in anticipation of that moment of need. While circulation staff draw on their connections with the library catalog and stack-maintenance experience to locate a known item, the reference librarians are trained to identify materials and research strategies on a particular topic, regardless of whether the library collection contains the needed material. This service requires a solid understanding of legal research skills and even of the law itself. Many larger law libraries, particularly academic law libraries, require the reference librarians to hold both the graduate library degree and a law degree, enabling the librarians to speak the same language as law professors and law students. In addition to legal information, reference librarians may be asked to help in locating other types of information. For example, attorneys may require a search of public records to prepare for cross-examination of a witness, or law students may seek background information about a hiring attorney or about a particular community in preparation for a job interview. Law professors may need help finding information about a particular technology, opinion survey results, or scholarship from different disciplines.

A number of services grow out of reference and vary depending on the type of library and the priority given to the particular category of library user.

The Reference Interview

The reference interview is a classic component of reference service. Good interview techniques help the librarian assist the library user. Frequently, questions that come to the reference librarian appear to be straightforward, such as "Where is the *Foreign Law Guide*?" If this resource is unavailable, the librarian might suggest other tools that contain the information the user is seeking. The librarian could follow up and ask whether the user is looking for information about a particular country's legal system. The answer to this question and subsequent dialogue could lead the user to a research guide about doing research in that country or to another resource with broad coverage of the country's legal system.

A fine line exists between invading the privacy of the library user and gaining enough information to help him or her locate the needed information. The public services provider should take care not to respond simply, "We don't have the *Foreign Law Guide*," since the need that the user has expressed may mask a different goal. But the researcher needs to feel comfortable knowing that the librarian is offering a service, not collecting personal information. A fine line divides the follow-up questions, "Why do you want to know about this country?" and "What type of information on this country's legal system do you need? Would you be comfortable looking for that information through an online research guide? I could show you the GlobaLex Web site. . . ."

In the busy law firm or corporate environment, the reference librarian should be especially careful to get a full description of the information or item sought. These reference questions are often requests for the delivery of material or information, rather than advice on research strategies. Deadlines and cost may be important pieces of information that shape the librarian's response. In the court library, reference librarians likely have the same need to clarify requests from judges. Reference librarians in academic libraries may also provide this level of service to law professors, and sometimes the reference interview is an ongoing process during the librarians' research. At times, discoveries lead to the need for further clarification from the attorney, judge, or professor, and the request is refined in response to uncovered information. When the information is elusive and the librarian feels confident that the answer does not exist, the professor or attorney should be consulted as quickly as possible to ask if he or she would like the next best thing. When an attorney says, "What do you mean there is no case on point in Florida?" the librarian might offer to find a case on the topic in a neighboring state. In some situations, the answer may exist but only for a price, so the clarification needed is how much can be spent on obtaining the information.

The form of communication also influences the reference interview. A face-to-face discussion includes body language and the opportunity for immediate back-and-forth discussion. Of course, the researcher may return for further explanation after examining the offered resources, and the librarian may need to follow up with the researcher as further questions develop. Telephone, e-mail, and chat reference, and increasingly, video chat, are options with advantages and disadvantages. E-mail and traditional chat reference provide full typed descriptions that some find easier to comprehend than communications in conversation in person or by telephone, but some reference librarians find the constant typing and absence of body language to be challenging.

Specialized Knowledge

Knowledge of legal research techniques is the basic tool that enables a law librarian to provide a high level of reference services. In many academic law libraries and sometimes in other types of law libraries, the law degree is required of reference librarians. The processes of legal research and legal analysis inform each other, and a full legal education strengthens the reference librarian's ability to engage fully in these processes, to help users develop a research strategy, or, if appropriate, to help the library user by performing legal research.

At all times, the lawyer must work with the most current information because to do otherwise is to fail to represent the client properly and could constitute malpractice. Given the importance of legal authority in the practice of law, legal research cannot be treated casually. Entire courses address legal analysis and legal research, while lengthy books and sets of books provide guidance on legal bibliography and legal research strategies. As lawmakers and commercial publishers make more legal information available, attorneys and other legal researchers rely on reference librarians to keep current with the changing options. Reference librarians can track and evaluate legal research options that support attorneys, judges, academic researchers, and the general public. With this expertise, the reference librarian can recommend new tools and strategies to meet the needs of particular library users, such as attorneys in the law firm, judges in the court library, and professors in the law school library.

In addition to changes in legal publishing, reference librarians are advised to keep current on major changes and trends in the law. Legal trends such as the increase in administrative law and use of social science data increase the number of types of resources that reference librarians should be comfortable using. In some academic settings, law libraries are hiring experts in empirical research to expand the range of support that public services can provide.

Beyond ongoing learning about general legal research and trends in the law, the reference librarian may need to develop an expertise in a particular area of law and/or to have foreign language skills. For example, legal reference librarians may need to be savvy about medical or business research, or they may need to have a sophisticated understanding of patent or tax law research. In a law firm doing plaintiff or business work, a reference librarian may do a significant amount of business-related research, such as acquiring copies of corporate filings or conducting public-records background research on individuals or businesses. The trend toward globalization has made foreign and international law research an important area of specialization as well. Some larger law firms and law schools employ law librarians who have foreign language skills. Law librarians with expertise in a special area serve as resources for their colleagues, as well as for the library users they serve in their own library.

Many publish research guides in journals or on library Web sites. Some publish chapters or books on specialized legal research. Law library e-mail discussion lists are also a resource through which experts share their knowledge in response to questions. When an attorney asks, "Where can I find a form for service of process in Mexico?" the reference librarian may draw on his own experience and knowledge, consult a research guide, or seek advice from colleagues with special expertise.

Law librarians build their understanding of legal research and of the law through formal education, professional development workshops, conferences, law and library publications, and through networking and collegial support.

Practicing Law and the Pro Se Patron

Law librarians in state, court, and county libraries and many academic libraries include service to the general public in their missions. This noble effort helps make the law accessible to all and helps to justify the expenditure of tax funds to support the library. The law librarian has special concerns in serving this group because of the risk of crossing the line from library assistance to practicing law. Numerous articles have debated the nature of this risk. Although the danger may be overstated, reference librarians should take care not to offer legal advice, as this is the province of the licensed and practicing attorney. Reference librarians who have law degrees and who are licensed to practice law in the state in which they work may need to be particularly cautious about establishing that their services are offered as a librarian and not as a free attorney. After three years of law school and perhaps a stressful bar examination experience, the licensed holder of a JD may be tempted to assert these qualifications at the reference desk. When a library user asks, "Are you a lawyer?" the proper response may be, "I am a librarian, and I have a legal education that will help me help you use the library resources. What are you looking for?"

The library user who is representing herself in some legal matter or in litigation is referred to by courts as a *pro se* litigant. In law libraries, the pro se patron may be fairly self-sufficient or may ask for a great deal of help. The reference librarian should take care not to interpret the law but should provide only instruction on finding legal information. The distinction can be quite tricky if a pro se litigant knows little about the law. Court opinions and court rules, legislation, administrative law, and persuasive secondary sources in federal and state jurisdictions may be needed, as might municipal law or institutional policies. Even identifying the relevant area of law for the patron could constitute legal advice, so the reference librarian must be cautious. Some libraries outline the boundaries of their services in prominent locations in the library and on the library Web site in order to avoid misunderstandings and to discourage library users from attempting to obtain free legal advice from a law librarian.

Levels of Service

All law libraries have policies, written or unwritten, about levels of service offered to different library users or categories of users. If the library has a fairly restricted community of users to support, the levels of support may be more a matter of user preferences than actual library policy. Academic and court libraries are likely to have the most stratified user communities. Law school libraries tend to provide a higher level of support to law faculty, and court libraries may devote most of their attention to delivering information to judges. Reference librarians in the law school setting may do fairly extensive research for law professors, either through a system of library-supervised law student research assistants or by the reference librarians themselves. Academic research for professors may focus on strictly legal points or might include historical or other law-related points such as, "What is the source of the phrase 'the devil is in the details'?"

In some situations, teaching the researcher is a better approach than delivering the answer. In academic law libraries, law students and other students are generally helped in this way because research instruction is part of their legal education. Teaching at the point of need provides an opportunity to convey research methods when the student is most likely to internalize and remember the strategy. Reference librarians delight in sharing stories of the teachable moment, that time when the researcher is truly receptive to learning. Law firm librarians make judgment calls about when the moment is right for teaching and when simply delivering the answer is most helpful. Some attorneys are interested in learning about new resources, while others are content to have material retrieved for them. Personality, comfort with the resource format, and the time pressure of the moment are all factors that play into the attorneys' and other researchers' receptivity to instruction.

Levels of service are determined not just during the reference service interaction but also in negotiating the purchase of electronic resources. In some large law firms, the cost of licensing a particular tax resource for the entire firm would be prohibitive, whereas licensing it only for the tax group is more feasible and meets the most important needs in the firm. Similarly, in law school libraries, some electronic resources are marketed only to law schools, to the exclusion of faculty and students in other campus programs. At many universities, when a journalism student approaches the law reference librarian and asks for access to Westlaw, the librarian is likely to have to apologize and explain that this service is available only to current law students and faculty at the institution. When an attorney or student is excluded from access in these ways, the reference librarian should provide guidance in finding alternative resources and should convey these needs to those in the library who manage both the law library collection and the main campus library collection.

Technology

Technology continues to expand information-delivery options that impact the method of providing reference services. Thus, technology is expanding the reference librarian's role. The shift away from print toward electronic resources means that reference librarians now teach research strategies and help patrons evaluate resources. Some reference librarians are creating Web sites with research guides and providing feeds of breaking news from other sources.

Library users communicate with reference librarians through an ever-expanding list of options, moving beyond face-to-face and telephone conversations to e-mail reference, instant messaging, and blogs. Each form has advantages and disadvantages. User groups are not consistent in their willingness to embrace each new option. Some law libraries attempt to offer off-hours reference service by providing their librarians with cell phones or by scheduling librarians to participate in deadline-sensitive projects and litigation. After-hours expectations are more the norm in law firms, where deadlines dominate.

Law firm librarians are using technology to handle new tasks such as internal document management, knowledge management, conflict checks, client development, and competitive intelligence. Client development means identifying potential clients based on the firm's areas of expertise, or identifying additional areas of legal advice that the firm might provide to an existing client. Competitive intelligence requires acquiring additional information about competitor law firms, based on public records or on marketing available through the Web.

Technology is transforming the way law librarians locate themselves within the parent institution. Many law firm librarians are housed within the department they support, rather than in a central information center. In academic law libraries, the 24/7 remote availability of online resources has allowed public services to reduce library hours and refocus staff time on services such as teaching or improving document delivery.

Marketing, Teaching, Breaking New Ground

Law firm librarians are leading the way into new information-management areas. Many lawyers and law librarians see the legal profession moving toward a business model in which a greater percentage of billing is based on projects completed, rather than hourly billing based on the number of hours required to complete the project. Clients and attorneys are also shifting allegiances from one firm to another much more than in the past. Law librarians are promoting themselves as information managers and simply as managers, taking on additional administrative and management roles as the law firm becomes more businesslike. Law firm librarians have assumed responsibility for records management and conflict checking in many firms. They also assist the firm with business development and competitive intelligence.

Law school librarians are moving into new roles too. In a growing number of law schools, the law library handles information technology support. Many schools now have a reference librarian who specializes in emerging technologies. Academic law librarians are teaching more courses on legal research, particularly advanced legal research courses. In a number of law schools, law librarians with law degrees are also teaching a wide range of substantive law courses and serving on law school committees. Because of their demonstrated competencies in administration and management, some academic law librarians are even tapped for appointments as assistant and associate deans and even as deans. As law schools become more focused on teaching skills, law librarians can become more involved in clinical and other skills instruction. For example, a law librarian might be embedded in the law school clinics.

Publicly funded state, court, and county law libraries increasingly promote their services to citizens and to key decision makers who have become convinced that such libraries may not be necessary because "it is all on the Web." As more *free* legal information becomes available on Web sites, law librarians find that they must remind chief administrators and the general public that many key legal materials are only available in print, microform, or subscription-based electronic sources. Although more primary law is now available on the Web, much work remains to make this online law official, reliable, and capable of citation in a court.

In all settings, the law reference librarian is observing the needs of users, monitoring and examining the opportunities to shift and expand information-management services. Reference librarians in all types of law libraries are positioned to be their institution's experts on research with new technologies, such as mobile device apps and developing platforms such as WestlawNext and Bloomberg Law.

Policies

Like circulation, the reference department benefits from having clear written policies, with the ability to make exceptions to serve the greater good of the institution. Policies in reference may include levels of service, limitations on service, and hours of service. Other policies may address expectations of library users to help maintain an environment conducive to research and preservation of library materials. Many libraries, either on their own or in conjunction with an information technology department, have policies outlining permissible and impermissible uses of the computers and of the Internet. Law libraries are also likely to include in their policies the confidentiality of library research. In law firms and court libraries, the policy may be a component of protecting attorney-client confidentiality, an important obligation of the attorney to the client. In law school libraries and in public libraries, state laws require the library to maintain the confidentiality of circulation records and other information about users' research.

INTERLIBRARY LOAN AND OTHER COOPERATIVE AGREEMENTS

Interlibrary Loan and Document Retrieval

Interlibrary loan is sometimes linked to circulation and sometimes to reference. This service is based on the kindness of other libraries. Many law libraries have agreements with other libraries to share materials with or without fees for the service. When a library does not own a title that one of its users wants to use, that library sends a request to other libraries to borrow the material to meet the local user's needs. Interlibrary loan, or ILL, as it is commonly called, developed during a time when libraries were based on books, journals, microform, and other physical types of collections. In recent years, electronic resources replaced some of these materials, and ILL adjusted. The interlibrary loan staff now check not only the library catalog to make sure requested material is not in the collection; they also check the library's electronic journal indexes and search the library's databases for the requested material. This initial search of the local resources prevents the library from using interlibrary loan except when the library does not have access to the material or when the material is already in use by another library user.

Licenses

As law libraries replace print materials with electronic options, interlibrary loan can become difficult. Although copyright law allows for legally owned copies of copyrighted material to be shared through limited ILL photocopy services, publishers generally avoid copyright law by selling access to electronic databases that require libraries to agree to license contracts governing the use of these materials. Often, interlibrary lending is not permitted under the publisher's license agreement. As the chapter on "Collection Development, Acquisitions, and Licensing" outlines, librarians should anticipate this restriction on use and negotiate for ILL use that is consistent with copyright law.[2] All public services staff should be aware of licenses and be trained to comply with them. Some law libraries include license information relating to ILL (both lending and borrowing) in their catalog or other electronic resource-management systems.

Universities, Consortia, Informal Sharing

Law libraries may participate in a variety of collaborative efforts that include interlibrary loan agreements. These groups may agree to share resources and may even agree to share without a fee. In the academic law library, the most common sharing is among libraries on the same campus, where sharing may include the electronic catalog and borrowing privileges for all law school and other university library users. In some academic law libraries, the law professors are provided a document-retrieval service that delivers campus library materials to the faculty member. Regional law library consortia provide varying levels of collaborative support, including interlibrary loan, to their members. The chapter on "The World of Consortia" provides an in-depth view of these arrangements.

Other types of cooperation that affect interlibrary loan may be formal or informal. Law firm librarians geographically or institutionally linked may simply telephone each other to borrow needed materials. These services may draw on institutional traditions or on a collegial relationship between the librarians at each firm.

Law librarians must be ever mindful, though, of the adversarial nature of legal practice and the need for confidentiality. Before posting a question on a listserv or approaching a colleague outside of the law firm, the law firm librarian must ensure that doing so will not injure the client or violate confidentiality. In the long run, purchase of the needed materials may be much less costly.

From ILL to Document Retrieval to Collection Development

Interlibrary loan is a library service that supports and draws on other library services, such as collection development, circulation, and reference. A small law library can easily make connections between an ILL request, a missing item, and collection development because only a few staff members are involved. In a larger law library, communication among staff and departments may be required to make these connections. The ILL staff should consider forwarding selected or all ILL requests to the librarian who selects materials for purchase, particularly if the material is new and can be obtained quickly. Similarly, if the material is supposed to be in the library but is missing from the collection, the interlibrary loan staff member should alert other librarians who might search for the missing item, adjust the catalog record, and/or purchase a replacement.

Some ILL requests may trigger the purchase of specialized material that should be obtained through ILL or purchased just for the interested library user, rather than for the library collection. Such materials might be documents held by a government agency but not published or posted electronically. If the library has a large and specialized staff, the task of locating this material might be forwarded to a reference librarian.

Policies

Like circulation and reference, interlibrary loan also benefits greatly from written policies. The lending function is very like circulation, so loan periods, as well as fines or fees for late or missing items, should be incorporated into posted policies for the library. In addition, the cost for the service should be outlined, and any stratification of user groups, such as consortia members, public libraries, law firms, etc., should be detailed. Having a policy, of course, does not mean that exceptions are unwise. When a borrowing library reports that its library user has lost an interlibrary loaned book, the lending library should consider past behavior of the borrowing library before applying a lost-book fee. Libraries that do each other favors can preserve that goodwill with a flexible approach to policy enforcement.

SHAPING THE PHYSICAL ENVIRONMENT

The law library physical environment shapes and reflects library use. Those served by the library may be inside the library facility, or they may be in a remote location, using electronic resources at any time of the day or requesting that print materials be delivered directly to their location. Many law libraries struggle to retain their space, given the shift toward electronic materials. The popular misconception that legal information is all on the Internet at no charge puts the law library on the defensive as administrators in the firm, court, or law school eye library space to meet other space needs. The best offense is to maintain an attractive, comfortable space that provides amenities appropriate for most of the users. Wireless Internet access, small rooms for group study or for conferences, and even areas for coffee and food are approaches used in a variety of law libraries. Safety, too, is an important component of the library as place. Law libraries work toward safety with policies about appropriate user behavior, staff emergency procedures and training, and physical approaches ranging from architectural openness, to installation of emergency phones, to the hiring of security personnel.

The physical environment should also accommodate disabled library users and disabled library employees to the extent that the budget can reasonably support. A variety of enabling designs and adaptive technologies can improve access to the library space and to library collections. In the spirit of service and in response to the Americans with Disabilities Act,[3] many libraries develop accommodations both in anticipation of the need and in response to specific requests.

WHEN PEOPLE AND MACHINES BEHAVE BADLY

"What do you mean, I can't have my pizza delivered here in the library?"
"I just spent five dollars at the scanner, and the copies are blurred."

The details and logistics of maintaining an environment supportive of research can be as important as the intellectual challenges of providing public services in the law library. Sometimes people behave badly, and so do machines. In these situations, the public services library staff must respond.

The problem patron has inspired a number of articles on how to manage the situation. Just as the reference interview requires both strategy and finesse, dealing with difficult people can be a matter of training and natural interpersonal skills. Written policies, active listening, and, ultimately, referral to a supervisor are useful approaches. In some extreme cases, calling the police is in order.

Machines, too, can misbehave, and the public services staff may be called upon to teach the user how to connect with the wireless service, attempt a minor repair, or call in experts. A reference librarian may shift from patent research instruction to locating paper misfeeds in a matter of minutes. And the most pleasant discovery of a key resource for a researcher can be followed by having to ask another library user to finish eating the pizza outside the library. The reality is that work in public services is unpredictable, and those in this area must have some sense of adventure to embrace the full gamut of possibilities.

AALL CORE COMPETENCIES, SPECIALIZED COMPETENCIES

Many law librarians are members of the American Association of Law Libraries, which has a set of core competencies and specialized competencies that includes lists for reference, research, and client services. These two sections are reproduced in the appendix to this chapter. A separate section addresses competencies for teaching, an activity closely aligned with public services. The full document is available at the association's Web site at http://www.aallnet.org.

CONCLUSION

The unpredictability of law library public service work is both challeng-ing and exhilarating. Individual and typical user needs may vary widely and are constantly evolving, and the resources library staff rely on to meet those needs also constantly change. Not long ago, resources on many types of law, from municipal law to foreign law, were difficult to find, but now many of these jurisdictions provide free access online. Once users had to travel to the library to use print resources, but now they can download apps to their mobile devices to view the laws of a state or nation. Public services staff stay on top of all of these changes in order to guide judges, faculty, students, attorneys, and others interested in the law. Ongoing shifts in information publishing, access, and use will con-tinue to make law library public services an endeavor for those who are alert, adventurous, and sympathetic to all who engage with evolving law and legal information.

NOTES

1. The phrase *public services* is a common one in law libraries, particularly academ-ic law libraries. It is used to describe services that normally involve interaction with the persons using the library. Other services, such as technical services, information technology services, and administration, are distinguished as being usually behind-the-scenes activities. Terms such as *user services* or even *reader services* are similar to *public services*. Sometimes the distinction is a matter of fashion; sometimes it is a matter of environment. Those whom the library serves are addressed with a variety of names, including *the public, library users, the readers, library patrons, library customers,* and *library clients* or *clientele*. Each of these has its own nuances. In this chapter, the terms *public services, researchers,* and *library user* will predominate.

2. 17 U.S.C. §§107–112 (2006 & Supps.).

3. 42 U.S.C. §12101 (2006 & Supps.).

FIVE

State Law Libraries in the Twenty-First Century

Steven P. Anderson

One of the most profound experiences I ever had at the reference desk was the day that a young mother, who happened to be a self-represented litigant, walked into the Maryland State Law Library and asked to speak to the director. After I told her that she had found the right person, she said that she wanted to return to the library to thank me for having such a helpful, talented, and caring staff. With tears starting in her eyes, she told me how one of my librarians, the day before, had provided her with just the right information on a child custody modification issue and that, because of that assistance, she had prevailed in a court hearing that allowed her to maintain custody of her children. Close to tears myself, I responded—fairly emotionally and modestly—that I was grateful that she was pleased with our service and that I certainly would pass along her kind words of gratitude to the accommodating librarian, who was out of the office that day. The entire exchange could not have lasted longer than a few minutes, but the encounter is indelibly etched in my recollection as the very best that public law librarianship can offer—to both the customer and the library professional.

Of course, most customer interactions in state law libraries are far less dramatic and result in considerably less unambiguous outcomes. Nevertheless, it is worthwhile for a librarian to remember that singular, extraordinary experience in his or her career to use as a goal, marking the finest service a library can provide. What if all customer interactions could be as remarkable? How can law libraries create systems, procedures, and services that will make exceptional customer interactions?

The Maryland State Law Library has made an effort to address such questions by defining its mission in an elemental way: "The Maryland State Law Library, a court-related agency of the Maryland Judiciary, serves the needs of Maryland's government and citizens by: building and preserving collections of legal information resources, promoting access to these collections, and creating educational opportunities that enhance the understanding of legal information."[1] Thus, the statement captures three basic components of library work: (1) the creation and management of collections; (2) reference assistance and accessibility services; and (3) instruction on the usage of information resources.

Many states operate their own state law libraries or state appellate court libraries, which usually have similar functions. The major differences among this set of libraries are those relating to administrative oversight (a few come under the auspices of a state library rather than the courts) and the prioritization of services by customer group (some state law libraries place greater emphasis on service to the bench or bar rather than to the public). Generally speaking, however, Maryland's is the archetypal state law library. As such, it is hoped that this review of the Maryland State Law Library's operations will serve as a useful example of the services and management of this type of library.

CREATION AND MANAGEMENT OF COLLECTIONS

Library collection policies serve as crucial blueprints for defining the scope of libraries' missions. They not only provide an essential framework for libraries' services, but they also provide justifications for adequate funding and direction throughout the budget-planning process. As government-funded institutions, state law libraries especially should strive to be accountable to the public for their expenditures.

The Maryland State Law Library's collection-development policy, like many others, builds on its own institutional history. Seldom do libraries change their missions so dramatically that whole new collections are required or that older parts of the collection must be withdrawn entirely. The library's policy reflects this fact and thus includes holdings of Maryland history materials and other "special collections," which are legacies from the library's predecessor entity.[2]

It is also useful to take into account the various constituent parts of a library's collection. For example, librarians should consider whether a noncirculating reference collection or a limited-circulation reserve collection merit selection criteria different from the main part of the collection. Similarly, there may be different requirements for selections from the Federal Depository Library Program or a state government library depository program in which the library participates, as does the Maryland State Law Library.

Law libraries must also consider how their collections will meet the research requirements of different groups of customers. Those serving the public should ensure that collection-development policies are broad enough to cover the information needs of self-represented litigants,[3] including the goal of providing materials in languages appropriate for this population. Attorneys, for example, typically find practice-oriented handbooks and continuing legal education materials to be quite useful. Judges, of course, require primary sources and well-regarded treatises.

The American Association of Law Libraries' *Standards for Appellate Court Libraries & State Law Libraries*,[4] which the Maryland State Law Library's policy incorporates, mandates that a library of this type make available a significant number of legal materials from the library's home state, as well as legislative and judicial primary sources from other states. Therefore, it should be noted that the need to provide such primary materials significantly expands the fiscal and administrative resources that a library requires. Although these standards are voluntary, library managers should maintain ongoing dialogue with their oversight boards about adherence to applicable standards.

Another consideration for materials-selection policies is the choice of the appropriate media format. While online sources make information readily accessible, the licensing of information content in database systems typically precludes a library's individual ability to preserve such information. Print and microform materials, on the other hand, although sometimes more cumbersome to use, can be owned and, therefore, preserved for as long as the owner wishes.

For these reasons, one of the greatest challenges facing law libraries today is finding the specific balance between print and digital publications that is the most resource efficient and useful for the library's customers.[5] As a practical matter, one of the most crucial factors in this regard is the availability of funding to purchase the same or similar items in duplicate formats. Some vendors, of course, offer discounts on bundled print and database subscriptions, but occasionally these costs are still too high for the individual library. The Maryland State Law Library typically duplicates coverage of primary legal sources, because online subscription costs for this material usually can be held to a manageable level and Maryland's appellate courts will be best served by the long-term retention of printed case law precedent. By contrast, the library replaces secondary source loose-leaf subscriptions with online access, so long as the pricing for the online service is approximately equal to or less than the print version. One major factor contributing to this decision is the desire to have the library's clerical staff oriented more toward direct customer service and away from tedious filing tasks whenever possible.

State law libraries such as Maryland's often boast extensive and wide-ranging holdings of secondary sources.[6] The selection process for these materials should account for changes in the law, such as developments in the technology and health fields, and should also give due consideration to all publishers, and not merely those that sell the greatest number of titles to law libraries. For example, state-based bar associations and continuing legal education providers often produce some of the most practical and useful information for local practitioners. It is not enough to conclude the selection inquiry after consulting the catalogs of just two or three major publishers.

Libraries should draft procedures for the acquisitions process itself. The Maryland State Law Library essentially follows a two-step process. First, the Collection Development Committee, appointed by the director and composed of professional staff, meets regularly to decide on the merits of proposed new title purchases and reviews title lists upon subscription renewal time. Once a decision has been made, the library follows the purchasing procedures of its parent institution, the Maryland Judiciary. As is now common with many government entities, court libraries typically adhere to the pertinent procurement regulations. Chief among these are spending limits for departmental authorizations, bidding requirements for government contracts, and justifications for the use of "sole source" suppliers. Because of the uniqueness of many legal publications, it is likely that many purchases by law libraries would fall into this latter category. Whatever the purchasing rules might be, it is crucial that libraries work cooperatively with their parent institutions' procurement departments for the public's benefit. The outcome of this situation is that governmental law libraries frequently spend a significant amount of time ensuring that procurements flow smoothly. For example, the Maryland State Law Library employs one full-time "fiscal services coordinator."

After purchasing, the next most crucial aspect of building a collection is its logical organization through cataloging processes. At the Maryland State Law Library, as with most law libraries, secondary source materials are cataloged according to Library of Congress classification. Primary sources, such as case law reporters and statutes, are grouped by jurisdiction. However, there are other cataloging standards to consider. As a member of the Federal Depository Library Program, the Maryland State Law Library uses the Superintendent of Documents (SuDoc) classification scheme for its federal documents collection.[7] Additionally, many years ago, the Maryland State Law Library adapted the SuDoc system to catalog its local collection of Maryland state agency publications, which it receives through the State Publications Depository and Distribution Program.[8]

After a library selects the appropriate classification system for its collection, it should create local cataloging guidelines that are appropriate for its customers. For example, the Maryland State Law Library chooses to provide hypertext links to available online sources for any materials that also are available physically in the library. Therefore, a customer can locate an old law book in the library's Special Collections Room or access directly the same resource in digital form from Gale's "Making of Modern Law" database. The notes field in the library's catalog is also used to identify a resource as being on the *List of Recommended Treatises for Maryland Court Libraries.*[9]

The Maryland State Law Library also intends to make its holdings as widely available as possible. Therefore, many of the library's records are available via OCLC. State law libraries also may elect to join various local or regional union catalogs. Technical services processing is an integral, but often-overlooked, part of collection development. Some law libraries, given their relatively modest size, have no check-in procedures for the processing of incoming publications. Although this may work efficiently for some, larger libraries continue to track the receipt of incoming materials. One might argue that such a process is somewhat inefficient, given the amount of duplicate material available online and the accuracy with which publishers now distribute subscriptions. Nevertheless, in most government libraries, there is a requirement that a staff member verify the receipt of all incoming items purchased at taxpayers' expense. When one staff member verifies receipt and another staff member relies on that verification in order to process payment, as occurs at the Maryland State Law Library, then a formal check-in procedure is advisable. Libraries can greatly streamline serials check-in and publications-ordering procedures by using integrated library systems (ILS).

ILSs are ubiquitous now for another reason, of course—the ability to provide detailed catalog records to library customers via the Internet. Customers typically expect libraries to provide access as a matter of course. In fact, for state law libraries, they are required by the American Association of Law Libraries' standards.[10] This, in turn, means that significant staffing and fiscal resources must be allocated for the maintenance and development of such a system. Currently, the ILS industry seems to be in a significant period of flux, with the rise of "open source" software and the continuing innovations being made to "discovery" platforms that can integrate catalog records with search results from other databases. Whatever ILS a library selects, one primary consideration should be its ease of use by library customers. Another important evaluation factor for government libraries to consider is the ability of the ILS to produce catalog information as an inventory list of the library's collection. In this way, the catalog record doubles as a property record that can be used for valuation and insurance purposes.

After materials are selected, processed, cataloged, and placed on the shelves, the work of collection management and preservation begins. Two basic elements to management are the intertwined tasks of space allocation and deaccessioning. Usually, a library does not withdraw an item unless the need to do so is triggered by some occurrence, such as irreparable damage to the book, supersedence by a newer edition, or lack of space. Collection management requires continuous planning to make new space available and to ensure that the collection is relevant for the library's customers. The Maryland State Law Library's deaccessioning guidelines are part of its collection-development policy and generally use the same criteria as the acquisition selection process. As a practical matter, the library evaluates items for withdrawal on a periodic basis, depending on the unavailability of sufficient growth space in a particular shelving area. The library is very conservative about the material it discards. For example, a legal treatise will remain in the collection if it was ever cited in Maryland case law or widely cited in court opinions from other jurisdictions. Most of the library's withdrawn material is offered to other libraries. For the present, the library is quite fortunate to have access to on-site storage with compact shelving, which will provide enough space for the next several years. Many libraries, on the other hand, are facing significant limitations to space availability and storage capability. For these libraries, the need for accurate collection-management planning is much more consequential.

Library materials deteriorate with the passage of time and frequent handling. Therefore, in order to ensure that items continue to be available for their customers, libraries should take some preventative and remedial preservation measures. Two key components of the Maryland State Law Library's preservation initiative for physical holdings are ongoing book-binding and continued support for its climate-controlled Special Collections Room, which houses rare and fragile materials. Municipal codes and ordinances, state agency publications, and continuing legal education handbooks often are originally published in softbound or loose-leaf formats, both of which are highly prone to loss or damage. Because it is one of the few with extensive and historical collections of these works, the library routinely ensures that these materials are bound, either when received as new or when discovered on the shelf retrospectively. The library is fortunate to have custom-built space to house its rare and antique materials. The Special Collections Room features temperature and humidity control separate from the rest of the building, a ceiling-mounted leak-detection system, and an FM-200 chemical fire-suppression system. This allows the library to serve as a careful steward of these valuable and unique items, which ultimately are owned by the public.

In recent years, the Maryland State Law Library has used considerable resources for the conservation of two highly prized works, one of which happens to be nonlegal. The library's predecessor entity, the State Library, was an original subscriber to well-known naturalist John James Audubon's "Birds of America" hand-colored lithographs. After 170 years of usage and display, the library was able to send all of its 431 prints for professional cleaning and conservation. The library did the same for its copies of Acts of Congress, from 1789 to 1791, signed by then-Secretary of State Thomas Jefferson. The library likely will be evaluating other similar large-scale preservation needs in the future. At present, the library is focusing on smaller preservation projects, such as book repair and archival boxing.

The library, in recent years, also has come to recognize the crucial importance of the preservation and stewardship of digital materials. In 2007, the library became a founding member of the Chesapeake Digital Preservation Group,[11] a collaborative digital archive from the Legal Information Preservation Alliance.[12] Through this system, the library has been able to store in a secure environment over 3,800 "born digital" Maryland state agency publications, many of which are at risk of loss as webmasters revise sites or inadvertently cause the documents to be unavailable.[13] The library expects to continue "harvesting" and saving law-related state government reports for the foreseeable future. Additionally, the library embarked on its own digitization efforts for both preservation and access purposes. At the present time, the library offers three collections online: Proceedings of the Maryland Judicial Conference, Maryland Task Force Reports, and Maryland Rules Committee Meeting Minutes and Agendas.[14] These sets, the print copies of which are sometimes unique to the library, are important for the understanding of the historical development of Maryland legislation and the state's court system. Documents are full-text searchable and available in PDF/A, the current standard format for digital preservation. The library hopes to share other similar resources in the near future.

Library equipment plays a significant role in the ongoing management of collections, especially when one considers the multiplicity of available formats. For example, a library will only be able to balance digital materials with printed works if there is adequate space for public access terminals, funding for computer hardware and software, availability of high-speed network connections, and ongoing technical support. Similarly, a library cannot maintain a microform collection without reading machines and cabinet storage, which often can be placed only on load-bearing floors.

Many institutions have designed continuity-of-operations plans to manage a coordinated response to natural disasters and man-made security incidents. In order to better protect their collections, government libraries may work with other departments within their institutions to draft such plans. For libraries without more broadly coordinated efforts, library managers should, at a minimum, draft some kind of disaster-preparedness document. Before the Maryland State Law Library became a part of judiciary-wide efforts, it used the resources of "dPlan: The Online Disaster-Planning Tool for Cultural and Civic Institutions."[15] This template should be useful for most libraries that need to plan independently for their disaster response.

The oldest books in the library's collections date back more than four hundred years. Therefore, the goal of the library's collection-management and preservation efforts is to do everything possible to ensure that core holdings, in both print and digital formats, endure another four centuries—or longer.

REFERENCE ASSISTANCE AND ACCESSIBILITY

The second part of the Maryland State Law Library's mission is to provide access to the library's collections. At first glance, this would appear to be quite easily accomplished. However, *meaningful* access requires both strategic planning and engaged management. More is required of libraries than simply opening their doors to customers.

The Maryland State Law Library employs a full-time staff of thirteen, including me, and five part-time staff. Of these, three professional part-time librarians and five professional full-time librarians have four-hour shifts on a rotating basis at the library's information desk. One paraprofessional fills in on a regular basis. Usually, this means that each librarian trained in legal reference work manages the intake of all in-person, telephone, and e-mail customer contacts during his or her shift, about eight hours total a week. Additionally, the same staff members are assigned coverage of hour-long live chat reference shifts, performed in conjunction with the Maryland AskUsNow program.[16] The library's outreach services librarian schedules the calendar at least monthly, taking into consideration librarians' leave requests and out-of-office meetings. At present, staff finds that a shared calendar on Google is the most straightforward way to manage scheduling. It is also worth mentioning that two of the part-time librarians have primary responsibility for the solo management of the library during its extended hours of operation on Tuesday and Thursday evenings and Saturdays. The intent behind this balance of staffing duties is to ensure that librarians will continue to sharpen their reference skills and still have sufficient time to work on other projects and position responsibilities, without burnout due to overwork in a particular area.

On an average day, customers will ask the reference staff a total of thirty to forty questions. Approximately 30 percent of these will be in-person contact, with another 30 percent being telephone calls. Customers pose the remainder of the questions via e-mail and live chat. The library's customers seek information at the reference desk more than 9,000 times each year.

Generally speaking, in-person and telephonic reference interviews are easier to conduct than those that are negotiated via e-mail.[17] Because many of the questions posed via e-mail appear to come from self-represented litigants, clarifying a request usually requires follow-up exchanges and consumes additional time.[18] Voice-based communication frequently permits the librarian to clarify his or her role in the research process, thereby more easily avoiding the unauthorized practice of law, such is not the case with e-mail.

There is abundant professional literature on ethics issues in law libraries.[19] Indeed, three key issues impact on a daily basis how law librarians provide reference service, especially to self-represented litigants. First, of course, is the fact that librarians who are not attorneys cannot dispense legal advice. Doing so is considered to be the unauthorized practice of law. Second, court librarians, as employees of the judicial branch of government, cannot demonstrate bias in the provision of services. All court staff must remain neutral in the performance of their duties in order to provide equal access to the justice system. Third, in most states, by statute, a customer's use of a library's collections must remain confidential.[20]

Because all three of these ethics issues uniquely impact online communications with library customers, the library in 2011 adopted "Guidelines for E-mail Reference Service" to identify the best practices for the handling of these communications.[21] These guidelines, for example, require a librarian to determine if a particular request for information contains an unambiguous description of the sought-after material. If not, then staff shall provide general information by performing the following tasks:

1. Consult an appropriate finding aid, such as a Web site, database, index, or digest, to assess the feasibility of locating the discrete part of the information resource that is most narrowly tailored to addressing the general question (e.g., whenever appropriate or feasible, provide a subtitle of the Maryland Annotated Code, a topic heading for a West Digest, a topic section of a legal encyclopedia, or a book chapter).
2. Evaluate the need to remind the requester of the existence of other resources that may provide additional information on the general topic.
3. Evaluate the need to instruct the requester on how to use information resources (e.g., whenever appropriate or feasible, explain finding aids, topic arrangement, authorship, publication cycles, official status or precedential value, etc.).
4. Evaluate the need to instruct the requester about court procedures.
5. Evaluate the need to provide the requester with referral sources.

Additional provisions include privacy in communications, a sample template for an e-mail reply to the customer, and a requirement that a reference staff coworker review the prospective reply before sending. The purpose for these directives is to identify affirmative steps that a librarian should take to foster the most effective use by self-represented litigants of the library's collections, while remaining neutral in the provision of information.

State law libraries can provide additional access services to their customers. The Maryland State Law Library, for example, provides, for a small charge to the general public, a document-delivery service. Customers complete an online request form, which includes a copyright statement, and can pay for copies via credit card once the library staff member locates the item and verifies the number of pages to be copied. The fees charged by the library follow the fee schedule for copies made by circuit court clerks' offices. The library does not charge other state government entities, however. A related service is interlibrary lending. The library uses OCLC to find materials in other libraries and frequently fulfills requests, as well.

Many state law libraries offer borrowing privileges to various user groups. Historically, the Maryland State Law Library has served as a reference library. Interestingly, this mandate is codified by statute: "The Director of the State Law Library may . . . [n]ot allow any book, map, or documents to be removed from the State Law Library, except by the executive and legislative departments, other State agencies located in Annapolis, members of the General Assembly, and judges of the Court of Appeals and Court of Special Appeals, or on interlibrary loan to other libraries."[22] Consequently, the library's circulation policy extends primarily to judges and their staff members. The library's circulation "system" is thus exceedingly simple—it consists of check-out cards at the reference desk. Another advantage of this statutory policy, of course, is the security of the library's collection, much of which is unique.

The Maryland State Law Library is fortunate to have a highly skilled and innovative staff, which makes customers appreciate the library's reference and access services. It is logical, of course, to invest in the creation and enhancement of such services in order to get the most out of libraries' collections. Every time a needed book is left unopened or a necessary database remains unsearched, an opportunity to provide the appropriate resource is missed. Publicly supported institutions such as state law libraries should strive to maximize the utilization of their resources. Consequently, information access is a crucial component of the Maryland State Law Library's mission.

INSTRUCTION ON THE USAGE OF INFORMATION RESOURCES

Instructional programming for library customers is closely linked to the provision of reference. In practice, most reference interactions contain some element of education. For example, a recommendation to use a case law digest may conclude with some instruction on how to use an available "words and phrases" volume as a research shortcut. Nevertheless, any formal steps a library may take toward the establishment of an ongoing training program require different resources and skills. The same is true for library marketing and promotional efforts, which at the Maryland State Law Library generally fall under the label of "outreach."

The library's approach to formal training makes effective use of partnership opportunities with other court departments, and is therefore rather narrowly focused. For example, the library offers basic legal research classes several times a year to any judiciary employee through the Office of Professional Development of the Human Resources Department. The office centrally manages registration, internal advertising, and other administrative details, so that librarians can concentrate on course development and instruction. The library works with appellate court clerks' offices to schedule annual orientations for judicial law clerks. It also schedules occasional training sessions on legal research databases, primarily targeted to judiciary staff. The Maryland Judicial Institute, the entity responsible for judges' continuing education, extends presentation opportunities to the library and asks the library to prepare supplemental bibliographies for topic-specific programs.

At present, the library does not offer formal training to members of the public or to the bar. One reason for this is the likely prospect of limited in-person attendance at such a program. Another, perhaps more fundamental, justification is that many library customers are more engaged in learning about the research process at the time of need. It is not uncommon for librarians to spend extended periods of time discussing with attorneys or self-represented litigants the organization of legal information. This tailored approach seems to meet the needs of the library's customers for now. Other state law libraries, however, do have training programs that are targeted for audiences of practitioners.

One of the most respected educational and outreach services offered by the library is the People's Law Library of Maryland Web site.[23] The library assumed responsibility for the site from the Maryland Legal Aid Bureau in 2007. It continues to operate as the premier legal "self-help" Web site for Maryland residents and enjoys the support of Maryland's nonprofit legal services providers. The library devotes substantial time and human resources to the project, including one full-time lawyer-librarian staff member. In order to direct the development of information on the Web site, the library convenes regular meetings of a Content Advisory Committee of legal professionals, including representatives of judiciary departments and conferences, bar associations, law school legal clinics, and Maryland Legal Services Corporation grantee organizations. The Content Advisory Committee has adopted protocols and guidelines for content development, akin to a library's collection-development policy. Accordingly, the People's Law Library focuses on meeting the information needs of self-represented litigants with civil cases in Maryland state courts. As a secondary priority, the site provides resources on Maryland criminal and administrative law and federal law. Usage is significant, with over 250,000 page views, 80,000 visits, and 1.3 million hits per month.[24]

Although the library maintains the People's Law Library for the basic legal information needs of the public, it also has developed a more traditional site for the promotion of the library's collections and services. The role of the library Web site is to provide more research-specific information, such as guides to Maryland legislative history research, links to online municipal codes, the Library's digital collections, and the online catalog.

The library's outreach efforts, although somewhat less formalized than its training programs and legal self-help Web site, are extensive and sustained. The library hired its first outreach services librarian over a decade ago, with the primary purpose of serving as a liaison to Maryland's county circuit court law libraries and public libraries. This networking relationship has solidified the library's participation in a number of organizations and programs, including an oversight committee for statewide public library services, the Maryland AskUsNow chat reference service, continuing education programs on legal topics for public librarians, and, perhaps most importantly, the Conference of Maryland Court Law Library Directors.

The conference, established by the chief judge of the Maryland Court of Appeals, is a forum through which circuit court librarians and State Law Library staff can discuss topics of shared interest and advise the chief judge on matters important to court libraries.[25] Maryland's trial courts are not part of a completely unified court system; rather, local court library staff members are county employees and supervised by the county administrative judge.[26] The creation of a judiciary-wide conference helps to coordinate communications, while maintaining local authority. Since its foundation, the conference, through regular meetings, has adopted the following: *Maryland County Public Law Library Standards*, *Maryland Titles Recommended for County Law Libraries*, and *General Treatises Recommended for the Core Collection*.[27] Additionally, it has offered to its members numerous templates and best practices, and promulgated mutual aid agreements for coordinated disaster-response planning.

Another organic outreach opportunity for the library has developed in recent years with the creation of the Maryland Access to Justice Commission. Both the conference chair and I, as director of the State Law Library, are appointees, as is a representative of the Maryland Association of Public Library Administrators. The commission plays an active role in the monitoring of court services to ensure a fair and open system of justice, support for the delivery of legal services to those in need, and the development of court-based self-help clinics. The commission plays a key role in the promotion of the People's Law Library and includes endorsement of the site in many of its public communications. Several members of the site's Content Advisory Committee also happen to serve on the commission.

A similar natural relationship has developed with the local Anne Arundel Community College. For many years, the library's conference room has served as the classroom for the school's paralegal studies program's legal research courses. In this way, area paralegals gain a great deal of familiarity with the library, frequently returning to visit and endorse the library's services.

Because the library is embedded in all of these networks, it enjoys substantial recognition among both the Maryland bar and the library community. The Maryland State Law Library makes every effort to enhance this visibility, for example, by frequently exhibiting at bar association conferences and having staff present at library association conferences. Of course, more can always be done, but the library strives to make effective use of its resources. Striking the appropriate balance of resources between building collections and promoting them to prospective customers is an ongoing challenge.

LIBRARY ADMINISTRATION

None of the Maryland State Law Library's growth and services would be possible without cooperation and assistance from its parent institution, the Maryland Judiciary, or the support of its oversight body, the statutory State Law Library Committee.[28] Institutional support has always been important to libraries, but today, for the government library, it is absolutely essential. Of course, a comprehensive understanding of the corollary—that libraries exist to further serve the mission of the main institution—is crucial, as well.[29]

The State Law Library Committee, chaired by the chief judge of the Court of Appeals, the state's highest court, enjoys a broad definition of supervision. In practice, however, it offers guidance on matters of policy and approves significant expenditures for the creation of new services. It gives me, as library director, discretion to decide on most day-to-day activities, ranging from subscription renewals to staff performance evaluations. I report to the chief judge for individual matters or urgent concerns.

The library benefits greatly from the services provided by the Administrative Office of the Courts. The Department of Human Resources assists with the library's recruitment needs and administers payroll. The Department of Procurement and Contracts Administration ensures that purchases are made fairly and according to policy. The Department of Budget and Finance offers guidance on budget planning and processes the library's invoices for payment. Other Judiciary entities make sure that the library remains accountable for the maintenance of its equipment and assets, the stewardship of its collections, and the handling of fiscal trans-actions. This cooperative and professional assistance allows the library to better focus on its mission, rather than forcing its staff to develop competencies possibly beyond the scope of their interests.

CONCLUSION

State law libraries today continue to harbor enormous potential to serve their local communities. With rich collections, talented staff, and rapid developments in technology, libraries have never before been able to provide such an effective level of access to legal information. The Maryland State Law Library offers one view of how state law libraries can use their resources to provide exceptional customer service. Collection development and management, reference and access services, and the promotion of educational opportunities are the core elements of the library's mission. Challenges exist, of course. However, the establishment of processes and procedures, collaboration with other entities with similar goals, and innovation all contribute to the successful provision of exceptional customer service at state law libraries.

NOTES

1. See "About Us: Maryland State Law Library," http://www.lawlib.state.md.us/aboutus/aboutus.html.

2. Like several other state law libraries, Maryland's earlier institution was known as the State Library.

3. See Merrilee Harrell, "Self-Help Legal Materials in the Law Library: Going a Step Further for the Public Patron," *Legal Reference Services Quarterly* 27, no. 4 (2008): 283–304.

4. "Standards for Appellate Court Libraries & State Law Libraries," American Association of Law Libraries, http://www.aallnet.org/sis/sccll/docs/Sccll%20Appellate%20Standards%20Mar%202005.pdf.

5. For a useful analysis of this topic as it pertains to academic law libraries, see Elizabeth R. Breakstone, "Now How Much of Your Print Collection Is Really Online? An Analysis of the Overlap of Print and Digital Holdings at the University of Oregon Law Library," *Legal Reference Services Quarterly* 29, no. 4 (October–December 2010): 255–75.

6. The Maryland State Law Library consists of approximately 235,000 volumes in print and audiovisual formats and 125,000 microform volume equivalents.

7. "Superintendant of Documents (SuDoc) Classification Scheme," http://www.fdlp.gov/cataloging/856-sudoc-classification-scheme.

8. Md. Code Ann., Educ. § 23-301 (LexisNexis 2008).

9. "Maryland Circuit Court Law Libraries: Maryland State Law Library," http://www.lawlib.state.md.us/audiences/cclib/cclib.html.

10. "The library should maintain a web site that provides information about the library and its services. The web site should also provide access to the library's online catalog, maintain links to law-related sites, particularly for its own state or jurisdiction, and provide information on topics of frequent interest to users." "Standards for Appellate Court Libraries & State Law Libraries," Paragraph V.D.

11. "The Chesapeake Digital Preservation Group," http://www.legalinfoarchive.org/.

12. "Legal Information Preservation Alliance," http://www.aallnet.org/lipa/.

13. Sarah Rhodes, "Breaking Down Link Rot: The Chesapeake Project Legal Information Archive's Examination of URL Stability," *Law Library Journal* 102, no. 4 (Fall 2010): 581–97.

14. See "Digital Collections: Maryland State Law Library," http://www.lawlib.state.md.us/collections/digitalcollections.html.

15. "dPlan™: The Online Disaster-Planning Tool for Cultural and Civic Institutions," http://www.dplan.org/.

16. "AskUsNow!" is the statewide interactive information service, available twenty-four hours a day, seven days a week, that uses the expertise of librarians to provide answers to questions, research guidance, and help navigating the Internet. AskUsNow! is a cooperative service of Maryland libraries and available for any resident or student of Maryland." "Maryland AskUsNow! Information Experts Available 24/7," http://www.askusnow.info/.

17. See Luis M. Acosta and Anna M. Cherry, "Reference Services in Courts and Governmental Settings," *Legal Reference Services Quarterly* 26, nos. 1–2 (2007): 113–34.

18. For additional general information related to self-represented litigants, see Amy Hale-Janeke and Sharon Blackburn, "Law Librarians and the Self-Represented Litigant," *Legal Reference Services Quarterly* 27, no. 1 (2008): 65–88.

19. For background information, see Paul D. Healey, "Pro Se Users, Reference Liability, and the Unauthorized Practice of Law: Twenty-Five Selected Readings," *Law Library Journal* 94, no. 1 (Winter 2002): 133–39.

20. In Maryland, a library staff member may not divulge customer records under the state's Public Information Act. See Md. Code Ann., State Gov't § 10-616(e) (LexisNexis 2009 & Supp. 2012).

21. "Guidelines for E-Mail Reference Service at the Maryland State Law Library," http://www.lawlib.state.md.us/aboutus/policies/EmailReferenceGuidelinesMSLL.pdf.

22. Md. Code Ann., Cts. & Jud. Proc. § 13-504 (LexisNexis 2006).

23. "The People's Law Library of Maryland," http://www.peoples-law.org/.

24. "About Us: The People's Law Library," http://www.peoples-law.org/about/.

25. "Administrative Order Creating the Conference of Maryland Court Law Library Directors," http://www.mdcourts.gov/lawlib/audiences/cclib/conference/2008_order.pdf.

26. Md. Code Ann., Cts. & Jud. Proc. § 2-501 (2006).

27. All documents are available at "Maryland Circuit Court Law Libraries: Maryland State Law Library," http://www.lawlib.state.md.us/audiences/cclib/cclib.html.

28. Md. Code Ann., Cts. & Jud. Proc. § 13-501 (2006).

29. For a useful, current discussion of libraries' relationships with their parent institutions, see John Palfrey, "Cornerstones of Law Libraries for an Era of Digital-Plus," *Law Library Journal* 102, no. 2 (Spring 2010): 185.

SIX

The Curious Case of County Law Libraries

Robert Riger

"NEITHER FISH NOR FOWL"

Although county law libraries have existed in some form since the latter part of the nineteenth century, they are arguably still the most unique and mystifying type of law library. This chapter will attempt to address and clarify some of this confusion.

One of the main reasons for the confusion lies in the very label, "county law library," which is often misleading, since these law libraries are usually not part of the general public library systems of the county where they are located, nor are they special divisions of those systems. Some states, such as California, specifically mandate that "There is in each county of this State a board of law library trustees, which governs the law library established for the county under the provisions of this chapter" (Business and Professions Code Sections 6300 et seq.).[1] In contrast, other states don't have county law libraries per se, such as New York, where the law provides that each county within the state have a *court* law library accessible to the general public.

The real connection between the counties and their public law libraries was the one established through an unfunded mandate by the state legislatures for support of these libraries. These statutes specified that the principal source of funding for county law libraries was a dedicated portion of the civil filing fees collected in the county where the library was located and allocated to the county's law library trust fund, for the provision and maintenance of a law library.[2] The term "maintenance" could cover a wide range of support, including rooms, suitable furniture, window shades, floor coverings, lighting, heat, telephone, janitorial service, approval of fee increases, and budgetary oversight.[3] The standards for meeting these requirements were never explicitly defined, and the counties were often permitted to provide what they deemed "sufficient" housing for their libraries. Obviously, this vague and unpopular mandate would cause friction between the counties and the state, and ultimately between the counties and their law libraries.

Another source of confusion was the creation of boards of trustees to govern these libraries, sometimes referred to as "special districts" or "independent public agencies." These hybrids were "neither fish nor fowl"—neither full county departments nor part of their local court systems—although both the courts and county often shared indirect oversight authority through a preset formula of judicial and/or county appointment.

Without a genuine connection to either the courts or the county (and the full protection and support that accompanies such a connection), county law libraries would be particularly vulnerable during funding crises.

1990–2000—A DECADE OF CHANGE FOR COUNTY LAW LIBRARIES

County law libraries grew during the latter part of the twentieth century, and by the 1950s, many county law libraries had shed their original space and moved into newer and larger space, while others added branches to accommodate the population shifts. Collections and personnel were added to staff so that these main and branch libraries could handle a steady demand for cases, statutes, treatises, journals, and photocopies of court documents, from attorneys, law firms, and county and court legal departments.

However, by the new millennium, the winds of change swept through county law libraries, and "business as usual" was never going to be the same. Key factors in this change are described below.

The online database revolution

County law libraries had thrived in a print environment by serving as repositories of paper resources (including current and historical materials and specialty treatises) for their users, who often lacked the space or resources to house them themselves. In the 1990s, Lexis and Westlaw penetrated the law firms with their online products. By the end of the decade, Lexis and Westlaw were offering desktop access to their products to county and court legal departments, in addition to law firms of all sizes and solo practitioners, and they followed that option by offering pay-as-you-go access via credit card to anyone (with restrictions on some content for non-attorney users) who wanted to access their services. Even database training could be conducted online without the need for the physical presence of a trainer or a classroom. Thus, patronage at county law libraries from three key user groups—law firms, county departments, and the courts' legal staff—began to decline, except for in relation to items that were unavailable or too costly to obtain online. Meanwhile, many county law libraries got left behind in the revolution. Database vendors such as Lexis and Westlaw were slow to offer public access contracts to county law libraries, fearing that these types of agreements would cannibalize their existing and future business with attorneys and private law firms. County law libraries were also limited in their ability to charge back database costs, limiting their return on the investment—an important factor particularly during budgetary and usage downturns.

Rise of the self-represented

Contrary to popular belief, the self-represented are not a homogeneous group, but rather a diverse mix of those who can afford to have representation, but choose not to, and those who wish to have it, but cannot afford it. The latter group often consists of the poor, the ill (mentally and/or physically challenged), and the homeless. As the attorneys began to transition in the last decade from research performed in the law library to online research performed from their desktops, they were replaced and/or supplemented in county law libraries with a rapidly growing population of self-represented litigants. This group seemed to multiply exponentially in the new millennium as the financial and housing situations worsened, mental facilities no longer kept patients hospitalized as they used to, and a wave of immigrants arrived.

This new user group descended on an unprepared legal system. In contrast to the familiar attorney user base, this new group lacked a basic understanding of the complex legal system and how it operated. Needless to say, they also lacked familiarity with legal terminology and both print and online legal research tools. This placed a heavy burden on both the courts and county law libraries in terms of resources and services to assist the self-represented in navigating the court system. County law libraries had to devote additional staff time to provide reference service and create self-help guides for the self-represented. They also had to use budget dollars to add online and print resources specifically designed for the self-represented. Courts had to provide resources and space for self-help centers. Sometimes county law libraries partnered with the courts by providing space, computers, and videos within their branches for the self-help centers and legal clinics, in addition to print and video resource guides for distribution by the courts.

Deterioration of facilities

County law libraries that were built in the 1950s and 1960s as state-of-the-art facilities were now aging and poorly lit, rather than bright and open in design. Heating and cooling systems and mechanical infrastructures were breaking down, while relations between the counties and the libraries sometimes became contentious over maintenance issues. Security was poor, particularly in the dark and isolated study carrels. Furniture was old and nonergonomic. Electrical outlets were inadequate for computers and printers. Mold, asbestos, and water leakage became concerns. The wiring in the buildings was too old and brittle for IT functions. Signage was poor, particularly for those users who were new to law libraries. Parking in downtown areas and crowded courthouse branches was problematic at best. The influx of the homeless and the mentally challenged often prompted fears—of real or imagined threats—on the part of other users. A trip to the local county law library became less attractive for many potential users.

Demographic changes

The population also shifted during this period. The housing market boomed before crashing in the first decade of the new millennium. Buyers took advantage of the boom to leave crowded urban areas and purchase newer homes in less congested suburban areas. Established ethnic groups migrated from old neighborhoods and were replaced by a new wave of immigrants.

Many of these population shifts (particularly in the larger counties), did not correspond to the locations of county law library branches, so potential users in these areas had to contend with commuting time, traffic, gas costs, and parking issues, in addition to facility and safety concerns. To compound matters, database vendors like Lexis and Westlaw did not offer remote access to their products for county law libraries, eliminating that alternative for those who didn't want to commute to use a county law library.

Florida's Revision 7

Florida voters approved Revision 7 of Article V of the Florida Constitution as a constitutional amendment in 1998.[4] It was proposed originally by the Florida Constitution Revision Commission to provide a uniform funding system for the trial courts of Florida. Prior to Revision 7, Florida's trial courts were funded by the county that the court was associated with, while the appellate courts were funded by the state. This created an imbalance across the state, with the wealthier counties being able to afford to provide better funding for court services, while the poorer counties were only able to provide a minimum level of service.[5] Revision 7 required that both the appellate courts and the trial courts be funded by the state, equalizing the funding levels across the counties.

The revision was designed to shift the costs of the state courts system from the counties to the state. Although efforts were begun as early as 1972 to accomplish this shift, the state had not assumed these costs until it was specifically assigned that responsibility with the passage of Revision 7 in 1998.[6]

How did Revision 7 affect Florida's county law libraries? Although Revision 7 was passed in 1998, the state had six years to pass the legislation to implement it. In 2004, the Florida legislature passed a law providing for the state to fund the state courts system, state attorneys' offices, public defenders' offices, and court-appointed counsel.[7] Funding for the offices of the clerks of the circuit and county courts performing court-related functions was to be provided primarily by users of the courts, through filing fees, service charges, and other costs.[8] Absent from this funding plan were county law libraries.[9]

A TALE OF TWO STATES—CALIFORNIA AND FLORIDA

There were two watershed challenges to the counties' unfunded mandate in the early part of the twenty-first century. Both had major consequences. One challenge was successfully defeated (at least in the short term), and the other resulted in a crushing defeat for county law libraries. Here is their story:

In 2002, Assemblyman Wyland of San Diego, California, introduced AB 2648, amending the existing law that required: (1) a county board of supervisors to provide sufficient quarters for the use of the public law library in that county, and (2) a county board of supervisors to pay for the necessary operation and maintenance expenses for such quarters. Wyland's amendment allowed San Diego County to review claims and expenses for law library facilities' operation and maintenance to determine whether the costs in question are necessary in order for the county to meet its statutory duty to provide sufficient quarters for the law library.[10]

The Senate amendments to the bill:[11] (1) permitted the San Diego County Board of Supervisors to review any claims, expenses, or requests for reimbursement received from county law libraries and reduce or deny those claims; (2) allowed the county to review all claims and expenses for law library facilities' operation and maintenance to determine whether the costs are beyond the obligation of the county to provide sufficient quarters for the law library; (3) allowed the law library board of trustees to file a formal protest to the county board of supervisors, should the county reduce or deny a claim, expense, or reimbursement of operation and maintenance costs; and (4) entitled the library's board of trustees to have the protest considered before the county board of supervisors. This bill provided a forum to define and clarify some important aspects of the unfunded county mandate for supporting county law libraries. Key points of the legislative discussion were:[12]

- The law (California Business and Professions Code 6360 et seq.) provides that a county must provide *sufficient* quarters and pay for *necessary* operation and maintenance expenses [my italics].
- Although the terms *sufficient* and *necessary* can be viewed as subjective by the layperson, the legislative analysts interpreted them as implying a standard for what is *reasonable* for meeting the counties' obligations to the law libraries for their facilities' operation and maintenance. Therefore, the counties are not required to pay for any expenses above and beyond what is considered *sufficient* or *necessary*.
- The bill would give San Diego County more authority over county law library expenditures by granting the board of supervisors the right to review reimbursement claims submitted by the law library trustees and to reject any claims the board considers to be above and beyond the county's obligation to the law library.

In his veto message, then-Governor Gray Davis said: "Current law already gives county supervisors discretion in funding law library operations and requires law library trustees use law library fund monies, when available, toward maintenance costs. A law library is an essential component of any court facility, and the local court system would be seriously weakened without county support. This bill creates a poor precedent for counties to follow in providing support for county law libraries."[13] The defeat of the bill was not only a major victory for the San Diego and other California county law libraries, but also served as a national model for effective legislative advocacy on behalf of county law libraries.

However, just two years later, on July 1, 2004, Florida's county law libraries were dealt a crushing blow when the state legislature enacted the provisions of Revision 7. In HB 0113A, the legislature, under pressure from the counties, eliminated the counties' obligations for support for the law libraries by striking the following statutory language: "Service charges in excess of those fixed in this section may be imposed by the governing authority of the county by ordinance, or by special or local law . . . to provide and maintain facilities, including a law library, for the use of the courts of the county wherein the service charges are collected; to provide and maintain equipment; or for a legal aid program in such county."[14]

In contrast to the California scenario, Florida's county law libraries did not play an active role in the 2004 legislative session, being preempted by the larger and more powerful players—the counties, the courts, and the county clerks—all of whom were pushing for their own funding needs. When the state asked the counties and the courts to indicate which functions were essential to their respective operations (and thus entitled to state funding), law libraries were conspicuously absent from both lists. County law libraries transitioned to nonessential or optional components of the court system, as opposed to Gray Davis's view, and unlike Davis, Florida's Governor Jeb Bush did not veto the legislation. The county law libraries' status of being "neither fish nor fowl" came back to bite them, since neither the counties nor the courts provided adequate protection for them.

Why did one effort succeed while another failed? Here are some reasons:

- *Intent*—The California bill appeared to be designed to protect the financial interests of San Diego County, rather than to contest the county's obligations for the facilities for the law library.[15] In contrast, the Florida bill was designed to remove the counties' obligation.
- *Interest*—The California bill had limited interest and little appeal. It appeared duplicative to the governor, and wasn't a "hot issue" or a pressing need for most Californians. On the other hand, court-funding equality was a pressing need in Florida, particularly as the deadline for enactment of the Revision 7 legislation had arrived.
- *Political climate*—Things were relatively calm in California in 2002. In contrast, the nation's eyes and ears were focused on Florida in 2004 after the bitterly contested 2000 presidential election that was decided on Florida's votes. It was also the sixth and final year for enactment of Revision 7, and people were getting anxious for change. The legislature was dominated by the northern counties, many of whom were in dire need of court funding reform. The courts, counties, and the state were all squabbling on what the landscape should look like after Revision 7 implementation. Counties were anxious to shed court costs, the judiciary needed funding for courthouses, and the clerks wanted a piece of the fading filing fees. The plight of law libraries hardly received any attention.
- *Legislative preparedness*—In 2002, California county law libraries had a strong legislative advocate in their established and well-organized professional association, the Council of California County Law Librarians (CCCLL). The CCCLL charged annual membership dues in proportion to the members' size and financial resources, affording benefits and protection to all, regardless of size and wealth. They retained a paid professional lobbyist and a capable volunteer legislative committee to monitor any developments in the capitol that could help or harm their members. Therefore, they could respond proactively to any challenges. However, in 2004, the

name, mission, history, organizational structure, legislative experience, and resources of CCCLL's Florida counterpart—the Florida
State, Court & County Law Libraries (FSCCLL)—made it a far more
vulnerable target than its western cousin. FSCCLL had more informal origins and format than the CCCLL, and included the three
main types of governmental libraries in the state—county, court,
and state—as opposed to focusing exclusively on the needs of
county law libraries. Membership was voluntary and by individual, rather than by library, resulting in lower annual revenue from
dues, and in 2005, FSCCLL's coffers were too low for mounting a
successful legislative defense against the attack on the filing fees. In
contrast to CCCLL, FSCCLL did not retain a paid professional lobbyist, nor was their legislative committee as well organized and
experienced. Although Floridians were aware of the raging storm
as early as 1998, there was a lack of clarity as far as the final outcome, and in my view, a lack of belief and preparedness, which
made the Florida effort a reactive rather than proactive response. I
base this view partially on the twenty-sixth annual FSCCLL meeting held October 16–18, 2003, and optimistically titled, "Article V,
Revision 7—Challenges and Opportunities." Unfortunately, the reality of Revision 7 proved to be many challenges for most Florida
county law libraries, with few opportunities for any.

- *Unrealistic expectations*—County libraries in Florida were given false
  hope that the "omissions" could be corrected at the 2005 legislative
  session, when in fact, any attempts at overturning the results would
  be met with overwhelming opposition.

As 2004 turned into 2005, stormy weather was on the horizon for both
states—although in somewhat different forms once again. Florida was
attempting to create a "no frills," "one size fits all" template for its county
law libraries, to conform to the theme of uniformity of Revision 7, while
California was creating its own uniform court filing system.

In Florida, the legislature attempted to define the minimum standards
for a county law library, in order to determine what, if anything, the state
was going to fund. They proposed a bare-bones collection consisting of
official federal and state reporters and statutes, along with a legal dictionary. The county law librarians countered with the American Association
of Law Libraries (AALL) standards. Rumors came and went that the state
was negotiating with LexisNexis and/or Westlaw to replace physical
county law libraries with staffed kiosks located in the capital in Tallahas-
see, and proposals were put forth to merge some of the county law libraries with their local city or county libraries. Another plan that was floated
briefly called for a partnership between one county law library and its
nearby state law school, so that the state monies could come to the law

school and then be distributed to the county law library. Unfortunately, this idea and others failed to find traction.

The transition in funding from civil filing fees to the new source—a portion of the criminal fees—proved to be difficult and painful for most of Florida's county law libraries. The Miami-Dade County Law Library, the state's largest county law library, was devastated by a 75-percent funding cut because of Revision 7.[16] For Miami, the situation was compounded by the fact that the collection rate for the new funding source was poor—only 25 percent of all criminal fines were being collected, according to the Hon. Gill S. Freeman, board president.[17] Staff and materials had to be cut to a bare minimum. Miami has attempted to find alternative funding sources, such as subsidies from the county, but even these plans have faced difficulties; new property tax legislation and lower revenues have forced cutbacks and endangered the continued operation of the library.

Meanwhile, California established its own Uniform Civil Filing Fee plan (UCFF), to transition responsibility for court funding from the counties to the state. Although the California plan did not remove civil filing fees as the primary funding source, it did make some important changes that impacted county law libraries. These included:

- Transferring the administration of the fees from the counties to the Judicial Council's Administrative Office of the Courts (AOC).
- Establishing a moratorium on fee increases for county law libraries from January 1, 2008, to January 1, 2012.

Although these changes were less dramatic and drastic than those in Florida, they were nonetheless significant in their own right for California's county law libraries.

Initially, library revenues improved under the AOC stewardship, in sharp contrast to the worsening economic condition of the state and the nation, and 2007 (the last year that filing-fee increases were allowed) became a benchmark year. However, shortly afterward, the moratorium on fee increases, combined with the cyclical nature of filing fees, took its toll on all the libraries, large and small, rich and poor. Without these periodic increases, medium and large county libraries had a harder time staying ahead of the inflationary curve, while the smaller and poorer ones just fell further behind. In addition, the cyclical nature of this funding source created the dizzying pattern of revving up resources and projects during the good times, only to have to cut back during the leaner times.

During this moratorium, the CCCLL had looked at a committee plan to consolidate and restructure California county law libraries into regional groupings, with the smaller and poorer libraries coming under the umbrella of the appropriate larger neighbor. Each of these new regional groups would be assigned a large regional library center (e.g., Los Angeles). The regional centers would then form a new library consortium under an executive director, and a statewide board would then replace the local law library boards.

The perceived benefits of the plan were relief for the smaller libraries under regionalization, cost savings for all members through consortium purchasing of print and online resources, and the potential for making the county law libraries more self-reliant and less dependent on other entities, specifically the courts and the counties. However, concerns about loss of local control of the law libraries, questions about the feasibility of the plan, and worries about startup and annual administrative costs caused the CCCLL executive board to send the proposal back to committee.

2010 AND BEYOND

While Florida's county law libraries were reeling from funding cuts, the State of California was experiencing severe budget problems of its own. Among the many victims of the budget deficits were the state courts, which suffered a $360 million shortfall from state general funds. In the spring of 2010, the courts looked to the county law library filing fees as a potential revenue source to bridge the gap. Once again, California's county law libraries were in jeopardy.

In April of 2010, the AOC (the administrator of the county law library filing fees) met with the CCCLL leadership and their lobbyist to present a proposal to "sweep" county law library filing fees each year to help bridge the courts' shortfall.[18] This was a sudden and unprecedented move, since California's county law libraries and their filing fees had never been part of the state budgetary process. CCCLL once again geared up to combat a dangerous precedent that would devastate their libraries' resources and services.

According to a report by CCCLL Legislative Committee chair Anne Bernardo, the AOC proposal called for:[19]

- Taking approximately $3.67 million from the county law libraries each year.
- Capping the amount of filing fees that each library can receive at the FY 2007–08 level.
- Redirecting fees in excess of the FY 2007–08 level to the trial courts.
- Distributing to each law library one-twelfth of its FY 2007–08 total each month for the first eleven months.
- Maintaining either an equal payment or an adjustment downward for the twelfth month if paid filings were lower for the year.
- Including this plan in a bill to accompany the FY 2010–11 state budget on July 1.

CCCLL negotiated with the AOC and reached an agreement to limit the redirection of the fees to a period of three years (until 2013), and to include provisions permitting the redirected fee amounts to be adjusted when the economy improved.[20] However, because of the onerous nature of the proposal and the small window of opportunity to challenge it prior to the July 1 deadline, CCCLL had to move quickly. They chose to oppose the proposal in its entirety, while still "keeping the door open" with the AOC in case they had to make concessions.[21]

CCCLL marshaled their forces to fight the proposal, and their lobbyist was directed to contact key legislators to build support for their position, while the CCCLL leadership reached out for support from allies such as patrons, and state and local library and bar associations. CCCLL's efforts proved to be successful, and the proposal was defeated. Another bullet was dodged. Perhaps the legislature saw the futility of devastating the libraries in order to collect a relatively small amount to fill the courts' coffers. Perhaps some members could see the value of the county law libraries to their communities. There is no guarantee that the proposal won't be reintroduced in the future.

Meanwhile, the combination of a poor economy and the lack of fee increases have hurt California's county law libraries for the period from FY 2009–10 to FY 2011–12. I recently spoke to current CCCLL president and former treasurer Chris Christman about filing-fee income. Chris was kind enough to share the distressing news. The figures show an average decrease in income of 13.69 percent from FY 2010–11 to 2011–12, with more than a handful of libraries (mostly the smaller ones), experiencing losses in the 20-percent range or higher.[22] The change from FY 2009–10 to 2011–12 is even steeper, with an average decrease of 16.29 percent.[23] In this comparison, the figures are even gloomier, with more than a dozen libraries experiencing a 20-percent or more decrease in income and including at least two medium to large libraries in this group.[24]

California's county law libraries once again find themselves in the downward cycle of furloughs, off days, layoffs, and resource cutting, while Florida struggles with lower county revenues. What to do? In both states, additional funding at either the state or county level is unlikely. Filing-fee increases are also unlikely in California, with the courts hurting so much. Plans for consolidation have not gained traction. Some libraries in Florida, such as Miami-Dade, have survived on the largesse of donors, but fundraising only goes so far, particularly in a bad economy. California has been looking at joint purchasing agreements and union catalogs to save money, but neither of these ideas are major revenue generators.

County law libraries lack a long-term, dedicated, predictable, and sustainable funding source that is safe from potential poachers. Without this ingredient, the outlook continues to be uncertain.

NOTES

1. Official California Legislative Information, California Business and Professions Code, Sections 6300 et seq., available at http://www.leginfo.ca.gov/cgi-bin/display-code?section=bpc&group=06001-07000&file=6300-6307.

2. Official California Legislative Information, California Business and Professions Code, Sections 6360 et seq., available at http://www.leginfo.ca.gov/cgi-bin/display-code?section=bpc&group=06001-07000&file=6360-6363.

3. Ibid.

4. Revision 7 of Article V out of Florida Legislation, available at http://www.govcollect.org/files/FL_Court_Article%20_V_Revision_7.pdf.

5. Ibid.

6. Ibid.

7. "An Act Relating to the Judicial System; Amending s.25.073, F.S.," Florida House of Representatives, 2003 Legislature, available at http://archive.flsenate.gov/data/session/2003A/House/bills/billtext/pdf/h0113Aer.pdf.

8. Ibid.

9. Ibid.

10. Official California Legislative Information, AB 2648 Assembly Bill—Bill Analysis, available at http://www.leginfo.ca.gov/pub/01-02/bill/asm/ab_2601-2650/ab_2648_cfa_20021008_165850_asm_floor.html.

11. Ibid.

12. Ibid.

13. Official California Legislative Information, AB 2648 Assembly Bill—Governor's Veto Message, available at http://www.leginfo.ca.gov/pub/01-02/bill/asm/ab_2601-2650/ab_2648_vt_20020911.html, 09/11/2002.

14. "An Act Relating to the Judicial System; Amending s.25.073," Florida House of Representatives, 2003 Legislature, available at http://archive.flsenate.gov/data/session/2003A/House/bills/billtext/pdf/h0113Aer.pdf.

15. Official California Legislative Information, AB 2648 Assembly Bill—Bill Analysis, available at http://www.leginfo.ca.gov/pub/01-02/bill/asm/ab_2601-2650/ab_2648_cfa_20021008_165850_asm_floor.html.

16. Miami Dade County Law Library Web page, "News about the Law Library," available at http://www.mdcll.org/html/News.htm.

17. Ibid.

18. Anne Bernardo, *AALL Case Study: California County Law Librarians Fend Off Courts' Proposal to Sweep Law Library Funds* (Chicago: American Association of Law Libraries, 2010).

19. Ibid.

20. Ibid.

21. Ibid.

22. Chris Christman, ="CA Law Library Income—Statewide Filing Fee Income Last Three Fiscal Years (FY=May-Apr income received Jul-Jun)," Excel spreadsheet, August 12, 2012.

23. Ibid.

24. Ibid.

SEVEN

Law Firm Librarianship

Money, Dashboards, Strategic Planning, and a Dash of
Patience Are What It Is All About

Abigail E. Ross

There are many things that set law firm libraries and librarians apart: corporate culture, rules and processes not seen elsewhere, peculiar copyright and resource licensing issues, and even basic financial management. We take the law students produced by our academic brothers and sisters and continue their molding into full-fledged attorneys. We "bridge the gap." That is, we help law students move from their academic environment to the "real world" of practicing law. Many law programs are designed around teaching their students the theory of law or giving them the knowledge they need to pass the bar—these do not always translate into the actual practice of law. Many firm librarians fill this role when it comes to teaching legal research. Though most law students now use online legal research tools for their classes, they are not using them in the ways that they will at a law firm, and they are certainly not using them in the cost-effective manner necessary in a law firm. We employ our resources and skills to turn these students into lawyers who then embody the idea of representation for all. Law firms—and the librarians who work in them—are the ones who put that lofty theory into practice.

This can be particularly exciting for librarians. Law firm libraries have flat employee hierarchies, which gives us the opportunity to involve all employees, and to be personally involved in all aspects of librarianship. Unless you work at a very large law firm, you will be expected to perform many different tasks. An employee may be hired for one job (e.g., reference librarian), but be expected to participate in shelving, database mining, project management, cataloging, loose-leaf filing, tablet trouble-shooting, or anything else that comes up in the course of a day. No two days are ever alike. I enjoy it because if I don't like one task, I know that in a few hours I will be doing something completely different.

A decision in a law firm library cannot ever be made in departmental isolation; our success is tied to the success of the firm, and the two are inseparable. Law firm librarians must take all aspects of librarianship into account when making decisions. The determination of whether or not to purchase a particular monograph must consider the library's collection-development policy, the firm's practice areas, the revenue those specific groups produce, marketing that item to attorneys located in offices around the world, access, licensing agreements, copyright restrictions, disaster planning, and a host of other topics.

To that end, I have divided this chapter into two parts. The first provides a brief overview of law firm librarianship and information that a potential or new firm librarian may want to know. The second part offers more practical advice, structured along the lines of my personal checklist. These are the big-picture items I have in the back of my mind as I go about my duties—the matters I know I need to account for as a law firm librarian, and the items I have found to be the most influential in my day-to-day decision making. Many of these may overlap with other types of law librarianship; some will be completely different. While I have included the most important considerations, I have left out or only briefly touched on those that are similar across all types of law libraries. Marketing, for example, is vital in all law libraries, but the general principles are the same and so do not warrant much discussion here. Some references on this and other topics that are firm specific will be included so the reader can delve into those subjects if desired.

EDUCATION AND PROFESSIONAL DEVELOPMENT

Unlike many types of law libraries, most law firms do not require librarians to have a JD. In some cases it is even actively discouraged, as there is still an outdated perception that librarians with JDs are trying to practice at the firm by getting in the "back door." This view seems to be fading, but it may still linger in some markets. There are exceptions to the no-JD concept—either by position or office location or firm preference—but for the most part, a law degree is not required to work in a law firm library. The masters in library information science (MLIS) or its equivalent is usually required, and attending a school accredited by the American Library Association (ALA) is a must. The skills needed most, though, are not always those learned in school. Working with busy, stressed, Type A, practicing attorneys is not for the faint of heart—a thick skin, a cool head, a disinclination to panic even when all around are doing so, and high-level legal research skills are what firm librarians really need.

Also valuable are a firm grounding in Excel (or whatever the latest spreadsheet program may be) and at least a passing knowledge of (or interest in) high-level business and management concepts. Firm libraries and librarians must stay on the cutting edge of information manage-ment—if not in actual practice, then at least in knowledge of librarians on staff. Maintaining a library solely for information's sake is no longer enough. The staff needs to actively leverage themselves and their re-sources to *increase shareholder value* in some definable way, or else they will be pushed to the side.[1] The resources that can be most useful to stay on top of such trends are those read by your C-level executives (COO, CIO, CEO). Take the time to read what they read and to think outside their box, and apply this thinking to your library.[2] Browse the *Harvard Business Review, American Lawyer,* and any local publications that might be of interest. The head of the information technology department is also a good place to look for market trends. These resources will contribute to your background knowledge of what motivates upper-level management and can give you the buzzwords to use, such as being able to discuss why project-portfolio management and document-management system (DMS) taxonomies all naturally fall under the library's purview. These are the issues the shareholders in your firm are discussing, and the li-brary can be actively involved in the research, selection, and implementa-tion of such systems, but only if you can participate in the discussion.

Many firms struggle with professional development for librarians. Unlike librarians in many academic institutions, we are often actively discouraged from taking part in associations, volunteering for commit-tees, or attending conferences, because they are seen as distractions from our jobs, not supplements to our institutional knowledge. Many firm librarians I know pay for their own association memberships and confer-ence attendance. Do not let this discourage you! Even if national partici-pation is not an option, most markets have a local association, and firm librarians are always welcome. Scholarships and reduced fees are there for the taking, if you can take the time to fill out the form. Ask older firm librarians how they manage such obstacles, as assistance for national events and local opportunities' is available, but not always well adver-tised.

Getting that first position as a firm librarian can be challenging. Many jobs require a legal background that can be difficult to obtain without first working in a firm. This circular problem exists everywhere. The best advice here is to be persistent. I have found that it is much easier to teach legal research than it is to teach the library and organizational concepts taught to an MLIS student, and many other managers feel the same. They will give you the opportunity if you can show your willingness to work hard and master the specifics of business and legal research.

If you are in a position to interview new candidates, ask questions that will elicit answers that demonstrate mastery of certain skills. Look for tenacity—if a reference librarian pursues one avenue of inquiry that does not produce results, is that person willing to brainstorm additional avenues? Determine whether the candidate has a customer-service orientation and can find creative ways to offer alternative avenues of inquiry without saying "no, we cannot find that" (something attorneys hate to hear).

FINANCIAL MANAGEMENT

Let's talk about money. Unlike the other large library associations, the American Association of Law Libraries' (AALL) Ethical Principles specifically mentions fiscal responsibility, and nowhere is this more apparent than in law firms.[3] The emphasis on the bottom line can be tough sometimes, but it also gives law firm librarians the chance to be flexible—to display adaptability in ways not necessarily taught in library school. Creative use of resources, staff, negotiation of alternative contracts, or even the creative interpretation of a licensing agreement can help that bottom line and cast the library in a positive light.

Budget issues are important to all types of libraries, but law firms are for-profit entities. This affects how decisions are made, how revenue is used and budgets are viewed. The importance of the bottom line determines not only the budget the library has to work with, but also how, and sometimes even by whom, those resources can be disbursed. Frequently, very little transparency exists in the budget decision-making process, which can leave librarians feeling like they are groping around in the dark. This is not to say firm stakeholders make capricious decisions—no firm would last very long with that decision-making model—but to note that librarians may not be as involved in these decisions as they would prefer.

Law firm library financial management advice can be boiled down to one phrase: *Are the library services/staff/decisions/resources increasing shareholder value?* That is, are you directly contributing to the success of the firm? Those two important words, "value" and "success," may translate to dollar amounts or they may be measured in other ways (efficiencies, brand recognition, helping a client, winning a case). However you define them, keep those goals in mind at all times.

Firm librarians often have to cut corners, and asking yourself this question of shareholder value over and over can help you identify where those corners can be cut without loss of service or quality to the firm. One example I see in law firms is cataloging standards. An integrated library system (ILS) is a must, but what system you use, how you structure it, and which rules you follow to the letter and which you can skip—all of that varies by the size of your firm and your mission. Though important to all librarians, following the minutiae of cataloging rules is not always practical in a law firm—we rely on the academic and government institutions to create those perfect records and then we cherry-pick from them which items/records/MARC headings are most useful. Is spending the staff's time on these minutiae really increasing shareholder value? Probably not in a firm—though useful to our profession, the large majority of cataloging fields may never be used by our patrons, and our time may be better spent elsewhere.

This idea of increasing shareholder value is also closely tied to the fiscal responsibility needed during the budget-writing process, usually done once a year at all levels. The goal of this process is to set a number for all library expenses. Preparing a law firm library budget is much easier now with spreadsheet applications and online tools to help. There are also some general best practices you can follow when going through this process.

For starters, get to know your accounting department. They are the first and last line of defense as you travel through the fiscal year, and they should be allies. Sometimes a process can be tweaked in the accounting department that will make your life easier, rather than involving the attorney or practice group directly. This can help with my next bit of advice: you should be coding the library invoices yourself rather than relying on anyone else to do it. When an invoice needs to be paid by the firm, it must first be reviewed by someone who can determine which firm account the money should be drawn from. This is referred to as "coding," and actively participating in this process helps the library staff see where the money comes from and how it should be allocated. Once all those bills are coded and processed and paid, ask your accounting department to send you a monthly reconciliation report for each ledger number the library utilizes. This gives you a snapshot of what amount of money is going out the door for certain library resource categories. It can also help spot problems far in advance. If attorneys code invoices to the library numbers, then you may have money moving out that you are not aware of, which can wreak havoc with your carefully prepared budget. That kind of issue can be seen on monthly reconciliations. Moving from resource category to practice group accounting can help solve that kind of issue. Each group is budgeted a certain amount of money for library resources, which gives the library a better idea of who is using these items and gives the firm a better picture of return on investment. If the smallest practice group is spending the most amount of library money, then some adjustment is needed. But without that information, it is difficult to determine where the resources are best spent.

The budget itself may take many forms; the specific form chosen will be determined by your particular firm's preferences. It should be attractive, easy to read, and actively demonstrate your attentiveness to detail and fiscal responsibility.[4] One way to do this is through a trend that has recently crossed over from the financial industry to librarianship: a dashboard, often defined as a visually appealing set of graphs that are carefully selected to underscore the goal of the presentation.[5] For our purposes, dashboards are dynamic representations of the workings of the library—from its budget to its spending to its overhead research charges, broken down by attorney.[6] Many different types of programs can be used to create these dashboards, but Excel is usually the easiest.

All of the other issues discussed below can even be incorporated into your dashboard to give your staff, the management committee, or the chief financial officer a clear snapshot of where their pennies (or millions) are being spent.

Whether you use a spreadsheet, a dashboard, or some other visualization tool for your budget, be sure to crunch your numbers. In an ideal setting, the library is tasked with providing resources and research, given a realistic budget with which to make this happen, and then generally trusted to do that in a responsible manner. This does not mean that your decision makers do not want to see your numbers, just that they will not ask for them every week. Preparing them in advance as you go through your fiscal year makes it much easier when they do ask to see them.

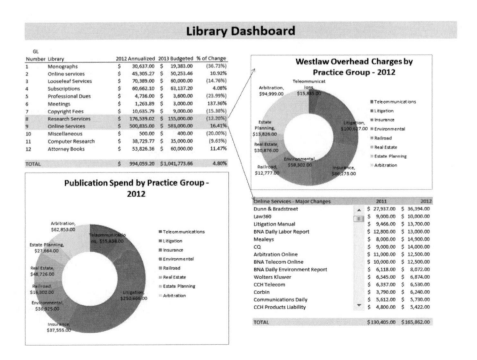

Figure 7.1.

Anticipate what numbers they may want to see—or use past questions to determine what numbers they *should* be looking at but would not know or consider to request.

They may want to know the cost of online resources per attorney, or which groups are purchasing more print titles, or which attorneys are using expensive online resources for overhead matters instead of client matters. There are resources available online, via existing software and from your vendors, that can answer most of these questions.

One question often asked is: Where do we stand on library spending when compared to other law firms in our city/practice area/size? You can glean some information from firm surveys or local legal news publications. But often the best way is to do an informal survey of your local firm librarians. You can then build a radial chart to show your attorneys where they stand in terms of library spending per attorney in relation to other firms. This can help your decision makers visualize where they stand in relation to the industry—and it can also help the library's cause. You can demonstrate how fiscally savvy you are if your numbers are lower—or you can demonstrate that you are spending the average amount if cuts are looming.

STRATEGIC PLANNING

If running a law firm and its library is now more akin to running a business, then you will need the resource-management tools of a business. These include development of a strategic plan that details not merely the goals or objectives, but the course required to achieve those goals. Establishing a strategic plan helps to avoid getting caught in the black holes of day-to-day activity and to remember *why* you are doing these routine tasks. In fact, many consider strategic planning and project management to be two sides of the same coin. Projects (day-to-day activities) are managed and finished in order to move the organization down the road toward the ultimate objective, whatever that may be. The strategic plan helps the librarian to choose or reject projects and to manage them in such a way that the ultimate objective is not lost in the noise of everyday work. The law firm library's strategic plan should be modeled after the firm's strategic and/or business plan and should include many of the same goals.

Many strategic plans are written and then thrown into a drawer and forgotten (and hence, fail). The key to making your plan a successful one is to make it dynamic. This is not a word-processing text you save to a folder and forget about. The plan should be a document that you refer to regularly, tweaking it every month or so. Even better, create a spreadsheet strategic plan, and open it as often as you open your financial management documents. More simply, use a whiteboard on the wall, or

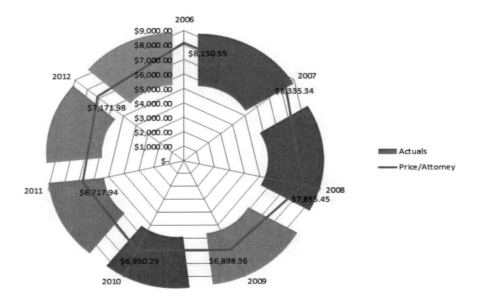

Figure 7.2.

even a flipchart that you and your staff update as needed. Whatever format you choose, if you refer to your plan on a regular basis, then you can avoid many of the mistakes commonly made in failed plans. These pitfalls include having no written plan at all, neglecting to name a person in charge of the plan, giving no benchmarks or checkpoints, or choosing unrealistic goals.

Every project added to the strategic plan should be in line with the narrative description of your organization, its mission, and its goals or objectives. The plan must also take into account a realistic assessment of the resources you have available. Every project should have a timeline, one that contains checkpoints and specific consequences for the failure to meet those checkpoints. The word "consequence" generally has a negative connotation, but in this context a consequence is simply an opportunity to correct an issue. These remedies take many forms: reevaluating the goal or the checkpoints on the timeline, reassigning roles, or even scrapping the project completely if it no longer fits in with the larger framework.

All of this effort is designed to help firm librarians answer the question: Is whatever I am doing at this moment increasing shareholder value? That can certainly refer to the bottom line on a spreadsheet, but it can also refer to more intangible values. Law firm libraries will always be limited by restrictions beyond their control—square footage leased, revenue earned by attorneys, and legal publishing industry pricing, to name a few—so instead of trying to be all things to *all* people, try being excellent at some things to *most* people. Examples include: (1) quality (providing the best pathfinders anywhere so patrons start with you and know the information they receive is authoritative); (2) customer service; (3) innovation; (4) technical superiority; etc.[7]

COLLECTION

One of the noteworthy differences between law firm librarians and other types of librarians is our detachment from format. Given all of the restrictions we face—budget, expensive square footage, conflicting requests from many bosses—we cannot be sentimental about the format of our information.[8] For the most part, so long as all agree that the source is authoritative and trustworthy, then the format of our information is irrelevant. Print, digital, hosted, cloud, mobile, written on the back of a napkin—all can be accepted and utilized. Law firm libraries are *not* archives in any sense of the word and any particular format must be chosen because of its utility, not because we (or the attorneys!) prefer one over the other. If the library resources are in-sourced to a central location serving all offices worldwide, then print publications are impractical for general use, despite our preference to use print for certain types of research.[9]

Firm libraries are also very involved in the issue of grey literature, often defined as "document types produced on all levels of government, academics, business, and organization in electronic and print formats not controlled by commercial publishing, i.e., where publishing is not the primary activity of the producing body."[10] Much of what firm libraries collect can fall under this definition if it: (1) is not produced by commercial publishing house; (2) usually does not include table of contents, index, or other finding aids; (3) does not have cataloging in publication or other bibliographic controls; and/or (4) has no, or very limited, publishing information.[11]

Grey literature and other collection quirks can wreak havoc with a firm library's integrated library system (ILS, or catalog). The notes and description fields are often the most utilized, as general information on grey literature or other types of bibliographic details that may not fit into other categories can be noted there. Keep in mind, too, that many of those ILSs are designed for academic institutions, so the serials management component does not take legal publication oddities into account. Many firm librarians also play fast and loose with the copy and item levels of the bibliographic record. Many use one record for a certain title and then create a new copy for each annual edition, which is supposed to go under the serials module, but using the copy level for this often creates a nice neat list that an attorney in a hurry can glance at without having to add more clicks. This type of ILS "work-around" is not ideal, but spending time on the proper setup may not always *increase shareholder value* on the library's end or help the attorney, if they have to page through multiple records to reach the same information. This is especially true when it comes to the grey literature we collect and house.

One area in which firm libraries can make the most of their library systems is disaster preparedness. Again, given the firm librarian's disinterest in format, a firm disaster plan can gloss over the rescue of the print collection and focus instead on password recovery and remote access. A judge or agency will not allow a firm to skip a required filing because of natural disaster or because the print collection was flooded by a broken pipe—backing up all important data in the ILS can save firm time and money, and can allow the ILS to essentially serve as the library's disaster-preparedness database.

VENDOR RELATIONS AND CONTRACT NEGOTIATIONS

Maintaining a good relationship with your vendors is key to your success. Vendors can assist with training, usage, research, and a myriad of other issues. As more and more firm librarian jobs tie in with resource management, vendors will play an increasingly important role. Although you might feel that you and your vendor are at times working at cross-purposes, remember that civility goes a long way. Be nice to your vendors, and they will be nice to you. This does not preclude being unyielding when necessary, or standing up for the firm's needs, just do so in a way that will not make the next interaction difficult.

All of this history can become a factor when contracts come up for renewal. At some point in a law firm, you will be involved in the negotiation for access to an online resource. This may be a multimillion dollar contract for one of the larger legal information services (Westlaw, Lexis, CCH, BloombergLaw/BNA) or just a small publication. Negotiation is an art, and many librarians dread the process. This is often made more difficult by the fact that the legal publishing industry is an oligopoly,[12] and one cannot always walk away from the table or select a different vendor. The process can be stressful, but it does not need to be antagonistic. It can even be a fun challenge: given the parameters of the game, how many of your goals can you achieve? It may not be the next World of Warcraft, but it may offer just as much strategy and maneuvering.

Few are the firms that have enough buying power to dictate all terms of an agreement; the rest of us have to approach the process as a symbiotic relationship. We need them just as much as they need us, even if that particular contract is not worth a lot of money. To that end, here are some rules to help you keep your cool:

1. Know your ideal outcome in advance—if you do not know what you are trying to accomplish, then the vendor certainly cannot help you get there.
2. Reality check—once you have an ideal outcome, be honest with yourself about how realistic that outcome may be.
3. Draw your line in the sand—know at which point you will have to end the conversation. Although that may be difficult and painful, if you have a very strict budget and the vendor cannot make it work for that amount of money, then further discussion is pointless. This is not to say that you should storm out of the room, just that you should know at which point you stop the process and say, "Let's try again next year."
4. Do your research—collect whatever information you can on your end before you walk into the room with the vendor. How much is this product currently used by your patrons? How much would a new product be used, and by whom? Crunch your numbers.
5. Try to be on the same team—it may not always seem so, but the vendor really is trying to find an equitable solution. They have their limitations, just as we have ours.

COPYRIGHT AND LICENSING

The relationships you have with your vendors will come into play when discussing the copyright restrictions for publications or the licensing agreements you must sign to obtain access to certain information, particularly since the copyright restrictions law firm libraries face can often be summed up in one general catch-all statement: the fair use exemptions usually do not apply in for-profit environments. Without going into the complexities and exceptions of this statement at this time (better suited for an entire book itself), it is a good idea for firm librarians to generally accept this statement as true and to plan and act accordingly. Every case or article copied, every book chapter scanned into PDF, every current awareness e-mail forwarded can cause huge, expensive issues and even spawn lawsuits.

To that end, a copyright policy and implementation guide is essential. This can take many forms, but the guide should generally lay out the policy for the firm, warn of potential consequences to the individual and to the organization, discuss the proper procedure for making copies or sharing copyrighted information, suggest alternatives if those policies do not tie into current workflow, and make some preparations for working with the Copyright Clearance Center or other copyright administrative bodies.

Copyright often goes hand in hand with licensing, which refers to the license terms or agreements that come along with access to certain types of materials. Sometimes these terms are included in the negotiations discussed above; at other times you must consent to any and all publisher licensing agreements when the resource is purchased or when logging in or using it online, depending on the type of resource.

Tracking all the license agreements, explicit or not, can be very difficult to manage, and an entire industry of electronic resource-management tools (ERMs) has sprung up to help librarians deal with these issues. Be sure to read the license agreement very carefully, and ask yourself the following:

- Are the terms favorable to the user/firm/librarian, or to the publisher?
- If the agreement is terminated, does the user/firm/librarian still own or have access to any of the content?
- Can you provide your users with the information they need from this publication and still abide by the terms of this agreement?
- Are all terms clearly defined (*user*, *site*, etc.)?
- If not, could there be any confusion?
- Are terms set forth for early cancellation and refunds? Are there terms for automatic renewal?
- Is there information about price increases?
- Are copyright terms/breaks clearly defined?
- Are distribution terms delineated?

The answers to these questions can make or break a deal. Not having access to a certain publication can translate into real loss of money in law firms. Often the information is needed immediately, so waiting the few hours—or even days—to obtain something from somewhere else is not an option. Keep a close eye on license terms, as they still dictate certain types of workflow, rather than vice versa.[13]

E-BOOKS/E-RESOURCES/MOBILE APPLICATIONS/SOCIAL NETWORKING

Navigating the licensing pitfalls has led to an unexpectedly slow switch from print to e-books/tablets/mobile platforms in law firms.[14] Due in large part to the complete misalignment of vendor licensing and attorney workflow, what is being heralded as the new format for future libraries currently falls far short.[15] Agreeing to pay twice as much for a format that limits number of users, amount of usage, and even hardware is difficult, if not impossible, given firm library budgets these days. Look for changes in this arena as vendors play catch-up.

Law firms, and hence the librarians who serve them, can often be slow to adopt new social networking tools. This is not because the individuals aren't using them or aren't excited about them, but rather because our duties do not always lend themselves well to such tools. Second Life is a great example of this—it is a wonderful tool, and when it was introduced many academic libraries utilized it for teaching and student outreach. Everyone needed an avatar, and discussions were held at the annual library conferences about what names and forms the librarians would choose. And yet amidst all that, I never once heard of a law firm library using this resource to much avail. These days, you barely hear of it at all. Then along came Twitter, another wonderful current awareness and news tool. The Law Library of Congress has a Twitter feed, and again, many academic librarians are leading the charge in finding uses for this new tool. But I haven't seen a law firm library (or even many law firms) that can use this tool as effectively. Where law firms do use these resources is in services you won't hear about on tech forums—client collaboration or extranet sites that play the same role as social networking sites but limit the participants to project members or particular clients. Firm librarians are often instrumental in leveraging these types of tools for best results.

WHAT THE FUTURE MAY HOLD

Change is certainly coming, and it is gathering speed given the recent economic and industry troubles. Firm librarians are now more involved in knowledge management, practice area specialization, competitive intelligence solutions, and a host of other exciting topics that ten years ago either did not exist or would not have fallen under the typical "library" umbrella.[16] We are moving from just managing the format or housing our information to supervising all steps of knowledge evolution—from the existence of data, to the processing of that data into information, to the application of that data in knowledge (management).

We have always been information gatekeepers, and that role gains strength and prominence as the legal field floods with new resources and documents. We manage virtual libraries—we don't just pick the best resource for the shelf, we pick the best resources for the firm's intranet, the attorneys' tablets, their current awareness tools and client development books, and we even help the IT department pick the best software to run all this.[17] Turning this pile of raw information, raw students, random technology, and arbitrary license agreements into a coherent plan, and strategically leveraging that plan on behalf of our patrons and clients, is what being a law firm librarian is all about.

NOTES

1. I will be using the term *shareholder value* throughout the article as a way to show the increasingly important relationship between law firm librarians and the bottom

line. The term *shareholder* can be defined in many ways, and that definition may even change from day to day or from project to project, but the underlying assumption is the same: we must be actively involved in the strategic and fiscal management of our resources in order to survive.

2. The legal literature abounds with case studies on running your law firm like a business. But I would recommend the following to start: Richard Susskind, "The End of Lawyers? Rethinking the Nature of Legal Services" (2008); one my favorites, Joseph Esposito, "What if Wal-Mart Ran a Library?" *Journal of Electronic Publishing* (Winter 2006), available online: http://www.hti.umich.edu/cgi/t/text/text-idx?c=jep;view=text;rgn=main;idno=3336451.0009.104; Sarah L. Nichols, "Aligning Library Service Lines with Business Strategy," in Aspatore Books, *How to Manage a Law Firm Library: Leading Librarians on Updating Resources, Managing Budgets, and Meeting Expectations*, 7–18 (Boston: Aspatore Books (2008).

3. See, for comparison, "AALL Ethical Principles," http://www.aallnet.org/main-menu/Leadership-Governance/policies/PublicPolicies/policy-ethics.html and "SLA Professional Ethics Guidelines," http://www.sla.org/content/SLA/ethics_guidelines.cfm and "Code of Ethics of the American Library Association," http://www.ala.org/advocacy/proethics/codeofethics/codeethics.

4. For examples of law firm library budgets, feel free to e-mail me at afeross@hotmail.com and I would be happy to share my formats.

5. For a great definition of a dashboard, see http://www.dummies.com/how-to/content/defining-excel-dashboards-and-reports.html.

6. For some excellent examples of dashboards on other topics, see http://chandoo.org/wp/excel-dashboards/ and http://chandoo.org/wp/2012/07/30/excel-salary-survey-contest-results/.

7. For a general overview of strategic planning for libraries, see Joseph R. Matthews, *Strategic Planning and Management for Library Managers* (Santa Barbara, CA: Libraries Unlimited, 2005). See pages 47–50 for a discussion of how libraries can differentiate themselves from other services in the organization.

8. For an interesting discussion of online research services available to law firms, see Laura K. Justiss, "A Survey of Electronic Research Alternatives to LexisNexis and Westlaw in Law Firms," *Law Library Journal* 103, no. 1 (Winter 2011): 71–85. Available online: http://www.aallnet.org/main-menu/Publications/llj/LLJ-Archives/Vol-103/2011-01/2011-04.pdf.

9. This is one area where the quality of "adaptability" can shine. I prefer to do my legislative history research in print—but we are moving away from such print sources because they take up too much space. So now it is up to us to create ways to manage this complicated process in a digital world. We have done so by creating a flowchart to help navigate the various documents involved in this type of research. From multiple bills to transcripts and hearings a hundred pages long, the flowchart helps us track what documents should be found, read, and analyzed. Showing this flowchart to attorneys reassures them that we are taking the limitations of the format into account when we do our research and that we are being as thorough as possible.

10. See http://www.greynet.org/greynethome.html for a more in-depth discussion of grey literature, along with articles, studies, and participant forums.

11. Michael Lines, "Are Legal Texts Grey Literature? Towards an Understanding of Grey Literature that Invites the Preservation of Authentic and Genuine Originals." Available online: https://dspace.library.uvic.ca:8443/bitstream/handle/1828/3221/2010-01-GL11Lines-AreLegalTexts.pdf?sequence=1.

12. Defined as a market form in which a market or industry is dominated by a small number of sellers, where three or fewer sellers comprise 50 percent of the market share. Thompson Reuters alone has almost 50 percent of the legal publishing market share.

13. For a general discussion of licensing in all types of libraries, see Karen Rupp-Serrano, ed., *Licensing in Libraries: Practical and Ethical Aspects* (Binghamton, NY: Haw-

orth Press, 2005). Also reprinted in *Journal of Library Administration* 42, nos. 3 & 4 (2005).

14. See Alan Cohen, "Law Librarian Survey," *The American Lawyer* 34, no. 8 (August 1, 2012): 39.

15. "eBooks: Why are Publishers Pouring Digital Content into 19th Century Wineskins?" 2012, http://deweybstrategic.blogspot.com/2011/09/ebooks-why-are-publishers-pouring.html.

16. Heather Heen, "Law Libraries," *Law Technology News*, September 10, 2012.

17. Steven A. Meyerowitz, " The Changing Role of the Law Firm Librarian, " *Pennsylvania Lawyer* 26 (May/June 2004): 28.

EIGHT

Collection Development, Acquisitions, and Licensing

Frederick W. Dingledy, Benjamin J. Keele, and Jennifer E. Sekula

LIBRARY MISSION, GOALS, AND RESPONSIBILITY

S. R. Ranganathan's second law of library science: Every reader his or her book.[1] Librarians should know the needs of the community they serve, and the library's collection should reflect and satisfy those needs.[2]

When building a collection-development policy for a law library, the second law means that one size does not fit all. Different categories of law libraries (academic, government, and private) have different types of users with different needs. Even libraries within the same category may serve multiple user groups. A government law library located in the heart of a major city will have collection requirements that may only slightly overlap with those of one located in a rural county. Law schools can range in size from three hundred students to over two thousand. Most law schools are affiliated with colleges or universities, but some are independent and cannot rely on a main campus library to provide easy access to important materials in other disciplines. A librarian may work in a boutique firm with ten attorneys or may be at a firm with over a thousand lawyers in multiple branch offices across the country—or the world.

Thus, there is only one guideline the law librarian must follow when deciding the composition of the library's collection: meet the users' needs. A good place to start is by deciding what the library's mission is. The mission is the library's foundation and the justification for its existence. Everything a librarian will need to consider when developing the library's collection ultimately flows from it.

A law school library might have a mission statement that reads:

> The fundamental mission of the Law School Library is to serve the educational and research needs of the Law School community.

A county law library that is open to the public might create a mission statement like this:

> The mission of the County Law Library is to provide current, practice-oriented law and law-related information to attorneys, judges, other county officials, and members of the public.

A law firm library's mission statement will usually be much narrower:

> The Law Firm Library serves the information needs of the firm, including its attorneys and paralegals, other staff members, and clients.

The mission statement is the broadest description of what the library does: what major groups of people does it serve, and what type of information does it provide? The mission statement will lead to the library's goals—a more detailed explanation of the objectives that the library must achieve in order to fulfill its mission. Once the mission and goals are established, they will serve as the framework the law librarian uses to decide what the library's collection policy should be. A law school library's goal statement might look like this:

> The goal of the law library's collection-development program is to maintain and provide access to a collection of information resources that support law school programs, research, the curriculum, and the needs of library users. The primary objective of the law library is to select, organize, preserve, and make available to members of the law school community information resources that will aid them in these pursuits. The collection shall support the law school curriculum and faculty and student research, and meet the standards set forth by the American Bar Association and the Association of American Law Schools. As a secondary objective, the law library will select materials for use by the college community, the bench and bar, and other library users, in that order of priority.

A county law library might have these goals:

> The law library's primary goal is to select, organize, and make legal information available to the county bench and bar, to other members of the local legal community, and to county residents. As a secondary goal, the library serves other members of the state bench and bar and residents of the state who do not live in the county.

A law firm library might use this goal statement:

> The law library's goal is to collect, maintain, and provide access to legal information necessary to satisfy the research needs of the attorneys and paralegals at the firm.

One of the most important things the library's goal statement must do is establish who the library's primary users will be, since a library's collection-development policy should clearly state that the library will acquire the resources those users need. In this case, "acquire" does not necessarily mean purchase. It can refer to licensing a digital resource or obtaining materials through interlibrary loan. A collection-development policy must acknowledge that the library's budget is not large enough to build an in-depth collection in every subject. Libraries that are open to the public will not be able to meet the needs of every user. Most libraries establish hierarchies among their patron groups, giving top priority to their primary users. A law school library centers its collection-development efforts on resources needed by the law faculty and students. A public law library focuses on the resources needed by the legal community and by the public in its jurisdiction. Since a law firm library is not usually open to the public, it will not need to identify who its primary users are—all of the firm's employees are primary, and there are no other users. If a law firm library participates in interlibrary loan and document-delivery activities with other libraries, though, it should acknowledge that fact and be sure to mention that the library's users benefit by its participation.

The collection-development policy should identify who is responsible for implementing it. The director is ultimately responsible for all library activities, but developing and maintaining the collection may fall to another librarian. In some libraries, several staff members may share responsibility for collection development and maintenance. Each librarian might have different specialties or areas of interest, and the director may find it useful to assign responsibility for a subject to a librarian with expertise in that field. A director who chooses to have multiple staff members share responsibility should ensure that at least one person is responsible for covering the entire range of subjects the library collects. It may also be a good idea to allocate overlapping subject responsibilities between librarians. Multiple selectors in the same subject will result in a more complete array of collection decisions. In addition, while librarians are usually responsible for collection development, they don't have to be. A non-librarian film aficionado on staff might be an excellent person to select movies.

TOOLS FOR SELECTING MATERIALS

Librarians have several tools at their disposal to identify new materials to add to the library's collection. Some have been around for many years, while others are more recent additions to the collection developer's tool-box.

Vendor Collection Profiles

Many libraries order a large portion of their materials through vendors, usually library services companies such as YBP or Ingram. Vendors offer the convenience of ordering and handling paperwork from one company instead of multiple stores, and they often include discounts on purchases. For a small fee, vendors may also provide extra services, such as covering books with dust jackets before shipping them, saving time and effort for the library. A vendor can also notify librarians about publications and publishers they otherwise might not know about. Many government and law firm libraries may not find their collection large enough to warrant dealing with a library services company, but a firm library with multiple branches may want to consider one, especially if some of those branches are in nations where the acquisitions librarians do not speak the local language. Library services companies can help locate useful resources in those countries.

In the past, the library services vendor would mail an envelope full of slips identifying new publications available for purchase. This practice has been largely replaced by online interfaces for ordering publications, which typically feature announcements of new offerings. The library can customize these announcements by creating a profile—a list of categories of materials the librarians would like to know about. Each vendor may have a different system of categories. Some will use the Library of Congress call numbers, while others may use home-brewed subjects. When setting up a profile, consult the collection-development policy to be sure that every possible subject of interest is covered, keeping in mind that it is better to err on the side of overinclusion. Depending on the vendor's system, each selector may be able to create a "wish list," which can be useful if selections must be approved by a designated person. In that situation, the librarian in charge of collection development can decide which of the items on the lists to order. Ask the vendor if staff members' profiles can be set up so that everyone can see each other's profiles, as well as which materials were ordered. This can help guide future acquisition decisions as they learn which types of books on the wish lists are being purchased, and which are not.

Publisher Catalogs

A traditional method for identifying new materials to add to the library's collection is by browsing through publishers' catalogs. These are still an excellent way to find out what books are new and forthcoming, and will often describe the publisher's lineup farther into the future than the vendor announcements discussed above. Publishers still send out print catalogs—often whether the librarian requests them or not. Catalogs, however, have also migrated online. The librarian can go to most publishers' Web sites and browse their available selection, and can usually request e-mail updates listing new titles.

Book Reviews

Book reviews are another useful source for keeping up with new materials. Book reviews have a couple of benefits that make them a useful supplement to vendor sites and publisher catalogs. A review offers a more detailed, and possibly more objective, description of the book's content and intended audience, both of which may be hard to discern from vendor sites. A review might reveal that a book that sounded perfect from the vendor's promotional materials is actually intended for high school students. The disadvantage of using reviews is that they usually do not appear until several weeks or months after the publisher has given information on a book to vendors. Overall, though, reviews can give the librarian an idea as to whether a book is a worthy addition to the collection. Academic journals, the popular press, and news Web sites are all good sources of reviews.

Demand-Driven Acquisition

Demand-driven acquisition (DDA), also known as patron-driven acquisition, has gained momentum among libraries over the past decade. Put simply, DDA is a formal system that includes library patrons in the collection-development process. It is collection development's version of "just-in-time" production.[3]

There are several ways to implement DDA in a library. One method libraries frequently use is to tie DDA to the interlibrary loan (ILL) process; if a patron requests an item through ILL and it falls within a set of parameters determined beforehand, the library will instead order a print copy of the book and add it to its collection.[4] Libraries may also choose to work with e-book vendors so that samples of e-books are made available to students through the library's catalog, and a certain amount of reading or checkouts by patrons will trigger an instant purchase of the e-book.

Some libraries that have experimented with DDA have found it to be a useful supplement to their collection-development techniques—Purdue University and Bucknell University libraries found that books they bought through DDA had higher circulation and use rates than those books acquired through traditional methods.[5] Purdue also discovered that DDA titles often came from interdisciplinary fields that the library's acquisitions staff considered outside their normal responsibility.[6]

When implementing DDA, set out guidelines ahead of time as to what materials can be acquired. A price ceiling for each item is usually recommended for automated purchases—some libraries may choose $50; some may go higher. An important consideration is what activity will trigger a DDA purchase. For example, the University of Florida and Florida State University's law libraries worked with a vendor to make a large selection of e-books in certain subjects available through their catalogs. If users checked an e-book out three times or read more than sixty pages from the book, then the libraries purchased the e-book for their collections.[7]

Libraries may wish to place limits on the types of materials that can be ordered through DDA, such as textbooks, which can be expensive and contribute little to the library's research mission but may be frequently requested by students. It may also be a good idea to exclude journal issues from DDA to avoid a piecemeal collection, or to avoid DDA purchases of serials altogether because of the ongoing cost of maintenance and upkeep. Libraries should make sure that DDA orders do not duplicate items already available to their patrons through other sources, such as blanket subscriptions to e-book services like NetLibrary (now EBSCOhost).[8]

If the library is worried about adding too many marginal titles, the DDA plan could also include a "yellow light" category of materials that require library approval before being acquired through DDA. If a library will automatically buy books under $50, maybe it can create a "yellow light" for books between $50 and $100. That way, most materials requested through DDA are quickly acquired and in the hands of patrons, and the library can avoid spending money on unwise purchases.

Set a separate budget for DDA materials, especially in the beginning, to ensure that they do not unduly drain funds for items acquired in more traditional manners—at least until the library determines how well DDA is working. By the same token, it is a good idea to have a policy stating that librarians cannot use DDA as a way to get books that were rejected through other collection-development processes.[9]

COLLECTION INTENSITY, SCOPE, GUIDELINES, AND CRITERIA

Most libraries do not assign the same priority to all of the materials they would like to acquire. Libraries' budgets are too small to buy everything they want, and some items are more important to the collection than others. Consider creating levels of intensity within the collection-development policy for different subjects, from "minimal" to "research." The levels in a law school library's policy might look like this:

> Current and anticipated courses, individual research projects, and other law school activities will be identified to help establish the degree of

acquisitions intensity in specific areas. Depending on the area, the law library collects on the following levels:

- *Minimal Level:* An extremely selective collection that is very limited in both scope and depth.
- *Basic Level:* A selective collection that provides the user with a basic introduction to and outline of the subject. This collection includes introductory books such as hornbooks and nutshells, a few selected treatises, and only the most widely used specialized periodicals. Collection at this level will support only general research into the subject area.
- *Instructional Level:* A collection that adequately supports JD course-work and somewhat broader research into the subject area than is provided at the basic level. Collection at this level will contain the most authoritative multijurisdictional treatises, the most important treatises, several widely used specialized periodicals, and access to specialized digital information services and databases.
- *Research Level:* A collection that includes major published source materials required for independent scholarly research by law school faculty and students. Included are all significant multijurisdictional treatises, the best historical and current treatises, all widely used specialized periodicals, the major reference works in the area, significant nonlegal treatises that will aid in the understanding of the subject area, and access to specialized digital information services and databases.
- *Comprehensive Level:* At this level the library attempts to collect, as far as possible, all major works on a given subject, both current and retrospective. This collection will support the most rigorous, in-depth research. Materials may be either print or digital, but need not be in both formats.

In most academic law libraries, the bulk of collection development will probably take place at the instructional or research levels. If the school or one of its faculty members is well known for expertise in a particular area of law, then the library may want to collect items under that subject at the comprehensive level. The library may acquire materials at the basic or introductory level for subjects rarely taught at the school and in which the faculty do little research—foreign jurisdictions, for example.

A law firm's library will probably have a very strong collection in any fields in which their attorneys specialize (a bankruptcy firm, for example, would have an excellent bankruptcy and debtor-creditor collection), with only a minimal or basic collection, if any, in other areas of law.

Government libraries will normally not have comprehensive collections in specific subjects. Instead, they will often have a strong collection of primary and secondary sources covering the law of their jurisdiction.

There are exceptions to this rule, however; the library of a probate court will likely have a robust collection of materials on estate law.

Along with intensity considerations, the library's development policy should also address the collection's general scope and the types of materials the collection contains. A portion of a law school library's scope statement might look like this:

> Most treatise acquisitions are in the area of American law. New treatises are selected in accordance with the priorities outlined in this policy. As a general matter, the library attempts to collect one copy of each multijurisdictional or federal legal treatise by reputable publishers that support the curriculum, or faculty or student research. The library will acquire all state continuing legal education materials; however, other materials designed exclusively for practitioners will be acquired very selectively. The library will consider the availability of treatises in databases available to its patrons when making acquisition decisions.
>
> Acquiring materials published within the past three years is a much higher priority than acquiring retrospective materials. Generally, little attempt is made to purchase retrospectively, except for in specific subject areas in which there is a demonstrable need for historical materials, or areas in which there is special funding.
>
> Print serials involve a commitment to ongoing costs, binding, and storage. The large number of law and law-related serials makes it impossible to purchase every title, and they are acquired selectively. The library will consider the availability of a journal title in databases available to its patrons when making a decision on whether to subscribe to it in print.

The collection scope statement in a law firm may appear as follows:

> The collection consists of a variety of formats, including a balance of print and digital resources. It includes both current materials and, more selectively, historical materials as needed. Information resources are provided within the budgetary, space, and technological constraints outlined by the Library Committee and the firm's CEO. In all cases, acquisition of resources will take into account the research skills of and amount of use by attorneys and paralegals. The library will use interlibrary loan as a substitute for purchase for infrequently used titles.

A state law library's scope statement might read like this:

> Generally, the library will collect primary legal materials from the federal government, U.S. territories, and the states. We will acquire secondary materials on a wide variety of legal subjects, especially practical materials that will be used by attorneys and citizens of the state. The library will maintain a comprehensive collection of this state's legal materials, both current and historical. The library will not acquire international law materials or foreign law materials.
>
> The library will collect basic materials on the law of the United States and of the state in languages used by a significant minority of the

state's population, but otherwise will only collect English-language materials. The law library relies heavily on interlibrary loan and document delivery for materials not within the scope of this policy.

The policy should also include guidelines that address issues such as cost, currency, language, format, and institutional priorities. If others must approve the policy—for example, the library committee in a law school or law firm, trustees in a county law library, or the chief judge and clerk of court in a court library—the guidelines will both explain and justify collection-development decisions. A law school library's collection-development policy may include the following statements:

- Current publications of lasting and scholarly value are given priority over retrospective materials.
- With minor exceptions, foreign language publications are not collected.
- Availability of materials online (e.g., Lexis, Westlaw, HeinOnline, or free Internet resources) or in other libraries through cooperative acquisition programs will be considered for infrequently used material and, in particular, for the laws of foreign countries.
- Duplicate copies are purchased for heavily used materials, and for items likely to be checked out indefinitely to a faculty member's office.
- In-depth materials for specific student research products, or for short-term faculty research projects, are not purchased unless the library's acquisition policy specifies collection development at the "research" or "comprehensive" level in that area. Such materials will be borrowed from other libraries as needed.
- Materials in support of the instructional and research needs of the law school faculty and students are favored over those for use by the rest of the university community, by the bench and bar, or by the general public.

Selection criteria also help the people responsible for collection development. Decisions to acquire or not to acquire an item are both collection-development decisions. Some criteria any type of law library might use include:

- Author and publisher reputation
- Significance of the subject matter
- Accuracy and timeliness of material
- Usefulness of title with respect to other materials already in the collection in print or digital format
- Appearance of the title in important bibliographies, lists, and other review sources
- Current and permanent value of the material
- Cost, including storage and maintaining currency

- Frequency, substance, and quality of updating and supplementation
- Format
- If digital, terms of the license
- Availability of the material in other libraries

STANDARDS AND ACCREDITATION

The only mandatory collection standards for law libraries involve those at law schools accredited by the American Bar Association (ABA) and/or the American Association of Law Schools (AALS). The American Association of Law Libraries (AALL), however, has created advisory standards governing appellate court, state, and county law libraries.

Law School Library Standards

The ABA most recently revised its standards for law school libraries in 2005 to recognize the deepening connection between technology and legal information. In 2008, the ABA initiated another comprehensive review of its accreditation standards, which is still ongoing. Since the last revision, technology has become an even bigger factor, and space and budgets have become even tighter in many libraries. The proposed amendments may lead to some substantial changes to meet these challenges.

Current ABA and AALS Standards

The library must be an "active and responsive force" in the law school, and must have sufficient financial resources to support the institution's teaching, scholarship, research, and service programs.[10]

The library must have a "core collection of essential materials" accessible in the library itself, as well as a collection that satisfies the law school's curriculum and the educational, research, and service needs of its students and professors. The materials must also be current, complete, and in sufficient quantity or accessibility for faculty and student use. The library also has to create and regularly update a written collection-development plan, and provide sufficient space and equipment to access the collection.[11] The appropriate mix of formats depends on the needs of the library and its patrons, but using only one format may not be enough.[12]

Libraries can enter into written agreements to share information resources if those agreements give faculty and students the necessary ease of access and availability to support the school's programs, but those agreements cannot be used to satisfy the core collection requirement. Schools cannot simply point their students to other law libraries for all of their research and education needs (not to mention that this would not endear the school to other members of their legal community).[13] The standards do permit the library to use off-site storage for "non-essential" items, so long as those items are "organized and readily accessible in a timely manner."[14]

Interpretation 606-5 provides much more detail as to what specific types of materials the library's "core collection" must contain.[15] The core collection cannot consist entirely of digital materials, but a substantial portion of the core collection requirements may be fulfilled using digital resources. While the interpretations prohibit libraries from making the majority of their resources available online only, they do allow for a fair amount of flexibility to fit each school's particular needs.

AALS's bylaws address the law library's collection requirements in much broader terms. Section 6-8 states that the library must be "adequate to support and encourage the instruction and research of its faculty and students," and that it "shall possess or have ready access to a physical collection and other information resources" to meet the research needs of students and faculty, satisfy curricular demands, allow the proper training of students in research methodologies, and serve the school's special educational and research needs.[16] As with the ABA rules, the AALS standards give libraries considerable leeway in meeting the overall requirements as they see fit.

Proposed Changes to ABA Standards

The ABA's Standards Review Committee is currently revisiting the accreditation standards for law schools. At the time this chapter was written, the proposed changes to chapter 6, covering libraries, were still in draft form. Some of the proposals are related to housekeeping—tasks like renumbering and moving some Interpretations. More substantially, the revised standards would require all libraries to include the U.S. territories' primary legal materials in their core collections.[17]

Other changes expand the flexibility libraries have when developing their collections. The revisions would still indicate that using one format for the entire collection may not be sufficient to meet the standard, and that schools must provide on-site access to materials. On the other hand, the proposed changes remove the language that states that the standards cannot be met solely by providing digital access. The new language would also allow libraries to provide a core collection through the sharing of digital and print resources, and would even permit the use of free databases as part of that core collection, as long as those databases are likely to remain free to the public. The proposed new language also says that the standard can be met through "reliable access" as well as ownership.[18]

Public Law Library Standards

In July 2005, AALL's State Court and County Special Interest Section (SCC-SIS) and the AALL executive board issued the *Appellate Court Libraries and State Law Libraries Standards.*[19] The *County Public Law Library Standards* followed in July 2009.[20] These are not binding in the way the ABA and AALS standards are for law school libraries; they are only suggested guidelines for a public law library's operation.

In their commentaries, AALL and SCC-SIS describe both sets of standards as recommendations to help provide a strong core law library collection. Each set includes a specific list of materials that AALL and SCC-SIS consider to be the minimum requirements for the core collection, covering legal resources from the library's state, federal law, and national materials. They also take pains to make clear that these lists should be considered a collection-development floor, not a ceiling. Both sets of standards also state that cooperative resource-sharing agreements with other libraries within a "reasonable geographic area" will satisfy the standards, as long as staff are available to help users access off-site resources. Both sets of standards call for a mix of print and digital resources.

FORMAT ISSUES

Digital Resources

In law libraries, the term "digital collections" usually brings to mind enormous databases of case law, statutes, regulations, and secondary sources.[21] Most of these materials were first published in paper or as microforms and were later digitized. As government and secondary publishers switch to digital publishing, more new materials are "born digital" and have no analog predecessor.

Features

A major advantage of most digital resources is the ability to search for specific words and phrases. Some databases use complex, proprietary algorithms to help researchers sift through massive amounts of text, while others offer little more than the ability to find a specific word. Examine all the different methods researchers can use for searching. Natural language searches, with the database's search engine doing much of the work, are more familiar and comfortable for many researchers. However, if these searches produce unexpected results, it is difficult to know precisely what terms were sought by the search algorithm. In those cases, carefully crafted Boolean searches permit more precise searching. Browsing through an index and similar subject-based listings can also be very useful, if the database offers such features.

Evaluating Digital Products

Librarians are often responsible for teaching researchers how to use resources. It is unrealistic to expect a legal database to be as simple and intuitive as a Google search, but a product that is difficult to use will either go unused or require plenty of training. Librarians who regularly use databases may forget how intimidating and challenging an unfamiliar database can be for novices. As you test out a potential acquisition or watch a vendor demonstration, imagine how a digital resource will seem to new researchers. Will the navigation and resource names and symbols make sense? Are the tools for common tasks prominently labeled and easy to locate? Select a known document you want to retrieve, and see how many ways the database can lead you to it. Then choose a topic that is interesting to you and see how much relevant material you can find. Expect to hit some dead ends; they are probably obstacles your researchers will run into, too. Analyzing the user experience this way will help you decide whether the product is a good fit for your patrons and how you will teach researchers to use the product. If it will present challenges to your researchers, can you mitigate any problems through proactive training or just-in-time assistance from librarians?

Cost is, of course, always an important consideration, but for reasons besides the library's collections budget. Private and government law librarians have to justify expenditures for databases by showing how they contribute to the organization's mission, and must demonstrate that the product is being used in a cost-effective way. This makes cost-containment training crucial, and not just for researchers in the law firm or at the court. Academic librarians need to be aware of the expense of digital research and teach their students to develop cost-effective habits while still in law school.

Accessibility

It is fair to expect most online resources to be readable by Web browsers. Mobile devices, such as tablet computers, e-readers, and smart phones, are also often used to access resources. Are mobile-optimized Web sites or applications available for the product you are reviewing? WestlawNext, LexisAdvance, and Fastcase have apps for phones and tablets. WestlawNext also lets a user send documents to her e-reader for later review. Researchers use a variety of devices, so databases that can transfer content between devices and across operating systems are attractive.

Some databases, especially e-book collections, permit limited downloads or viewing, and place digital rights management (DRM) controls on users' downloaded copies. Others prevent printing or e-mailing more than a set number of pages. The vendors' desire to prevent unauthorized copying is understandable, but such limitations can also decrease the value of the resource. An e-book database that only allows researchers to download or print ten pages might be frustrating for those who like to make notes on their copies. A database of legal forms should let researchers download forms in an editable format so they can complete and prepare them for filing.

Use the process of evaluating digital resources for acquisition as an opportunity to talk with your core patrons about how they access digital information in their research processes. Ask them how they conduct their research and what features make their work better. In addition to informing librarians about what resources and research training their patrons need, such discussions also reinforce perceptions of librarians as knowledgeable and responsive legal information specialists.

Perpetual Access

Unlike print materials that the library purchases and then owns indefinitely, most digital resources are covered by license agreements. If you sign a license agreement to gain access to a digital product, you do not own it; you are merely renting it, and do not have the same rights as you would for a typical book. Under U.S. copyright law's first-sale doctrine,[22] someone who buys a copy of a copyrighted work can sell the copy, lend it, or rent it. The first-sale doctrine is the legal basis for most library lending.

The first-sale doctrine does not apply to copies that are lent or rented, nor to licensed databases. What you can do with licensed content depends completely on the contract between the library and the vendor. The license may prevent you from printing or saving backup copies of the content, or sending copies of journal articles from a database to other libraries like you could from a print journal. The default rules contained in the Copyright Act are fairly friendly to libraries, but those rights can be signed away by license.

Another important aspect of ownership is continuing access. If you can no longer afford the digital product, you will likely lose access to all the information in that resource. On the other hand, if you had to cancel a subscription to a print law journal or a loose-leaf service, at least after the subscription ended you would still possess the issues and updates you had received. Additionally, many vendors are aggregators that license material from other publishers, and if that license ends, the vendors have no choice but to remove the content.

These scenarios are not inevitable, but they can only be prevented through appropriate provisions in the license agreement. Some vendors offer post-cancellation access (also called *perpetual access* or *digital ownership*), and it is an option that is worth watching for. Under these arrangements, the library owns a copy of the digital files that were in the database during the subscription term. The catch is that the files may not be provided to you in the same format or with the same user interface as those that you could access through an active subscription. Still, perpetual access is better than nothing—just make sure you understand how you will receive your content. Having a hard drive holding thousands of text documents or PDF files may not be especially useful to your researchers. You will probably need an access mechanism through a locally maintained portal, the vendor's Web site, or a third-party provider.

The University of Pittsburgh Barco Law Library faced this situation when the contents of a database it canceled arrived in several digital tape cartridges. The library recruited a computer engineering student to develop a basic user interface to provide access to the content.[23] Companies exist that can build and maintain user interfaces for libraries. The cost of doing so will depend on what sort of features you want to offer your users.

Some vendors, such as JSTOR and Project MUSE, promise perpetual access to the digital content available to your library during the subscription period. Other publishers have contracted with Portico, a digital preservation organization that provides post-cancellation access to member libraries for a fee (but probably much less than the cost of a current subscription). On the other hand, perpetual access to print items requires continuing investments as well. Keeping everything in good condition and organized requires space, materials, and personnel, so be sure to include all access costs in your expense calculations.

Microforms

Poor microforms. Just a few decades ago, they were being hailed as the format of the future. Print books in libraries would move aside, replaced on the shelves by reels of microfilm, drawers of microfiche, and plenty of microform readers. Today, tell someone that the information they seek is only available on microform, and their reaction says that you may as well have told them they must journey to the deepest fires of Mount Doom.

Microform does have its advantages. It has a long life expectancy (around five hundred years for the current generation meeting international standards); it takes up very little space compared to print; and once the library has bought the microform, it is the library's to keep. Many libraries still have a large number of microform documents; in fact, a substantial portion of a law library's volume count may be in microform. Microforms also capture the original page images, giving the format an advantage over text-only databases when searching for some types of content, such as advertisements, maps, and charts.

That said, microform has a number of disadvantages as well. Microform can be a pain to read; it is not easily searchable, the way digital

documents are, or as easy to browse as print materials. Microform readers are expensive, easily costing several thousand dollars each. Patrons
may think twice about how crucial it is to use the resource if they are told
it is only on microform.

A library might address microforms in its collection-development policy like this:

> The library collects materials in microform primarily when:
>
> The materials are infrequently used, and one of the following is true:
>
> - The materials would take up a great deal of shelf space, were they in
>   paper format, or
> - The materials are not available in paper format, or
> - Preservation in microform is superior to paper, or
> - The cost of the materials in microform is significantly less than the
>   cost of the materials in paper format.
>
> In all cases, the library will consider the digital availability of the mate-
> rial—especially when in PDF—as an alternative to microforms. Digital
> information may be a cost-effective alternative to microform when the
> library is confident that the digital materials will be available indefi-
> nitely.

PARTICULAR SELECTION ISSUES

Newsletters and Loose-leaf Services

Newsletters can eat your budget alive, if you let them. They are often
expensive and have limited usefulness beyond being a current awareness
tool. Many libraries subscribe just to those newsletters that are routed to
someone—an attorney in the firm, a judge, or a faculty member, for example—and renew a subscription only after verifying that it is still
needed. Online alternatives to traditional print newsletters abound at
various price points. Commerce Clearinghouse (CCH) and BloombergB-
NA's offerings may make sense for firms and schools with practitioners
and faculty who research within the topics covered by those services.
Lexis and Westlaw also offer current awareness notification features
within their main products, and boutique legal news companies, mem-
bership-based groups such as the American Bar Association's various
special interest sections, and nongovernmental organizations may provide low-cost or free newsletters for customers, members, or subscribers.
For example, the American Society of International Law's semimonthly
newsletter, *International Law in Brief*, covers recent developments in international law, and is e-mailed to subscribers (who do not have to be members) free of charge.

A law firm's policy on newsletters might look like this:

> The library only subscribes to newsletters that are being used by attorneys, paralegals, or staff. Every newsletter is reviewed annually to assess current use. Where possible, online subscriptions are preferred to print. BloombergBNA, CCH, and other providers offer summaries of daily and weekly reports sent via e-mail links to full-text documents. Lexis and Westlaw also can be used to keep current.
>
> Depending on the practice area and the needs of individual attorneys, an online subscription to a newsletter might include only highlights and summaries, or it could include access to the full text of each issue. Attorneys are encouraged to investigate current awareness options offered by associations and organizations to which they belong.

The burgeoning expansion of the administrative branch of government in the early to mid-1900s created the need for lawyers to find statutory, administrative, and judicial materials in one place. Enter the loose-leaf service, which gathered these disparate forms of law on a given subject into one set, and often included editorial commentary and extensive indexing in a comparatively compact, easy-to-update package. Two of the biggest loose-leaf publishers, CCH and BloombergBNA, each offered dozens of titles that were once a print mainstay in all types of law libraries. Both companies have shifted and modernized their loose-leaf content for online consumption.

Whether a library chooses to continue to subscribe to print loose-leafs or to online versions (or both) depends on its resources. Factors to consider include subscription costs, shelf space (some sets, especially those covering tax and labor, are quite large), the availability of staff to file updates, and how the library's users prefer to research. Regarding this last issue, it may be difficult to migrate to online services if the lawyers in your firm, judges in your court, or faculty in your school insist on using the print. Old habits sometimes die hard, so seek input from users, and use online trials to evaluate the advantages and disadvantages of various products. (See "Evaluating Digital Products," within this chapter.)

POPULAR READING

Most libraries have a casual reading area that includes newspapers and magazines. Typically, a library might subscribe to local papers and national publications such as the *New York Times, Washington Post, Los Angeles Times,* and the *Wall Street Journal.* Although these are all available online, many readers still prefer the tangible pages of newsprint. The library likely will offer the local and state legal newspapers, *The American Lawyer, Legal Times,* and the *National Law Journal.*

The magazines to which you subscribe should be those that your patrons want to read. You might offer the popular newsweeklies; business, entertainment, and sports magazines; and policy-related magazines. Depending on your patron base, you might also include technology, fitness, or local interest publications—whatever appeals to your users. If you don't know what they'd like, ask them! Magazines are inexpensive, and they give the library a lot of goodwill for little money.

Many law libraries have popular book collections that include fiction and mystery; current events, biography, and history; and humor. Keep the book jackets on the books; they attract readers and make for eye-catching displays. Like popular magazines, these inexpensive additions to your collection are a great value. Some libraries also offer a popular film collection tailored to their core user groups. Selections might range from the latest TV dramas and award-winning films to classic comedies and children's features that users can take home to their families. [24]

Reserve

Many libraries, especially those in law schools, have a reserve collection that remains under the control of library staff. Items within this collection are usually subject to shorter circulation periods and stiffer overdue fines in order to facilitate accessibility. Patrons may be permitted to browse the shelves (open reserve) or may have to request items from a staff member (closed reserve). The access method you choose depends on how closely you want your reserve collection to be monitored, as well as other considerations, such as your physical layout and availability of the staff to retrieve materials.

A law school library's reserve collection usually has materials placed there by faculty for classes or general use, heavily used items such as study guides, and items that are at a higher risk of theft. The collection may include practice and continuing legal education titles from the home jurisdiction, hornbooks and nutshells, and audiovisual materials. Some libraries keep current issues of law journals on reserve, too. The collection should be dynamic; materials no longer needed on reserve should be moved to the open stacks.

Reference

Most libraries' reference collections have shrunk significantly due to the ubiquity of reliable resources online. Information that used to be found only in a print directory may now be available on a Web site for free or for a nominal subscription fee. The collection policy should recognize that reference materials include information in both print and digital formats, and that the "reference collection" provides users with current, useful, and authoritative resources for frequently researched issues. Some libraries will include every reference source in a discrete collection that typically is located near the reference desk, while others spread some of their reference books throughout the library. An institution that takes the latter approach may have a policy as seen in table 8.1.

Foreign and International Law Collections

"International law" refers to the law between nations, such as treaties on every topic from the environment to extradition, the decisions of international courts, and the activities of intergovernmental institutions like the World Trade Organization. "Foreign law" is the law of any jurisdiction that is not your own. The size of a law library's foreign and international law (FIL) collection may range from microscopic to an entire floor or wing, and in some cases may be in a separate branch of the library. FIL materials are typically much more expensive than their domestic counterparts, and can be a real challenge to buy and maintain on a limited budget.

You will need to decide whether to collect FIL materials at all, and if so, whether to do so broadly, deeply, or both.[25] For example, a library in a law firm with a significant international presence may provide attorneys with a thorough collection of primary and secondary materials covering the countries and areas of law in which the firm or its clients conduct business, plus a smattering of general FIL materials. A law school may develop a broad foreign law collection covering each individual country's legal system (books such as *Introduction to German Law* and *The Nigerian Legal System*), and only purchase additional materials for those countries and legal systems that faculty are actively teaching or researching. That same library may also offer a collection of materials on international law that is both broad and deep.

Whichever you choose, investigate online options and periodically revisit those options as new Web sites are launched and existing ones decay or disappear. Documents from intergovernmental organizations (such as the United Nations and the European Union) and some countries are available online at no cost, but secondary materials generally require a subscription for access. Some products cover single jurisdictions, such as Chinalawinfo, while others, like vLex, are multijurisdictional. Pricing varies widely, as does the quality of translations, when available.

By being selective and creative, the library can stretch its budget. Carefully investigate potential purchases, avoiding books that are nothing more than collections of previously published articles you already own or compilations of freely available primary documents. Talk with other law libraries in your region to see if there is any interest in cooperatively collecting materials, perhaps by agreeing to split jurisdictional responsibilities. For instance, one library could collect European law, while another collects Asian law. Above all, closely monitor your firm's prac-

Table 8.1.

This policy offers guidelines on which materials should and should not be included in the library's reference collection.

Works shelved in the reference collection. These include those used frequently by librarians and a wide variety of patrons. The reference collection will comprise:

1. Authoritative general reference works, including:

- Well-regarded, general-purpose nonlegal works, such as general dictionaries, encyclopedias, and biographical dictionaries and encyclopedias.

- General-purpose legal works, such as *Black's Law Dictionary* and *American Jurisprudence 2d.*

- Selected style, grammar, usage, and citation guides pertaining to law and general writing.

2. General reference works pertaining to the state, including frequently used works specifically relating to the court system and political science.

3. Current statistical resources.

4. Whether they are general purpose or subject specific, the current editions of statistical resources are shelved in the reference section.

5. Current general legal bibliographies.

6. Subject-specific and general-purpose directories.

Reference-type works shelved in the stacks. These include works that are easy to shelve in a specific category, and those that are normally accessed and used with other works on that subject. Reference-type materials shelved in the stacks include:

1. Subject-specific works, including dictionaries and encyclopedias, and

2. Subject-specific bibliographies.

Prior editions. The library will only keep the newest edition of a reference work in the reference collection. Prior editions are kept selectively, and will be shelved in the stacks. Superseded reference materials retained in the stacks indefinitely include:

1. Publications with a significant change in coverage between editions.

2. Selected biographical materials.

3. State materials.

4. Fact-based annual publications, such as almanacs.

tice areas or your faculty's research interests, and acquire only high-quality products that fit those needs.

Annex and Remote Collections

Some libraries maintain annex or remote collections within the larger institution, such as a job-hunter's library in a law school's career placement office. A library that provides materials for other locations—whether it is a judge's chambers or a legal writing department—should maintain some control over those items. Process the materials through the library: use the library stamp, label them to indicate their location, and check them out to the unit or office in which they are kept. Purchase and manage online subscriptions as well. For password-protected services, set up or keep a copy of the log-in credentials.

Gifts

Beware of patrons bearing gifts. As harsh as that may sound, the truth is that donors rarely read a collection-development policy before making a tangible donation. Your policy should include a statement on gifts, including the right to refrain from accepting ones that don't conform to the library's selection parameters.

Accept only those donations that you know will be of interest to the library, and refuse up front those that will not (as opposed to accepting all gifts and sorting them out after the fact). If a patron calls to inquire about a donation or stops by to drop one off, explain what parts of the gift you can and cannot accept. If, despite this, you are given something that doesn't fit the collection, be clear that you will not add it. Offer the donor alternatives if you have any, such as making the item available to students on a "free books" cart. This proactive approach will reduce the number of donors who return to "visit" their gifts, only to find that they were disposed of without ever touching a shelf.

Any donation that fits within the collection's scope should be processed and added to the library's holdings. Commonly, a bookplate is affixed inside (or a sticker might be placed on the front or back cover of a DVD) indicating who donated the item, unless anonymity is preferred. You can choose to include donation information on the item's record in the catalog: information about the gift can be detailed in the staff notes, and a small notation can appear in the public view if desired. Remember to send the donor an appreciative acknowledgement of the gift. If the donor asks you to appraise the value of the gift, politely say that you cannot. You may, however, refer the donor to professional appraisers.

Here is an example of a collection-development policy's statement on gifts:

The library encourages gifts of useful materials. Before accepting such gifts, the library will request a list or general statement of the materials offered. The director of the library is responsible for accepting all gifts and will only accept those materials that conform to the selection guidelines or if the director finds them useful.

The library will not accept gifts with conditions as to their disposition or location except by express permission of the director. The director retains the right to determine the disposition of the materials at any time and in any manner deemed appropriate.

The library will not appraise the value of gifts for tax purposes. However, the library may assist a donor in obtaining prices located in catalogs of second-hand dealers or procuring the services of a professional appraiser.

Special Collections

Some types of special collections begin with a gift, but on a grander scale than usual. A faculty member, prominent attorney, or esteemed jurist or statesperson might retire and donate a package of collected notes, books, manuscripts, trial documents, photographs, or other materials to a library. In the best circumstance, the donor and receiving library will have discussed and negotiated the transaction before the actual handoff, so the library can prepare for staff and space considerations tied to processing the materials and determine where the collection will ultimately be located and how and to what degree patrons will access it.

The rare book collection, another type of special collection, is most commonly found in academic or large court libraries. Rare book collections may be themed (such as those which reconstruct the libraries of notable historical figures) or not, but in all cases will require specific ambient conditions and other long-term preservation accommodations. The process of selecting and caring for rare books is both an art and a science, and preferably should be carried out by someone with a background in it. If you want to build a rare book collection but no one on staff has any experience in the area, consider investing in special classes or training. It will pay off in the long run in terms of well-reasoned purchase and access decisions and proper display and maintenance techniques.

Either of these types of special collections, archives or rare books, may require hundreds or thousands of hours of staff time to organize, prepare, and catalog the materials, and in some cases may necessitate remodeling or adding on to the library. Hardware, software (off the shelf or custom-designed), and technological expertise may be needed if the materials will be digitized or hand-indexed. In return for these significant investments, the library preserves information that otherwise could be irretrievably lost, and receives the prestige of holding a completely unique collection that may attract researchers from all over.

Lost Materials

Sadly, sometimes books disappear. A library typically will declare an item to be lost when it has been off the shelf for a certain span of time without being checked out, and it cannot be located. Some libraries define an item as lost when it has been gone for three or four months, while others may wait as long as a year. Occasionally, a patron may confess to losing an item as well.

Decisions about replacing a lost item should be made using the selection criteria set forth in the collection-development policy. You might assume that if a book was selected pursuant to the development policy, it should be reselected under the same criteria. However, don't automatically replace a lost item; instead, determine whether you still need it. Factors to consider include:

- the age of the item,
- circulation information, if available,
- whether you have additional copies in the collection,
- the importance of the item to your collection and to the topic in general,
- if an older work, whether it imparts a historical perspective that might be of value to researchers, and
- replacement cost.

If an item is no longer in print, the library may need to search both new and used book dealers' Web sites to locate a replacement.

WEEDING, UPDATING, MONITORING

Weeding

Judicious and systematic discarding of certain materials is important for the health and usefulness of any collection. The decision to weed (remove items from) a collection can depend on a number of factors. The most common of these are space issues and financial constraints. Weeding frees up shelf space to make room for materials that are more germane to the purpose of the collection. Likewise, the cancellation and removal of items that have an ongoing cost—such as loose-leafs, journals, and heavily supplemented treatises—makes fiscal room for materials that the library places a higher value on.

Even libraries that enjoy ample space and an adequate budget benefit from periodic weeding. Just because a library has the space to keep each item it has ever purchased does not mean that it should. Clearing the unused, unneeded, or no longer useful materials from the collection allows users and librarians to more easily find relevant items.[26] The perfect treatise for your patron's needs might be buried among multiple copies of every edition of *Income Taxation of Individuals in a Nutshell* dating back to 1972 and thirty-five volumes of an out-of-date copy of RIA's *Federal Tax Coordinator*, but who could find it?

Another benefit of regular weeding—collection pruning, if you will—is that it will prolong the time before there is no room to jam another book on the shelf, triggering a massive, all-hands-on-deck collection purge. A trimmed collection is a more agile collection, making stacks shifts (spatial adjustments of materials due to growth) a more pleasant undertaking for staff.

Finally, weeding provides one additional benefit: walking the stacks and examining the collection keeps librarians in touch with what the library owns and where various topics are physically located.[27] Some libraries even ask new librarians to weed or shelf-read part of the collection just for this purpose. The alert librarian might notice if a section of the collection seems underdeveloped or overemphasized, and may uncover works that are missing, misshelved, or that should be classified elsewhere.

The collection-development policy should include the library's practices regarding weeding.[28] Items that law libraries typically weed include multiple copies of infrequently used materials (such as those old *Nutshells*), superseded replacement volumes of current works, substantially incomplete runs of journals in peripheral subject areas, and loose-leaf services to which the library no longer subscribes.

Depending on space availability, a library will likely keep superseded volumes, supplements, and pocket parts of the United States Code and its own state laws. To avoid confusion, superseded materials often are shelved in a different location than current ones, and should be prominently marked "superseded."

Materials that are available online, especially from the publisher or an aggregator like EBSCO, are also candidates for removal. However, when evaluating whether to cancel and withdraw print in favor of online access, consider the following questions:

- When the contract with the vendor ends, will access to some or all titles be lost, or is there a provision for permanent access rights? How is post-cancellation access provided? (See "Perpetual Access" within this chapter.)
- In the case of serials, is the online product subject to embargos of recent issues, and if so, can the material be found elsewhere? For example, a vendor may not provide access to the latest volume of a law review, but Lexis and Westlaw generally do. Does the vendor

offer a complete run of the title, and if not, are you able to retain the print you already own to fill in the gaps? [29]

• Do your patrons have a strong preference to use certain titles or types of materials in print or online? Note that this should not necessarily be the decisive factor when considering whether to cancel print in favor of online access. People tend to adapt when faced with the need to do so.

Even a digital product chosen to replace print is not immune from future weeding. Monitor it using the criteria discussed in the next subsection, and if it is no longer useful to your patrons, cancel your subscription.

Many librarians cringe at the thought of tossing withdrawn materials into the recycle bin. While much of what you weed will not be of use to anyone, you may be able to donate some items to charities that accept books for resale or for stocking libraries in remote, underserved areas around the world. Many libraries, especially government-affiliated ones, may have specific procedures to follow when disposing of weeded materials, so check those first. If space is your primary motivator for weeding and you think some of the materials might still have some life left in them, consider temporary or long-term off-site storage. With this sort of halfway-house setup, you can watch for items that are requested repeatedly. These would be obvious candidates for returning to the main stacks. If you opt for off-site storage, remember to weed that collection once in a while, too.

Updating and Monitoring

For a long time, legal publishers believed that the philosophy of "if you build it, they will come" [30] would also apply to librarians: "If you sell it, they will buy." This was generally true until the late twentieth century, when updating costs started to spike. Faced with static or shrinking budgets, libraries began deciding not to acquire every update on the market.

Whether a library chooses to receive every update to a title depends on its budget, its philosophy on updating, and the update's content. To some librarians, the integrity of a publication is compromised when it lacks the most recent information; others skip purchasing updates for certain titles, especially if the update does not include substantive changes to the text, but instead, only citations to newer court decisions.

In deciding whether to update a certain title, determine how useful the item will be if it is not updated, and whether researchers will be harmed if they do not have the current update. In fact, during this process you may find that you do not need the title at all. (See "Weeding" as mentioned within this chapter.) Some items are logical targets for non-regular updates, such as a title on trial practice. Each of the publisher's annual updates may contain very few noteworthy changes, since topics such as opening statements, closing arguments, witness examination, and so on are likely to remain substantially the same over the short run. Such a work would probably not suffer in terms of usefulness if updated only every two to three years. Always keep users informed, and include a notice where the supplement would normally be found that the update in the book is not the most current one available.

As the faculty changes in a law school, and practice areas shift in a firm, the library's collection will evolve over time. Most legal publications have ongoing costs, so frequently review your collection policy and subscriptions. The following law firm policy statement reflects the dynamic nature of collection development, and the need to review the collection and seek input from library users.

> In order to provide attorneys and paralegals with the information that they need, and to adhere to the library's budget, the library will:
>
> Monitor changes in practice areas
>
> - Add to the budget for titles in new practice areas
> - Cancel subscriptions for titles no longer being used
>
> Continuously review subscriptions
>
> - Before renewal, ask attorneys in the practice area if they still need the item
> - As supplements are received, verify that the item is still needed
> - As attorneys are added to routing lists, add more subscriptions as needed
>
> Identify little-used but still-needed titles
>
> - If available via interlibrary loan or online, consider canceling
> - Review the need for continuous supplementation; alternatives include occasional updates, or periodic purchase of replacement sets
>
> Review current awareness routing
>
> - Review number of copies requested
> - Change number of subscriptions as appropriate
> - Compare e-mail and print subscriptions

COPYRIGHT AND LICENSING

Digital resources and license agreements are almost inextricably intertwined. This is primarily due to the confluence of copyright law and digital technologies. While equipment can enable the manufacture of infringing copies of paper books and journals, it would not be very convenient to do so. Digital files, on the other hand, can be perfectly copied quickly and easily. This difference has led vendors of digital resources to prefer licensing, instead of outright selling, their products to libraries.

As mentioned within this chapter (see "Perpetual Access"), copyright law is fairly generous to libraries and enables them, under certain circumstances, to make copies for their patrons. For instance, the section 108 library exception expressly authorizes libraries to make single copies of some resources for research purposes.[31] The first-sale doctrine, as mentioned within this chapter, permits libraries to lend copies that they own. Additionally, libraries rely heavily on the fair-use doctrine, a broad defense that may allow copying when social interests outweigh those of the copyright holder.

License agreements override these default copyright protections, so when evaluating one, see what duplication it authorizes, and what it does not. Ideally, the license will acknowledge and maintain the library's rights under the fair-use doctrine and other statutory provisions. You should read all license agreements closely, but be especially careful with provisions covering authorized access and copying. Does the definition of an authorized user cover all the categories of researchers who come to your library? If you have a professor or attorney who prefers articles to be printed and routed to her, does the license have language that clearly authorizes that? You do not have to accept the vendor's form contract. Write your changes on the agreement, initial them, and send it back. The vendor may resist some amendments, but it cannot hurt to negotiate.

Avoid license provisions that seek to make your library liable for any infringement that researchers may commit. It is unreasonable to expect all researchers to perfectly comply with the publisher's interpretation of copyright law. The precise boundaries between infringing and permitted duplication are unclear and contested.[32] Experts do not agree on the exact rules, so it should come as no surprise that sometimes researchers, out of ignorance, thoughtlessness, or misunderstanding, make infringing copies. It is impractical to expect librarians to closely monitor patron use of resources, and even if it were feasible, too much monitoring would infringe on researchers' privacy interests. Libraries can, and should, take reasonable measures to educate users about their rights and obligations under copyright law and to mitigate infringement, but they should not be responsible for patrons' actions.

Licenses cover many other matters than copyright. Check whether the vendor provides any guarantees that it will keep the database and all of its content online. If the database is down for an extended period of time or a significant amount of content disappears, you should have an option to cancel the subscription early or be reimbursed for the lost access. Do not let vendors disclaim the implied warranties of merchantability and fitness for a particular purpose. These warranties give you important protections if the database changes and is no longer useful to you. Many contracts will specify that they will be interpreted under a particular

jurisdiction's laws. You will probably prefer that the contract be interpreted under your state's laws, and your organization may have a policy
against contracts that apply the laws of another jurisdiction, especially if
you work for a public institution.

Also, be sure that appropriate privacy protections are included for
your researchers. Both vendors and libraries benefit from aggregated usage data, but records on each individual's research should be retained for
a limited time and, ideally, remain under the control of the individual.
WestlawNext and Lexis Advance, for example, keep research trails for
each user, but the trails eventually expire unless the user saves them.
Records that are retained should be kept confidential. State laws often
shield library patron records, but they may not apply to private vendors'
databases, so the same rules should be set out in contracts.[33]

DIGITIZATION PROJECTS

Aside from leasing and purchasing digital resources, libraries can build
their own digital collections. These efforts come in many varieties and are
a locus of innovation in academic law librarianship. The least technologically demanding of these types of projects is creating a digital repository
of the law school's faculty scholarship and journals, or an online brief
bank for a firm's attorneys. Most of these documents have already been
digitized, so assembling such a collection generally requires acquiring
and cleaning up the appropriate files, ascertaining intellectual property
rights, and then loading them into a vendor-provided or open source
digital repository platform. A more ambitious collection could involve
digitizing materials that thus far only exist in analog format. Institutional
archives, court records, records relating to local legal history, and faculty
papers are good candidates for local digitization projects.

The costs of local digitization projects are mostly due to personnel and
equipment, because the materials to be digitized are either readily available to librarians or, in the case of law journal articles, relatively inexpensive. You may need to invest in digitization equipment and software.
What you will need depends heavily on the materials you wish to digitize and the access features you wish to provide, such as search and
indexing. Digitization work can be outsourced to specialized vendors,
and your project may benefit from the economy of scale that some of
these vendors can achieve.

You will need some sort of public access platform. Vendor-hosted
platforms are dominant in the law library market at present. Open source
platforms are available, but require qualified staff to install and maintain
both the servers and repository software. Law libraries have successfully
implemented both vendor- and self-hosted repositories, either independently or in cooperation with university library systems.[34]

Digitization projects can easily mushroom into an unmanageable amount of work, so it is important to add a section on local digital collections to your library's collection-development policy. It is better to start small and set achievable goals. Once those are accomplished, your goals can become more ambitious. For example, you can expand the scope of your faculty publications to those written by adjunct professors and faculty who used to teach at your institution, but later left. You can move from journal articles to book chapters, pieces written for the popular press, congressional testimony, drafts that have been posted on the Social Science Research Network, or lecture notes. Perhaps the library will dive into multimedia, collecting images, audio recordings, and video recordings of lectures and conferences held at the school. Such an effort would present a new host of challenges, compared with collections that are predominantly text. You might need additional editing software or a new platform to preserve and provide access to the content, and you may need to hire a qualified vendor to handle some of the work.

To keep digitization projects manageable and to justify the expense, set criteria for what will be included. Assuming you are not planning a massive quest to digitize everything in your library's collection, good candidates for projects will have a defined scope, require relatively little permission collecting, fill a niche, and align with institutional strengths.

INTERLIBRARY LOAN AND CONSORTIA

No library can own every bit of legal information. Fortunately, libraries share with each other. Through the interlibrary loan system, libraries can obtain materials for researchers that are not in their own collections. This frees you from worrying about items that will rarely be accessed. You do not need to buy it if another library will lend it to you the few times you need it.

Interlibrary loan is not a panacea, of course. Libraries decide what parts of their collections they are willing to lend to other libraries. If you are hoping to borrow a current casebook, a popular movie, or a rare or fragile item, you will probably have a difficult time finding a library that will mail it to you. For those kinds of items, you should plan to purchase them or send the researcher to the other library to access the resource on-site. If a user's needs can be met by a scan or photocopy, then you are more likely to have the request filled. Additionally, license agreements for digital materials can sometimes limit interlibrary lending (another reason to carefully read and negotiate your licenses).

Interlibrary loan requests highlight holes in your collection, so use them as a tool to find weaknesses that can be remedied and to predict topics for which you are going to see more interest in the future. ILL statistics constitute a useful set of data that, along with patron input and your library collection-development policy, can help you choose worthwhile purchases.[35] For example, if a book is requested for interlibrary loan several times by different researchers, that is a strong indication that there is enough demand to justify a purchase. In 1978, the National Commission on New Technological Uses of Copyright Works (CONTU) issued guidelines for copies of articles made to fulfill interlibrary loan requests.[36] These guidelines include what is called the "suggestion of five": a library can request five copies of articles from a given periodical in a calendar year without worrying about copyright infringement. This is not a strict rule, and more than five copies might be fine, but if you are requesting more than five articles from a journal in a year, consider a subscription.

Purchases through library consortia are another way libraries share resources. Through consortia, libraries pool their funds to purchase or license materials that would not otherwise be affordable. Such acquisitions are shared among all the members, so in addition to understanding any licenses with vendors, make sure you understand the relationships you will have with other member libraries. Joining a consortium is essentially another collection-development decision. Use the same tools and information to decide whether spending funds on a membership is a good value for your library and will give you access to materials that are in step with your collection-development policy.

CONCLUSION

A law library is designed to meet the needs of its present and future researchers. To cultivate a collection that serves their patrons well, law librarians must select relevant, authoritative materials in appropriate formats. This means choosing from a wide variety of options while carefully managing a budget.

With a clear collection-development policy, librarians can make principled decisions that best use the library's acquisition funds. The development policy is an important document that should not be allowed to ossify into a relic of obsolete practices. Pay close attention to changes in publishers' offerings and your patrons' research needs, and use that information to regularly reevaluate and revise the policy. This will help your library's collection meet the aspirations of Ranganathan's second law by providing every reader his or her information source.

NOTES

1. S. R. Ranganathan, *The Five Laws of Library Science* (Bombay: Asia Pub. House, 1957), 9.

2. Richard E. Rubin, *Foundations of Library and Information Science* (New York: Neal-Schuman, 2000), 251.

3. Jennifer Perdue and James A. Van Fleet, "Borrow or Buy? Cost-Effective Delivery of Monographs," *Journal of Interlibrary Loan, Document Delivery and Information Supply* 9 (1999): 24.

4. See, e.g., Perdue and Van Fleet, "Borrow or Buy?"; Kristine J. Anderson et al., "Buy, Don't Borrow," *Collection Management* 27 (2002): 1.

5. Anderson et al., "Buy, Don't Borrow," 9–10; Perdue and Van Fleet, "Borrow or Buy?" 24–27.

6. See, e.g., Anderson et al., "Buy, Don't Borrow," 5, 7.

7. Sarah Pearson, Erin Gallagher, and Edward Hart, "Seminoles and Gators: Can Shared Patron Driven Acquisitions of EBooks Overcome the Rivalry?" Presentation at the annual meeting of the Southeastern Chapter of the American Association of Law Libraries, Clearwater Beach, Florida, March 22–24, 2012.

8. Ibid.

9. Ibid.

10. Standard 606, *2011–2012 Standards and Rules of Procedure for Approval of Law Schools*, http://www.americanbar.org/groups/legal_education/resources/standards.html.

11. Standard 606, *2011–2012 Standards and Rules of Procedure for Approval of Law Schools*.

12. Interpretation 606-2, *2011–2012 Standards and Rules of Procedure for Approval of Law Schools*.

13. Interpretation 606-3, *2011–2012 Standards and Rules of Procedure for Approval of Law Schools*.

14. Interpretation 606-4, *2011–2012 Standards and Rules of Procedure for Approval of Law Schools*.

15. Interpretation 606-5, *2011–2012 Standards and Rules of Procedure for Approval of Law Schools*.

16. "Bylaws and Executive Committee Regulations Pertaining to the Requirements of Membership—The Association of American Law Schools," http://www.aals.org/about_handbook_requirements.php.

17. "Standards Review, April 27–28, 2012," http://www.americanbar.org/content/dam/aba/migrated/2011_build/legal_education/committees/standards_review_documents/april2012/20120404_april12_src_meeting_materials.authcheckdam.pdf, 71, 73.

18. "Standards Review, April 27–28, 2012," 71–73.

19. "Appellate Court Libraries and State Law Libraries Standards," http://www.aallnet.org/main-menu/Leadership-Governance/policies/PublicPolicies/policy-county-standards.html.

20. "County Public Law Library Standards," http://www.aallnet.org/main-menu/Leadership-Governance/policies/PublicPolicies/policy-county-standards.html.

21. A useful article on print and digital collection development is Michelle M. Wu, "Why Print and Electronic Resources Are Essential to the Academic Law Library," *Law Library Journal* 97 (2005): 233.

22. 17 U.S.C. § 109 (2006).

23. Sallie Smith, Susanna Leers, and Patricia Roncevich, "Database Ownership: Myth or Reality?" *Law Library Journal* 103 (2011): 233.

24. If you do choose to collect movies, evaluate your willingness to lend them through interlibrary loan—they are wildly popular. If you want to ensure that your movies are available for your users, update your lending policy to reflect that you won't loan them through ILL, and consider automatically deflecting the requests to save staff processing time.

25. For discussions of the realities of putting together an FIL collection and considerations to take into account when doing so, see Holger Knudsen, "Collection Building: Foreign, Comparative and International Law in Print," and Marylin J. Raisch,

"Shaping Electronic Collections in Foreign, Comparative and International Law," both in *The IALL International Handbook of Legal Information Management*, ed. Richard A. Danner and Jules Winterton, (Surrey, UK: Ashgate, 2011).

26. Vicki L. Gregory, *Collection Development and Management for 21st Century Library Collections: An Introduction* (New York: Neal-Schuman, 2011), 120.

27. Joyce Saricks, "At Leisure: The Lessons of Weeding," *Booklist* 108 (2011): 43.

28. For a practical example of how to plan and implement a systematic collection-weeding project, see Amy K. Soma and Lisa M. Sjoberg, "More than Just Low-Hanging Fruit: A Collaborative Approach to Weeding in Academic Libraries," *Collection Management* 36 (2011): 17.

29. For more information about cancellation and retention issues pertaining to serials, including implications of different digitization scenarios, such as the use of inadequate preservation-quality standards and converting image-intensive sources, see Roger C. Schonfeld and Ross Housewright, "What to Withdraw? Print Collections Management in the Wake of Digitization," *Ithaka S+R*, September 29, 2009.

30. *Field of Dreams*, directed by Phil Alden Robinson (Los Angeles, CA: Gordon Co., 1989).

31. 17 U.S.C. § 108 (2006).

32. Melville B. Nimmer and David Nimmer, *Nimmer on Copyright* (New Providence, NJ: Matthew Bender, 1963, 2012), § 13.05.

33. There is plenty of worthwhile reading on libraries, copyright, and licensing. Two solid options are James S. Heller, Paul Hellyer, and Benjamin J. Keele, *The Librarian's Copyright Companion*, 2nd ed. (Buffalo, NY: Hein, 2012); and Kenneth D. Crews, *Copyright Law for Librarians and Educators: Creative Strategies and Practical Solutions*, 3rd ed. (Chicago: American Library Association, 2011).

34. A law library's implementation of an open source repository is described in Fang Wang, "Building an Open Source Institutional Repository at a Small Law School Library: Is It Realistic or Unattainable?" *Information Technology and Libraries* 30 (2011): 81.

35. A library's use of interlibrary loan data to make collection development decisions is in Amy Burchfield and Kevin Garewal, "Meeting Evolving Research and Curriculum Needs: A Survey of Interlibrary Loan and OhioLINK Borrowing at an Academic Law Library," *Journal of Interlibrary Loan, Document Delivery and Electronic Reserve* 19 (2009): 137.

36. "CONTU Guidelines on Photocopying under Interlibrary Loan Arrangements," http://old.cni.org/docs/infopols/CONTU.html.

NINE

Foreign, Comparative, and International Law Librarianship

Mary Rumsey

One vibrant and growing field is foreign, comparative, and international law librarianship. Librarians who work in this area are often called "FCIL" librarians. If you have an interest or background in foreign cultures, languages, or international affairs, FCIL librarianship might be for you.

WHAT IS FCIL LIBRARIANSHIP?

Foreign Law

Three areas fall under the "FCIL" umbrella. The first, foreign law, covers the national and subnational laws of other countries. ("Subnational" means the law of political subdivisions, such as Canadian provinces, Australian states and territories, and German *Länder*.) Now that people and businesses frequently cross national borders, questions about foreign law come up all the time. For example, U.S. immigrants with family back at home may need to prove that a foreign adoption, marriage, or divorce satisfies U.S. requirements. It's not unusual for FCIL librarians to get requests for information on Vietnamese adoption law, Moroccan divorces, or Eritrean marriages.

Businesses also run into legal questions when they move into foreign markets, outsource work, or make contracts with foreign suppliers. They want to know things like:

- "Are there any legal hoops we have to jump through before we can sell our software in France?"
- "What is the best way to work with a Chinese company to distribute our product—a distributorship, a joint venture, an acquisition or merger, or something else?"
- "Are foreign companies allowed to buy land in Poland?"

Comparative Law

Comparative law, the second FCIL component, isn't really a kind of law. It's a way of studying law. People who do comparative law study the similarities and differences between the legal systems of different countries. For example, a law professor might write an article comparing the U.S. law on products liability with the law in Japan. Practicing lawyers do not usually do comparative law; most often, it is law professors or law students who make scholarly comparisons between legal systems.

From the FCIL librarian's perspective, comparative law usually plays out as a foreign law question. In other words, when aiding a comparative law researcher, the FCIL librarian must identify and locate foreign law sources.

International Law

The third area of FCIL librarianship, international law, has grown much more important since World War II and the birth of the United Nations. International law represents the idea that countries must follow certain rules in dealing with each other, with people, and with entities like companies or international organizations. After World War II and the Holocaust, countries even agreed that international law affected what they could do to their own citizens—at least in the extreme case of genocide.[1] Human rights, international trade, and the environment are among the new subjects of international law.

Fifty years ago, or even thirty years ago, the area of foreign, comparative, and international law was a quiet backwater. A handful of law professors thought about it and wrote about it, but few lawyers or law students, let alone anyone else, paid much attention. But the rise of international organizations like the World Trade Organization, increased immigration, and increasing economic interdependence between countries have all focused attention on this area.

WHO ARE FCIL LIBRARIANS?

Nearly all law librarians get asked foreign and international questions. Few of them, however, specialize in FCIL work. In the United States, about 80 law librarians have job titles that reflect their FCIL responsibilities. More librarians—perhaps 150—are the unofficial FCIL librarians at their workplace. Most of them work at law school libraries, but large law firms often have a librarian who handles most of the foreign and international law work. A couple of large county law libraries, in Chicago and Los Angeles, also have librarians with "foreign and international" in their job titles. Even most librarians with FCIL job titles, however, do not work exclusively on foreign and international projects.

THE WORK OF FCIL LIBRARIANS

Duties vary widely, but generally fall under the headings of reference, collection development, teaching, or cataloging. Most FCIL librarians do at least some reference.

Reference

Foreign law reference questions range from "Here's a citation to a foreign law—can you find me a copy?" to "What is the law on doctor-patient confidentiality in Chad?" Some patrons may just need help deciphering a foreign citation, such as "Loi fédérale sur les brevets d'invention du 25 juin 1954 (état le 1er juillet 2009)." Other patrons may need to dig deeply into the inner workings of a foreign legal system—to identify the relevant sources of law, such as a civil code and regulations, and then to find the necessary materials on a topic.

Foreign Legal Systems

One aspect of foreign law that makes it harder for U.S. law researchers is that many foreign countries have very different legal systems. For example, most countries have what is called a "civil law" system. Civil law systems differ from the U.S. system in several ways. One key difference is that court opinions are much less important in civil law systems. In such systems, courts still decide criminal cases and disputes between parties, but courts rarely establish general legal rules. Perhaps even more surprising to Americans, these legal systems do not have civil trials by jury.

FCIL librarians often spend time explaining foreign legal systems to researchers who have not yet learned about them. If a researcher assumes that a foreign country has a legal system that matches the U.S. system, he or she may ask for information that is not available, or is not useful. For example, American lawyers sometimes research civil jury instructions—summaries of the law that a judge reads to the jury before the jury makes its decision. An American lawyer who wanted German jury instructions would learn that no such materials exist!

For many foreign law questions, the librarian can use English-language books, articles, research guides, and databases to identify the relevant sources of law. One source that many FCIL librarians call the "Bible" of foreign law research is Thomas A. Reynolds and Arturo Flores, *Foreign Law Guide* (1989–). This title, formerly a loose-leaf publication, is available as a Web database. The *Foreign Law Guide* is arranged by country. For each country, the authors provide a brief summary of the legal system and a list of basic legal publications. This list is followed by a longer list of legal subjects, from abortion to worker's compensation. For most subjects, the authors list citations to the relevant law in the country.

The *Foreign Law Guide* helps librarians identify the material their patrons need. For example, suppose a U.S. lawyer asks the librarian to find the Austrian laws on investment funds. The *Foreign Law Guide*'s chapter on Austria has the index entry "Securities and Stock Exchange," which gives the following useful information: "Investmentfondsgesetz. Law of 2011 (investment funds) in Bundesgesetzblatt 2011 no. 77." This is the name and citation of the law in German. Where the authors of the *Foreign Law Guide* have found no English translation, their entries usually stop here. With this citation, the librarian could probably retrieve the German text from the Web, or at least make an interlibrary loan request for it.

In this case, the *Foreign Law Guide* entry continues: "Official text, consolidated to current date, on the website of the Finance Market Authority at http://www.fma.gv.at/ (click on Verordnungen for all regulations and ordinances). Abrogates and replaces, as of 31 Aug 2011, the Investmentfondsgesetz of 1993." From this information, the librarian learns that the 1993 law is no longer in force. Also, knowing the effective date will help the researcher distinguish between discussions of Austria's old law and its new one. (Too often, especially on the Web, legal commentary does not include citations to the law.)

The entry continues: "English translation at http://checkpoint.riag.com." For most patrons, an English translation or summary is the Holy Grail of their research. The *Foreign Law Guide* does a great service to foreign-law researchers by pointing to English-language translations and summaries, where available.

Of course, the *Foreign Law Guide* does not provide citations to every foreign law. Its focus is on those laws most likely to be required by U.S. legal researchers; moreover, not all countries are covered. If the *Foreign Law Guide* does not provide a citation, the librarian embarks on a much more difficult search. The librarian may need to search indexes or digests of foreign laws, Internet sources, article indexes, or other sources. For these searches, the librarian will probably need at least a working knowledge of other languages.

Many of the *Foreign Law Guide*'s references to translations point to "subject collections." This term of art describes databases or loose-leaf sets on a particular topic, such as business law or copyright law, offering

English translations of laws from a variety of countries. Good examples include the World Intellectual Property Organization's online WIPO Lex, which has copyright, patent, trademark, and other related laws from over 100 countries; and *Investment Laws of the World*, a large set of loose-leaf volumes that covers basic investment laws from about 150 countries.

The Web has made foreign law research much easier. One useful tool is the country or regional research guide. Usually written by librarians or lawyers from the area in question, these guides make great starting points. For example, a librarian confronted with a question about Caribbean law can refer to Yemisi Dina's *Guide to Caribbean Law Research* (updated 2010),[2] published at the GlobaLex site. Like most such guides, Dina's guide gives an introduction to the legal system, lists major legal publications, and points to online sources where available. Web sites such GlobaLex offer large collections of research guides.

International Law

International law questions have grabbed headlines in the twenty-first century. For example, does the United States' targeted killing program, using drone aircraft, violate the laws of war? Does international law offer remedies for damage from global warming? More and more patrons are asking law librarians for help with international law research.

Most reference work in international law can be conducted using English-language sources. Nonetheless, international law research poses its own hazards. The variety of sources used in international law can overwhelm researchers. International law differs from national law in that there is no real international government. In other words, there is no legislative body like the U.S. Congress, no executive like the U.S. president, and no executive agencies like the Environmental Protection Agency. The United Nations General Assembly and the secretary-general, which sound a bit like Congress and the president, lack the power to make laws. And although the International Court of Justice, sometimes called the "World Court," can decide cases between countries if they agree to go before it, its decisions are not binding on future disputes. Thus, the World Court is much less powerful than the U.S. Supreme Court.

If bodies like the United Nations do not pass laws, where do the rules of international law come from? Treaties form the clearest source of international law. For example, the Convention on International Trade in Endangered Species of Wild Flora and Fauna regulates the buying, selling, and shipping of endangered plants and animals.[3]

Another major source of international rules is "customary law." Customary law refers to general practices of states (i.e., countries) and intergovernmental organizations that are legally binding and generally recognized by all states. An example of customary law is the practice of not executing juvenile offenders. Although a couple of nations still impose the death penalty on juveniles, the "general practice" of nearly every country forbids this punishment.

Other sources of international law include "general principles of law," judicial decisions, and the teachings of the most highly qualified legal scholars (called "publicists") of the various nations. General principles of law include concepts found in nearly all legal systems, such as the idea that a party can lose a right by repeatedly failing to assert it ("waiver"). Judicial decisions and scholarly writings can be used in international law to argue that states should follow a certain rule described in those decisions or writings.

International law lacks a clear ladder of authority. This makes international law research more confusing than studying U.S. law. In researching U.S. law, the Constitution trumps statutes, which trump regulations. By contrast, researching international law often involves identifying a hodgepodge of documents from which the lawyer infers a general principle of international law.

Even though treaties are the clearest source of international law, they are not like a contract between the signatories. A state may add a "reservation" when it signs a treaty, saying that it refuses to be bound by certain parts of the treaty. Even more confusingly, a non-party may find itself bound by rules in a treaty that it never signed. For example, even states that never signed the Genocide Treaty are considered bound by it.

Because international law is based, in part, on what states do, FCIL librarians must often track down examples of "state practice" in international law. State practice is found in treaties, decisions of national courts and international tribunals, national laws, diplomatic correspondence, opinions of national legal advisors, and the practice of international organizations. Identifying state practice can be so difficult that some distinguished FCIL librarians have published a loose-leaf set designed to simplify this research.[4] Nonetheless, researching state practice remains a challenging task; generally, starting with secondary sources, such as the *Max Planck Encyclopedia of Public International Law*,[5] works best.

Another important resource is the American Society of International Law's *Electronic Resource Guide*.[6] This guide, prepared by law librarians, consists of a series of research guides on various international law topics, including human rights, European Union, law of the sea, environmental law, criminal law, and intellectual property law. The *Electronic Resource Guide* can help researchers sort out the important online resources from the flood of less useful information.

Reference work in international law, like foreign law, has become easier with the advent of Web sources. For example, many treaties can be found online. In addition to excellent online searching skills, however, an understanding of older, paper-based tools plays a part in most FCIL librarians' work.

Teaching

Some FCIL librarians teach formal classes on international and foreign legal research. Such teaching may consist of guest appearances in substantive law courses, such as a human rights, international law, or comparative constitutional law class. Or the librarian may teach a session on FCIL research as part of an advanced legal research class. A few law schools offer a regular class or seminar focusing on FCIL research. Other schools offer shorter courses on the topic.

In a 2011 survey of FCIL librarians, Neel Kant Agrawal found that over 80 percent of them reported giving at least periodic presentations on FCIL research.[7] Half of the respondents reported teaching or having taught a course on FCIL research.[8] To support librarians who teach FCIL research, the Foreign, Comparative and International Law Special Interest Section of AALL maintains a page of syllabi, presentations, handouts, exercises, and other class materials.[9]

Collection Development

Another task for many FCIL librarians is collection development—the selection and acquisition of paper and electronic resources on foreign and international law. FCIL collection development has become increasingly expensive. With the upsurge in transnational and international law interest, publication of FCIL titles is booming. Also, the number of independent countries has increased threefold since World War II.[10] This increase means more countries from which law libraries might collect materials. In addition, new organizations and legal systems have sprung up, including the European Union (EU), the World Trade Organization, and the North American Free Trade Agreement system. These three organizations have created whole new areas of law to which FCIL collection development must respond. With new titles on EU law numbering in the hundreds each year, collection librarians must choose carefully.

The 2008 economic crisis and ensuing fallout have changed law libraries' collection-development policies, probably forever. Bridget Reischer, collection development librarian at Harvard Law Library, recently stated that Harvard is "no longer collecting for the ages."[11] Other law libraries with major foreign law collections, such as Columbia and the University of Michigan, have also made significant cuts. Collection-development librarians struggle with how to direct their foreign law budgets. Most of their patrons seek information about major western European countries. Thus, libraries tend to duplicate one another's holdings. Partly because of this duplication, libraries have less money to buy materials from other jurisdictions. So while several libraries own the current German Civil Code, far fewer have codes from Latvia, or Ugandan statutes. In an attempt to resolve this dilemma, Harvard's Law Library has cut some foreign law materials held by other Boston-area law libraries, while maintaining more obscure holdings.

Generally, everything that is hard about collecting U.S. legal materials applies to FCIL work. But collection of foreign and international legal materials adds new headaches to the usual problems. In addition to agonizing over whether to switch to electronic formats, librarians must cope with foreign currency fluctuations and transactions, overseas shipping costs, advertisements and catalogs in foreign languages, and vendors whose first language is something other than English.

Recently, the dollar's weakness against foreign currencies has made acquiring these materials even more expensive, increasing the budget woes suffered by most law librarians. Also, libraries that collect from developing countries, such as most African jurisdictions, must deal with erratic publication schedules, unreliable vendors, and logistical obstacles such as poor communication and shipping infrastructures. Because of the high cost and wide range of possible materials, few libraries can afford to collect them from every jurisdiction. Harvard and the Law Library of Congress come the closest to a comprehensive global law library;[12] however, recent budget cuts have eroded their ability to collect comprehensively.

Collection development may include extensive work in foreign languages at law libraries that acquire foreign monographs, but FCIL librarians in smaller libraries may look only at English-language publications. Most of the demand from U.S. patrons is for materials in English, making those materials the first priority for many collection librarians. And after spending money on the first priority, little cash may remain for others. A couple of companies have sprung up recently, trying to provide English-language, practitioner-oriented legal information from numerous countries.[13] Another company, vLex, provides "as-needed" access to individual laws, court opinions, and other legal documents.[14] These models may be the future of collection development for foreign law.

Cataloging

Of course, once someone selects a foreign title, it will have to be cataloged. Cataloging foreign titles often requires special skills and training. Fortunately, records for most titles are available through OCLC, making copy-cataloging possible. Changes to the Library of Congress classification system for international law have made more work for FCIL catalogers. The "JX" class, established in 1910, originally covered both international relations and international law. As international organizations and international law grew in importance, works on these topics no longer fit neatly into the JX class. A drastic change was needed. In 1997, the Library of Congress split the class into Political Science (JZ) and Law (KZ).[15] In

2011, the KZ class was also expanded to include more international criminal law.

Islamic law and other religious law have presented another challenge to FCIL catalogers. Until recently, the Library of Congress classification schedule had no place for it. Therefore, catalogers used a variety of approaches to works on Islamic law, scattering them among classes such as BP (Islam), or not classifying them at all.[16] For the last several years, the Library of Congress has been adding classification schedules on religious law. Reclassifying books on Islamic, Hindu, canon law, and general religious law will keep some FCIL catalogers busy for at least a few years.

ATTRACTIONS OF FOREIGN AND INTERNATIONAL LIBRARIANSHIP

Variety

Most librarians who do FCIL work cite its variety and challenge as the reasons they enjoy it.[17] Of course, law librarianship itself is characterized by variety.[18] FCIL librarianship, however, widens the scope of work dramatically. Foreign law questions can cover almost two hundred countries; international law reaches from the deep seabed to outer space. FCIL research pulls librarians into foreign legal systems, calls on their foreign language skills, exposes them to different cultures and different approaches to legal problems, and takes place in an ever-changing landscape of print and electronic resources.

Collegiality

Another benefit of FCIL work stems from the relatively small number of librarians in the field. New FCIL librarians often comment on how warmly their seasoned colleagues welcome them.[19] Because few libraries' foreign and international law collections come close to being complete, librarians tend to cooperate and share resources readily.

Employment Prospects

Generally, the market for FCIL librarians is strong.[20] American Association of Law Libraries salary surveys show FCIL librarians making more money than law librarians in nearly all other positions—more than reference librarians, computer/automation librarians, and government documents librarians.[21] Probably much of this difference reflects the greater size and resources of libraries with large FCIL collections; in other words, the type of library that has a dedicated FCIL librarian is the type of library that pays all of its librarians more than average. Recent job postings, however, suggest that FCIL positions pay better than comparable positions at the same library.

Moreover, the globalization of law practice will continue to increase demand for foreign and international legal information and for the people who know how to find it. Lawyers whose practices never reached farther than the next state now find their clients doing business in foreign countries, inheriting property in other countries, or fighting child custody battles with ex-spouses overseas.

QUALIFICATIONS OF FCIL LIBRARIANS

Education

Most FCIL librarians work in reference at law school libraries. For reference librarian positions, law libraries prefer to hire applicants with law degrees. However, not all academic FCIL librarians have them.[22] Few of the law firm librarians who specialize in FCIL work have law degrees, although some do.

As with U.S. legal research, FCIL research may be easier for librarians with law degrees. Law school gives librarians a useful vocabulary, overviews of legislative and regulatory processes, and familiarity with dispute-resolution mechanisms such as courts. But many law librarians have acquired an excellent understanding of law-making institutions and legal concepts without a legal education. Moreover, the typical law school education does not include classes in foreign or international law,[23] though students may take them as electives.

Like most law librarians, most FCIL librarians have a master's degree in library and information science.[24] Academic law libraries usually require this degree. Exceptions usually arise when talented paraprofessionals get promoted into jobs that ordinarily require the degree, or when law libraries hire a lawyer based on his or her research skills.

Languages

Foreign language skills are one of the "necessary strengths" for FCIL work.[25] Historically, French, German, Spanish, and Italian have been the most common languages used by FCIL librarians.[26] With increasing legal and financial interest in China, however, knowledge of Chinese may be even more marketable.

But librarians without strong foreign language skills should not despair of their FCIL prospects. The most common use of foreign languages is the slow deciphering of written words—the easiest of the four basic language skills (reading, writing, listening, and speaking). Generally, librarians do not translate material for patrons. Translating legal documents requires specialized training and a great deal of time—more than librarians have. Willingness to wade through foreign-language documents with a bilingual legal dictionary, however, is definitely required.

Online translators, such as Google Translate, cannot substitute for translations by humans, but they can help librarians get the gist of a document or Web page. If an English translation of a foreign law is unavailable, the best a librarian can do is provide the law in its original language, and online translators can help find that. For example, foreign news stories about a recently passed law often contain a link to the law. By using a Web translator to help identify likely search terms, librarians can find these news stories, get the gist of them with a translator, and use the link to retrieve the full text.

Curiosity and Intelligence

Many FCIL librarians share an interest in foreign countries, international relations, or history. Librarians who like to grapple with new concepts, and who are willing to learn some background before jumping into search mode, flourish as FCIL librarians.

Training

Training in FCIL librarianship can be hard to get.[27] The best way to learn is by working with an experienced FCIL librarian. In large cities, it may be possible to set up an internship. More commonly, law librarians learn FCIL librarianship by combining on-the-job experience (relying on books, research guides, and dogged persistence), and attending educational programs.

In the mid-1990s, AALL and Oceana Publishing sponsored a series of workshops on foreign and international research. The papers from those workshops were published as several volumes that still offer invaluable guidance on FCIL librarianship. Unfortunately, they largely pre-date the Web, making them an incomplete resource.

At its annual meeting, AALL usually has from three to five programs relating to international or foreign legal research. In addition, programs at other organizations offer some FCIL training. The International Association of Law Librarians (IALL)[28] has an annual meeting, usually held outside the United States, that features detailed, substantive legal topics. For the past several years, the Law Library of Congress has offered inexpensive, valuable, one-day workshops the day before the American Society of International Law meeting opens in Washington, D.C. Topics have ranged from Latin American legal systems to the problems of legal translation and court interpretation. Finally, some AALL chapters occasionally hold programs on foreign or international topics.

CALI, the Center for Computer-Assisted Legal Instruction, has several tutorials on FCIL research. Topics include customary international law, international environmental law, foreign law, private international law, foreign constitutions, human rights, U.N. documentation, and others. Those lessons, however, are open only to students and staff at CALI member law schools.

A DAY IN THE LIFE

The variety of FCIL work means that no day is typical. To give an idea of what my work is like, however, I kept track of the work I did one day as the University of Minnesota's foreign, comparative and international law librarian. On another day, I might have taught a session of my class on FCIL research, or spent a shift at the reference desk.

I started my day, like most of us do, by looking at my e-mail. I found a request for help from a former student. He writes: "I am researching whether Korea has any laws, statutes, etc. regarding costs, fines, etc. of a business terminating a distributor. The distributorship contract has a provision addressing termination, but I am wondering whether Korea has any laws that supersede or otherwise affect that contractual provision. I have tried Google scholar and Westlaw Next, but I have not had success."

Distributorship agreements are used often enough that legal publishers have responded with some excellent products. We have several looseleaf publications in the library, and we subscribe to a database called *International Encyclopaedia of Agency Distribution Agreements*. A quick check of that database shows that it covers Korea; I send the student an e-mail with references to the database and to some of the other books we have on this topic.

The next e-mail is from a law librarian friend at Michigan State University Law Library. She needs a copy of an old statute from India. The University of Minnesota has a large collection of Indian materials, most of which are stored in our basement. I take the e-mail downstairs, find the statute, and ask our interlibrary loan librarian to scan it as a .pdf file. Soon I'm replying to my friend's e-mail with a copy of the law.

One useful practice for FCIL librarians is to subscribe to various electronic discussion lists (listservs) and blogs. On the INT-LAW discussion list, I see a note from an Australian law librarian who needs an old decision from Canada. I get the reporter, scan the case, and send it off. By helping other librarians when I can, I feel better about asking the list for help now and then.

After dealing with the rest of my e-mail and skimming my blog feeds, I pick up a folder of publishers' advertisements and catalogs. Collection development never ends—at least until the money runs out for the fiscal year. I'm amazed by the number of new books on European competition law—four in this catalog alone, with an average price of over $200. We collect heavily in this area, but we cannot buy everything. I'm going to have to look more closely at these books before deciding what to get. Before I can pick up the next flyer, the phone rings.

One of our professors, who teaches international intellectual property law, wants some quick research on comparative patent law. (Helpful translation tip: when a professor says she has a "quick question," it means, "I want a quick answer.") This research requires getting information on the concept of "inventive step" in various jurisdictions. I can get some leads by searching full-text law review articles and Google Book Search, but will also need to spend some time looking at articles in the journal *IIC: International Review of Intellectual Property and Competition Law*, which we don't have in electronic format.

I've made a little progress on the question when a student knocks on my door. He wants to write a law review article about Julian Assange, the Wikileaks founder, seeking asylum in Ecuador. He has a collection of news articles and blog postings gathered by Google searching. I start him with some background information from the *Max Planck Encyclopedia of Public International Law*, one of my favorite research sources. We also look at the law library catalog together and select some monographs on extradition and asylum; as usual, using books is going to make his research more efficient.

Next the phone rings again; this time it's the reference librarian on duty. An immigration attorney needs help figuring out if a customary marriage in Liberia would be legally valid if the marriage were not registered with the government. In other words, is a marriage in Liberia only legally valid if registered with the government? Knowing that this will be a hard question to research, I ask the reference librarian to get the attorney's contact information so I can get back to her later. Several Web, law review database, and Google Book searches later, I identify the relevant Liberian laws. Unfortunately, we don't have them at this library, so I send the attorney the citation information and some suggestions on law libraries (Harvard, UC-Berkeley) that offer fee-based document-delivery services.

It wouldn't be a true FCIL day without striking out, however; failure is never far away. A local law firm librarian calls me to find out about getting court filings from a German court in a bankruptcy case. I consult by e-mail with a wonderful law librarian in Germany, whom I've become acquainted with via the INT-LAW discussion list. He tells me these documents are not publicly available.

I finish skimming through various articles on the patent law issue, and mark some sections for the professor to read. I take a couple of volumes of *IIC: International Review of Intellectual Property and Competition Law* down to the circulation desk so they can be checked out and delivered to the professor.

Meanwhile, more e-mail questions have come in. A student needs help finding an international law topic for a law review article. I refer her to a few of the international law blogs, including a favorite of mine, IntLawGrrls. Another professor wants a bibliography of articles on fair trial principles. I search online periodicals indexes, including the *Index to Foreign Legal Periodicals*. This professor reads French and some Spanish, so I include articles in those languages. The index terms in the *Index to Foreign Legal Periodicals* are in English, and I know French and Spanish well enough to decide which citations to include. I also search full-text articles in Westlaw and LexisNexis's database of law reviews—in addition to the most recent articles, I always find a few older articles that didn't show up in the periodical indexes. I finish by checking some more obscure indexes—*Public International Law: A Current Bibliography of Books and Articles* on the Max Planck Institute Web site, the *Legal Journals Index*, and *PAIS*.

While I'm working, an LLM student stops by my office. The LLM is a master's degree in law. At the University of Minnesota and many other law schools, foreign lawyers study U.S. law for a year, earning an LLM degree. The student needs help finding European and U.S. sources for a paper comparing parents' responsibility for their children's torts. Like many LLM students, she can read several languages—English, French, and Spanish, in this case. We navigate through the *Index to Foreign Legal Periodicals*, and I show her how she can link to full-text articles for some of the citations we find. I'm able to load the student down with useful material, and show her how to navigate through some indexes and other databases. Before leaving, she also asks me about exams, so I show her the old exams that the law library puts on its Web site.

I spend the rest of the afternoon preparing to lecture about human rights research next week. I have given a similar lecture for several years, but the databases and other resources are always changing, and I have to change my materials accordingly. I also like to replace older examples with up-to-date ones, so I take new examples from human rights blogs and news stories.

CONCLUSION

FCIL work is never boring. Foreign and international law librarianship offers all the rewards of law librarianship, with an extra dose of challenge. Trends in the globalization of law practice make employment prospects attractive. To become an FCIL librarian, learn foreign languages, seek out educational opportunities, and find opportunities to develop FCIL reference, acquisition, or cataloging skills at your current or future job.

NOTES

1. Convention on the Prevention and Punishment of the Crime of Genocide, December 9, 1948, 78 U.N.T.S. 277.

2. Yemisi Dina, UPDATE: Guide to Caribbean Law Research (2010), http://www.nyulawglobal.org/globalex/Caribbean1.htm.

3. Convention on International Trade in Endangered Species of Wild Fauna and Flora, March 3, 1973, 27 U.S.T. 1087, 993 U.N.T.S. 243.

4. Ralph Gaebler and Maria Smolka-Day, eds., *Sources of State Practice in International Law* (Ardsley, NY: Transnational Publishers, 2002).

5. Rüdiger Wolfrum, ed., *Max Planck Encyclopedia of Public International Law* (Oxford: Oxford University Press, 2012).

6. American Society of International Law, *Electronic Resource Guide*, http://www.asil.org/erg.

7. Neel Kant Agrawal, *Training in FCIL Librarianship for Tomorrow's World*, App. 1, "Survey Instrument and Results," at 3, http://works.bepress.com/aallcallforpapers/70 (January 2012).

8. Ibid.

9. FCIL-SIS, 2011 Syllabi and Course Materials Database, http://www.aallnet.org/sis/fcilsis/syllabi.html.

10. "Harper's Index," *Harper's Magazine*, February 2001, 13.

11. Statement of Bridget Reischer, FCIL-SIS Foreign Law Selectors Interest Group Meeting, American Association of Law Librarians Annual Meeting, July 22, 2012.

12. Andrew Grossman, "Towards Cooperation in Access to Foreign Primary Law," *International Journal of Legal Information* 30 (2002): 28 (table 2).

13. These companies include the Practical Law Company (http://us.practicallaw.com) and Getting the Deal Through (http://www.gettingthedealthrough.com).

14. vLex, http://vlex.com.

15. Katherina R. Lin and Erin Murphy, "Reflections on a JX Reclassification Project," *Law Library Journal* 92 (2000): 459.

16. M. Lesley Wilkins, "Harvard Law School Library Collections & Services Related to Law of the Islamic World," *International Journal of Legal Information* 31 (2003): 383–84.

17. See, e.g., Mary Rumsey, "Strangers in a Strange Land: How to Answer Foreign Law Research Questions," *AALL Spectrum*, July 2004, 17.

18. Mary Whisner, "Choosing Law Librarianship: Thoughts for People Contemplating a Career Move (1999)," http://www.llrx.com.features/librarian.htm. Whisner's article serves as an excellent overview for anyone considering becoming a law librarian.

19. See, e.g., "New Member Profile: Julie Horst," *FCIL-SIS Newsletter*, February 2005, 17.

20. In an informal 2005 e-mail survey of law library directors, twenty-one of the forty respondents said that their libraries had an FCIL position. Of those, seven, or 33 percent, were created in the last five years. (Laura N. Gasaway, director of the Law Library and professor of law, University of North Carolina, sent out the e-mail inquiry; results are summarized in an e-mail from Teresa Stanton, reference/foreign and international law librarian, University of North Carolina, to Mary Rumsey, foreign, comparative and international law librarian, University of Minnesota Law School (Nov. 7, 2005) [on file with author.]) Similarly, the number of FCIL positions listed in the *AALL Directory & Handbook* grew from thirty-six in 1991 to seventy-eight in 2012, an increase of over 100 percent. The membership of the FCIL-SIS has increased from 134 in 1985 to 399 in 2012.

21. Am. Ass'n of Law Libraries, AALL 2011 Annual Salary Survey, Annual Salary Summary—Academic Libraries, available to members only at http://www.aallnet.org/Documents/Publications/Salary-Survey/AALL-Salary-Survey-2011/s-3.pdf; Am. Ass'n of Law Libraries, AALL 2005 Annual Salary Survey, Summary—All Library Types, available to members only at http://www.aall.org/members/pub_salary05/s-7.pdf; Am.

Ass'n of Law Libraries, AALL 2003 Annual Salary Survey, Summary—All Library Types, available to members only at http://www.aall.org/members/pub_salary03/s-7-s-8.pdf.

22. Among FCIL librarians surveyed, about 87 percent had law degrees. Agrawal, "Training in FCIL Librarianship for Tomorrow's World," App. 1, 5.

23. The University of Michigan is one exception to this generalization, as it requires its law students to take a class on transnational law. Jeffrey Lehman, "International Law and the Legal Curriculum," *American Society of International Law Proceedings* 96 (2002): 55. Nonetheless, "very few [law schools] require students to take it as part of a law degree." Bassina Farbenblum, "Executive Deference in U.S. Refugee Law: Internationalist Paths through and beyond Chevron," *Duke Law Journal* 60 (2011): 1119, n.325.

24. In Neel Kant Agrawal's survey, about 95 percent of the respondents stated that they had a degree in library or information science. Agrawal, "Training in FCIL Librarianship for Tomorrow's World," 4.

25. Marylin J. Raisch, review of *Toward a Cyberlegal Culture*, by Mirela Roznovschi (2001), *International Journal of Legal Information* 30 (2002): 370.

26. David McFadden, "Survey of FCIL Membership: Results," *FCIL Newsletter*, February 1992, 17.

27. Neel Kant Agrawal presents an excellent survey of FCIL training, and the need for additional training options, in Agrawal, "Training in FCIL Librarianship for Tomorrow's World."

28. Silke Sahl, "Introduction," *International Journal of Legal Information* 31 (2003): 151. "The program offers countless learning opportunities, including scholarly lectures, visits to libraries and information centers, and meetings with publishers and vendors. Last but not least, it offers the chance to meet new colleagues as well as to renew friendships and contacts with law librarians from around the world."

TEN

Technical Services

Sonia Luna-Lamas

In an academic law library, traditional technical services include the functions of acquiring, processing, classifying, and organizing information for retrieval. Acquisitions, cataloging, and serials/continuations almost always fall within the purview of this department. Occasionally stacks maintenance, circulation, and resource sharing, which includes interlibrary loan (ILL) functions, also fall under the umbrella of technical services. Even when these departments are not directly under technical services, they will certainly work closely together on projects that will affect not only the individual departments but also the law library as a whole. Technical services librarians also often serve as systems librarians, closely interacting with the integrated library system (ILS) effectively and efficiently.

Historically, change came slowly to technical services departments. Technology brought the first changes. Many technical services functions, such as ordering, check-in of serials, claiming, and processing materials were automated. This automation, coupled with the integration of these functions into integrated library systems, meant that technical services librarians were the first librarians within the library to experience, use, embrace, and often assist in the development of technology.

While technology has altered the workflow and processes in technical services, it has not eliminated the need for technical services librarians. Instead, it has increased the need for well-trained, technology-savvy, and highly inventive librarians who are not afraid to embrace changes and to implement new ideas and concepts. Acquisitions librarians must not only concern themselves and their departments with the negotiation of contracts, selection of simultaneous users, and the acquisition of IP ranges for EZ proxy servers. With the advent of different electronic formats, they must also associate themselves with different methods of acquiring and delivering materials using the newer electronic formats available. Catalogers routinely include URLs in the 856 field and include electronic resources within the catalog in order to create direct links to materials as they are discovered by the patrons.

Changes in technical services departments include several common trends. Some of these trends are:

- the outsourcing of formerly in-house processes, such as cataloging, physical processing, authority control, and database maintenance services;
- the development of digital collections, moving away from the emphasis on print collections;
- the reliance on digital periodicals such as HeinOnline,[1] which means that traditional print periodicals are no longer bound;
- switching from manual or online ordering to the use of an electronic data interchange (EDI);
- and most recently, with the advent of e-books, determining how to handle their acquisition and their availability to patrons for discovery.

Some of these trends create questions. Are law libraries building online catalogs for the use of patrons or for the use of librarians? Are law libraries saving money by outsourcing technical service responsibilities? Will law libraries continue purchasing and binding periodicals or will digitization products that provide large collections of online periodicals, such as HeinOnline, be used instead? Should law libraries stop manual ordering and claiming, and rely on electronic data interchange? Should law libraries provide links to electronic resources on Web pages, in catalogs, or in both places? Should law libraries purchase MARC records to add individual titles to their online catalogs? What formats should be collected? Why? How should law library's titles and volumes be counted? Should these items be counted? Should electronic resources be included in these counts? If so, how? What is the American Bar Association (ABA) annual report attempting to measure with its counting requirements?

Technical services will be involved in answering the above questions. Why? Because I believe that technical services is the heart of the library. Without technical services, the library could not function. Without technical services, materials are not ordered, checked in, processed, classified, or organized and made accessible. Thus, information retrieval by public services librarians and patrons becomes impossible. In technical services, materials are purchased and paid for via acquisitions, an initial bibliographic description is provided for correct accessibility via cataloging, and then materials are placed on the shelves for use. Or, if acquired digitally, material is made accessible for discovery by the patrons. Lastly, these tasks are all counted, creating statistics. In order for an academic law library to effectively function, the above tasks must transpire smoothly and seamlessly, creating a continuous workflow.

ACQUISITIONS

Some would say that libraries begin in the acquisitions department. This department is responsible for the ordering, purchasing, and receiving of new library materials. While a collection-development team selects the materials for acquisitions based on the collection-development policy that the library has instituted, the acquisitions department actually orders, checks in, and approves invoices for payment of the materials selected and purchased.

After the material is selected, the acquisitions department will engage in *preorder searching*, which weeds out duplicate orders and identifies any series titles and or serials the library may already hold. What is the difference between a series and a serial? Anglo-American Cataloging Rules (AACR2) defines the terms as follows:[2]

> *Series:* A group of separate resources related to one another by the fact that each resource bears, in addition to its own title proper, a collective title applying to the group as a whole. The individual resources may or may not be numbered. A separately numbered sequence of volumes or issues within a series or serial (e.g., notes and queries, 1st series, 2nd series, etc.).

> *Serial:* A continuing resource issued in a succession of discrete parts, usually bearing numbering, that has no predetermined conclusion. It is material that is uniquely identified with enumeration, chronology, and possibly a date that is usually issued in successive parts and is intended to be continued indefinitely.

If the library already owns the series title, it will usually have a standing order with a vendor for that title. The vendor will automatically ship to the library any successive parts of the multipart publication as they are published. If the title is a serial, it will likely be a periodical, such as a journal or law review, and will be handled directly by the serials/continuations department. In law libraries, all materials seem to be serials.

In order to make certain that the title is not held by the library, the library checks its holdings by searching the law library's online catalog. Thorough searching is done using many different access points, such as title, author, ISBN, ISSN, and series statement. Finally, an online bibliographic utility, such as OCLC WorldCat (Online Computer Library Center) is searched to verify once more that the law library does not already hold the title in question. WorldCat is the world's most comprehensive catalog of bibliographic entries or titles. It includes several million items held in libraries around the world.[3]

Once it is determined that the law library does not hold the materials, vendor selection begins. There are publishers, vendors, and jobbers. What do these terms mean? Can they be used interchangeably? According to the *Serials Acquisitions Glossary*, revised in 2005 by the Association for Library Collections and Technical Services (ALCTS), these terms are defined as follows:[4]

> *Publisher:* A company or service that prepares and distributes books, newspapers, journals, or music (usually for sale to the public).

> *Vendor:* Individuals or companies, other than publishers, from whom library materials are purchased. There is a distinction made between book and serial vendors. *Book vendors* provide law libraries the convenience of buying the books of numerous publishers and receiving a consolidated invoice for their purchase. They may also provide the library with standing orders, electronic ordering, claiming, and shelf-ready book processing. *Serial vendors* place and renew a library's serial orders and offer the benefits of consolidated billing and claiming. They will both provide customer service.

> *Jobber:* Can be used synonymously with *vendor*. A jobber is also commonly referred to as a *purchasing agent*, a middleman who will purchase the material for the library from the publisher, invoice the library, and take care of any customer service issues, such as claims.

The decision may be made to go directly through the publisher, vendor, or jobber. It is much easier to deal with a few vendors and jobbers rather than with several hundred publishers. This decision is dependent on the nature of the material, its subject matter, the country of publication, and whether a need exists to expedite the acquisitions of the materials. Common law library publishers, vendors, and jobbers include ABA, Hein, BNA, CCH, West Group, LexisNexis, Ebsco, Puvill, Gaunt, Oxford, Coutts, and YBP (Yankee). Many others exist, and YBP Library Services and Coutts Library even offer shelf-ready delivery of materials to a law library. Shelf-ready materials are received from a vendor or publisher with catalog records for the integrated library system and physical processing already done. This means that the library property stamps, barcodes, spine labels and security devices have already been attached to the books when they arrive at the library.

Because of the variety of formats that are currently available for purchase, librarians also need to make a decision about what format is to be purchased. Not only do librarians need to decide whether they will be choosing paperback or hardcover, but now they need to decide whether an item will even be acquired in print. Who will be reading it? How will they be accessing it? How many copies will they need? If it is electronic, the licensing and the simultaneous-users issues will need to be addressed as well.

Two other decisions that need to be made are about the funds to be used for and the location to be assigned to the item that is to be purchased. Library budgets are usually assigned at the beginning of the fiscal year. The library often divides the budget in order to make purchases based on its collection-development policy. These budgets may be assigned by material format, by the final physical or virtual location of the item, or even by department or faculty member's name. So the acquisitions department then decides where the item will be placed after it is processed and to what fund the purchase will be assigned.

After this process, the order is placed. A purchase order is commonly entered into the acquisitions module of the integrated library system. The order is then placed with the chosen vendor. This may be done in a variety of ways. The order can be mailed, phoned, faxed, e-mailed, placed online through the vendor's Web page or sent via electronic data interchange (EDI). EDI is a set of computer interchange standards that replaces traditional paper documents for items such as invoices, bills, and purchase orders. Paperwork is eliminated, and time is saved with EDI. When a purchase order is entered into a law library's integrated library system's acquisitions module, an order is sent electronically to the vendor via EDI. Most of the major integrated library systems and major vendors support this type of ordering.

At the time the purchase order is created in the acquisitions module, a bibliographic record is selected in a bibliographic utility such as OCLC and downloaded. It can also be manually keyed in to the integrated library system's acquisitions module. Some of the new integrated library systems will allow searching and downloading to be done directly from the integrated library system, so independent searching in the bibliographic utility is unnecessary. Once the law library receives the materials , the order record is compared to the item and verified for accuracy. After receiving the item, it is sent to the cataloging department for cataloging, classification, and physical processing.

Finally, the acquisitions department is responsible for claiming materials not received by the library. The acquisitions department compares what was ordered to what it has received. It will claim materials that do not arrive in a timely manner. Just like orders, claims may be mailed, phoned, faxed, e-mailed, placed online through the vendor's Web page or sent via EDI. When invoices are received, they also will be compared with the order record to verify that the law library is correctly and accurately invoiced for materials ordered and received. Invoices are signed and approved and then turned over for payment to the accounts payable department in the law library or university.

CATALOGING

The cataloging department is responsible for the cataloging, classification, authority control, and physical processing of library materials. Through this process, print materials that are not received in a shelf-ready format are prepared for access by patrons. Will the library be *cataloging* or *classifying* these materials? Cataloging requires the description of an item's physical appearance. It is done following specific rules that will allow the patron to retrieve it. To physically describe materials, cataloging departments will be following the new Resource Description and Access (RDA)[5] standards that are replacing Anglo-American Cataloging Rules (AACR2)[6] . RDA standards follow functional standards for bibliographic records (FRBR). These rules are designed to aid in the construction of library catalogs. They cover the description of the material and provide access points for the material. The rules answer these questions:

- What does the material look like?
- Who published it?
- What are the *access points* — title, author, subjects?

The RDA standards are fairly new and are now being adopted by the national libraries, which are libraries that are established by the government of a nation to serve as the repository of information for the country. These libraries are currently conducting intensive training for full implementation. The adoption of RDA standards by these libraries will certainly lead to adoption by all libraries. RDA standards use FRBR, a system that attempts to improve our access to bibliographic records in the online environment.[7] It attempts to establish a bibliographic relationship using the following four concepts: item, manifestation, expression, and work. It is a "one bibliographic record with many formats" approach, which makes it easier to search for and discover items in the online catalogs that we all widely depend on, instead of using the traditional system of one bibliographic record for each format. Standards are finally being put in place that will allow easier search discovery of items using online catalogs.

The process of classification attempts to determine what materials will be shelved together, as well as what *call number* will be assigned. If the correct subject analysis is not done on the material, then the correct call number will not be assigned. If this happens, the material may not be found and could be lost on the law library shelves. If the acquisitions department did not decide on the physical location of the material, it is decided now. Again, this depends on the collection-development policy of the library, the arrangement of the physical library collection, and the type of material that was selected.

Authority control is another function of the cataloging department. Authority control is the consistent use and maintenance of the access points or forms of names, subjects, and uniform titles. These access points are usually revised against an online bibliographic utility, such as OCLC, for accuracy. The library's copy-cataloger or cataloger can perform authority control at the same time that they are are revising and editing the bibliographic record for addition to the library catalog. Authority control should be done regularly as part of database maintenance. Many integrated library systems run reports that advise the users of authority conflicts. If authority control has been outsourced, the cataloging department periodically sends copies of the most recent bibliographic records to vendors for authority-control processing. Vendors that offer this service include Marcive,[8] Library Technologies,[9] and Backstage Library Works (MARS Automated Authority Control).[10] These services offer law libraries name and subject authority records based on the Library of Congress name and subject authority databases. The authority-control process standardizes name, subject, series, and uniform title headings. During this process, copies of bibliographic records are sent to the vendors. Corrections are then made to the bibliographic records. The corrected bibliographic records are then returned to the law library electronically, and then the incorrect records are replaced in the integrated library system.

When materials arrive from the acquisitions department, they may be divided into shelf-ready materials, copy-cataloging materials, or materials that need to be routed directly to a professional cataloger for review. The shelf-ready materials need minimal processing. Shelf-ready materials arrive at the law library with property stamps, barcodes, and call number spine labels. Barcodes must be entered into the law library's local catalogs for easy access; call numbers are shelf listed. In the process of shelf listing, the call numbers that are on the spine will be compared to the law library's local catalogs for conflicts with other works, multiple copies, and other library-specific location changes. Many law libraries have copy-catalogers, who may revise and review materials received before forwarding these materials to professional catalogers. These individuals usually catalog the materials—that is, physically describe them—but leave the subject analysis and the call number assignment to the professional catalogers. If the materials that are purchased are in an electronic format, they obviously do not have a physical manifestation. Catalogers will need to make such titles accessible for discovery by library patrons. Links to the materials will need to be created and often revised to make sure that they are valid.

Most law libraries are arranged according to the Library of Congress classification system and Library of Congress subject headings. Currently, both the schedules and the subject headings are available in a variety of formats. For the benefit of space and accessibility, many law libraries opt to access the schedules and subject headings electronically, via the Library of Congress Classification Web (LC).[11] What are these, and how can they assist in cataloging? Classification Web is currently the only

Web-based subscription service that features the entire Library of Congress classification system and the complete list of Library of Congress subject headings and name headings. You can construct, verify, and assign classification numbers, subject headings, and name headings to library material using the most current data. This is a paid subscription service that is updated on a daily basis. The benefit of this electronic format is that updates are immediate and that libraries can purchase licenses for multiple users, allowing usage by more that one cataloging staff member at a time. The downside is that browsing generally tends to be more difficult, and network availability is essential for working with up-to-date schedules or subject headings.

Most law libraries are members of computer library services, such as OCLC (Online Computer Library Center). OCLC provides catalogers with bibliographic utilities and online union catalogs, as well as support in the form of training and tutorials. Member catalogers may use these networks to assist them with bibliographic data. Member libraries share in the editing of bibliographic records and holdings and the input of such records into this online union catalog, and these records are then exported and made available to the general public via their online catalogs. OCLC offers its members WorldCat, which is the world's largest online union catalog. WorldCat allows law libraries to process, manage, and share information resources. WorldCat makes its records available to Internet users on popular search sites, allows linking to contents in library collections, and makes member-library collections more visible. [12]

Another function of the cataloging department is database maintenance. Database maintenance involves location changes of materials, removal from the catalog of titles withdrawn from the shelves, addition of added copies, and general cleanup of bibliographic records that may be duplicates or just obsolete. This process assures the integrity of the data loaded into the integrated library system database. Due to the advent of online integrated library systems, an interrelated environment has been created in which data placed in one module of the library system directly affects how other modules are able to utilize the data. For example, the library staff member in cataloging who handles these issues needs to work closely with the acquisitions department as well as the serials/continuations departments when there is a location change. The item's records—including bibliographic, item, and location holdings—not only need to be updated, but if the item is a serial, the check-in record and the purchase order record need to be updated as well. If this is not done, materials will not go to their proper location when they are updated again. If the library decides to cancel a title and withdraw it from the collection, not only must librarians physically discard the item, but the acquisitions and or serials/continuations departments also need to be notified to cancel their records; otherwise, they will be claiming materials from vendors for which they have cancelled their subscriptions. The cataloging department needs to remove the item's holdings from their online catalog, as well as make sure that the item has been physically removed from the library's physical collection. All of the departments within the library, not only within technical services, must work together and communicate effectively to ensure the smooth and proper functioning of the law library.

Budget cuts and downsizing are very common in law libraries. In order to minimize spending and optimize staffing, some law libraries are outsourcing many technical services functions, such as cataloging, processing of materials, and authority control. Although in theory outsourcing is a good idea, libraries should realize that sometimes this outsourcing may create more work and generate more problems that need to be resolved. The law library should fully understand what services it is getting when it outsources. It should maintain open communication channels with the service provider in order to ensure a smooth and productive relationship. Profiles need to be carefully created and reviewed regularly, not only when there seems to be a problem. Several trial runs should be conducted before any service agreements are entered into. When these services are successful, they greatly benefit the library. But if the services become a burden, the law library should review the decision and the relationship. If outsourcing is decided upon, it is essential that law library administration involve technical services personnel in the planned-outsourcing process. These staff members are great assets during the profiling and trial period. Because they have experience doing the work, the staff can identify potential problems.

Another area that is usually handled within the technical services department, and specifically by the cataloger or technical services librarian, is the maintenance, implementation, and migration of the integrated library system. These librarians often serve as systems librarians, especially in the smaller law libraries, where staffing and contact with IT or information service departments are limited. Because maintenance, implementation, and migration usually involve many decisions that are based on bibliographic data, the technical services librarian and their staff are the most qualified individuals to assist and make suggestions. Data migration has specific parameters that need to be decided upon before any data are loaded into a current database for use. If the data are not correctly identified and transferred into the appropriate fields or parameters, they will be useless for the library's staff and its patrons. In many law libraries, the cataloger is the one involved with technical software issues concerning the new integrated library system, as well as training staff to use the various integrated library system modules, such as circulation, acquisitions, and serials.

The technical services professional is usually the one responsible for monitoring the availability of the integrated library system on a daily basis. This individual puts together any information or training that may be needed after there is an upgrade or migration from one system to another. These are related to staffing issues and workflow reassignment within the specific library. This position may also coordinate in-house training by the library vendor when deemed necessary. Few technical services professionals have any formal training in systems operations, but they are an invaluable source of information for the IT departments, which usually handle the hardware issues involving the integrated library systems. Technical services staff have an understanding of how materials are arranged in an online environment and how these items can best be searched. This, if coordinated and properly addressed in an online environment, will ensure the success of any integrated library system that is implemented.

SERIALS/CONTINUATIONS

The majority of the materials that law libraries acquire and collect fall into the following formats: monographs, serials/continuations, integrating resources, electronic resources, and microforms. For purposes of budgeting and statistics, they are divided into these categories as well. How are these different formats defined? The Anglo-American Cataloging Rules (AACR2) defines the terms as follows:[13]

> *Serial:* A continuing resource issued in a succession of discrete parts, usually bearing numbering, that has no predetermined conclusion. It is material that is uniquely identified with enumeration, chronology, and possibly a date, that is usually issued in successive parts and is intended to be continued indefinitely.

> *Monograph:* A bibliographic resource that is complete or is intended to be completed within a finite number of parts or within a fixed period of time—meaning, nonserial in nature. These are works that are either complete in one part or intended to be completed in a finite number of separate parts, with no intention of updating or supplementing.

> *Integrating Resource:* A bibliographic resource that is added or changed by means of updates that do not remain discrete and are integrated in the whole. Integrating resources can be finite or continuing. Examples include updating loose-leafs and updating Web sites.

> *Electronic Resources:* Materials (date and/or programs) encoded for manipulation by a computerized device. These materials may require the use of a peripheral directly connected to a computerized device or a computer network. These materials may be in the form of CD-ROMs, databases, or Web sites.

Microform: Any medium, transparent or opaque, bearing images. In this format we find microfilm and microfiche.

Because law is dynamic in nature, most of the materials will fall into the serials/continuations category. Serials subscriptions will be in the form of periodicals, such as law reviews, newsletters, and journals, as well as annuals of different types. There are also pocket parts and supplements to law library monographs. Check-in of materials in the serials department provides technical services professionals with an endless amount of work. Proper check-in of materials into the integrated library system enables the librarian and the online catalog user to locate the most current issue, update, or supplement that the library has received. The check-in process also assists the law library with invoicing. It helps to ensure that the law library is only paying for materials that it has received and currently owns.

Law libraries spend a great deal of time keeping services up to date and subscriptions to periodicals current. Print reporters, loose-leaf services, and periodicals all require continuous updating and monitoring. Sometimes these services are also outsourced. In order to effectively outsource these services, law libraries should randomly monitor the services to ensure that they follow library procedures concerning discards, duplicates, and missing issues.

The serials/continuations departments often handle binding. Traditionally, law libraries have bound periodicals. With reduced budgets, space restrictions, and the advent of online electronic periodicals, many law libraries no longer bind their periodicals, and may even withdraw large print collections in order to provide more reading and study space for their patrons. Should a law library decide to continue binding periodical issues, there are several commercial binderies available for their use.

ELECTRONIC RESOURCES

Futurists are positing that the library of the future will be a *virtual library.* Virtual libraries provide patrons with electronic access to information. While law libraries are still required to maintain collections in a variety of formats, most still offer access to both print and electronic materials. How are technical services departments affected by electronic resources?

Electronic resources present significant issues for acquisitions, cataloging, and serials/continuations. In acquisitions, librarians are faced with licensing issues. In cataloging, decisions need to be made as to whether the item will be listed on only the law library's Web page or also included in the library's catalog. If the library decides to allow individual title access within the catalog, adding individual records to the library databases may be cumbersome, and the linked sites must be regularly checked for new, deleted, and updated titles, in order to keep the catalogs up to date. Who will be responsible for checking the accuracy of the links? Will this be the responsibility of the cataloging department? If so, they will need to engage the assistance of commercial link-checking software if the integrated library system does not supply one. In the serials/continuations department, check-in records can be created to track annual renewals for electronic subscriptions so that there is no service interruption for the library user.

STATISTICS

What are we counting? What should we be counting? How are we counting? For whom are we counting? To whom should we be reporting our counting?

What are we counting? In technical services, everything is counted. The workflow is methodical and concrete. Materials arrive, they are handled, and they are put out on the shelves. When the materials arrived, to what categories did they correspond? Were monographs or serials purchased? If it is an electronic resource, is it a database? Does it provide access to full texts or simply citations?

What should we be counting? Again, *everything!* The counts seem to be used to justify law library budgets; to help us rethink collection-development policies; to validate the need for extra personnel by evaluating and reevaluating jobs in order to eliminate unnecessary procedures and incorporate new ones; and to create new and update current job descriptions that accurately assess and describe what library staff currently spend their time doing.[14] Law librarians have devised several methods of counting. Most law libraries are moving to keeping statistics using the aid of their online integrated library systems (ILS). Usually the ILS will report statistics for usage; added bibliographic records; deleted item records; purchase orders entered; items ordered, received, or checked in; and titles cataloged in a certain classification.

The information reported by the online library systems is accurate if the input has been standardized. In other words, the quality of what you input equals the quality of your output. Do all online library systems count the same things the same way? If the codes used are not standardized, the output for statistics will be unreliable. Most law libraries have devised local statistics on spreadsheets that allow them to customize what and how they want things counted. Librarians count to justify the need for an increase in law library budgets. They are also required to report annual statistics to the ABA (American Bar Association), as well as to any law library consortia in which they are members. If the law libraries are part of a university system, they will also need to supply certain statistics for the governing bodies of the university as well. Numbers are important, and we will probably have to keep counting forever. Innovative as we are, we will keep devising ingenious ways of keeping statistics in the future that will not involve individuals keeping manual counts of any type.

What should we be counting?[15] The ABA no longer requires law libraries to report on volume or title counts, and has recently asked that the number of electronic titles be reported. For years, the volume and title counts seemed insignificant compared to the overall collection. The age of the collection and the quality of what was being reported were never addressed, making the numbers meaningless and not a useful tool for any kind of qualitative analysis. Most law libraries continue to count all materials received and cataloged in order to justify workflow and for reporting to bodies other than the ABA.

The ABA's decision to ask us to report electronic titles has once again faced us with a new dilemma. What do we count?[16] Do we count what is accessible, what is licensed, or only titles that the library has actually purchased? How do we count titles that are jointly purchased with our university campus libraries? What exactly is ownership, and how do we define it? The ABA has attempted to address these questions. But in reviewing their suggestions, what are seen as answers are actually guidelines. At this time, there is no clear answer as to what we should be counting. Therefore, a rule of thumb is to keep copious notes of what materials your library counts and how, and to make sure that it is consistent from report to report and year to year, so that the how and why of your statistics can be justified if questioned by anyone at any time.

CONCLUSION

Technical service in law libraries has traditionally involved the acquisition, processing, and classification of materials. While technology has changed the workflow of the department, as well as some of the job tasks, it has not eliminated the need for technical services librarians. Instead it has made the job of the technical services librarians more technically oriented. Acquisitions, cataloging, and serials/continuation continue to require the presence of trained professional librarians. Technology may be changing how these jobs are done, but it is not eradicating the need for these jobs to be done.

NOTES

1. HeinOnline. www.heinonline.org.

2. Joint Steering Committee for Revision of AACR, *Anglo-American Cataloging Rules* (AACR2), 2nd ed. (Ottawa, ON: Canadian Library Association, 2002).

3. WorldCat (OCLC). www.worldcat.org.

4. Serials Section, Acquisitions Committee Association for Library Collections & Technical Services, "Serials Acquisitions Glossary," 3rd ed., rev. (American Library

Association, 2005). http://www.ala.org/alcts/sites/ala.org.alcts/files/content/resources/collect/serials/acqglossary/05seracq_glo.pdf.

5. Chris Oliver, *Introducing RDA: A Guide to the Basics* (London: Facet Publishing, 2010).

6. Joint Steering Committee for Revision of AACR, *Anglo-American Cataloging Rules*.

7. Oliver, *Introducing RDA*.

8. Marcive, Inc. www.marcive.com.

9. Library Technologies, Inc. www.librarytech.com.

10. Backstage Library Works. http://www.bslw.com.

11. Library of Congress, "Classification Web: World Wide Web Access to Library of Congress Classification and Library of Congress Subject Headings," http://classificationweb.net.

12. WorldCat (OCLC). www.worldcat.org.

13. Joint Steering Committee for Revision of AACR, *Anglo-American Cataloging Rules*.

14. T. Fitchett, J. Hambleton, P. Hazelton, A. Klinefelter, and J. Wright, "Law Library Budgets in Hard Times," *Law Library Journal* 103, no. 1 (2011): 91–111.

15. American Association of Law Libraries, "Report to Law Library Directors on Upcoming Changes in the ABA Questionnaires," http://www.aallnet.org/sis/allsis/committees/liaisons/abachanges2008.asp.

16. Ibid.

ELEVEN

The Evolution of Government Documents

Federal Documents — A Brief Historical Overview

Jennifer Bryan Morgan

FOUNDATIONS AND THE NINETEENTH CENTURY

The evolution of government documents is intertwined with the history of government printing. In the formative era of the United States, government printing was handled by private printers and newspaper publishers.[1] Following the American Revolution, public printing was first mentioned in a House recommendation in 1789; proposals were invited for "printing the acts and other proceedings of Congress."[2] Private printers were hired, and in turn, followed Congress from New York to Philadelphia in 1790 and then to Washington in 1800. The first inkling of a federal depository library program became evident in 1813, when Congress authorized legislation to ensure the distribution of congressional documents. The Resolution of 1813 provided that the journals of Congress would be furnished to certain universities, colleges, historical societies, and state libraries.[3] Thus, today's U.S. Government Printing Office dates their core mission ("Keeping America Informed") back to 1813, when Congress specified the need to make information regarding the work of the three branches of government available to all Americans.[4] The United States Congressional Serial Set (the earliest continuous and longest-lived publication compiled under directive of the Congress) began publication in 1817 with the fifteenth Congress.[5] Today's Serial Set contains the House and Senate documents and reports and is bound by session of

Congress. Historically, congressional material in the Serial Set included the committee reports, journals, manuals, and administrative reports of both chambers, in addition to a variety of directories, orations, and special publications (such as illustrated descriptions of the Capitol). During the late nineteenth and early twentieth centuries, executive-branch materials were also published in the Serial Set, including messages of the president of the United States, annual administrative reports of departments and agencies, series publications (such as the *Geological Survey Bulletins*), and periodicals (such as the *Monthly Summary of Foreign Commerce* and *Monthly Consular Reports*). Other types of serialized executive documents published in the Serial Set included Bureau of Labor and Bureau of Labor Statistics bulletins, Census Bureau *Statistical Abstracts*, Smithsonian Institution's Bureau of Ethnology reports and bulletins, and Department of State commercial relations, commercial policy, and foreign relations series.[6] In 1818, concerned that its proceedings be accurately and promptly recorded, Congress appointed a joint committee to consider whether a statutory requirement was "necessary to ensure despatch [sic], accuracy, and neatness, in the printing done by order of the two Houses [of Congress]."[7] And in 1819 the committee's report recommended that Congress establish

> a National Printing Office (with a bindery and stationery annexed,) which should execute the work of Congress while in session, and that of the various Departments of Government during the recess; and should do all the binding, and furnish the stationery, for the Departments, as well as for Congress. The committee are of opinion that such an establishment under the superintendence of a man of activity, integrity, and discretion, would be likely to produce promptitude, uniformity, accuracy, and elegance, in the execution of public printing.[8]

The advice of the committee was not heeded, and a resolution of March 3, 1819, directed the House and the Senate to elect their own printers, instruct their work, and establish what price to pay for the press work.[9]

In the years that followed, numerous printers petitioned for employment by the Congress, bidding wars followed, a failed contract system of printing was operated, appropriations continued to be made for "printing, stationery, and fuel," and various committees were appointed to investigate the subject of public printing.[10] These investigations into printing activities uncovered corruption, profiteering, excessive and useless printing, and exorbitant political contributions paid by printers.[11] Records describe how members of Congress contentiously debated the election of printers. "In 1827 the debates show that the public printing was regarded as patronage used by the party in power to aid in supporting its 'organ.' The abuse of this patronage, however, became so flagrant that the House in 1828 ordered an investigation upon the subject of public printing. This investigation exposed a most extraordinary condition of

things and led to wholesome reforms."[12] Yet future investigations continued to expose further corruptions, and the committees continued to recommend the establishment of a public printing office. Finally, in 1852, an
act of Congress provided for the appointment of a superintendent of
public printing and directed that he supervise the work done by the
elected printers.[13] The superintendent position, however, became a political plum, as "[p]oliticians who had no practical knowledge of printing
succeeded in securing the place of printer, and farmed out the work to
practical printers at a percentage of the receipts. The dominant party
elected the printer with a positive understanding that he would devote
specified sums out of his own profits for partisan purposes."[14] The act
also appointed a Joint Committee on the Public Printing, and empowered
it to mediate disputes between the superintendent and printers, and to
use any measures deemed necessary to remedy any neglect or delay in
the execution of the public printing.[15]

By 1860, several House and Senate committees were investigating all
phases of public printing and binding,[16] and thus provoked the proposal
of a reform bill calling for the establishment of a government printing
office. The *Joint Resolution in Relation to the Public Printing* (No. 25) was
signed into law by President James Buchanan on June 23, 1860, and provided that the superintendent of public printing be "authorized and directed to have executed the printing and binding authorized by the Senate and House of Representatives, the executive and judicial departments, and the Court of Claims. And to enable him to carry out the
provisions of this act, he is authorized and directed to contract for the
erection or purchase of the necessary buildings, machinery, and materials
for that purpose."[17] The government purchased a private printing plant
near the Capitol, and the Government Printing Office (GPO) opened for
business on March 4, 1861, the same day that Abraham Lincoln was
inaugurated president. The first GPO presses were steam powered, and
ink was made from a mixture of oil and lampblack. In the composing
room, where gas fixtures illuminated the night, composers set type by
hand, and women were employed in the bindery to fold printed sheets
by hand.[18]

During the nineteenth century, a succession of public printers oversaw the Government Printing Office through important events such as
the Civil War, Reconstruction, presidential assassinations, the installation
of an electrical power plant, World War I, the Spanish–American War,
advances in printing technology, building additions and construction,
and innovations in personnel management and accounting systems.[19]
During the Reconstruction years, the GPO acquired the responsibility for
printing the *Congressional Record*,[20] taking over the reporting of the debate and proceedings of Congress from the newspaper trade. GPO produced its first issue of the *Record* on March 5, 1873. However, the most
significant event to occur during the nineteenth century was perhaps the

passage of the Printing Act of 1895.[21] The act codified all of the laws relating to the GPO and to public printing in general. (Today, Title 44 of the United States Code includes chapters that define the activities of the GPO and form the foundation for government printing and public dissemination.) The Printing Act of 1895 centralized in the GPO the printing and binding required by the three branches of government and attempted to prevent printing at private plants. At that time, the GPO truly became the federal government's primary centralized resource for gathering, cataloging, producing, providing, and preserving published information in all its forms. The Printing Act of 1895 also created the office of the superintendent of documents in the Government Printing Office. Prior to 1895, the secretary of the interior was responsible for the general distribution of government printed materials,[22] until the act of 1869[23] created the office of the superintendent of public documents in the Department of the Interior. In 1895, "[t]he new officer succeeded to the duty of distributing publications to depository libraries, was given authority to sell government publications, and was charged with the duty of preparing monthly, annual, and biennial indexes."[24]

In May 1895, Adelaide Hasse became the first documents librarian at the GPO. Her duties included caring for the documents in the GPO library, as well as pulling together collections that were stored around the Capitol. Within six weeks of her arrival at the GPO, she organized and classified nearly three hundred thousand documents, including duplicates.[25] But her most significant accomplishment was that during her employment at the GPO, Hasse developed the superintendent of documents (SuDocs) classification system.[26] The SuDocs system is still used by libraries today to classify and organize federal government publications.

The Twentieth Century

In 1912, the public printer replaced GPO's horses and wagons with electric trucks. Throughout the twentieth century, the public printers initiated many more modern transitions and oversaw important activities, such as instating hot metal technology, constructing skylights, providing better ventilation and a new cafeteria in the GPO building, installing a five-color offset press, collective bargaining, traveling overseas, and becoming active in the international community of printers.[27] World War I resulted in the largest production in GPO's history, as a rush was made for government printing from 1911 to 1918. Important changes were also in store for the Depository Library Program. Since 1895, all publications had been distributed to all designated depository libraries. Language in an appropriations bill for fiscal year 1923 allowed depositories to select particular publications by providing that, "no part of [the appropriation for the Office of the Superintendent of Documents] shall be used to supply to depository libraries any documents, books, or other printed matter not requested by such libraries."[28] The superintendent of documents then sent to depositories a classified list of documents from which they could select the materials that best suited the needs of their patrons.[29] During the Great Depression, the public printer, under the Economy Act of June 30, 1932, adopted a five-day (forty-hour) workweek and instituted a reduction in pay for GPO employees.[30]

A new public printer, Augustus E. Giegengack, at last, was able to convince Congress that the existing GPO buildings were hazardous firetraps. Construction was completed on the new eight-story GPO building in February 1940. Giegengack's other significant accomplishments during his tenure included modernizing and improving the appearance of publications by creating a Typography and Design Division and obtaining a reduction in costs through changes in makeup and typographic detail.[31] World War II brought increased production, as the GPO began to receive war-related orders and Public Printer Giegengack conferred with leaders in the printing industry to arrange partnerships to secure supplemental commercial production. After the war, printing-press technology evolved and the GPO shifted from hot metal to offset printing.[32]

During the second half of the twentieth century, the public printers shepherded the GPO through the Korean War, civil defense concerns, modern improvements in lighting systems, the addition of new presses, McCarthyism, modernization of printing equipment and procedures, the installation of a new page photocomposition system, internal reorganizations, the assassination of President Kennedy, studies on the commercial procurement of printing, new technologies (such as microforms), and the "computer age."[33] The Federal Depository Library Program continued to grow; from 555 designated depositories in 1945 to 1,200 depositories in 1977.[34] In the early 1970s, concerns arose involving the lack of modernization in the Depository Library Program and the Document Sales Service.[35] Problems were addressed by boosting appropriations; increasing the number of full-time employees; automating the *Monthly Catalog*, mailing lists, and order processing; and creating the online Publications Reference File. At this time, the Depository Library Council to the public printer was formalized.[36] The council consists of fifteen documents librarians who are appointed by the public printer. "The purpose of the Depository Library Council to the Public Printer is to provide advice on policy matters dealing with the Depository Library Program as provided in Title 44 U.S.C. The primary focus of Council's work will be to advise the Public Printer, the Superintendent of Documents, and appropriate members of GPO staff on practical options for the efficient management and operation of the DLP."[37]

In 1977, advances in technology allowed for the production of the *Federal Register* to shift from hot metal to photocomposition, and for the conversion of the entire text of the *Code of Federal Regulations* to an electronic database.[38] Technology also allowed the public printer to effect cost-saving measures, such as the use of microforms in sales and in the Depository Library Program. The Depository Library Council undertook the Microform Project Initiatives, and in March 1977, the Joint Committee on Printing authorized the GPO to produce microfilm publications "to determine if there could be cost savings and/or better service provided to the library distribution program through the use of microfilm."[39] Coopers and Lybrand, the consulting firm that performed the study on GPO operations in 1978, observed that micrographics was the subject of intense debate at the time, and argued that microform distribution would increase the number of documents distributed and would save money (first-year savings estimated to be in excess of one million dollars).[40] Coopers and Lybrand concluded "that GPO should be allowed to expand its use of microfilm technology to include sales by the Superintendent of Documents and allow micropublishing to be offered as a general GPO service."[41] In 1979, as a cost-reduction strategy, GPO offered depository libraries the choice of receiving the Serial Set in paper or as a microfilmed edition.[42]

During the 1980s, more and more of the congressional print work shifted to electronic processing, and GPO facilities were converted to accommodate the ongoing computerization of the trade.[43] Public printers throughout the history of the U.S. Government Printing Office have set their goals on reducing the cost of printing, applying new technologies, and increasing productivity. However, during the last two decades of the twentieth century, GPO's production of printed documents decreased. The reason was twofold: federal budgetary constraints and the electronic transformation of government information.[44] Actions to reduce the amount of paperwork and to lower government expenditures curtailed funds for printing and publishing.[45] In the 1980s and 1990s, as federal agencies were expected to justify their printing needs in an era of rising inflation, the number of publications that were available declined—titles were terminated, consolidated, or made available only on the Internet or on electronic bulletin boards, and as a result, GPO's revenues dropped.[46] It became evident that GPO was facing serious challenges in "keeping America informed," as desktop publishing and electronic formats contributed to the deterioration of GPO's centralization and control of printing.[47] Focusing on the challenges posed by the developing electronic information phenomenon, Congress held hearings in 1985 to examine the status of federal information-collection and dissemination technology and the surrounding policy issues, and in 1986 produced an assessment with their findings and recommendations.[48] "These findings revealed a relatively new technology of growing use and application, one conveying considerable discretionary capability to federal agencies concerning government information management, while simultaneously outstripping the existing practical limitations and legal structures governing many aspects of the government information life cycle."[49] Then in 1988 the Office of Technology Assessment (OTA) published a report addressing the opportunities for improving the dissemination of federal information, which highlighted two major problems: "maintaining equity in public access to Federal information in electronic formats, and defining the respective roles of Federal agencies and the private sector in the electronic dissemination process."[50] Focusing on the current and future roles of the GPO and the superintendent of documents, and the Depository Library Program,

> [the] OTA concluded that the government needs to set in motion a comprehensive planning process for creatively exploring the long-term future (e.g., 10 to 20 years from now) when the information infrastructure of the public and private sectors could be quite different. At the same time, the government needs to provide short-term direction to existing agencies and institutions with respect to electronic information dissemination. A central challenge is setting future directions for the governmentwide [sic] information dissemination institutions.[51]

Congress mandated GPO's official transition into electronic publishing by enacting the Government Printing Office Electronic Information Access Enhancement Act of 1993.[52] The act amended Title 44 U.S.C. to require GPO to disseminate government information products online, to maintain an online directory or locator of federal information sources in electronic format, and to address permanent public access by establishing a storage facility for electronic information files. GPO launched its Internet information service site one year later, in June 1994, and, in addition to providing online versions of the *Federal Register* and *Congressional Record*, GPO created a legislative database that would contain all published versions of House and Senate bills starting with the 103rd Congress. GPO Access provided free online access to more than three hundred thousand federal government document titles, and the information offered through this service was considered the official, published version.[53] Developments concerning the challenges and opportunities of increased federal government use of the Internet continued to arise into the 1990s, and further studies examined issues such as preserving electronic material, ensuring public access, and "the erosion of the Public Printer's authority to supervise the public printing system."[54] GPO had become as much a procurement agency as a printer, with the majority of noncongressional production being obtained under standing contracts negotiated by GPO with the private sector.[55]

During the era of government downsizing and economizing in the mid-90s, Congress, working with the staff of the Joint Committee on Printing, held hearings to examine issues affecting the reform of Title 44 U.S.C., the provisions of which were seen as arcane and not accommodating of changing technology and policy developments.[56] In the 104th Congress, proposals were made to downsize GPO, reduce its resources, privatize public printing, and abolish the Joint Committee on Printing.[57] The 105th Congress revisited the issue of printing reform and formed a legislative working group, consisting of staff from the Joint Committee on Printing, the Office of Management and Budget, and the Senate Committee on Rules and Administration. The three main goals for reform of Title 44 U.S.C. were to:

- Resolve constitutional issues regarding the appropriate roles of the legislative, judicial, and executive Branches in the production of government publications and other printing.
- Improve efficiency and economy in the production of government publications and the printing of government materials, including relying increasingly on private sector procurement.
- Enhance public access to government publications in the electronic era, while ensuring that a safety net exists for those without computer technology.[58]

Subsequently, a consensus reform bill, the Wendell H. Ford Government Publications Reform Act of 1998,[59] was introduced on July 10, 1998. The bill initially enjoyed broad support, including support from the library community, which was "united in the belief that [the Act] must be passed to strengthen the current Federal Depository Library Program and to enhance public access to both tangible publications and those created or transmitted through an electronic communications system or network."[60] However, the proposed legislation was not enacted before the close of the 105th Congress, and due to leadership changes in the 106th Congress, efforts were not made to renew the reform effort.

During this same period, librarians began to discuss their vision of a reinvented Federal Depository Library Program (FDLP). In 1993 two documents were reported out of these discussions that articulated the tenets of a model federal information program:

- The FDLP would be characterized by timely, equitable, and no-fee provision of government information to the public with a cooperative network of information-producing agencies, geographically dispersed participating libraries, and a central coordinating government authority.
- The information would be made available in formats most appropriate to content, use, and audience, and defining legislation would be broadly inclusive of all types of information in all formats and media.
- Agency participation would be assured, and the program should facilitate partnerships between its constituents. [61]

In 1995, Congress directed the public printer to initiate a cooperative study to help redefine a new and strengthened federal information-dissemination policy and program. The study involved representatives from the legislative, executive, and judicial branches of the government, as well as the depository library community, the national library associations, the information industry, and other appropriate government and public entities. [62] A draft report was issued after the study concluded in March 1996. The basic principles for federal government information, developed as part of the study, are as follows:

- Principle 1: The public has the right of access to government information.
- Principle 2: The government has an obligation to disseminate and provide broad public access to its information.
- Principle 3: The government has an obligation to guarantee the authenticity and integrity of its information.
- Principle 4: The government has an obligation to preserve its information.
- Principle 5: Government information created or compiled by government employees or at government expense should remain in the public domain. [63]

Public comment was invited in response to the document, and the public printer issued his final report and the strategic "Transition Plan" for completing the move from print to electronic format in June 1996. The implementation timetable initially projected a two-and-a-half year conversion schedule, but after receiving input from publishing agencies and depository libraries, the public printer extended the timeframe to a more realistic and cost-effective five- to seven-year transition schedule. [64] The transition plan resulted in an aggressive program of conversion to electronic formats, both at the production level and at the distribution level. GPO's transformation became swiftly evident. For example, within two years of the final report's issuance, the percentage of paper products distributed to depository libraries dropped from 45 percent to 30 percent, and microfiche dropped from 50 percent to 20 percent, while electronic products increased from 5 percent to 50 percent. [65] By 2006, more than 92 percent of new titles made available through the FDLP were electronic, whether or not they were also available in tangible form. [66] In fiscal year 2005, GPO distributed a total of 5,285,169 tangible copies of 10,301 titles to depository libraries (7,714 of these titles were on paper). [67]

GOVERNMENT DOCUMENTS IN THE TWENTY-FIRST CENTURY

At the beginning of the twentieth century, the activities of the Government Printing Office fell into three classes: public printing and binding, the furnishing of blank paper, and the distribution of printed publications. [68] By 1978, GPO distributed publications in microfiche; CD-ROM products followed in 1988, the GPO Access Web site for online publications was developed in 1994, and other initiatives to harness government information on the Internet soon followed. While the *Congressional Record* and *Federal Register* continued to be produced at its main plant, GPO transformed into a digital information-processing facility at the dawn of the twenty-first century.[69] At the end of 2004, GPO released a document, "Strategic Vision for the 21st Century," which provided a framework for how it would carry out and fund its transformation goals—to develop a future digital system to anchor all future operations, to reorganize the agency into new product- and service-oriented business lines, along with investment in the necessary technologies; to adopt management best practices across the agency, including retraining to provide needed skills, and to relocate the GPO to facilities that are sized and equipped to meet future needs.[70] So, in an attempt to cope with economic realities, GPO concentrated on disseminating information rather than on printing it, and made plans to bring revenues in the door. Law librarians expressed concerns with some of the policies proposed in the "Strategic Vision"— that the policies didn't ensure GPO's commitment to no-fee public access, that changes in the distribution of print materials would have a negative impact on authentic government information, and, primarily, that "the important issues of version control, authenticity, and permanent public access [would] not [be] addressed."[71]

The information environment changed rapidly in the last decade of the twentieth century. The federal government continued to develop its Internet presence and offer emergent electronic services to the public, and as the twenty-first century dawned, depository librarians and libraries again considered redefining their roles. In 2001, Shuler argued that "a national system of depository libraries [was] no longer needed"[72] to distribute government information, because "the Internet has redefined and displaced the concepts of 'ownership' and accessibility."[73] Jacobs, Jacobs, and Yeo, on the other hand, asserted in 2005 that in the digital age, the traditional roles of FDLP libraries in selecting, acquiring, organizing, preserving, and providing access to and services for government information are more important than ever.[74] In 2005, the Depository Library Council (DLC) drafted a discussion paper that envisioned the future of the provision of government information and the role of the federal depository libraries in it.[75] The DLC held conversations with GPO staff and solicited input from librarians at its meetings in the fall of 2005. At the fall meeting, the DLC presented the major points of the discussion paper to the public printer, GPO staff, and attending librarians. The DLC identified the following four issues for strategic planning: roles of federal depository libraries in the nonexclusive environment of the Internet, managing collections and delivering content, deploying expertise, and adding value.[76] For further discussion about the best practices and responsibilities of a new depository library, GPO's education and outreach, library services and content management provided a "Top-10 List" for new depository staff, which is provided at the end of the book.

RECENT GPO INITIATIVES

By 2006, GPO was working on multiple enterprises to continue its transformation from a nineteenth-century printing-press operation to a twenty-first-century electronic information agency. Such transformational projects included the following examples:[77]

- An integrated library system (ILS) to modernize GPO's older legacy systems. One component of the ILS, the new *Catalog of Government Publications* (CGP), is part of the *National Bibliography of U.S. Publications* (a comprehensive index of public documents from all three branches of the federal government). On March 9, 2006, GPO launched the enhanced version of the CGP at http://catalog.gpo.gov/. This version of the CGP is the online public access catalog (OPAC) module of the Government Printing Office's new integrated library system. With the availability of the new CGP, phase one of a larger modernization plan to replace older legacy systems is complete.[78]
- An authentication initiative to procure the necessary tools and capabilities for GPO to automate the application of digital signatures on Adobe Acrobat portable document format (PDF) files. In March 2008, GPO began providing authenticated electronic documents on GPO Access. The first documents available in authenticated form were public and private laws from the 110th Congress and the Fiscal Year 2009 Budget. Online PDF documents contain visible digital signatures, which serve the same purpose as handwritten signatures or traditional wax seals on printed documents.[79] A digital signature, viewed through the GPO seal of authenticity, verifies document integrity and authenticity on GPO online federal documents.[80]
- A future digital system to manage, preserve, version, provide access to, and disseminate authentic digital content. In February 2009, GPO's Federal Digital System (FDsys) became operational and eventually replaced GPO Access in March 2012. The Office of the Federal Register's new publication, *Daily Compilation of Presidential Documents*, was specifically engineered for FDsys.[81]
- A digital legacy collection, in which GPO would partner with the Library of Congress and the National Archives and Records Administration to implement a plan to digitize tangible collections of historical documents in federal depository libraries. In 2011, GPO and the Library of Congress collaborated to digitize legislative documents that were then authenticated and made available on FDsys

and THOMAS.gov. The project included public and private laws, proposed constitutional amendments published in *Statutes at Large* from 1951 to 2002, and *Congressional Record* permanent edition volumes from 1873 to 1998.[82] In 2012, GPO and the U.S. Department of the Treasury partnered on a pilot project to make digitized historical documents from the treasury library available on FDsys.[83]

- GPO developed a registry that is a locator tool for publicly accessible collections of digitized U.S. government publications (the Digitization Projects Registry is located at http://registry.fdlp.gov/).
- A revision of the list of *Essential Titles for Public Use in Paper Format* and a next-generation *Federal Depository Library Manual* and *Instructions to Depository Libraries*. In 2010, GPO established its first preservation librarian position, tasked with updating the FDLP collection-management plan for the preservation of federal government documents.[84] In 2012, GPO launched a new e-learning tool to conduct virtual trainings and hold virtual meetings with members of the FDLP.[85]
- The GPO LOCKSS Pilot Project (a digital preservation alliance), which at the time made five government e-journals available to participating pilot libraries. LOCKSS (Lots of Copies Keep Stuff Safe) is open-source software that provides institutions with a way to collect, store, and preserve access to their own local copies of e-journal content. In June 2010, GPO joined LOCKSS to collaborate with federal depository libraries and other organizations on preservation initiatives.[86]
- A pilot project for Web discovery and harvesting, in which efforts were made to discover and retrieve publications from federal agency Web sites that fell within the scope of the FDLP and the National Bibliography Program.
- A review and proposed model for revision of the item-number system used by libraries in the FDLP to select tangible and electronic titles.[87] On February 14, 2006, GPO published revised versions of the briefing papers outlining proposed changes to the system used by federal depository libraries to select tangible and online titles.[88]

The U.S. Government Printing Office began its sesquicentennial anniversary celebration on June 23, 2010, and marked the year by setting up social media sites (YouTube, Twitter, and Facebook) and by launching the "Government Book Talk" blog as a means of bringing more attention to federal publications and GPO operations. In 2011 and 2012, GPO expanded its offering of formats for the public to access federal government information by partnering with Google, Barnes & Noble, and Apple to sell federal e-books. GPO worked with federal agencies to produce their publications, books, and reports in print and digital formats, and made titles available in PDF and e-book formats for the iPad, e-readers, PCs, and Macs. GPO continued to provide the public with new options for accessing federal government information by releasing its first mobile Web application (app) on November 15, 2011. The Mobile Member Guide app is for the *Guide to House and Senate Members*, and features a congressional pictorial directory, as well as other information on every member of the 112th Congress.[89] Other free downloadable apps created by GPO include apps for the FY 2013 Budget, presidential documents, and the "Plum Book" (*United States Policy and Supporting Positions*).[90]

In October 2011, GPO developed a study of the Federal Depository Library Program, "to effectively assess the current needs and future direction of the FDLP for both individual libraries and states." Questionnaires were sent to individual depository libraries, and the responses of individual libraries were incorporated into state-focused action plans, which would "document initiatives and activities that FDLP members in states or Federal depository regions plan to implement in the next five years."[91] In addition, the FDLP study will look at laws governing the program, possible program models, and other data before decisions are made on formulating the FDLP national plan for the future of the program.[92] The Fall 2012 Depository Library Council Meeting and Federal Depository Library Conference included presentations of preliminary results of the FDLP Forecast Study. These sessions provided an overview of the forecast study, information on how the quantitative and qualitative data were analyzed, preliminary findings of the analysis of the thirty-eight state forecasts received by the deadline, state-focused action plans, and a community discussion on the future.[93]

DIGITAL, BUT ALSO TANGIBLE

The U.S. Government Printing Office still produces the daily and permanent editions of the *Congressional Record*, bills, resolutions, amendments, hearings, committee reports, committee prints, documents, stationery, the *Federal Register*, the *President's Budget of the United States Government* for the Office of Management and Budget, the *Public Papers of the President*, and a wide variety of other products in both online and print formats. GPO also produces U.S. passports for the Department of State and a line of secure identification "smart cards" used by a number of federal agencies. All of the work GPO performs for Congress is funded through the annual appropriation for congressional printing and binding.[94]

Tangible government publications are still being distributed to depository libraries; in FY 2011, GPO distributed approximately two million copies of 10,200 individual tangible items to depository libraries.[95] The superintendent of documents maintains the "Essential Titles List," which includes titles that "contain critical information about the U.S. Government or are important reference publications for libraries and the public, and their availability for selection in paper format has been deemed essential for the purposes of the FDLP."[96] However, today the FDLP is predominantly a digital program, as "approximately 97 percent of Federal Government documents are born digitally and published only to the Internet[,] making FDsys the place to go to access authentic, published Government information."[97]

GPO's Federal Digital System (FDsys) provides permanent public access to federal government information from all three branches of the federal government at no charge. FDsys is:

- A content-management system. FDsys provides free online access to official federal government publications and securely controls digital content throughout its lifecycle to ensure content integrity and authenticity.
- A preservation repository. The repository guarantees long-term preservation and access to digital government content.
- An advanced search engine. FDsys combines modern search technology with extensive metadata creation to ensure the highest quality search experience.[98]

Since going live in January 2009, FDsys has achieved 200 million retrievals. Approximately seven million searchable government documents across fifty collections are freely available to the public on FDsys,[99] and more than twenty-five million documents are downloaded every month.[100]

OFFICIAL. DIGITAL. SECURE.

As depository librarians continue to consider the future of the Federal Depository Library Program and to reinvent themselves to accommodate the transformation of government information products, we can only be certain of one thing: "the 19th Century is not coming back. The times have changed and the GPO must change with them if it is to continue carrying out its core mission to keep America informed."[101] The U.S. Government Printing Office has proven its commitment to embracing evolving technologies as the information needs of Congress, federal agencies, and the public have changed. "During a time in which information is increasingly created, disseminated, and stored electronically, GPO will continue to leverage its historical strengths to sustain and advance openness in Government," said Acting Public Printer Davita Vance-Cooks. "We will continue to adapt to and overcome these challenges as we transform ourselves into the Official, Digital Information Platform for the Federal Government and Provider of Secure Credentials."[102]

CHRONOLOGY OF SIGNIFICANT EVENTS AND PUBLIC LAWS
RELATING TO GOVERNMENT PRINTING

1777 In October, the Continental Congress adopts a resolution authorizing the Committee of Intelligence to take measures for getting a printing press erected in Yorktown.[103]

1789 The subject of printing the acts and proceedings of Congress is referred to a special joint committee.[104] A report is adopted by both houses, in which it is left for the secretary of the Senate and the clerk of the House to contract for printing and binding.

1789 From 1789 to 1872, Congress orders that laws be printed in newspapers.[105]

1801 The District of Columbia becomes the seat of the national government. A committee is appointed to expedite the printing of the House. The committee's report directs that a printer for the House be appointed, but this is not carried through.

1803 Departing from tradition, President Jefferson sends a message in writing to Congress with accompanying documents, spurring violent debate over the proposal to have it printed. Five hundred copies of the "Message and Documents" are printed.

1804 Congress empowers the secretary of the Senate and clerk of the House to advertise for proposals for printing.[106] Until 1819 government printing is done under contracts made with the lowest bidder.

1813 On December 27, the first act to specifically authorize the distribution of government publications to libraries in the United States (3 Stat. 140) provides that one copy of the journals and documents of the Senate and House of Representatives be sent to each university and college and to each historical society incorporated in each state. The secretary of state is responsible for distributing publications.

1818 A joint committee is appointed in December to consider the need for further printing laws, and recommends the establishment of a national printing office.

1819 The passage of a joint resolution (3 Stat. 538) provides for each house to elect its own printer. Gales & Seaton of the *National Intelligencer* are elected printers by both houses.

1828 The House orders an investigation into public printing, exposing political corruption, excessive and useless printing, and exorbitant profits obtained by trickery.

1845 The government contracts with Little, Brown & Co. to produce a collection of all public and private laws, foreign treaties, and Indian treaties, chronologically arranged by session of Congress, a series known as *Statutes at Large*.[107]

1846 In hopes of preventing fraud, a joint resolution is passed to establish the contract system of printing.[108]

1852 The Printing Act of 1852 (10 Stat. 30) provides for the appointment of a superintendent of public printing (within the Department of the Interior) to oversee the work done by the printers selected by the Senate and House.

1857 The secretary of the interior is authorized (11 Stat. 253) to distribute government publications and to designate the libraries that receive publications.

1858 A joint resolution (11 Stat. 368) provides that the representative from each district and the delegate from each territory may designate a depository library.

1859 An act (11 Stat. 379) provides that each senator may designate one library to receive government publications. The secretary of the interior is charged with the distribution of all books printed or purchased for the government, with some exceptions (11 Stat. 379). Distribution includes the shipping of documents to depository libraries.

1860 An investigative committee (Select Committee on Public Printing) reports to Congress that the contract system of public printing is a corrupt failure. The Government Printing Office is established by the 1860 Printing Act (12 Stat. 118). The act authorizes the superintendent of public printing to purchase the buildings, machinery, and materials needed to execute the public printing.

1861 The Government Printing Office opens for business on March 4. Abraham Lincoln is inaugurated sixteenth president of the United States on the same day.

1867 On February 22, the office of the superintendent of public printing was abolished, and the office of congressional printer was created. "That person so elected shall be deemed an officer of the Senate, and shall be designated 'congressional printer.'" [109]

1869 On March 3, the office of the superintendent of public documents is created at the Department of the Interior (15 Stat. 292) and is charged with the general distribution of certain government publications.

1873 GPO takes over compiling and printing the *Statutes at Large*. The first GPO-produced issue of the *Congressional Record* appears on March 5.

1874 Dr. John G. Ames becomes superintendent of public documents and retains the post until it is abolished in 1895. "The three great contributions of Dr. Ames were his checklists, with serial numbers assigned to all Congressional Documents from the First to the Fifty-third Congresses, the comprehensive index of government publications covering the years 1881 to 1893, and his work in developing sentiment in Congress for the creation of the office of Superintendent of Documents in the Government Printing Office." [110]

1882 An electrical lighting plant is installed at the GPO.

1895 The Printing Act of 1895 (28 Stat. 601–624) codifies the laws relating to the Government Printing Office and public printing in general. The act abolishes the office of superintendent of public documents in the

Department of the Interior and creates the office of superintendent of documents in the Government Printing Office. In addition to distributing publications to depository libraries, the superintendent is now authorized to sell government publications and is ordered to prepare monthly, annual, and biennial indexes. The act provides for executive department publications to be distributed to depository libraries and designates as depositories the state and territorial libraries, as well as the libraries of the existing (in 1895) executive departments, the Naval Academy, and the Military Academy. There are 420 depository libraries in 1895. The *Monthly Catalog* first appears in 1895. The first depository shipment, containing eleven congressional publications, is shipped on July 17. Congress authorizes the GPO to distribute the *Statutes at Large* to depository libraries. The superintendent of documents (SuDoc) classification system is developed by Adelaide Hasse (in the library of the GPO) between 1895 and 1903.

1896 With the implementation of a new electrical lighting plant, the GPO shifts from steam-powered presses to direct electrical-powered machinery.

1904 The superintendent of documents is given authority (33 Stat. 584) to reprint publications other than congressional documents.

1907 The library of the Philippine government is designated a depository (34 Stat. 850). The libraries of the land-grant colleges are designated depositories (34 Stat. 1014).

1910 The Printing Investigation Commission of Congress issues a preliminary report (61 Cong. 2 Sess., S. Doc. 652) on the subject of branch printing establishments and recommends that all public printing be centralized at the GPO. The printing office of the Weather Bureau is abolished by authorization of the Joint Committee on Printing.

1912 Additional responsibilities charged to the superintendent (37 Stat. 414) include the storing and mailing of executive department publications. The public printer replaces the majority of horses and wagons at the GPO with electric trucks.

1913 An act (38 Stat. 75) provides that the depository designation of a library shall remain permanent.

1917 The legislative, executive, and judicial appropriation act of March 3 (39 Stat. 1083) directs the abolishing of the State, War, and Navy departments' branch printing offices.

1919 Because printing is still being done outside the GPO, the legislative, executive, and judicial appropriation act of 1920 (approved March 1, 40 Stat. 1270) includes a clause to order the centralization of printing at the GPO, with a few exceptions.

1920 The Joint Committee on Printing (JCP) conducts a thorough investigation of the cost of work done at the GPO versus the cost of commercial printing (or private contractors). The JCP concludes (66 Cong. 2 Sess., S. Doc. 265) that "printing and binding can be done at the [GPO] at less cost to the government than printing of similar quality . . . obtained from commercial printers."

1922 An act (42 Stat. 436) provides that depository libraries can select the classes of publications that they wish to receive, instead of receiving every publication issued. For the first time, the superintendent of documents sends to depositories a "Classified list of United States public documents for selection by depository libraries, July 1, 1922." A joint resolution (42 Stat. 541) gives the superintendent of documents the authority to reprint congressional publications.

1923 There are 418 depositories in 1923.

1924 The GPO is charged (4 Stat. 592) with the new activity of supplying blank paper and envelopes to all government establishments in the District of Columbia. The geological and patent gazette depositories are discontinued.

1938 On June 27, the original building where GPO first opened for business on March 4, 1861, begins to be demolished. In its place is erected an eight-story building, comprising 481,975 square feet, completed in February 1940.

1943 The bullet and item number are added to the *Monthly Catalog* to indicate shipment of publications to depositories.

1945 There are 555 depositories. Research and development at the GPO during the postwar years leads to the shift from hot metal to offset printing.

1947 The first Biennial Survey of Depository Libraries is conducted.

1950 The first modern GPO shipping list begins around 1950.

1962 There are 594 depositories. The Depository Library Act of 1962 (PL 87-579) discontinues the payment of postage by depositories and allows depositories to discard materials after a five-year retention period. The act adds libraries of independent federal agencies and authorizes the designation of not more than two libraries in each state and in the Commonwealth of Puerto Rico as regional depositories.

1966 Freedom of Information Act (FOIA), 80 Stat. 250; 5 USC 552. Amended in 1974, 1976, 1986, and 1996.

1967 Modernization of printing at the GPO continues as the Linotron system is installed in October. The Linotron system utilizes computer-generated magnetic tape to produce page photocomposition.

1968 Title 44 United States Code (Public Printing and Documents) enacted. Provides that a depository designation can be removed by the superintendent of documents for failure to abide by the laws governing the depository program.[111]

1970 The GPO proposes studying the feasibility of making government publications available in microfiche.

1972 An act (86 Stat. 507) adds the highest appellate courts of the states to the depository program. The Depository Library Council to the Public Printer (consisting of fifteen documents librarians) is formalized.

At GPO, proposals are studied for the automation of a new order-processing system, production of the *Monthly Catalog*, mailing lists, and the creation of a publications reference file online.

1973 *Public Documents Highlights*, an irregular GPO newsletter for the depository community, begins in May. The publication is discontinued in September 1983.

1974 Privacy Act of 1974 enacted, 88 Stat. 1896; 5 USC 552a. Amended in 1986.

1977 There are over 1,200 depositories. GPO receives approval from the Joint Committee on Printing and begins to distribute microfiche to libraries. Production of the *Federal Register* converts from hot metal to photocomposition.

1978 An act (92 Stat. 199) adds law libraries to the depository program. GPO installs an interactive page makeup system, which facilitates computerization as page formatting shifts from metal-type to photocomposition and electronic processing. The entire text of the *Code of Federal Regulations* converts to an electronic database.

1979 The U.S. House of Representatives begins televising its proceedings on the Cable Satellite Public Affairs Network (C-SPAN) on March 19.

1980 Paperwork Reduction Act (PRA) of 1980, 94 Stat. 2812; 44 USC 3501 et seq. *Administrative Notes*, a GPO newsletter, begins in September to increase communications with the depository community.

1986 The U.S. Senate begins televising its proceedings on C-SPAN on June 2.

1993 On June 8, the Government Printing Office Electronic Information Access Enhancement Act of 1993 (PL 103-40; 107 Stat. 112; 44 USC § 4101 et seq.) requires the GPO to disseminate government information products online. In June, *Administrative Notes* makes its electronic debut on the listserv GOVDOC-L.

1994 The *Administrative Notes Technical Supplement* is first published in January. In March, GPO LPS adopts GOVDOC-L as a method of e-mail communication. GPO Access is launched in June, providing Internet access to information from all three branches of the government (http://www.gpoaccess.gov/).

1995 Paperwork Reduction Act of 1995, 109 Stat. 165-66; (44 U.S.C. 3501 et seq.).

1996 Electronic Freedom of Information Amendments (E-FOIA), 110 Stat. 3048; 5 USC 552.

1996 Report to Congress—*Study to Identify Measures Necessary for a Successful Transition to a More Electronic Federal Depository Library Program* (Washington: Government Printing Office, June 1996).

1998 Government Paperwork Elimination Act (GPEA), 112 Stat. 2681-749, Title XVII.

2000 FirstGov is launched on September 22—the single federal portal and search engine for all national government Web sites (www.firstgov.gov). FirstGov.gov officially changes its name to USA.gov in January 2007.

2003 Public Printer Bruce James establishes the Office of Innovation and New Technology (INT) in May to develop a plan to bring the Government Printing Office (GPO) into the digital age.[112]

2004 GPO publishes "Strategic Vision for the 21st Century" on December 1.[113]

2005 In March, 794 depositories participate in a survey to identify "essential titles" that should continue to be distributed in a tangible format.[114] GPO launches LOCKSS Pilot Project in June.[115]

2006 GPO launches its Registry of U.S. Government Publication Digitization Projects (http://registry.fdlp.gov/) in January.

2006 GPO discontinues paper distribution of *Administrative Notes*. GPO-FDLP-L becomes GPO's primary vehicle for communicating with depository library staff.

2006 GPO proceeds with plans to create a new content-management system, the "Future Digital System."[116] GPO advances its "Strategic Vision" with the creation of two new business lines: Library Services and Content Management, and Publication and Information Sales.[117]

2006 On March 9, GPO launches the enhanced version of the *Catalog of U.S. Government Publications*.

2006 GPO produces millionth electronic passport (e-passport) (December).

2007 GPO converts all passport production to the new electronic passport and produces its five millionth e-passport in May.[118]

2007 GPO creates its first ever online congressional directory in November.[119]

2007 In December, the U.S. Government Printing Office and the Federal Depository Library Program enter into a two-year pilot project with the Administrative Office of the U.S. Courts to provide access to its PACER (Public Access to Court Electronic Records) service.

2008 GPO authenticates the Budget of the U.S. Government Fiscal Year 2009 by digital signature (January).[120]

2008 The FDLP supersedes the *Instructions to Depository Libraries* manual and the *Guidelines for the Depository Library System* with its newly revised *Federal Depository Library Handbook*.[121]

2009 In February GPO launches the Federal Digital System (FDsys). FDsys replaces GPO Access in March 2012. There are 1,250 federal depository libraries.

2009 The White House, the National Archives, and the GPO achieve Open Government Milestone by publishing ten years of *Federal Register* data in XML (extensible markup language) format.[122]

2010 In February, the GPO and Cornell University Law School begin yearlong pilot project to evaluate converting *The Code of Federal Regulations* (CFR) into XML format.[123]

2010 GPO begins using the social media sites YouTube (http://www.youtube.com/user/gpoprinter) and Twitter (https://twitter.com/USGPO), and launches the "Government Book Talk" blog (http://gov-booktalk.gpo.gov/).

2010 GPO celebrates 150th anniversary on June 23.[124] There are 1,220 federal depository libraries.

2010 GPO and the National Archives launch Federal Register 2.0 (www.FederalRegister.gov), a user-friendly online version of the *Federal Register*,[125] and GPO receives awards for social media initiatives.[126]

2010 GPO partners with Google to offer federal e-books.[127]

2011 Mary Alice Baish becomes superintendent of documents for GPO on January 20. As a librarian and advocate of GPO and the library community, Baish previously served as the director of government relations for the American Association of Law Libraries.[128]

2011 GPO launches a Facebook page on February 7, "in an effort to continue to use social media as [a] way of increasing transparency and [to] engage with the public" on its operations.[129]

2011 March 4, 2011, marks the 150th anniversary of GPO operations.[130]

2011 In April, GPO and the General Services Administration (GSA) partner to offer consumer-related government publications for free electronic download through Google.[131] GPO and the federal judiciary launch one-year pilot program to provide free public access to court opinions through FDsys.[132]

2011 In March, the U.S. Census Bureau announces that budget cuts would cause the termination, after 133 years, of the *Statistical Abstract of the United States*.[133] In June, *The FDL Handbook* (2008) is superseded by the *Legal Requirements & Program Regulations of the Federal Depository Library Program*.[134]

2011 Public printer testifies at Congressional hearings on May 11,[135] and discusses first-ever GPO survey on congressional printing needs. "Boarman explained how GPO has transformed itself into a digital information platform for the entire Federal Government. Even though there are proposals to reduce Congressional printing, 70% of the cost is for the prepress functions to create the digital version of those publications."[136]

2011 GPO has produced one million Trusted Traveler Program cards for the Department of Homeland Security's U.S. Customs and Border Protection.[137]

2011 In June, GPO releases a new white paper[138] that describes GPO's authentication program and latest activities to ensure its role as a trusted source for disseminating official and authentic federal government publications to the public.

2011 On June 15, GPO publishes *Keeping America Informed: The U.S. Government Printing Office: 150 Years of Service to the Nation*, the first official GPO history to be released in fifty years.

2011 On July 13, GPO expands its collection of e-books available through Google's eBookstore.[139] GPO now produces Global Entry cards for the Department of Homeland Security, Customs and Border Protection.[140]

2011 GPO releases its first mobile Web application (app) on November 15, the "Mobile Member Guide."

2011 On December 20, the public printer appoints Davita Vance-Cooks as GPO's deputy public printer, the second-highest-ranking position at the agency. Vance-Cooks is the first woman ever to be appointed to that position.[141] The public printer reports positive financial results in GPO's 2011 Annual Report.[142]

2012 On January 3, Deputy Public Printer Davita Vance-Cooks becomes acting public printer for the U.S. Government Printing Office, the first woman to lead the agency.[143]

2012 On January 18, GPO assists the Library of Congress with the creation of a *Congressional Record* iPad application (app).[144]

2012 FDsys has received 4.3 million total visits since GPO launched the site in January 2009 (February 7). GPO adds new content to FDsys every day.[145] On February 13, GPO releases its second mobile Web application (app), President Barack Obama's Budget for the U.S. Government, FY 2013,[146] and it receives fifty-three thousand visits in its first twenty-four hours.[147]

2012 GPO Access is officially shut down on March 16, 2012, after sixteen years of "Keeping America Informed."[148]

2012 Since 2005, GPO has produced 75 million electronic passports at its secure production facilities in Washington, D.C., and Stennis Space Center in Mississippi.[149]

2012 GPO signs agreements with Barnes & Noble and Apple to sell federal e-books.[150]

2012 GPO adopts an internal XML system to manage and publish congressional bills, the *Federal Register*, and the *Congressional Record*. "The system also will make it easier to load GPO publications into new forms such as e-books and smartphone and tablet applications, according to [Chief Technology Officer Ric] Davis" (September 12).[151]

2012 On October 10, GPO releases a mobile Web application (app) for presidential documents.[152]

2012 October 22, GPO releases its Strategic Plan for FY 2013–2017,[153] "showing how GPO will continue to meet the information needs of Congress, Federal agencies, and the public with an emphasis on being Official, Digital, and Secure."[154]

2012 The next generation of the official Federal Depository Library Program (FDLP) Web site is released in beta at http://beta.fdlp.gov. There are 1,200 federal depository libraries (November).

2012 GPO releases its fourth mobile Web application (app) on December 3—the *United States Policy and Supporting Positions* (also known as "The Plum Book").[155]

2012 Science.gov celebrates its tenth anniversary. "This free gateway to government science information and research results from 13 federal agencies provides a search of over 55 scientific databases and 200 million pages of science information, including Library of Congress information from THOMAS, the Prints and Photographs Division, and the Science, Technology, and Business Division, with just one query."[156]

U.S. GOVERNMENT DOCUMENTS: A SELECTIVE LIST OF FINDING AIDS AND RESOURCES

Bibliographic Tools (Catalogs, Indexes, and Checklists)

Ames, John G. *Checklist of United States Public Documents, 1789–1909.* (Also called *The 1909 Checklist*). 3rd ed., rev. and enlarged. Vol. 1, *List of Congressional and Department Publications.* Washington: GPO, 1911. Arranged by publishing offices, classes of publications, and series, of all publications issued by the government during the period covered. Useful to research the breadth of an agency's publishing from 1789 to 1909, as it "records the first systematic effort to include within the limits of one publication an approximately complete checklist of all public documents issued by the United States Government during the first century and a quarter of its history." Introduction, v. 1A, p. VII (see also definition of "Public Document," Introduction, v. 1A, p. VII).

———. *Comprehensive Index to the Publications of the United States Government, 1881–1893.* House Document 754, 58th Congress, 2nd Session. An index prepared by Dr. John Griffith Ames, superintendent of documents, continues from 1881, where B. P. Poore's left off.

Catalog[ue] of the Public Documents of the [Fifty-third–Seventy-sixth] Congress and of All Departments of the Government of the United States. Washington, DC: GPO, 1893–1940. (Generally known as the *Document Catalog[ue].* A comprehensive index of public documents, the *Document Catalog* lists all publications issued in two-year periods. One volume contains the congressional publications of an entire Congress and the executive branch publications covering two fiscal years. Indexes proclamations and executive orders. Arrangement is alphabetical by personal and government author, subject, publishing office, and title. Includes cross-references to related topics. "The Ames comprehensive index of the documents of the Fifty-first and Fifty-second Congress is recognized as the most successful predecessor of the present volume." Preface, v. 1, p. 3.

Catalog of U.S. Government Publications (CGP), 1976– . Also known as CGP. http://catalog.gpo.gov/ or http://purl.access.gpo.gov/GPO/LPS844. Continues the print *Monthly Catalog* and is the online public access catalog (OPAC) module of GPO's integrated library system, offering more than five hundred thousand records of both historical and current government publications. These records have been created or updated daily since July 1976. Plans are underway to include records for publications dating back to the late 1800s. "The CGP was originally the online counterpart of the *Monthly Catalog of United States Government Publications*, which had been printed since the passage of the Printing Act of 1895. The print version of the *Monthly Catalog* was discontinued with the December 2004 edition. For publications issued prior to 1976, the printed *Monthly Catalog* should be consulted. Print editions of the *Monthly Catalog* and many of the publications indexed in it were distributed through the Federal Depository Library Program. To locate the depository library nearest you, use GPO's Locate Libraries service at: http://catalog.gpo.gov/fdlpdir/public.jsp." From about the *Catalog of U.S. Government Publications* (CGP).

CIS Index to Publications of the United States Congress (CIS Index). ProQuest, 1970–current. Provides access to congressional publications through abstracts, controlled vocabulary subject indexing, and bibliographic information. Publications covered include all House and Senate documents and reports, congressional committee hearings and prints, and Senate executive reports and treaty documents. Annual sets include abstracts and index volumes. For all years dating back to 1984, the hardbound set also includes a Legislative Histories volume. Additional historical index sets include:

- CIS Index to Presidential Executive Orders and Proclamations, 1789–1980
- CIS Index to Unpublished U.S. House of Representatives Committee Hearings, 1833–1972
- CIS Index to Unpublished U.S. Senate Committee Hearings, 1823–1980
- CIS Index to U.S. Senate Executive Documents and Reports: Covering Documents and Reports not Printed in the U.S. Serial Set, 1817–1969
- CIS U.S. Congressional Committee Hearings Index, 1833–1969
- CIS U.S. Congressional Committee Prints Index, 1830–1969
- CIS U.S. Serial Set Index, 1789–1969

A user guide to the CIS Index is published at http://www.lexisnexis.com/iw/pdfs/CISGuide_0105.pdf. ProQuest Congressional is an online service that provides access to the CIS Index, with hypertext links to the full text of related congressional documents dating back to 1789. It is the most comprehensive online resource available for congressional publications and legislative research. You can search ProQuest Congressional collections from 1789 to the present. Collections are indexed by committee, author, publication number, public law numbers, bill numbers, SuDoc numbers, and subject terms. Use a basic, advanced, or "search by number" form.

Clarke, Edith. "Bibliography [of government publications]." In *Guide to the Use of United States Government Publications*. Boston: Boston Book Co., 1918, 241–88.

Digitization Projects Registry. Registry of state and U.S. government publication-digitization projects (http://registry.fdlp.gov/); serves as a locator tool for publicly accessible collections of digitized U.S. government publications.

Guide to U.S. Government Publications. Detroit: Thomson Gale, published annually since 1959. (Generally known as *Andriot*). Arranged in SuDocs class number order; provides a brief history of the creation of agencies, their publication history, and a listing of current series issued by each agency. The "Agency Class Chronology" traces the history of all agencies current or defunct. Identifies the changes in SuDoc numbers over time. Indexed by both agency and title. Updated annually.

HathiTrust Digital Library. http://www.hathitrust.org/. A collaborative repository of digital content from research libraries administered by Indiana University and the University of Michigan. HathiTrust contains 10 million volumes, over 2.7 million of which are public domain (as of January 2012) and provides full-text searching and meta-access through its catalog (http://catalog.hathitrust.org/Search/Advanced).

Index to the Reports and Documents of the _____ Congress, with Numerical Lists and Schedule of Volumes. (Generally known as the *Document Index*). Washington, DC: GPO, annual 1908–1933. Contains only the documents and reports of Congress. Entries are arranged alphabetically by subject, names of publishing offices, and committees, and, in the case of reports, by the name of the senator or representative submitting that report. The documents and reports are also listed in numerical order.

Internet Archives. *CyberCemetery*, at the University of North Texas Libraries (http://govinfo.library.unt.edu/default.htm), provides permanent online access to electronic publications of selected federal government agencies that have ceased operation. The Internet Archive (http://www.archive.org/) is also useful for locating government Web pages that have disappeared. It contains multiple copies of the entire publicly available Web and has an index (the *Wayback Machine*) that allows surfing archived Web pages over multiple time periods back to 1996 (http://www.archive.org/web/web.php).

Internet Search Engines. Useful for locating federal (and state) agency documents. Use the Advanced Google search engine (http://www.google.ca/advanced_search) and narrow your results by domains .gov and .mil to find U.S. government and military documents. USA.gov is the U.S. government's official Web portal, where you can find information by topic or audience; find services, jobs, and government agencies; and contact officials. USA.gov's search engine has an advanced search option at http://search.usa.gov/search/advanced. Use general search engines to find collections of archived digital documents hosted by academic institutions or FDLP content partners, such as the "Historical Publications of the United States Commission on Civil Rights" at Thurgood Marshall Law Library or U.S. Census Bureau Data at Case Western Reserve Library.

Monthly Catalog (1895–2004). *Catalogue of United States Public Documents*. Washington, DC: GPO, 1895–1907. Continued by *Monthly Catalogue, United States Public Documents*. Washington, DC: GPO, 1907–1933. Continued by *Monthly Catalog of United States Public Documents*. Washington, DC: GPO, 1933–1939. Continued by *United States Government Publications Monthly Catalog*. Washington, DC: GPO, 1940–1951. Continued by *Monthly Catalog of United States Government Publications*. Washington, DC: GPO, 1951–2004. (Generally known as MoCat). Monthly, with semiannual and annual indexes. This is the most comprehensive ongoing source for federal publications and catalogs all publications of the United States government, including those of the Congress and all executive departments (with the exception of administrative and confidential or restricted documents). Publications are listed according to publishing offices. Each publication is listed by title and serial number. The digitized version from ProQuest LLC provides all issues of the *Monthly Catalog* from 1895 to June 1976, available online, both as keyed full-text records and as page images of the original printed catalog. The University of Illinois at Urbana-Champaign Library has digitized the pre-1976 volumes of the *Monthly Catalog*. Content is available via the Internet Archive's Web site (http://archive.org), the University of Illinois' online catalog (http://www.library.uiuc.edu/catalog/), the Illinois Harvest Web portal (http://illinoisharvest.grainger.uiuc.edu/index.asp), and WorldCat.

Poore, B. P. *A Descriptive Catalogue of the Government Publications of the United States, September 5, 1774–March 4, 1881*. Washington: GPO, 1885. Catalogs all federal government publications produced from the beginning of the republic to 1881.

Tables of and Annotated Index to the Congressional Series of United States Public Documents. (15th to 52d Congress.) Washington, DC: GPO, 1902. "Contains a list of, and an index to the documents of the Fifteenth to the Fifty-second Congress, both inclusive." Contents include: preface; congressional series tables; congressional series index; Appendixes—I. Table showing number of documents, II. List of title-pages and imprints, III. Reference tables (duration of sessions, etc.).

For information on additional finding aids, consult Morehead, *Introduction to United States Government Information Sources*, 6th edition (1999) and Forte et al., *Fundamentals of Government Information* (2011).

Electronic Databases

CQ.com—A full-service legislative tracking Web site from Congressional Quarterly Inc. Databases include the full text of bills, committee reports, the *Congressional Record*, committee testimony, congressional transcripts, and the *Federal Register*. Services include bill analysis and tracking, floor votes, *CQ News*, *CQ Today*, and *CQ Weekly*. Topical databases include the CQ Budget Tracker, Green Sheets, Health-Beat, House Action Reports, SenateWatch, and more. Databases are generally searchable by Congress number, word or phrase, bill numbers, member names, date, subject, and stage in legislative process. This commercial database is available at http://www.cq.com/.

FDsys.gov (U.S. Government Printing Office's Federal Digital System)—FDsys is a content-management system, preservation repository, and advanced search engine. FDsys provides free online access to official federal government publications, securely controls digital content to ensure content integrity and authenticity, guarantees long-term preservation and access to digital government content, and provides extensive metadata. Through FDsys, you can search (with the ability to refine and narrow your search) or browse (by collection, congressional committee, date, and government author) for documents and publications, access metadata about documents and publications, and download documents and publications in multiple renditions or file formats. Find more information about FDsys, including instructional videos, FAQs, and online help, at http://www.gpo.gov/fdsysinfo/aboutfdsys.htm.

HeinOnline—An online commercial database with over fifty "collections," containing some eighty million pages of legal information and federal government documents content, available in a fully searchable, image-based format. In addition to providing comprehensive coverage of more than 1,600 law and law-related periodicals from their inception, HeinOnline has digitized an impressive collection of government documents. Almost half of these collections contain significant U.S. government federal publication information. HeinOnline's current GPO-originated content includes complete collections of the following: federal statutes, federal regulations, the *Congressional Record* and its predecessors, U.S. Reports (bound volumes preliminary prints and slip opinions), public papers of the presidents of the United States (1931–2009) and similar titles, U.S. treaties and agreements, U.S. attorney general opinions and the opinions of the office of legal counsel of the United States Department of Justice, and *Manual of Patent Examining Procedure* (all eight editions). The "Federal Register Library" contains a full run of the *Federal Register* and its indexes, FR *List of Sections Affected*, *Weekly Compilation of Presidential Documents*, and the full run of the Code of Federal Regulations. The "U.S. Federal Legislative History Library" contains bibliographies and compiled full-text legislative histories on historically significant legislation. The "Treaties and Agreements Library" contains official and unofficial treaty publications, treaty guides and indexes, and other texts. The "U.S. Federal Agency Library" contains administrative decisions, FCC *Record*, *Tax Court Reports*, and a number of other notable U.S. federal agency publications. All documents are available in PDF format and are retrievable by citation, and by searching the full text and metadata. This commercial database is available at http://heinonline.org/.

LLSDC's Legislative Source Book—Maintained by the Law Librarians' Society of Washington, D.C., the Source Book provides a wide variety of resources and links to federal and state legislation and information pertaining to federal and state legislation. This resource is available at http://www.llsdc.org/sourcebook/index.html.

ProQuest Congressional—A Web-based service that provides access to indexing, abstracts, and full texts of congressional documents dating back to 1789. Indispensable to legislative research, ProQuest Congressional is the most comprehensive online resource available for locating congressional publications. Full-text collections in PDF include the following: committee reports (U.S. Congressional Serial Set and American State Papers, 1789 to current); committee prints (1830 to current); congressional hearings (1824 to current); statutes at large (1789 to current); *Congressional Record* (bound permanent edition and predecessors, 1873–2001; daily edition 1985 to current); and U.S. bills and resolutions (when fully loaded, by the end of 2013, this product will contain searchable PDFs of all versions of all bills and resolutions from 1789 to 2013). Collections are indexed by committee, author, publication number, public law numbers, bill numbers, SuDoc Numbers, and subject terms. Use the basic, advanced, or "search by number" form to retrieve indexing, abstracts, or full-text documents in PDF or text formats. This commercial database is available at http://congressional.proquest.com.

ProQuest Legislative Insight—A federal legislative history service that, upon completion, will contain approximately eighteen thousand compiled legislative histories dating back to 1929. PDF documents included with the public laws include bills (all versions), legislative reports, documents, CRS reports, committee prints, speeches in the *Congressional Record*, and presidential signing statements. Features include the following: full text searching, controlled vocabulary subject indexing, guided and search-by-number forms. This commercial database is available at http://www.conquest-leg-insight.com/legislativeinsight/LegHistMain.jsp.

THOMAS.gov—A free legislative tracking service from the Library of Congress, which provides summaries and full texts of congressional publications (bills, hearings, reports, debates, and statutes). THOMAS also contains committee information and information on the legislative process. Search a single Congress or across multiple Congresses; by keyword, bill number, law number, report number, committee, or sponsor name. Coverage extends back to 1967 for treaties, 1973 for bills and laws, 1995 for reports, 1989 for the *Congressional Record*. THOMAS is available at http://thomas.loc.gov.

Additional online resources for government documents at the Library of Congress include:

American Memory—A digital record of American history that provides free online access to written and spoken words, sound recordings, still and moving images, prints, maps, etc. To access the legal documents, go to "Browse Collections by Topic," choose "Government, Law," then select "Documents from the Continental Congress and the Constitutional Convention, 1774–1789" or "A Century of Lawmaking for a New Nation: U.S. Congressional Documents and Debates, 1774–1875." These documents include the early journals and debates of Congress, bills and statutes, the U.S. Serial Set, and more. The collections are searchable by number or word, and are available full-text in image (TIFF) or text format. American Memory is available at http://memory.loc.gov/ammem/index.html.

Congress.gov—A free service from the Library of Congress, in beta version, which contains legislation from the 107th Congress (2001) to the present, member profiles from the 93rd Congress (1973) to the present, and some member profiles from the 80th through the 92nd Congresses (1947 to 1972). The Legislative Process (http://beta.congress.gov/legislative-process) contains educational videos that provide a basic outline of the steps involved in the legislative process. The Legislative Glossary (http://beta.congress.gov/help/legislative-glossary/) provides brief explanations of legislative terms. Eventually, Congress.gov will incorporate all of the information available on THOMAS.gov.

Tools for Depository Management and Information

Administrative Notes Technical Supplement (ANTS)—The Library Programs Service's former monthly newsletter, which updated various FDLP-related publications, directories, and depository listings. The U.S. Government Printing Office ceased publication of ANTS, with its final print version released in December 2008 (http://www.fdlp.gov/collections/collection-tools/ants). Updates are now made directly in a Web-based system called WEBTech Notes. Available at http://www.fdlp.gov/webtechnotes.

Catalog of U.S. Government Publications (CGP)—A search-and-retrieval service that provides bibliographic records of U.S. government information products. Use it to link to federal agency online resources or to identify materials distributed to Federal Depository Libraries. Coverage begins with 1976, and new records are added daily. Available at http://catalog.gpo.gov/.

Documents Data Miner 2 (DDM2)—A Web-based "Library Management System for United States Government Documents," available at http://govdoc.wichita.edu/ddm2/gdocframes.asp. Provides tools for depository management, including a searchable list of classes, searchable shipping lists, searchable inactive/discontinued List, collection profiling tools, and the Item Lister's current item number selection profiles for depository libraries.

FDLP Desktop—News, information, and communication from and about the Federal Depository Library Program. Available at http://fdlp.gov. Categories of information and resources on this Web site include depository administration, collection management, outreach, cataloging, and help. Resources include information on the FDLP, the Depository Library Council to the Public Printer, the Biennial Survey of Depository Libraries, and GPO projects. Depository administration tools available include the Federal Depository Library Directory, Federal Depository Legal Requirements, the FDL Handbook, and collection-management tools (including the Item Lister, List of Classes, and shipping lists). Cataloging guidelines and polices are offered. Refer to the site map (http://www.fdlp.gov/sitemap) to see the full range of content. A beta version of the next generation of the official FDLP Web site was released in November 2012 and can be found at http://beta.fdlp.gov.

Government Documents Round Table (GODORT)—American Library Association Web site. Available at http://www.ala.org/godort/. Provides the GODORT directory of committee and task force membership; a list of GODORT committees; *DttP: Documents to the People* (the official publication of GODORT); and the GODORT wiki, where you can find GODORT-created resources (e.g., Toolbox for Processing and Cataloging Federal Government Documents), professional resources (e.g., government information periodicals and professional organizations), and the Government Information Clearinghouse and Handout Exchange (http://wikis.ala.org/godort/index.php/Exchange).

Government Documents Special Interest Section—American Association of Law Libraries Web site. Available at http://www.aallnet.org/sis/gd/. Provides information on state bibliographies (http://www.aallnet.org/sis/gd/stateb.html), section bylaws and business, the newsletter JURISDOCS, advocacy, and a government documents tutorial.

Government Printing Office. *GPO Annual Reports Archive*—Online at FDsys.gov, http://www.gpo.gov/congressional/reports.htm.

Government Printing Office. *GPO History*—Online at GPO Web site, http://www.gpo.gov/about/gpohistory/.

Government Printing Office. *GPO Mobile*—Site for GPO's mobile apps. Online at GPO Web site, http://www.gpo.gov/mobile/. Other mobile apps available from the federal government can be found at http://apps.usa.gov/.

Government Printing Office. *GPO Testimony Before Congress*—Online at FDsys.gov, http://www.gpo.gov/congressional/testimony.htm.

Government Printing Office. *Legal Requirements & Program Regulations of the Federal Depository Library Program* (June 2011)—Provides the current legal and program obligations for federal depository libraries. Available at http://fdlp.gov/administration/fdlp-legal-requirements.

Government Printing Office. Superintendent of Documents. *An Explanation of the Superintendent of Documents Classification System*, 1990—Available on the FDLP

Desktop at http://fdlp.gov/cataloging/856-sudoc-classification-scheme. See also "Superintendent of Documents (SuDocs) Classification Scheme." GP 3.2:C 56/8/990.

New Depository Coordinators—Available on the FDLP Desktop at http://fdlp.gov/help/tutorials/ndc. "These tutorials provide an overview of the basics of being a depository coordinator, a list of resources with descriptions of what they are and how they can be used, and more. They are intended to help new coordinators learn about their collections and the responsibilities of being a depository coordinator."

New Electronic Titles—A finding aid used to locate, by month, online federal government publications that were acquired for the Federal Depository Library Program Electronic Collection. Full bibliographic information for the titles in these lists can be found in the *Catalog of U.S. Government Publications*. The weekly lists may be found in the NET Archive after four weeks. These files are accessible from the New Titles section (http://catalog.gpo.gov/F/?func=file&file_name=find-net&local_base=NEWTITLE) of the *Catalog of U.S. Government Publications* (CGP).

"Resources for New Government Information Librarians"—Government Documents Round Table of Michigan. Available at http://godortmi.pbworks.com/w/page/8768963/Resources%20for%20new%20government%20information%20librarians.

"Twenty-One Things to Do When Assuming Responsibility for a Federal Depository Library."—University of North Texas Libraries. Available at http://www.library.unt.edu/govinfo/21things.

U.S. Government Online Bookstore—The official online bookstore for U.S. government publications for purchase from the U.S. Government Printing Office. Available at http://bookstore.gpo.gov/. A newly designed beta version (http://newbookstore.gpo.gov/) of the bookstore was launched in October 2012 and features e-books and digital products. Browse publications by topic or agency. Search by keyword, title, agency, ISBN, or stock number.

WEBTech Notes—An interactive, online resource for depository coordinators, catalogers, and reference librarians. Available at http://www.fdlp.gov/webtechnotes. Search or browse, and view updates to Superintendent of Documents classification numbers and to List of Classes information. The WEBTech Notes database is cumulated on a weekly basis and contains information on the four main components from ANTS, specifically: Classification/Cataloging Update; Whatever Happened to ?; Update to the List of Classes, New Items; and Update to the List of Classes, Misc. The data is updated weekly and is cumulative back to 1991.

Secondary Sources, Manuals, Guides

Boyd, Anne Morris, and Rae Elizabeth Rips. *United States Government Publications*. H. W. Wilson, 1949. A detailed review of government document series to the late 1940s.

Dwan, Ralph H., and Ernest R. Feidler. "The Federal Statutes—Their History and Use." *Minnesota Law Review* 22, no. 7 (1938): 1008–29.

Ennis, Lisa A. *Government Documents Librarianship: A Guide for the Neo-Depository Era*. Medford, NJ: Information Today, 2007.

Forte, Eric J., Cassandra J. Hartnett, and Andrea L. Sevetson. *Fundamentals of Government Information: Mining, Finding, Evaluating, and Using Government Resources*. New York: Neal-Schuman Publishers, 2011.

Herman, Edward. *Locating United States Government Information: A Guide To Sources*. W. S. Hein, 1997. "[T]he purpose of this book is to provide a practical how-to guide for locating United States government publications. Emphasis is upon locating and using government information, rather than policy issues" (Preface).

Maclay, Veronica. "Selected Sources of United States Agency Decisions." *Government Publications Review* 16, no. 3 (May/June 1989): 271–301.

McKinney, Richard J. "An Overview of the U.S. Congressional Serial Set." Law Librarians' Society of Washington, D.C. (available online at http://www.llsdc.org/sch-v/

#Overview). See other resources available in the LLSDC's Legislative Source Book at http://www.llsdc.org/sourcebook/.

Morehead, Joe. *Introduction to United States Government Information Sources*. Libraries Unlimited, 1999. An overview of the GPO and FDLP, general reference sources, and an overview of the publications, both print and electronic, of the legislative, executive, and judicial branches of government.

Morrison, Andrea, for the ALA Government Documents Round Table, ed. *Managing Electronic Government Information in Libraries: Issues and Practices*. Chicago: ALA, 2008.

Schmeckebier, Laurence F. *Government Publications and Their Use*. Brookings Institution, 1969. A thorough analysis of historical government document series.

Surrency, Erwin C. *History of the Federal Courts*. Oceana Publications, 1987.

———. "The Publication of Federal Laws: A Short History." *Law Library Journal* 79, no. 3 (Summer 1987): 469–84.

Treaties and Other International Agreements: The Role of the United States Senate, A Study. Government Printing Office, 1993.

United States Government Manual. "As the official handbook of the Federal Government, the United States Government Manual provides comprehensive information on the agencies of the legislative, judicial, and executive branches. It also includes information on quasi-official agencies; international organizations in which the United States participates; and boards, commissions, and committees." Published annually since 1935; available in print and online at http://www.gpo.gov/fdsys/browse/collection.action?collectionCode=GOVMAN.

Zinn, Charles J. *How Our Laws are Made*. Washington, DC: GPO, 2003. Also available online at Thomas, http://purl.access.gpo.gov/GPO/LPS4046, and http://thomas.loc.gov/home/lawsmade.toc.html.

Zwirn, Jerrold. *Congressional Publications: A Research Guide to Legislation, Budgets, and Treaties*. Libraries Unlimited, 1983.

STATE DOCUMENTS

Finding Aids and Resources

The Council of State Governments. *The Book of the States*. Annual since 1935. Contains information and data on challenging topics facing the states. "The Book of the States has been the reference tool of choice since 1935, providing relevant, accurate and timely information, answers and comparisons for all 56 states, commonwealths and territories of the United States. The 2012 volume includes 170 in-depth tables, charts and figures illustrating how state government operates. It also includes more than 30 articles from state leaders, innovative thinkers, noted scholars and CSG's in-house policy experts that analyze and report on the transformations taking place in state government. Staff members mined more than 500 sources to obtain the information shared in *The Book of the States*" (from http://knowledgecenter.csg.org/drupal/category/content-type/content-type/book-states). Available in print and online at http://knowledgecenter.csg.org/drupal/category/content-type/content-type/book-states.

Dow, Susan L. *State Document Checklists: A Historical Bibliography*, 2nd ed. Buffalo, NY: William S. Hein & Co., 2000.

Government Relations Committee and Washington Affairs Office. *State-by-State Report on Permanent Public Access to Electronic Government Information*. Chicago: American Association of Law Libraries, 2003. Available online at http://www.aallnet.org/Archived/Government-Relations/Issue-Briefs-and-Reports/2003/ppareport.html.

Hellebust, Lynn, ed. *State Legislative Sourcebook*. Topeka, KS: Government Research Service, Annual.

———, ed. *State Reference Publications: A Bibliographic Guide to State Blue Books, Legislative Manuals and Other General Reference Sources.* Topeka, KS: Government Research Service, 1999.

Hernon, Peter, John V. Richardson, Nancy P. Sanders, and Marjorie Shepley, eds. *Municipal Government Reference Sources: Publications and Collections.* New York: R. R. Bowker, 1978.

Manz, William H. *Guide to State Legislative and Administrative Materials,* 7th ed. Buffalo, NY: William S. Hein & Co., 2008.

Parish, David W. *State Government Reference Publications: An Annotated Bibliography,* 2nd ed. Littleton, CO: Libraries Unlimited, 1981.

Smith, Lori L., Daniel C. Barkley, Daniel D. Cornwall, Eric W. Johnson, and J. Louise Malcomb. *Tapping State Government Information Sources.* Westport, CT: Greenwood Press, 2003.

State Bibliographies. AALL Government Document Series. Various authors. Chicago: American Association of Law Libraries, Government Documents Special Interest Section, published in partnership with William S. Hein & Co., dates vary. For more information, see http://www.aallnet.org/sis/gd/stateb.html or https://www.wshein.com/catalog/?series=64.

Tulis, Susan E., and Daniel C. Barkley, eds. *Directory of Government Document Collections and Librarians,* 8th ed. American Library Association, 1974–.

Online State Resources

Council of State Governments (CSG)—Identifies issues common among state governments, provides directory of state government officials from all fifty states as well as territories, and lists research publications produced by CSG staff. Available at http://www.csg.org/).

Municode.com—A free online municipal code library. Available at http://www.municode.com/Library.

National Association of Secretaries of State (NASS)—Contains information on secretaries' responsibilities and such key NASS initiatives as election administration, voter participation, and electronic or e-government services. Provides biographies, contact information, and state Web links for all secretaries of state. Available at http://www.nass.org/.

National Conference of State Legislatures—Serves as a resource for those who draft legislation on the state level, providing a searchable database that accesses publications and court decisions on a variety of legislative issues. Available at http://www.ncsl.org/.

State and Local Documents Task Force, American Library Association, Government Documents Roundtable—Provides professional-development tools, links to state resources, and news on projects, issues, and initiatives. Available at http://www.ala.org/godort/taskforces/statelocaldocuments.

State and Local Documents Task Force Wiki (ALA GODORT Wiki)—Projects listed include links to state agency databases, state blue books, state depository systems, etc. Available at http://wikis.ala.org/godort/index.php/State_%26_Local_Documents.

State Constitutions—Information on researching state constitutions and their history. Includes a fifty-state A-to-Z list of resources for finding the full text of state constitutions, information on amendment processes, and pending and historical amendments, artifacts, and documents. Available at http://law.indiana.libguides.com/state-constitutions.

State Government Information from the Library of Congress—Contains general information on state and local government issues, state maps, and individual state Internet links. Available at http://www.loc.gov/rr/news/stategov/stategov.html.

State Legislative History Research Guides—An index of state legislatures and legislative history research guides that are available on the Web. Available at http://law.indiana.libguides.com/state-legislative-history-guides.

State Legislatures, State Laws, and State Regulations: Web Site Links and Telephone Numbers—Provides a comprehensive list of Web site links and telephone numbers, from the Law Librarians' Society of Washington, DC. Available at http://www.llsdc.org/state-leg/.

StateList—The Electronic Source for State Publication Lists. A joint project of the Documents and Law Libraries at the University of Illinois. Provides links to state publication checklists and shipping lists that are currently available on the Internet. Available at http://www.library.illinois.edu/doc/researchtools/guides/state/statelist.html.

NOTES

1. For more information on the early history of government printing, see Laurence F. Schmeckebier, *The Government Printing Office: Its History, Activities and Organization* (Baltimore: The Johns Hopkins Press, 1925), 1–16; and Daniel R. MacGilvray, "A Short History of GPO" (FDLP Desktop), http://www.access.gpo.gov/su_docs/fdlp/history/macgilvray.html (January 26, 2006).

2. *House Journal*, 1st Cong., 1st sess., May 15, 1789, 35.

3. Resolution of December 27, 1813, 13th Cong., 2nd sess., *Stats at Large of USA* 3 (1813): 140–41.

4. U.S. GPO. *About GPO*, http://www.gpo.gov/about/.

5. Documents before 1817 are found in the *American State Papers*.

6. For more information on the Serial Set, see Joe Morehead, *Introduction to United States Government Information Sources* (Englewood, CO: Libraries Unlimited, 1999), 146–57; "Library Resources for Administrative History: Congressional Serial Set" (Archives Library Information Center), http://www.archives.gov/research/alic/reference/admin-history/congressional-serial-set.html (November 10, 2005); Richard J. McKinney, "An Overview of the U.S. Congressional Serial Set" (LLSDC's Legislative Source Book), http://www.llsdc.org/sourcebook/sch-v.htm#over (November 10, 2005); and Virginia Saunders, "U.S. Congressional Serial Set: What It Is and Its History" (GPO Access), http://www.access.gpo.gov/su_docs/fdlp/history/sset/index.html (November 10, 2005).

7. 15th Cong., 2nd sess., 1818, S. Doc. 29, serial 14, 1.

8. 15th Cong., 2nd sess., 1819, H. Doc. 139, serial 24, 3.

9. Public Resolution 6, 15th Cong., 2nd sess. (March 3, 1819). *Stats at Large of USA* 3 (1819): 538.

10. Schmeckebier, *The Government Printing Office*, 1–9.

11. Ibid.

12. Ibid., 5.

13. Ch. 91, 32nd Cong., 1st sess. (August 26, 1852), *Stats at Large of USA* 10 (1852): 30.

14. Schmeckebier, *The Government Printing Office*, 7.

15. Ch. 91, 32nd Cong., 1st sess. (August 26, 1852), *Stats at Large of USA* 10 (1852): 35.

16. See, e.g., Senate Committee on Alleged Abuses of Printing, 36th Cong., 1st sess., 1860, S. Rep. 205; House Committee to Investigate Alleged Corruptions in Government, *The Covode Investigation*, 36th Cong., 1st sess., 1860, H. Rep. 648; Senate Committee to Inquire into Expenditures from the Public Printing for the Support of Newspapers, etc., *Resolution of Inquiry Whether Certain Sums of Money Were Paid by Public Printer, or Any Party who Executed Binding for 35th Congress [. . .] Testimony in Relation Thereto*, 36th Cong. 1st sess., 1860; House Committee on Public Expenditures, *Public Printing*, 36th Cong., 1st sess., 1860, H. Rep. 249.

17. *Joint Resolution in Relation to the Public Printing* 25, 36th Cong., 1st. sess. (June 23, 1860). *Stats at Large of USA* 12 (1860): 117.

18. MacGilvray, "A Short History of GPO."

19. Ibid.

20. For more information on the printing history of the *Congressional Record*, see Richard J. McKinney, "An Overview of the Congressional Record and Its Predecessor Publications" (*LLSDC's Legislative Source Book*), http://www.llsdc.org/cong-record/.

21. *Printing Act of 1895*, c. 23, *U.S. Statutes at Large* 28 (January 12, 1895): 601–24.

22. *An Act Providing for Keeping and Distributing all Public Documents*, c. 22, *Stats at Large of USA* 11 (1859): 379.

23. *An Act Making Appropriations for the Legislative, Executive, and Judicial Expenses of the Government for the Year Ending the Thirtieth of June 1870*, c. 57, *Stats at Large of USA* 15 (1869): 283, 292.

24. Schmeckebier, *The Government Printing Office*, 15.

25. James Cameron, "GPO's Living History: Adelaide R. Hasse" (FDLP Desktop), http://www.access.gpo.gov/su_docs/fdlp/history/hasse.html (January 12, 2006).

26. For more information, see "Superintendent of Documents (SuDocs) Classification Scheme," (FDLP Desktop), http://www.fdlp.gov/cataloging/856-sudoc-classification-scheme; and "Gov Docs Online Tutorial, Module 3: The Superintendent Of Documents (Sudocs) Classification System" (AALL Government Documents Special Interest Section), http://www.aallnet.org/sis/gd/tutorial/mod3a.html (January 11, 2006).

27. MacGilvray, "A Short History of GPO."

28. *Public Act 171*, c. 103, 67th Cong., 2nd sess. (March 20, 1922).

29. MacGilvray, "A Short History of GPO."

30. Ibid.

31. Ibid.

32. Ibid.

33. Ibid.

34. Sheila M. McGarr, "Snapshots of the Federal Depository Library Program" (FDLP Desktop), http://www.access.gpo.gov/su_docs/fdlp/history/snapshot.html (November 7, 2005).

35. Senate Committee on Appropriations, *Second Supplemental Appropriations for Fiscal Year 1976: Hearings Before Subcommittees [. . .]*, 94th Cong., 2nd sess., 1976. House Committee on Appropriations, *Second Supplemental Appropriation Bill, 1976: Hearings Before Subcommittees [. . .]*, 94th Cong., 2nd sess., 1976.

36. MacGilvray, "A Short History of GPO."

37. FDLP Desktop, "Depository Library Council: About." http://www.access.gpo.gov/su_docs/fdlp/council/aboutdlc.html (January 17, 2006).

38. For more information on the history of the *Federal Register* and *Code of Federal Regulations*, see Richard J. McKinney, "A Research Guide to the Federal Register and the Code of Federal Regulations" (*LLSDC's Legislative Source Book*), http://www.llsdc.org/fed-reg-cfr/.

39. Joint Committee on Printing, *Analysis and Evaluation of Selected Government Printing Office Operations*, report prepared by Coopers and Lybrand, 95th Cong., 2nd sess., 1978, Committee Print, 280.

40. Ibid., 280–81.

41. Ibid., 283.

42. Morehead, *Introduction to United States Government Information Sources*, 155.

43. MacGilvray, "A Short History of GPO."

44. For more information on the transformation of government information during the "electronic revolution," see Morehead, *Introduction to United States Government Information Sources*, 1–14.

45. *Paperwork Reduction Act of 1980*, Public Law 96-511, *U.S. Statutes at Large* 94 (1980): 2812.

46. McGarr, "Snapshots of the Federal Depository Library Program."

47. Ibid.

48. House Committee on Government Operations, *Electronic Collection and Dissemination of Information by Federal Agencies: A Policy Overview*, 99th Cong., 2nd sess., 1986, H.Rep. 560.

49. Harold C. Relyea, *Public Printing Reform: Issues and Actions* (Congressional Research Service: The Library of Congress, June 17, 2003), 3.

50. U.S. Congress, Office of Technology Assessment, *Informing the Nation: Federal Information Dissemination in an Electronic Age, OTA-C IT-396* (Washington, DC: U.S. Government Printing Office, October 1988), Foreword.

51. Ibid., 10.

52. *Government Printing Office Electronic Information Access Enhancement Act of 1993*, Public Law 103-40, *U.S. Statutes at Large* 107 (1993): 112.

53. U.S. Government Printing Office, Frequently Asked Questions, http://www.gpo.gov/factsheet/index.html#4 (January 3, 2006). Since its inception, GPO Access retrievals have exceeded 2.45 billion. June 2005 was the busiest month ever, with more than 39 million retrievals. The total number of retrievals in FY2005 was 431 million. GPO, "Update for ALA," http://www.access.gpo.gov/su_docs/fdlp/events/ala_update06.pdf (June 2006).

54. Harold C. Relyea, *Public Printing Reform*, 5.

55. Michael F. Di Mario, "Prepared Statement before the Committee on Rules and Administration, U.S. Senate," February 3, 1994.

56. Senate Committee on Rules and Administration, *Public Access to Government Information in the 21st Century*, 104th Cong., 2nd sess., 1996; Subcommittee on Government Management, Information, and Technology of the House Committee on Government Reform and Oversight, *The Government Printing Office and Executive Branch Information Dissemination*, 105th Cong., 1st sess., 1997; Senate Committee on Rules and Administration, *Title 44, U.S. Code—Proposals for Revision*, 105th Cong., 1st sess., 1997.

57. See, e.g., *Requiring the Appropriate Committees of the House to Report Legislation to Transfer Certain Functions of the Government Printing Office, and for Other Purposes*, H. Res. 24, 104th Cong., 1st sess. (January 4, 1995); *To Improve the Dissemination of Information and Printing Procedures of the Government*, H.R. 1024, 104th Cong., 1st sess. (February 23, 1995); *Government Printing Reform Act of 1996*, H.R. 4280, 104th Cong., 2nd sess. (September 28, 1996).

58. Eric Peterson, "Concepts for Reform of Title 44" (Comprehensive Assessment of Public Information Dissemination: Reports and Directives), http://www.nclis.gov/govt/assess/assess.html (March 1, 2006).

59. *Wendell H. Ford Government Publications Reform Act of 1998*, S. 2288, 105th Cong., 2nd sess. (July 10, 1998).

60. Testimony of Robert L. Oakley, Senate Committee on Rules and Administration, *Wendell H. Ford Government Publications Act of 1998: Hearings on S. 2288*, 105th Cong., 2nd sess., 1998, 12–20.

61. Dupont Circle Group, "The Future of the Federal Depository Library Program," Washington, D.C., April 16–18, 1993, http://www.arl.org/info/frn/gov/dupont.html; and "Chicago Conference on the Future of Federal Government Information, Chicago, October 29–31, 1993. Executive Summary [and] Report," *Documents to the People* 21, no. 4 (December 1993): 234–46. See also: http://www.arl.org/info/frn/gov/chicago.html.

62. *Study to Identify Measures Necessary for a Successful Transition to a More Electronic Federal Depository Program: As Required by Legislative Branch Appropriations Act, 1996, Public Law 104-53* (Washington, DC: U.S. Government Printing Office, June 1995).

63. Ibid., 4–5.

64. Ibid., 27.

65. "Progress Report on the Transition to a More Electronic FDLP 1996–1999," *Administrative Notes* 20, no. 8 (May 1, 1999): 26.

66. . U.S. Government Printing Office (Update for ALA) http://www.access.gpo.gov/su_docs/fdlp/events/ala_update06.pdf (January 12, 2006), 11.

67. Ibid., 11–12.

68. Schmeckebier, *The Government Printing Office*, 17.

69. U.S. GPO, 2006 Annual Report, http://www.gpo.gov/pdfs/congressional/archives/2006-GPOAnnualReport.pdf.

70. U.S. GPO, "A Strategic Vision for the 21st Century," 5–6; available at http://www.gpo.gov/congressional/pdfs/04strategicplan.pdf.

71. Mary Alice Baish, "Washington Brief: GPO Plan to Reduce Print Distribution to Depository Libraries," *AALL Spectrum* 9, no. 6 (April 2005): 4.

72. John A. Shuler, "Beyond the Depository Library Concept," *The Journal of Academic Librarianship* 27, no. 4 (July 2001): 299.

73. Ibid., 300.

74. James A. Jacobs, James R. Jacobs, and Shinjoung Yeo, "Government Information in the Digital Age: The Once and Future Federal Depository Library Program," *The Journal of Academic Librarianship* 31, no. 3 (May 2005): 205.

75. Depository Library Council, *The Federal Government Information Environment of the 21st Century: Towards a Vision Statement and Plan of Action for Federal Depository Libraries*, http://fdlp.gov/home/repository/doc_view/810-the-federal-government-information-environment-of-the-21st-century-discussion-paper (September 2005).

76. Ibid. The strategic documents of the Depository Library Council are located at http://fdlp.gov/home/about/237-strategicplan and at http://fdlp.gov/component/docman/cat_view/72-about-the-fdlp/77-federal-depository-library-council.

77. U.S. GPO, "American Library Association (ALA) Update (Midwinter 2006)," http://www.fdlp.gov/home/repository/doc_download/523-american-library-association-ala-update-midwinter-2006.

78. U.S. GPO, FDLP Desktop. http://www.access.gpo.gov/su_docs/fdlp/ (March 10, 2006).

79. Authentication of printed documents was mandated by the first Congress: Chap. XIV, *An Act to provide for the safe-keeping of the Acts, Records and Seal of the United States, and for other purposes.* 1 Stat. 68, September 15, 1789. Sec. 2, All enacted laws should be received by the secretary of state and "two printed copies duly authenticated to be sent to the Executive authority of each State."

80. U.S. GPO, FDsys.gov, "Authentication," available online at http://www.gpo.gov/authentication/.

81. U.S. GPO, "GPO's Federal Digital System (FDsys) Operational," press release at http://gpo.gov/pdfs/news-media/press/09news02.pdf (February 4, 2009).

82. U.S. GPO, "GPO and Library of Congress to Digitize Historic Documents," press release at http://gpo.gov/pdfs/news-media/press/11news13.pdf (February 16, 2011).

83. U.S. GPO, "GPO Partners with Treasury Department on Public Access to Digital Collections," press release at http://www.gpo.gov/pdfs/news-media/press/12news44.pdf (October 17, 2012).

84. U.S. GPO, "GPO Establishes First Preservation Librarian Position," press release at http://gpo.gov/pdfs/news-media/press/10news23.pdf (July 14, 2010).

85. U.S. GPO, "GPO Introduces New eLearning Tool for Federal Depository Libraries," press release at http://gpo.gov/pdfs/news-media/press/12news25.pdf (May 15, 2012).

86. U.S. GPO, "GPO Joins Alliance for Digital Preservation," press release at http://gpo.gov/pdfs/news-media/press/10news19.pdf (June 14, 2010).

87. U.S. GPO, *ALA Update 2006*, 2–10.

88. U.S. GPO, FDLP Desktop. "Study of FDLP Selection Mechanisms," http://fdlp.gov/component/content/article/184-gpoprojects/462-selection-mechanisms.

89. U.S. GPO, *GPO Mobile*, online http://www.gpo.gov/mobile/. Site for GPO's mobile apps.

90. Ibid.

91. U.S. GPO. *FDLP Forecast Study*, http://www.fdlp.gov/project-information.

92. Ibid.

93. 2012 Meeting Proceedings can be found in the Depository Library Council file repository at http://www.fdlp.gov/home/repository/cat_view/177-outreach/97-events/101-depository-library-council-dlc-meetings/357-2012-meeting-proceedings.

94. U.S. GPO , *2011 Annual Report* , 7, available online at http://www.gpo.gov/pdfs/congressional/archives/2011_AnnualReport.pdf. Technology changes over the past generation have reduced the cost of the *Congressional Record* by more than two-thirds, and today the vast majority of the cost to produce it—nearly 70 percent—is in the creation of the digital file for dissemination online and in print. For those print copies needed by Congress, federal agencies, and the public, production is on 100 percent recycled newsprint with vegetable oil-based ink. U.S. GPO, "The Congressional Record," press release, May 9, 2011, No. 11-24, available at http://www.gpo.gov/pdfs/news-media/press/11news24.pdf.

95. U.S. GPO, *Budget Justification, FY 2013*, January 25, 2012, p. F2, available at http://www.gpo.gov/pdfs/congressional/Budget_Justification_FY2013.pdf.

96. U.S. GPO, FDLP Desktop. "Essential Titles for Public Use in Paper or Other Tangible Format," http://www.fdlp.gov/collections/collection-tools/essential-titles-list.

97. Acting Public Printer Davita Vance-Cooks, "GPO's Federal Digital System Achieves Milestone," press release at http://gpo.gov/pdfs/news-media/press/12news27.pdf (June 5, 2012).

98. U.S. GPO, About FDsys, http://www.gpo.gov/fdsysinfo/aboutfdsys.htm.

99. U.S. GPO, "GPO's Federal Digital System Achieves Milestone," press release at http://gpo.gov/pdfs/news-media/press/12news27.pdf (June 5, 2012).

100. U.S. GPO, *Budget Justification, FY 2013*, January 25, 2012, p. F2, available at http://www.gpo.gov/pdfs/congressional/Budget_Justification_FY2013.pdf.

101. Bruce R. James, *Public Printer's Annual Report, Fiscal Year 2003* (Washington DC: GPO, 2003), Introduction.

102. U.S. GPO, *GPO Strategic Plan: FY 2013–2017*, http://www.gpo.gov/pdfs/about/2013-2017_StrategicPlan.pdf.

103. *Journals of the Continental Congress, 1774–1789*, Friday, October 17, 1777, vol. 9, p. 817. "Resolved, That the Committee of Intelligence be authorized to take the most speedy and effectual measures for getting a printing press erected in this town [York town,] for the purpose of conveying to the public, the intelligence that Congress may, from time to time, receive."

104. *Journal of the House of Representatives of the United States*, 1789 (Washington, DC: Gales & Seaton, 1826). May 28, 1789, vol. 1, p. 42. *Journal of the First Session of the Senate of the United States of America, 1789.* (Washington, DC: Gales & Seaton, 1820). June 2, 1789, p. 30.

105. "(a) The acts for the general promulgation of the laws of the United States have been: The act of March 3, 1795; act of December 31, 1796; act of March 2, 1799, chap. 30; act of November 21, 1814; act of April 20, 1818, chap. 80; act of May 1, 1820, chap. 92. By the 21st section of the act of August 26, 1842, chap. 202, the laws of the United States are required to be published in not less than two nor more than four newspapers in Washington. 1838, ch. 187." Chap. XIV, Sec. 3, 1 Stat. 68 (1789). Statutes were officially published in newspapers until March 4, 1875, when further publication in that manner was forbidden by statute. Act of June 20, 1874, ch. 328, 18 Stat. 85, 90.

106. No. 16, *Joint Resolution directing the Manner of procuring the Printing for the Two Houses of Congress*, 9 Stat. 113 (1846).

107. No. 10, *A Resolution to authorize the Attorney General to contract for copies of a proposed edition of the Law and Treaties of the United States*, 5 Stat. 798 (March 3, 1845).

108. No. 14, *A Resolution regulating the Printing of Congress, and establishing the Compensation of [for] the same*, 9 Stat. 112 (July 23, 1846).

109. Ch. LIX, *An Act providing for the Election of a Congressional Printer*, 14 Stat. 398 (February 22, 1867).

110. Schmeckebier, *The Government Printing Office*, 15.

111. P.L. 90-620, 82 Stat. 1238, H.R. 18612, October 22, 1968. *To enact title 44, United States Code, "Public Printing and Documents," codifying the general and permanent law relating to public printing and documents.*

112. U.S. GPO, "Future Digital System (FDsys) Facts and Timeline," press release at http://gpo.gov/pdfs/news-media/press/FDsysFactSheet.pdf.

113. U.S. GPO, "A Strategic Vision for the 21st Century," http://www.gpo.gov/congressional/pdfs/04strategicplan.pdf.

114. U.S. GPO, FDLP Desktop, "2005 Essential Titles Survey Initial Analysis," http://fdlp.gov/component/content/article/19-general/189-essentialtitles-survey2005.

115. U.S. GPO, FDLP Desktop, "GPO and the LOCKSS Alliance—Pilot Project," http://fdlp.gov/component/content/article/715-gpolockss?start=6.

116. U.S. GPO, "GPO Forges Ahead in Creation of Future Digital System," press release at http://gpo.gov/pdfs/news-media/press/06news08.pdf (April 4, 2006).

117. U.S. GPO, "GPO Advances Strategic Vision," press release at http://gpo.gov/pdfs/news-media/press/06news09.pdf (April 10, 2006).

118. U.S. GPO, "GPO Achieves Two Milestones in Producing E-Passports," press release at http://gpo.gov/pdfs/news-media/press/07news15.pdf (May 23, 2007).

119. U.S. GPO, "GPO Creates its First Ever On-Line Guide to Members of Congress," press release at http://gpo.gov/pdfs/news-media/press/07news32.pdf (November 13, 2007).

120. U.S. GPO, "GPO to Authenticate by Digital Signature and Distribute Printed Copies of the Budget of the U.S. Government Fiscal Year 2009," press release at http://gpo.gov/pdfs/news-media/press/08news02.pdf (January 16, 2008).

121. U.S. GPO, FDLP Desktop, "FDL Handbook," http://www.fdlp.gov/administration/handbook.

122. U.S. GPO, "The White House, National Archives and Government Printing Office Achieve Open Government Milestone," press release at http://gpo.gov/pdfs/news-media/press/09news40.pdf (October 5, 2009).

123. U.S. GPO, "GPO and Cornell University Pilot Open Government Initiative," press release at http://gpo.gov/pdfs/news-media/press/10news07.pdf (February 22, 2010).

124. U.S. GPO, "GPO Begins 150 Year Anniversary Celebration," press release at http://gpo.gov/pdfs/news-media/press/10news22.pdf (June 23, 2010).

125. U.S. GPO, "GPO and National Archives Launch Federal Register 2.0," press release at http://gpo.gov/pdfs/news-media/press/10news26.pdf (July 26, 2010).

126. U.S. GPO, "GPO Receives Top Honors for Social Media Initiatives," press release at http://gpo.gov/pdfs/news-media/press/10news45.pdf (December 13, 2010).

127. U.S. GPO, "GPO Partners with GPO to Offer Federal E-Books," press release at http://gpo.gov/pdfs/news-media/press/10news46.pdf (December 14, 2010).

128. U.S. GPO, "Library Advocate Becomes Superintendent of Documents," press release at http://gpo.gov/pdfs/news-media/press/11news04.pdf (January 20, 2011).

129. U.S. GPO, "GPO Launches Facebook Page," press release at http://gpo.gov/pdfs/news-media/press/11news09.pdf (February 7, 2011).

130. U.S. GPO, "GPO Celebrates 150 Years of Keeping America Informed," press release at http://gpo.gov/pdfs/news-media/press/11news14.pdf (March 3, 2011).

131. U.S. GPO, "GSA Turns to GPO's Partnership with Google to Offer Free Government Publications Online," press release at http://gpo.gov/pdfs/news-media/press/11news17.pdf (April 5, 2011).

132. U.S. GPO, "GPO & Federal Judiciary Enhance Public Access to Federal Court Opinions," press release at http://gpo.gov/pdfs/news-media/press/11news23.pdf (May 4, 2011).

133. U.S. Department of Commerce, United States Census Bureau, Web site of the *Statistical Abstract.* "The U.S. Census Bureau is terminating the collection of data for the Statistical Compendia program effective October 1, 2011. The Statistical Compendium program is comprised of the Statistical Abstract of the United States and its supplemental products—the State and Metropolitan Area Data Book and the County

and City Data Book. In preparation for the Fiscal Year 2012 (FY 2012) budget, the Census Bureau did a comprehensive review of a number of programs and had to make difficult proposals to terminate and reduce a number of existing programs in order to acquire funds for higher priority programs. The decision to propose the elimination of this program was not made lightly. To access the most current data, please refer to the organizations cited in the source notes for each table of the Statistical Abstract" (http://www.census.gov/compendia/statab/).

134. U.S. GPO, FDLP Desktop, *Legal Requirements & Program Regulations of the Federal Depository Library Program*, http://purl.fdlp.gov/GPO/gpo9182 (June 2011).

135. House Committee on House Administration, Subcommittee on Oversight, *GPO—Issues and Challenges: How Will GPO Transition to the Future?* 112th Cong., 1st sess. (May 11, 2011), 4–14, 114–331.

136. U.S. GPO, "Public Printer Testifies at Congressional Hearings," press release at http://gpo.gov/pdfs/news-media/press/11news27.pdf (May 12, 2011).

137. U.S. GPO, "GPO Produces One Million Trusted Traveler Program Cards," press release at http://gpo.gov/pdfs/news-media/press/11news28.pdf (May 17, 2011).

138. U.S. GPO, *Authenticity of Electronic Federal Government Publications* (Washington, DC: GPO, 2011). Available online at http://www.gpo.gov/pdfs/authentication/authenticationwhitepaper2011.pdf. In addition to the white paper, an overview document summarizing GPO's authentication program is available at http://www.gpo.gov/pdfs/authentication/authenticationoverview.pdf. For further information about GPO's authentication initiative, visit http://www.gpo.gov/authentication/index.htm.

139. U.S. GPO, "GPO Expands eBook Titles," press release at http://gpo.gov/pdfs/news-media/press/11news38.pdf (July 13, 2011).

140. U.S. GPO, "GPO Produces Global Entry Card for Expedited Airport Travel," press release at http://gpo.gov/pdfs/news-media/press/11news41.pdf (July 27, 2011).

141. U.S. GPO, "Public Printer Makes Historic Appointment," press release at http://gpo.gov/pdfs/news-media/press/11news74.pdf (December 20, 2011).

142. U.S. GPO, "Annual Report FY2011," available online at http://www.gpo.gov/pdfs/ig/FY-2011-Annual-Report.pdf.

143. U.S. GPO, "Public Printer Makes Historic Appointment," press release at http://gpo.gov/pdfs/news-media/press/12news01.pdf (January 3, 2012).

144. iTunes, *The Congressional Record App*. "Description: Read the daily edition of the Congressional Record on your iPad, iPhone or iPod touch. The Congressional Record App is presented by the Library of Congress using data provided by the Office of the Clerk of the U.S. House of Representatives, the Office of the Secretary of the Senate, and the Government Printing Office" (https://itunes.apple.com/us/app/the-congressional-record/id492077075).

145. U.S. GPO, "GPO's Federal Digital System Achieves Record Number of Visits," press release at http://gpo.gov/pdfs/news-media/press/12news09.pdf (February 7, 2012).

146. U.S. GPO, *GPO Mobile*, http://www.gpo.gov/mobile/. Site for GPO's mobile apps.

147. U.S. GPO. "GPO Makes Available the Federal Budget for the First Time as an App," press release at http://gpo.gov/pdfs/news-media/press/12news12.pdf (February 13, 2012).

148. "GPO's Federal Digital System (FDsys) is GPO's official system for free online access to information from all three branches of the Federal Government. The information on FDsys is current and updated daily." U.S. GPO, "The Phases of the GPO Access Shut-Down," http://www.gpo.gov/pdfs/fdsys-info/The-Phases_GPOAccessShut.pdf.

149. U.S. GPO, "GPO Produces 75 Million Electronic Passports," press release at http://gpo.gov/pdfs/news-media/press/12news21.pdf (April 24, 2012).

150. U.S. GPO, "GPO Teams with Barnes & Noble to Sell Federal eBooks," press release at http://gpo.gov/pdfs/news-media/press/12news26.pdf (May 22, 2012).

151. *Nextgov*, "Government Printing Office Adopts Internal XML System," http://www.nextgov.com/mobile/2012/09/government-printing-office-adopts-internal-xml-system/58065/ (September 12, 2012).

152. U.S. GPO, *GPO Mobile*.

153. U.S. GPO, *GPO Strategic Plan FY2013–2017* (Washington, DC: GPO, 2012). Available online at http://www.gpo.gov/pdfs/about/2013-2017_StrategicPlan.pdf.

154. U.S. GPO, "GPO Announces Five Year Strategic Plan," press release at http://gpo.gov/pdfs/news-media/press/12news46.pdf (October 22, 2012).

155. U.S. GPO, *GPO Mobile*.

156. Law Library of Congress, *In Custodia Legis: Law Librarians of Congress.* "Happy Birthday Science.gov!" http://blogs.loc.gov/law/2012/12/happy-birthday-science-gov/.

TWELVE

The Future of Law Libraries: Technology in the Age of Information

Roy Balleste and Billie Jo Kaufman

> If we have learned one thing from the history of invention and discovery, it is that, in the long run—and often in the short one—the most daring prophecies seem laughably conservative.—Arthur C. Clarke

Law libraries are admired and respected as institutions dedicated to safeguarding legal education. Within the law library, the future of legal education is understood as a scholastic achievement progressing toward a common goal. If law librarianship is going to fulfill its goal, it must redefine its legitimate place in legal education. Technology-driven changes have been particularly noticeable in the past two decades. As the twenty-first century continues, it is evident that, for better or worse, the future of computing will be more and more characterized by human-machine interaction. Humanity has started a new age, one in which humanity thrives when information is shared and disseminated for the benefit of all members of society. This chapter seeks to identify the intersection of technology and librarianship within the ambit of legal education.

Communication technologies now represent a new world of convenience, because the Internet has changed how we share information. The Internet, as an avenue of communication, has attributes that set it apart from any previous forms of technological innovation. Its infrastructure is based on scientific breakthroughs worthy of admiration and study. Its power has spread an international movement for innovation that now connects two billion people, with the potential to connect six billion.[1] In the process of its development, the Internet's technological power has become quite versatile. Against this background, law libraries face new challenges while still operating within their traditional atmosphere. The law librarianship world revolves around legal materials in a research-intensive system that continues to serve the research needs of faculty and law students.[2] Law librarianship has continued to evolve throughout the development of the legal profession. For that reason, two factors should be considered while reading this chapter. First, the Internet has become the tool of choice for the transmission of knowledge, delivering many kinds of information more effectively than past delivery methods. Second, while information technology has helped diversify and strengthen the access to law libraries, it is worth noticing that the rapid evolution of technology across the globe has been fueled not just by scientific developments, but also by the economic and technical processes that flow from these developments. It is within this theme of national and international significance that the challenges surrounding law librarianship become apparent. Today, the Internet has opened up the doors of social media, high-speed video, and global communications. The end result is a world in which the law library can serve patrons at any time and in any place.

While society questions the future of libraries, and some even predict their demise, libraries now provide services at all times, every day and in every location around the world where access to the Internet exists. The Working Group on Internet Governance, probably the most successful multistakeholder group to date under the rubric of the United Nations, noted that unequal access to the Internet constitutes a "digital divide." This division exists between developed and developing countries, as well as within nations, including between urban and rural communities.[3]

In 2011, the International Communication Union, one of the specialized agencies of the United Nations, reported that one-third of the world's population, or approximately 2.3 billion individuals,[4] was connected to the Internet; this meant that 65 percent of the world's population was not connected.[5] The good news is that since 2006, developing nations have increased their proportion of Internet users from 44 percent, to 62 percent as of 2011.[6] This achievement is not enough. There are still many people across the globe who lack access. This extremely large group of individuals reside behind a barrier known as the "digital divide." Access to knowledge has become an essential tool in economic, cultural, and social development. Education has empowered people to overcome poverty, and helped them bridge that "digital divide." Increased access to the Internet means an increased need for information professionals to serve these constituencies. Humanity has always been inclined to seek and to discover, while exploring its own existence. What then is the future role of technology in law libraries in this information age? This question is the basis of this chapter.

WINDS OF CHANGE

Information powers civilization. When examining the past, we learn that humanity has managed to achieve great levels of technological sophistication. If we look at our history closely, we learn that entire civilizations have disappeared, and with them, their valuable knowledge. Lost information has always been tied to a reversal of civilization. Are we today less technologically sophisticated than our predecessors? Did our civilization's development suffer from the loss of information available in antiquity? It is unclear how we should answer the first question with certainty. The second must always be answered in the affirmative. One of the most fascinating examples is the story of the Antikythera mechanism, which was designed to calculate the relative movements of the sun, planets, and moon. Today it is located at the National Museum of Greece in Athens.[7] Professor Derek J. de Solla Price suggested that the ancient computer was probably related to one of Archimedes's machines.[8] A masterpiece of the Hellenistic civilization, it is possible that its technical plans were preserved in the Library of Alexandria until the unfortunate destruction of this great center of learning. Technology should not only be used to develop the present; it is also a tool that preserves information for the future. Thousands of years ago, our predecessors lost valuable technical information. Perhaps they considered that information of consequence for only a *few*; perhaps some of that valuable information was destroyed by senseless wars. In this new century, library science reminds us that information is for the ages. This concept constitutes a professional responsibility. This idea does not belong in the world of the abstract, but rather in the present physical world. How can humanity avoid the mistakes of the past? How will it avoid losing knowledge? During the Ptolemy dynasty in the third century BCE, the Library of Alexandria came into existence.[9] The value of this library was appreciated for many centuries, as the great minds of antiquity poured all their knowledge into its vast archives. Unfortunately, a series of catastrophes slowly destroyed the library, until its final annihilation in the middle of the fifth century CE.[10] This terrible end for the library was not the result of a hurricane, volcano, or earthquake. This horrific catastrophe was caused by the "wars of men." Ignorance, fanaticism, and disregard for knowledge reduced the Library of Alexandria to ashes. Many of the great inventions preserved there were lost. Although some were rediscovered hundreds of years later, others were lost forever in time. What kind of knowledge did humanity lose? What types of technologies are now lost to us? The library's final destruction was one more sign of the end of the Roman Empire. The period that followed, the Dark Ages, represented a setback or a reverse in civilization. Whatever is said about the end of the Roman Empire, one thing is certain. A way of life was lost, one in which libraries were no longer maintained, and humanity was no longer learning new concepts

or spreading progressive ideas.[11] Examples of the loss of valuable information were also found across the ocean, in the fascinating civilizations
now known by the ruins at Tiahuanako, Bolivia; the great city of
Teotihuacán in Mexico; and the city of the high Andes, Machu Picchu in
Peru. These cities, along with their civilizations, disappeared, as did their
great architectural and astrophysical secrets. The destruction of these civilizations resulted in the loss of knowledge for posterity.

Yet, this loss of information is not confined to the ancient past. China's
destruction of the libraries of Tibet during the 1950s and 1960s, both after
their 1949 invasion and later during the Cultural Revolution, represents a
modern example and a tragedy that serves as a reminder that civilization
should guard information.[12] Unfortunately, this tragedy continues today
in the form of censorship online by governments that engage in activities
that contravene international human rights standards;[13] it demonstrates
censorship at its worst.

Today's knowledge is the responsibility of all librarians. What will be
the legacy of law librarianship to future generations? Forty years ago, our
computing technology world was dominated by massive machines. In
those days, the space rockets of the Mercury, Gemini, and Apollo missions dominated our imagination. In essence, computer technology was
accessible to a few selected groups of scientists and academics. Times
have changed, and today computer access is widely available to many
individuals. This is by no means equal, as many individuals still remain
behind the "digital divide." For instance, the Pew Internet Project of 2012
reported differences within groups in the United States, usually associated with age, household income, and educational attainment.[14] The data
reports, compiled in 2011, noted that one in five American adults did not
utilize the Internet because they concluded that the technology was not
relevant to them.[15] The report stated that in 1998 individuals relied mainly on bulky desktop computers; in 2012, Internet access increased due to
gadget ownership. Pew reported that today people connect differently to
the Internet, noting that these connections occur not only via desktop
computers, but also by cell phones, laptops, e-book readers, and tablet
computers.[16] Yet Internet accessibility has also been enhanced, in no
small part, by libraries. Consider that technology is forever tied to our
progressive vision, and its development is inevitably connected to the
landscape of law libraries. Computer technology has been directly related
to the processing of calculations, the organization of information, and the
storage of data. This technology now belongs to the world of intercon-
nected computers: the Internet. This human technological achievement, a
system of information and communication technology (ICT), is a network
formed by millions of servers and computers sharing data with one another.[17] This innovation has changed societies across the globe. It is the
most important and most fascinating tool for communication and research. Human beings live within a technological society that is now

known as the *information society.*[18] Arguably, many technological devices and related services will be invented or discovered in years to come, tapping into the imagination of human civilization. The impact and continuing nature of discovery tools, such as Encore and Decision Center, from Innovative Interfaces, or management tools, such as CONTENTdm from OCLC, are great examples of expanding the capabilities of the basic database to offer increased ease when accessing information, but also, to make statistics and other background data available for librarians as they provide greater services to users. These tools enable librarians to advocate and explain the use and cost of the collections being provided.

Today, law libraries enjoy the convenience of online library catalogs, as computers continue to make a direct impact on their daily operations. The "age of information" continues to develop, and law libraries face new challenges with additional breakthroughs in wireless standards, artificial intelligence, and quantum computing. These are relevant technology trends that will influence future libraries. All these considerations center on the importance of technological innovations, their influence in libraries, and the present and future technological landscape. This includes a future panorama, not yet realized, that has the potential to change how libraries deliver legal information.

The pressure of change is obvious in today's world of law librarianship. How much has law librarianship been changed by technology in the past ten years? Libraries participating in the design process for new buildings continue to consider the shrinking size of their print collections.

Figure 12.1.   Inside the Bibliotecha Alexandrina, Egypt. © Carsten Whimster "New Library of Alexandria"

With changes in technology, there is a need to create areas for information commons that materialize into reading rooms conducive to study and that also allow students to interact with technology.[19] Information delivery is transitioning and has been for over a decade. This is now an accepted reality. The electronic environment is the preferred method for a new generation of students. It is difficult to ignore the fact that electronic resources have become more prevalent. Because of this, another question has arisen: Will libraries permanently own or merely lease their access to information? This is an ongoing challenge. This challenge is made more difficult by university budgeting processes, which attach twentieth-century terminology, such as "capital expenditures," to twenty-first century acquisitions, such as online databases. Some librarians report that their budget officers just don't understand how their collections have changed over time; electronic collections may be accessed or licensed, but they may not be "owned."

How will this state of affairs shape the law librarianship landscape? These are very serious questions that will be debated for quite some time. For now, it is safe to say that we continue to need both print and electronic sources. Electronic resources will push away the need for print, making electronic sources the dominant format for information delivery in a not-too-distant future. The electronic delivery trend may dictate that publishers choose to offer fewer print publications. The future may also show that library users do not recognize print as a valuable resource. The accessibility and increased use of electronic treatises and casebooks will continue to make these resources cheaper and easier to use. In other words, electronic resources will continue to develop quickly. Yet we must not underestimate the power of old print collections. Some print collections have historical value; legal practitioners may find the answer to historical legislative questions only within these materials.

An example of lost print and missing knowledge involves the Olmecs. The efforts of archeologists and historians to understand the history of the Olmecs, the oldest Mesoamerican civilization, have been frustrated because of a lack of information. The Olmecs' history was preserved for many generations by the Aztecs. Unfortunately destroyed during the Spanish conquest, the Aztecs' historical records would have been priceless to historians of the present time.

MOBILE WIRELESS, QUANTUM COMPUTERS, AND THE WEB OF CONVENIENCE

The most beautiful experience we can have is the mysterious—the fundamental emotion which stands at the cradle of true art and true science.—Albert Einstein[20]

Around the year 2000, law libraries began to investigate and invest in wireless technologies. The wireless standards were improved from 802.11b to 802.11g around 2005. These standards opened a doorway to a world that had operated in concealment. Computers were connected to the Internet, but cables were no longer needed to connect to the wall outlet, and thus, to the network. Just twelve years ago, 802.11b, a standard for wireless local area networks (WLANs), was being used by libraries. The authority on wireless standards is the Institute of Electrical and Electronics Engineers (IEEE), which specifies the technical standards for wireless networking. As time passed, the 802.11n standard gained prominence, due to its ability to provide higher data speeds. As the next generation of wireless applications surfaces, it may take the form of 802.11ac. For the future, this means there will be faster delivery of information.

How exactly does this work? A workable wireless network, for example, requires access points throughout the library. Access points allow computers to connect to or access the network. In essence, the access points located in the roof of the library allow radio signals to communicate with the internal wireless cards in the computers of staff, faculty, and students. The access points are pieces of hardware connected to the wired network, which allow multiple computers to connect through them to the network. A router, or junction, connects the law library network, for example, with the rest of the university network. The bottom line is that devices connected to the network expand our ability to access information. This architecture allows faculty and law students to connect with their wireless-enabled devices from practically any location on campus. The wireless world of convenience has now become mobile. Our homes now have the option of having their own wireless routers. Many restaurants and airlines offer wireless access. In fact, wireless could now simply be comparable to electric power: consumers expect it. Since 2011, wireless services have expanded, allowing users to create their own "hotspots," and thus their own mobile networks. These capabilities are no longer the playground for scientists, librarians, or geeks; they are for everyone. It is not uncommon to encounter Wi-Fi-enabled facilities in places such as bookstores, restaurants, and airports. It is amazing to consider that McDonald's offers Wi-Fi services in thousands of their restaurants around the world. It is not surprising that McDonald's offers this service, however; what it is mind-boggling is that this company is not in the service of providing access to information. Understanding wireless possibilities brought librarians the realization that law libraries could go beyond their physical walls. The law library network was no longer restricted to the library building. Students could access library resources from the classrooms, lounges, and other buildings on a university campus, and even from the open spaces in between buildings. Wireless technologies, in essence, enhanced the reach of law libraries. This technology then expanded access to the Internet. Although it is not necessary for law librarians to have a detailed knowledge of wireless technology, it is helpful to have some basic knowledge of its inner workings, especially if one is interested in upper-management positions.

Wireless technologies have revolutionized our present mobile society. Patrons have learned the convenience of this service, whether in the library, classrooms, office, courthouse, law firm, or home. Across the country, law libraries continue to provide wireless connectivity, while keeping a close watch on the development of this technology. The ability to call, text, browse, and access e-mail in practically any location provides Wi-Fi with a loyal fan base. Academic law librarians can gauge the state of technology by the mere observation of technology usage by patrons in their daily lives. Today the usage of tablets is on the rise. Patrons are accustomed to having access to these services, just as they were once attracted, not too long ago, to the convenience offered by the typewriter or the pay phone. The use of technology has always influenced, and will continue to influence, the way business is handled at our law libraries.

This brings another consideration: Will computer labs be necessary in the future? It seems unlikely, but only time will tell. Indeed, many libraries continue to downsize their labs. Some have chosen that path out of necessity to make room for collections and collaborative learning environments. In this day and age, many students simply push aside the desktops to make room for their tablets or laptops. While there may be some type of a lab in the library of the future, it is possible that the computer labs will be replaced by convenience kiosks for e-mail look-up or for printing services. The Internet has opened up great possibilities for the future, and its graphical display, the browser, has expanded those possibilities even further. While the Internet created an international network of communications, this technology would have been much less useful without a graphical user interface (GUI). These interfaces became the center of development for human-computer interaction designs, and experts date the events back to 1970—the prehistory of modern Web browsing.[21] It all began with Xerox in 1970 and the later invention of the mouse.[22] It took nineteen years of technical developments for that final seed that would propel the rise of the World Wide Web. For it was in 1989 that Sir Tim Berners-Lee and Robert Cailliau, working at the European Center for High-Energy Physics (CERN) in Geneva, Switzerland, proposed the creation of HTML.[23] During the 1980s and 1990s, all the components of the modern browser were developed; from the introduction of the mouse by Xerox in 1974, to upgrades in design and addition of color, by various companies such as Microsoft and Apple.[24] Since then, Berners-Lee has played an active role in guiding the development of Web standards, and in recent years, has advocated his vision of a Semantic Web, a more intelligent web.[25] In 1991, Mark Cahill at the University of Minnesota led the development team of the Internet Gopher, the first widely-adopted menu-based browser for document delivery.[26] The following year, Mark Andreessen and his team from the National Center for Supercomputing Applications (NCSA) at the University of Illinois released Mosaic, the first graphical browser for the Web.[27] In 1994, they would leave NCSA to work on an improved commercial version of the browser called Netscape.[28] This type of browser was the precursor to the more popular Internet Explorer, Google Chrome, and Firefox. In the late 1990s, the Internet and its partner invention, the World Wide Web, experienced the commercialization and the development of new products and services that today we enjoy.

By 2002, the concept of artificial intelligence (AI) within the Internet was beginning to take form. Artificial intelligence is another frontier to be explored.[29] AI has been for many years a topic considered by science fiction writers. But today, AI technologies seem to be at a stage that allows librarians to contemplate their adoption within familiar Internet tools. Considering artificial intelligence tools within a browser would be a good example of applying cutting-edge technology within the Internet. AI is intended to work as a "virtual assistant" that adds "invisible" enhanced services to the browsing experience. Consider that AI has the potential to enhance the distribution and management of information. The future, no doubt, will belong to Internet searching enhanced by artificial intelligence.

Computer science continues to evolve, and with it, new ways of information delivery. One possible vehicle for this progress is development of quantum computers. The era of computing soon will become the age of quantum computers. The story of the Antikythera mechanism and Archimedes, if considered, would place the beginning of the history of computers hundreds of years further into the past.[30] In any case, the modern computing world began to be developed during the early 1800s with the mechanical devices of the English mathematician Charles Babbage. The modern era of computing evolved with the design of gears and wheels; then vacuum tubes redefined computers. Later, transistors revolutionized computing, and to our surprise, integrated circuits were even better. Now, in the twenty-first century, quantum particles will take computers to a higher level of performance. This is the quantum world that librarians will learn to embrace.

The science of quantum computing originates from quantum mechanics and the laws of physics. Because quantum particles exist at the atomic level, working with them will allow new computers to process calculations at speeds only found today in our imagination.[31] A computer, for example, transfers information or bits. This information is transferred based on the binary code, which in turn is based on a value in relation to another, as in the case of a 1 or a 0.[32] This is the limited existence of today's computers. On the other hand, quantum computers are not limited to two states, since information transfer is powered by quantum bits, or *qubits.* In quantum computers, information transfer is based on a 1 or a

0, or it can be a superposition that is simultaneously both 1 and 0.[33] Keep in mind that superposition is somewhat of a tricky concept to visualize. Developments in quantum mechanics have opened the door to the world of teleportation. Consider that in quantum computers, information may exist at the same time in two destinations, coexisting around that qubit. Now further consider that a qubit may be represented as a photon (a beam of light). In our universe an object exists in one place at a time; yet that is an assumption of conventional wisdom. A photon may exist in two places at once, allowing for the transmission of information at a speed faster than light. That is so because the qubit holds a relationship with its counterpart in another place of existence. This is called *entanglement*.[34] When two particles are entangled, they behave as one, regardless of how far apart they are. This is also the same principle being studied by scientists to develop further the science of teleportation. In essence, teleportation would facilitate the transmission of information between computers.[35]

To visualize further the inner workings of a quantum computer, consider for a moment this concept of teleportation. Quantum teleportation is a field of study that also belongs to quantum mechanics and quantum mechanics is a field of study that belongs to physics. Although this concept may be perceived as far-fetched, consider the theories presented by the German physicist Werner Heisenberg.[36] The ability to be transported, or being "beamed up" via a particle stream to another location in a matter of seconds, is certainly science fiction, reserved to shows such as the *Star Trek* series, correct? Heisenberg believed that it would be difficult to calibrate the position of an object (or person) as it traveled in the stream. In the *Star Trek* series, a device called the Heisenberg compensator is utilized to avoid the drawbacks presented by Heisenberg's principle. In the show, the transporters are equipped with a "compensator" to protect the integrity of the object while traveling in the stream, thus making teleportation a reality. Times have changed, and today progress has been made in the field of physics. The concept is now beyond science fiction. Quantum teleportation began its early stages of successful development in 1993 when a group of scientists from around the world managed to beam particles of light from one location to another thanks to the principle of entanglement, which helps to compensate for the shortcomings presented by Heisenberg, and sets the stage for a new category of computers.[37] Physicists found that a "fundamental feature of quantum mechanics, entanglement, could be used to circumvent the limitations imposed by Heisenberg's uncertainty principle without violating it."[38] Just as with teleportation, quantum computers could utilize entanglement to transfer information at super-fast speeds. Since quantum computers operate in more than one state at the same time, they promise to provide information billions of times faster than today's computers.

This technology is exciting. Our information universe, including the law library world, is on the verge of another major technological evolution. For example, while the inner components of a computer would consist of silicon-based circuits, cables, and screws, the inner components of a quantum computer would be based on some form of radio wave interface, magnetic fields, or lasers combined with crystals. A quantum computer could be designed with crystals catching information delivered by photons traveling on laser beams; in essence, a quantum memory.[39] Mathematically, quantum computers are a possibility. Preliminary laboratory trials around the world have produced interesting and positive results. Consider that around 2020, the first quantum computers could appear on some university campuses. A practical quantum computer for consumers could be available around 2030.

THE RISE OF INTERNET GOVERNANCE

The law library world does not operate in isolation. It must keep up with technology in order to serve its constituents. Librarians are also interested in openness and access to information. These two simple concepts establish the policies and regulations that constitute the world of Internet governance. Internet governance is a multifaceted field of standards and regulations. Scientific developments, commercial forces, and political interests have fueled the rapid development of information and communications technologies (ICTs). Thus, the history and controversies surrounding Internet governance traverse the interests of a wide range of actors (or stakeholders). Internet governance can be said to overlap with the values inherent in state sovereignty, social justice, security, human rights, technical standards, and ultimately human dignity. For law librarians and all librarians in general, it is important to have a grasp of this subject. For example, while a law library may own a *domain name*, how that entire domain is managed within its *top-level domain* (TLD) is equally relevant. Have you ever wondered what is needed to own a Web site within the ".edu" domain? Who manages the .edu TLD? To understand how a TLD works, it is helpful to visualize the Internet's architecture. Communications on the Internet are facilitated by unique Internet Protocol (IP) addresses.[40] These numbers consisting of four blocks of up to three digits each (for example, 123.456.789.11) identify a device connected to the network. Just as with telephones, the Internet requires that computers have a numerical identifier before a connection can be made.[41] The Internet works by recognizing this unique IP address on every computer. As a computer sends information to another, the data is broken down into packets that contain the address of the recipient, another IP address.[42] These addresses work within a particular top-level domain, and the domain is part of the overall domain name system, which is a hierarchical database that includes the IP addresses.[43] These IP addresses work under a subdivision scheme. An IP address is always divided in two parts: top-level domain (TLD) and second-level domain (SLD). The TLD represents the last segment of the domain name, which is its most authoritative subdivision.

Looking again at the .edu domain, all TLDs must follow rules managed by their particular *registrars*. The registrar is the entity that sells consumers a domain name. In the case of all domain names within .edu, EDUCAUSE is the exclusive registrar of these domains. This exclusivity was granted to EDUCAUSE by the U.S. Department of Commerce in 2001.[44] The Department of Commerce has been involved in Internet policymaking since 1998, when the U.S. government issued the "Memorandum of Understanding between the U.S. Department of Commerce and the Internet Corporation for Assigned Names and Numbers."[45] For law librarians, another key concept is essential: the *multistakeholder process* within Internet governance. While the Internet was an American marvel of engineering, this technology was shared with the world, and subjected to national governments' control over access, content, and security. There are nongovernment stakeholders who have advocated in other matters, including democratic legitimacy and human rights. While technology continues to change our way of life, the law and policy that surround these changes are equally important. There are various stakeholders involved in the debate, and for the most part, they are categorized as nation-states, the private sector, nongovernmental organizations (NGOs), intergovernmental organizations, and civil society, including academia. Internet-governance policies center around worldwide laws and technical standards for managing the domain name system (DNS), all top-level domains (TLDs), IP-address allocation, and the Internet's root zone. The Internet Corporation for Assigned Names and Numbers (ICANN) oversees those matters on behalf of the U.S. government. VeriSign, under contract with the U.S. government, oversees the management of the root of the Internet.

If a new law is going to be utilized to block a particular group of Web pages, then librarians need to be informed of the policies surrounding the drafting, development, and implementation of the new law, which may interfere with the delivery of information. There are those who believe that controlling the Internet allows them total authority to censor content in the name of public morals or security. While there are perfectly legitimate reasons why a government, or other entity, may decide to block a Web site or series of Web sites—such as for the protection of children, intellectual property, or national security—it is also true that political censorship is often disguised as something else. Indeed, in 2011 the United Nations Special Rapporteur on the promotion and protection of the right to freedom of opinion and expression noted that governments had criminalized legitimate online expression, as in the case of the imprisonment of bloggers, simply because those governments did not agree with the views expressed by those bloggers.[46] This is why decisions of control should be subject to a constant process of review in which all stakeholders participate. This is at the core of Internet governance. Representing libraries, the International Federation of Library Associations and Institutions has remained active within Internet-governance discussions.[47] IFLA is also concerned with governments that engage in activities that on the surface seem legitimate and necessary, but that are actually biased activities designed to limit, control, and curtail legitimate speech online.

The Internet remains under the technical control of the U.S. government. It is administered primarily by private U.S. entities, such as ICANN and Verisign, under contract with the U.S. Department of Commerce. Librarians willing to engage in this vital debate should familiarize themselves with all aspects of and participants in this important discussion. Internet governance recognizes the growing interaction and interdependence of individuals and technology. It is here that we find the future of Internet governance. Librarians should promote and support the current trend toward more diversity of participants in the Internet-governance process.

THE ELECTRONIC SERVICES LIBRARIAN

In today's law library world, library users expect interactivity with Web resources. Our libraries' Web pages provide numerous personalized services to students, faculty, staff, judges, attorneys, and members of the public. In cyberspace, electronic services librarians have become interactive players. Their skills have proven very effective in connecting the technological worlds of the libraries and their users. Librarians have always worked with library technology, from the rudimentary to the complex.

Today, the electronic services librarian is, to a greater degree, a product of the information age. What do they do? They spend a significant amount of time keeping patrons informed through Web page design efforts. They are involved with their IT departments. They acquire knowledge of hardware and software. Their days are filled with projects that may involve designing, maintaining, and updating library Web sites. They may also work with the online catalog; work in database management with Westlaw, Lexis, Bloomberg Law/BNA, HeinOnline, and Law360; track the installation of software versions; and attend conferences that discuss technology topics. They are librarians, and have the traditional duties of reference, legal research, and evaluation of print resources to make recommendations for future acquisitions. This position provides the opportunity to introduce and teach faculty, students, and/or attorneys about the electronic sources acquired by the library. The elec-

tronic services librarian works very closely with acquisitions of databases, licensing, use, and definition of users. In addition, this position
must market and work with library administration on user data statistics.
This librarian can be crucial in helping patrons understand the differences between databases, print resources that are delivered digitally, and
Web site links. Careful instruction helping patrons recognize these dis-
tinctions may seem unnecessary, but users should recognize the appropriate use of resources and tools and proper citation.

Electronic services librarians are not limited to these duties. The electronic services librarian's strength comes from the knowledge of technology. This can be difficult, since our technological world continues to
change at a very fast pace. Knowledge of HTML is inescapable, and in
some cases, these librarians must work with JavaScript and XML. It is
clear that traditional collection-development procedures no longer reflect
a complete picture of acquisition activity within a library. Libraries are
actively seeking new means to integrate electronic resources, while patrons are expanding their use of online databases and using the Internet
for an increasing amount of research. Financial allocations directed toward collection development have increased to acquire additional digital
formats. Today, virtual reference desk (VRD) services are mainstream—
an extension of reference services. VRD technology is an option to communicate with distant students, an instrument to attract law students to
the library resources, and a marketing tool. More than ever, librarians
must have a significant presence as the current generation of students
continues to rely on more electronic resources for information.

Similar to the role of professional futurists, we must take a holistic
approach to the future, considering the interrelationships between technology, our patrons, legal education, and the future of our collections.
That is the nature of the electronic age. Librarians must stay informed
about new trends in technology development while anticipating potential new trends. Participation in national and international events, membership in listservs, reviewing publications, and networking with colleagues allow librarians to stay up to date. Librarians have become the
bridge between technology and law school administration. They are sen-
tries who consider, analyze, review, and scout for new technologies that
will be beneficial to the law library, and ultimately to the patrons they
serve. It is worth noting that within AALL, the Computing Services Special Interest Section (CS-SIS) recognizes the importance of new technologies in law libraries. Many electronic services librarians are members of
the CS-SIS. Because technology continues to be such an important topic
for our future libraries, it is recommended that all librarians join the CS-
SIS. The Computing Services Special Interest Section has been helping
librarians improve services with the use of computers and the Internet. It
is here that we discover the importance of networking with colleagues—

to discover new ideas, meet librarians with equal interests, and participate in conferences that discuss the use of technology in librarianship.[48]

We could not leave this section without sharing the importance of the Center for Computer-Assisted Legal Instruction (CALI) and the CALI conference. This group of legal academics, professors, and law librarians has worked together for many years to find ways to apply technology to legal education. CALI is a nonprofit 501(c)(3) consortium incorporated in 1982 with membership from nearly every U.S. law school, paralegal programs, law firms, and individuals, and it is aimed at providing support in the use of technology and distance learning in legal education.[49] CALI is famous for its creative design and distribution of a DVD containing CALI lessons (computer-based tutorials) that are useful to all law students. CALI also promotes the creation of these lessons online. The CALI conference has become the place to discuss, analyze, and see into the future the use of technology in legal education.[50]

CONCLUSION

> . . . I shall be telling this with a sigh
> Somewhere ages and ages hence:
> Two roads diverged in a wood, and I,
> I took the one less traveled by,
> And that has made all the difference.
> —Robert Frost[51]

This chapter has sought to present an innovative way of seeing technology in libraries. Our goal as information professionals is to maximize research, teaching, and learning through educational technologies. To support this effort, librarians continue to utilize technology as the avenue of delivery for a superior learning experience. The ultimate purpose continues to be to gain a better understanding of technology and to develop effective services for our libraries. Long distances are no longer a barrier to information delivery and accessibility. Much work has been done over the past ten years to make information more accessible to law students and faculty. As educational technologies continue to be incorporated into higher education, it is important to understand how to maximize their utility. New devices and software programs have appeared on the market that promise to enhance our ability to help our patrons. Now the very existence and usability of these technologies present us with an opportunity to challenge ourselves as we seek to design new educational interfaces. These interfaces, in turn, allow us to provide better service to our patrons, as the law library continues to be the nerve center of the legal world: the place where all roads connect to information. As we consider this new technological realm, think for a moment about Roy Tennant's truths:[52]

1. You don't want to be the first or last in any technology.
2. Everything you do should be geared toward the user.
3. Don't expect users to know what they want until they see it.
4. Never underestimate the power of a prototype.
5. Always make a backup.
6. Buy hardware at the last possible moment.
7. Don't buy software with a zero at the end of the release number.
8. Never bother with Silo systems (they don't interact with anything else).
9. If you can't be with the operating system you love, love the one you're with.

There is no doubt that law librarians and computer science have intermingled and forever are connected in library operations. This chapter, therefore, has considered subjects such as wireless technologies, artificial intelligence, Internet governance, quantum computing, and finally, the role of the librarian in technology implementation. Consider that, as a profession, law librarianship is in transition. Our profession is rapidly developing and will require that law librarians continue to become familiar with some computing matters. More importantly, shifts in the profession require of librarians the desire to learn and adapt to these new changes. The survival of law librarians in the future will depend on just that, adaptability. We will humbly leave you with Balleste and Kaufman's postulates about the future. In twenty years. . .

1. Law libraries will continue to be centers of learning.
2. Law librarians will not be called *librarians*.
3. The power of print will be diminished.
4. Library science will merge with computer science.
5. There will be a futurist in all of us.

To you, the student of library and information science, we say, join our profession to discover a greater understanding of present and future technologies. Your findings might surprise you, or at the very least enlighten you. We have an opportunity here and now to gain a grasp of the different factors and dimensions that technology offers our profession, and to explore the ways in which these technologies take libraries into the ambit of the world of tomorrow. Similar to the role of professional futurists, librarians will take a holistic approach to the profession, considering the interrelationships between technology, patrons, legal education, and the future of law library collections. The driving force of law librarianship and technology will rest in honoring and contributing to the efforts of many who have worked and searched, and will continue to work and search, for better services.

NOTES

1. Chairman's Summary, Second Meeting of the Internet Governance Forum, Rio de Janeiro, November 12–15, 2007, available at http://www.intgovforum.org/cms/index.php/secondmeeting.

2. S. Matheson and S. Davidson, "The Evolution of Providing Access to Information: Is the Online Catalog Nearing Extinction?" *Legal Reference Services Quarterly* 26, no. 1 (2007), 57–89.

3. Working Group on Internet Governance, WGIG Background Report, June 2005, paragraph 191, available at http://www.wgig.org/WGIG-Report.html.

4. According to the U.S. Census Bureau, the estimated world population number was 7,057,349,019 as of December of 2012; available at http://www.census.gov/main/www/popclock.html.

5. International Telecommunication Union, "The World in 2011: ICT Facts and Figures," available at http://www.itu.int/ITU-D/ict/facts/2011/index.html.

6. Ibid.

7. See Derek J. de Solla Price, "An Ancient Greek Computer," *Scientific American* 200, no. 6 (June 1959): 60–7.

8. Ibid.

9. Luciano Canfora, *The Vanished Library* (Los Angeles: University of California Press, 1987), 119–22.

10. Ibid., 190.

11. Thomas Cahill, *How the Irish Saved Civilization* (New York: Anchor Books, 1995), 33.

12. Rebecca J. Knutt, "China's Destruction of the Libraries of Tibet," in *Lost Libraries: The Destruction of Great Book Collections since Antiquity*, ed. James Raven, 247–59 (New York: Palgrave Macmillan, 2004).

13. Jonathan Zittrain and John Palfrey, Introduction to *Access Denied: The Practice and Policy of Global Internet Filtering*, ed. Ronal Deibert, John Palfrey, Rafal Rohozinski, and Jonathan Zittrain, 5–9 (Cambridge, MA: MIT Press, 2008).

14. Pew Internet Project of 2012.

15. Ibid.

16. Ibid.

17. "Information and Communication Technology: The combination of both terms took place in the 1980s to emphasize the merging of both technologies." See Deutsche Telekom, available at https://www.telekom.com/dtag/cms/content/dt/en/258604;jsessionid=DF766904E7BB81C67011E75D2DD5B444#.

18. The information society is a political, social, and technological concept, based on the "digital revolution" in information and communication technologies, that promotes a free flow of information, ideas, and knowledge across the globe. From World Summit on the Information Society, "What Is the Information Society? Basic Information—Frequently Asked Questions," available at http://www.itu.int/wsis/basic/faqs.asp.

19. For example, http://www.aallnet.org/main-menu/Publications/spectrum/Archives/Vol-16/No-7/fsu.pdf; http://www.aallnet.org/main-menu/Publications/spectrum/Archives/Vol-16/No-7/pacific-mcgeorge.pdf.

20. Albert Einstein (1879–1955) was a physicist and one of the greatest scientists of the twentieth century. He proposed the famous theory of relativity.

21. Wilbert O. Galitz, *The Essential Guide to User Interface Design: An Introduction to GUI Design Principles and Techniques* (Indianapolis: Wiley, 2007), 6–8.

22. Ibid., 6.

23. Ibid., 8.

24. Ibid., 7–8.

25. The Semantic Web, also known as the World Wide Web 3, is designed to enhance connectivity of information on the Web. This new Web will help researchers

find and organize information efficiently. See the World Wide Web Consortium (W3C), "W3C Semantic Web Activity," available at http://www.w3.org/2001/sw/.

26. M. McCahill et al., Network Working Group, Request for Comments: 1436, The Internet Gopher Protocol (a distributed document search and retrieval protocol), University of Minnesota, March 1993. See also Janet Abbate, *Inventing the Internet* (Cambridge, MA: MIT Press, 2000), 213.

27. Abbate, *Inventing the Internet*, 216–18.

28. Ibid.

29. This section of the chapter is based on Roy Balleste's winning entry in the new member division of the 2004 AALL/LexisNexis Call for Papers Competition.

30. Derek De Solla Price, "Gears from the Greeks: The Antikythera Mechanism — A Calendar Computer from ca. 80 B.C.," *Transactions of the American Philosophical Society* 64, part 7 (1974).

31. George Johnson, *A Shortcut through Time: The Path to the Quantum Computer* (New York: Alfred A. Knopf, 2003), 5–8.

32. Ibid., 6–8.

33. Ibid.

34. Ibid., 41–44.

35. Anton Zeilinger, "Quantum Teleportation," *Scientific America*, special edition 13, no. 1 (May 2003): 34–43.

36. Ibid., 39.

37. Ibid., 40. For more information on entanglement, see Dirk Bouwmeester, Artur Ekert, and Anton Zeilinger, *The Physics of Quantum Information* (New York: Springer-Verlag, 2000).

38. Zeilinger, "Quantum Teleportation," 40.

39. Dr. Matthew J. Sellers, professor of physics and engineering in the Department of Quantum Science of the Australian National University, Canberra, illustrated in great detail this concept. For more information, see John Hudson, "This Laser Trick's a Quantum Leap," *Wired*, October 4, 2005, http://www.wired.com/science/discoveries/news/2005/10/69033.

40. William Stallings, *Data and Computer Communications* (2007), 166.

41. See Jon Postel and Zaw-Sing Su, *The Domain Naming Convention for Internet User Applications*, Network Working Group, Request for Comments: 819, August 1982. See also P. Mockapetris, *Domain Names: Implementation and Specification*, Network Working Group, Request for Comments: 1035, November 1987.

42. Stallings, *Data and Computer Communications*, 25.

43. Stallings, *Data and Computer Communications*, 777.

44. EDUCAUSE, http://net.educause.edu/edudomain/.

45. National Telecommunications and Information Administration, *Domain Names: Management of Internet Names and Addresses*, "Memorandum of Understanding Between the Department of Commerce and the Internet Corporation for Assigned Names and Numbers (ICANN)", available at http://www.ntia.doc.gov/ntiahome/domainname/icann.htm.

46. Frank La Rue, Report of the Special Rapporteur on key trends and challenges to the right of all individuals to seek, receive and impart information and ideas of all kinds through the Internet, ¶¶ 34-35, A/HRC/17/27, May 16, 2011.

47. International Federation of Library Associations and Institutions, "IFLA Position on Internet Governance," http://www.ifla.org/publications/ifla-position-on-internet-governance.

48. American Association of Law Libraries Computing Services Special Interest Section, "About the AALL Computing Services SIS," http://cssis.org/about/about-cssis.

49. See the Center for Computer-Assisted Legal Instruction (CALI) Web site, http://www.cali.org/content/about-cali.

50. See the Center for Computer-Assisted Legal Instruction (CALI) Web site, "Cali DVDs," http://www.cali.org/content/cali-dvds.

51. Robert L. Frost (1874–1963) was an American poet.

52. See Roy Tennant's professional Web site, http://roytennant.com/profession-al.html.

THIRTEEN

The Law Library of Congress

Christine Sellers[1]

The Library of Congress was built around the wise advice of Thomas Jefferson, who said: "There is no subject to which a member of Congress may not have occasion to refer."[2] The Law Library of Congress was established by Congress in 1832 as a branch of the Library of Congress. Today, the Law Library of Congress is not only the largest law collection in the world, with a collection of more than 2.82 million volumes, spanning the ages and covering virtually every jurisdiction of the world, it is also an institution serving Congress and the public with unparalleled research and reference services, and extensive electronic services and products.[3] The Law Library of Congress serves a wide range of functions; some are better known than others. It provides research and reference assistance, oversees the preeminent legal collection available, and houses an international staff of foreign law attorneys.[4]

HISTORY

Initiatives to establish a congressional library, begun as early as 1782, were unsuccessful. Why? Congress had access to libraries in New York and Philadelphia as it migrated between the two cities. However, before Congress made the move to Washington, President Adams signed a bill creating a congressional library, with an appropriation of $5,000. The following year, with a grand total of 728 volumes and three maps, the library arrived and was set up in the nation's capital, where it was to reside, with a short hiatus due to fire, for the next ninety-six years.[5] "Because the nascent American legal system was almost wholly depen-

255

dent on the court-based English common law, there were few American legal publications. Of the forty law titles contained in the original collection, only two were produced on American soil."[6] In the beginning, access to the collection was limited to the president, the vice president, and the members of Congress. As a result, the Supreme Court justices relied primarily on their own libraries to carry out their work. In 1812, President Madison signed a joint resolution that granted the justices the same access to the library as the members of Congress had.[7]

In 1814, the British attacked the capital. This resulted in a fire that completely destroyed the library and its 174 law titles. The library of Thomas Jefferson was then purchased for $23,950 to form the basis for the new Library. Jefferson's collection contained 6,487 volumes, of which 475 were law titles in 639 volumes.[8] Of these, 318 were published in England. The collection also "included Virginia laws and court decisions, but material from other states (which Jefferson had classified as 'foreign law') remained limited. Although the Library received copies of all federal laws and Supreme Court decisions, obtaining state laws and decisions of state courts remained a problem for decades."[9]

Initiatives to create a separate law department within the Library of Congress started in 1816 with the introduction of a bill by Senator Robert Goodloe Harper. Congress, the Court, lawyers, and others felt the need for a separate law library in Washington. On July 14, 1832, President Andrew Jackson signed a bill establishing the Law Library, placing it under the control of the Supreme Court justices.[10] "The books would be selected by the chief justice, which provided more consistent selection than that resulting from the changing membership of the Joint Committee on the library," which had previously selected the books.[11] The 2,011 law books that were segregated from the main collection at this time formed the core of what would become the world's largest law library. "The significance of the 1832 'charter' establishing a separate Law Library [was] a recognition of the special place that legal research should hold in a society whose government [was] based on democratic legal principles."[12] As a result, the Law Library was given a separate book fund from the main Library of Congress.[13] In 1833, the justices granted borrowing privileges to members of the bar with cases before the Court. That same year, Charles Henry Wharton Meehan was appointed the first law librarian of Congress. In 1839, the first separate catalog for law books was printed.[14]

"Throughout its history, the Law Library has been directly and immediately affected by world events and the involvement of the U.S. government in them."[15] After the war with Mexico, the U.S. Congress in 1848 instructed the Law Library to obtain all available Mexican constitutions. By 1870, the Law Library was the country's largest law library at the time, thanks to "the centralization of all of the U.S. copyright registrations and deposits in the Library of Congress."[16] As a result of the increased collection, the Law Library was moved to the Old Supreme Court Chamber in the U.S. Capitol in 1860. The Thomas Jefferson Building opened to house the Library of Congress, as well as the Congressional Library, in 1897, but the Law Library remained in the U.S. Capitol building.[17] In 1888, Congress passed a law that directed that the Law Library remain open whenever either house was in session.[18] The law collection was gradually transferred to the Thomas Jefferson Building's Northeast Pavilion in 1901. While the collection was moved, the Law Library itself remained in the U.S. Capitol as a reference center.[19] As a result, this meant that the law collections were held in several different places. The collection in the U.S. Capitol building and its reference librarian were maintained until 1988.[20]

In 1917, the Law Library assumed responsibility for foreign and comparative legal research, while American law and public policy research became the purview of the Legislative Reference Service, later known as the Congressional Research Service (CRS). This is when "the Law Library gradually makes the transition from a strictly legislative and government reference library to a legal research center, and the tasks of the staff evolve from merely 'finding the books' and 'finding the law' to producing written legal analyses and comparative studies for the use of Congress in its effort to legislative more effectively."[21] This transition was also marked in 1909 with the publication of the index to the United States federal statutes, which immediately became a standard reference work for law libraries. The Law Library also began to produce bibliographic guides to the laws of foreign countries. For the next several decades, major publications on the laws of Spain, France, the larger Latin American countries, Eastern Europe and East Asia were published.[22] "Initially the work was done by temporary staff or outside experts, but after the mid-1930s the Law Library gradually began adding permanent staff whose primary qualifications were in foreign rather than U.S. law."[23]

John T. Vance, scholar and diplomat, became the thirteenth law librarian in 1924. Under him, the size of the Law Library's collection doubled, and the Law Library's reputation was established as a foreign law research center. The Law Library turned one hundred in 1932. During this anniversary year, "the Law Library makes a concerted drive to publicize its needs and to seek the support it must have to become the national law library."[24] That same year, the American Bar Association established a Committee on the Facilities of the Law Library of Congress to increase support from Congress and the bar. George Wickersham founded the Friends of the Law Library in 1934 to support the Law Library as well.[25]

The historic ties between the Law Library and the Supreme Court were officially cut when the latter obtained its own library in its own building in 1935.[26] The Law Library continued to provide reference assistance to Congress after its move to a new Law Library Reading Room in the main Library of Congress building. The first law reading room in the main building was located in the northeast pavilion of the second floor.[27]

During the 1940s, the Law Library's Foreign Law Division was established. Through this division, the Law Library provided linguistic assistance, acted and testified as expert witnesses on points of foreign law, or submitted testimony used in court cases to U.S. government offices.[28]

The Library of Congress classification system was developed at the beginning of the twentieth century.[29] Class K was assigned to the field of law. It was not until March of 1967 that a detailed schedule for American law was completed, with Class KF call numbers being given to newly cataloged and retrospective materials. During the 1970s, schedules for Canada, the United Kingdom, Ireland, general law, and the Federal Republic of Germany were completed and assigned to new material.[30] "Due to the lack of sufficient funding for additional staff, the reclassification of retrospective material is greatly slowed, and priority is given to the work on new materials."[31] With advances in technology, a Microtext Reading Room in the Law Library was opened in 1972, as the legal microfilm collection had grown large enough to warrant one.

On Monday, February 2, 1981, the Law Library of Congress moved from the Thomas Jefferson Building to its present location in the James Madison Building.[32] The Law Library moved 1.7 million volumes across the street from the old Thomas Jefferson Building. The new quarters, still in use today, are located on the second floor in the east corner of the James Madison Building. They hold "the Reading Room with its own Rare Book Room and Microtext Reading Room, the administrative offices, research divisions, and Processing Section. Four floors below is the newly created Stack Service and Collection Maintenance Unit of the Processing Section. Also in this subbasement, in an area covering almost two football fields, are the compact book stacks," which was the largest installation of its kind in the world at the time.[33]

In 1991, the Global Legal Information Network (GLIN) was established. In 1995, the GLIN database, designed to share the laws of member nations in the vernacular, went online. The next year, GLIN debuted on the Library of Congress's Web site. A Memorandum of Understanding between the Law Library of Congress and the National Aeronautics and Space Administration (NASA) provided satellite technology assistance to GLIN partner countries.[34]

In 2007, the Law Library of Congress marked its 175th anniversary with a yearlong series of events. A significant milestone was reached when the collection grew to 2.6 million items. Roberta Shaffer was appointed the twenty-second law librarian of Congress on August 20, 2009.[35] David Mao, appointed deputy law librarian on May 5, 2010,[36] was then appointed the twenty-third law librarian of Congress on January 4, 2012, and remains the current law librarian.[37]

COLLECTION

The mission of the Law Library of Congress is to provide research and legal information to the U.S. Congress, as well as to U.S. federal courts and executive agencies, and to offer reference services to the public. To accomplish this mission, it has created the world's largest collection of law books and other legal resources from all countries, and now moves into the age of digitized information with online databases and guides to legal information worldwide.

The Law Library is the nation's custodian of legal and legislative collections from all countries and legal systems of the world. In addition to covering every region, the collection spans all periods of law, from the most ancient and primitive to the most contemporary and sophisticated. All systems of law, common, civil, customary, religious, and socialist, are represented. Combined, the collections include more than 2.82 million volumes, 2.44 million microfiche, and 87,000 reels of microfilm.[38] Some of the law collection has been transferred to the library's high-density storage facility at Fort Meade, Maryland.

> Legal materials have been a central component of the Library of Congress collections since 1800. In 1832, the Law Library was established as a separate entity within the Library of Congress with a distinct collection to be housed in separate quarters and with its own budget line for acquisitions. At the time 2,011 law books, 639 of which had belonged to Thomas Jefferson, were removed from the Library's general collection. These formed the nucleus for what is today the world's largest collection of legal materials.[39]

The collection of the Law Library of Congress

> is notable not only for its sheer size, but for its diversity. It includes American law and foreign law; primary materials and commentaries, reporting series, and other secondary sources; treaties and treatises; rare medieval codices and annual editions of state laws; decisions from U.S. federal and state courts, as well as many foreign courts; religious and customary law; and more complete collections of the past laws of some countries than can be had in their national capitals. About one-third of the collection consists of U.S. federal and state law; the rest is foreign and international material.[40]

"The first priority for the Law Library has always been the collection of as complete a record of American federal and state law as possible,"[41] which means that the Law Library is a repository for American law.[42] It possesses the largest and most complete general collection of American law, although other research libraries might hold larger collections in some specialized areas.[43] "The American material includes original editions of colonial, state, and territorial session laws, codes, and compilations. The holdings of Congressional publications are surpassed only by the collections of the House of Representatives and Senate themselves. Congressional holdings begin with the September 5, 1774, issue of the journals of the Continental Congress."[44] The Law Library, as well as the Supreme Court depository, has a complete set of the records and briefs of the Supreme Court. "The records go back to 1832; the briefs to 1854. It also has partial collections of the records and briefs of the thirteen Circuit Courts."[45]

"The Law Library attempts to collect primary legal material for every national-level jurisdiction in the world, as well as for some dependent areas such as Bermuda, Greenland, or the former colony of Hong Kong," for a total of about two hundred jurisdictions.[46] It also makes efforts to obtain official publications of state or provincial-level units of several large or federated nations, such as Australia, Canada, Germany, India, and Mexico. The materials include official gazettes, constitutions, session laws, administrative regulations, and court decisions and reports. Commentaries and indexes to laws are also collected, as are digests and reports of court decisions, treatises and legal periodicals."[47] The foreign and international law materials comprise the largest percentage of the total collection. The scope is broad and includes all major current and former national, state, and equivalent jurisdictions.[48] "This collection is used by a staff of specialists in foreign and international law to provide research and reference services to the United States Congress, the Supreme Court, Executive Branch Agencies, the legal profession, the academic community and the general public. The collection also supports the work of the Congressional Research Service's American Law Division."[49]

Additionally, the Law Library has one of the largest legal rare book collections in the world. It consists of approximately sixty thousand volumes of books and bound manuscripts, many issued prior to 1801.[50] Materials can be searched and requested through the library's online catalog.[51] Public patrons of the library must obtain a reader registration card.[52] Registered readers can request materials online through the LC online catalog using their individual account numbers, and can then view these materials at the library. Public patrons are not able to check out materials from the Library of Congress.[53]

SERVICES AND PRODUCTS

The Law Library serves as the nation's custodian of legal and legislative collections from all countries and legal systems of the world. These materials are housed in the Library of Congress. As custodian, the Law Library maintains, retrieves, preserves, and secures the print and microform collections. Maintenance includes the shelving of all incoming volumes and serial pieces; filing of incoming loose-leaf updates, advance sheets, and pocket parts; and the weeding of superseded volumes. Re-trieval includes the servicing of any material requested. Preservation in-cludes the preparation for binding of newly collated volumes, and the preparation of material to be digitized, microfilmed, or boxed. Security of the collection involves making sure all Library of Congress regulations on this topic are followed in the handling of the legal collection. [54]

"Since its establishment in 1832, the Law Library's first priority has been service to Congress." [55] The Law Library's Global Legal Research Center provides research services directly to Congress, the judiciary, the executive branch, and members of the public. The staff of legal scholars includes foreign-trained attorneys with a wide range of backgrounds and experiences relating to the laws of foreign jurisdictions. They also have linguistic capabilities to respond to all foreign, comparative, and interna-tional law questions that arise when using the library's collection. The collection covers the laws of over 240 countries and jurisdictions and includes materials in nearly 140 languages. [56] "Apart from immediate telephone assistance, it produces several hundred written reports every year." [57] The reports can vary from one- to two-page summaries to multi-author, multijurisdictional reports. "Congressional inquiries cover a wid-er range of topics than requests from any other source. Congress is inter-ested in broad political and constitutional questions, including the struc-ture of foreign governments and courts, procedures for elections, parlia-mentary immunity, and international law and treaties." [58] "Research ser-vices, especially in foreign, comparative, and international law, are also provided to the judiciary and a wide variety of U.S. government bod-ies." [59]

In addition to foreign and comparative legal information services, the Law Library also provides research assistance and reference services on United States federal and state legal issues to national and global constit-uents. Through its staff of skilled American-trained attorneys and law librarians, the Law Library guides patrons to appropriate print and elec-tronic resources and advises constituents on efficient and effective re-search techniques. The staff produce a variety of online products, includ-ing: Century of Lawmaking for a New Nation, Guide to Law Online, Legal Research and Collection Guides, and THOMAS. [60] The Law Library Reading Room law librarians provide direct reference services to mem-bers of Congress and their staffs, as well as the public. Law librarians serve patrons in person, by phone, or electronically through the *Ask-A-Librarian* service, through which "they provide legal and legislative re-search assistance on federal, state, foreign, and international law." [61] As mandated by law, the Law Library Reading Room is staffed by at least one attorney/librarian qualified in U.S. law whenever and for as long as either house of Congress is in session, which occasionally makes for late nights and weekends. [62]

The Law Library helps sponsor major events to honor achievements in law, such as the Kellogg Biennial Lecture on Jurisprudence. This lecture provides a forum for the most distinguished contributors to international jurisprudence. It also celebrates law-related observances, such as Constitution Day, Law Day, and Human Rights Day. Additionally, the Law Library hosts a number of lectures, meetings, and information sessions covering a range of legal topics throughout the year.[63]

Other services include *Current Legal Topics*, which is a Web page of legal commentary and recommended resources on issues and events with legal significance,[64] and the Global Legal Information Catalog (GLIC), which is a catalog aid to assist researchers with foreign, comparative, and international law.[65] The Global Legal Information Catalog includes information about publications that reprint the laws and regulations of multiple jurisdictions on a particular legal topic, and is searchable by jurisdiction, title, subject, and keyword. The Law Library of Congress also hosts the Global Legal Information Network (GLIN), which is a database of laws, regulations, and other complementary legal sources from around the globe.[66] "GLIN is an online parliament-to-parliament cooperative exchange of laws and legal materials from more than 40 countries and institutions, which began in 1996."[67]

The Law Library of Congress publishes the *Global Legal Monitor*, an online bulletin covering legal developments and news around the world.[68] Also published online is the Guide to Law Online, an annotated portal that links users to primary and secondary sources of government and law from 195 nations and the United States.[69] The Guide to Law Online is an annotated compendium of Internet links, providing a portal to Internet sources of interest to legal researchers. In compiling this list, emphasis wherever possible has been on sites offering the full texts of laws, regulations, and court decisions, along with commentary from lawyers writing primarily for other lawyers. Materials related to law and government that were written by or for laypersons also have been included, as have government sites that provide even quite general information about themselves or their agencies. Every direct source listed here was successfully tested before being added to the list. Users, however, should be aware that changes of Internet addresses and file names are frequent, and even sites that usually function well do not always do so. Thus a successful connection may sometimes require several attempts. If such an attempt to access a file indicates an error, the information can sometimes still be accessed by truncating the URL address to access a directory at the site.[70]

The Law Library of Congress also has a heavy social media presence. The Law Library has a Facebook account and two Twitter accounts. The Law Library's Facebook account was launched on October 21, 2009.[71] The Law Library's Twitter account[72] was launched on October 22, 2009.[73] The Law Library also has a Twitter account for THOMAS[74] that was launched on August 27, 2011.[75] The Law Library is also present on YouTube[76] and iTunesU.[77] The Law Library's blog, *In Custodia Legis*,[78] was launched on August 2, 2010.[79] Bloggers publish daily content related to global legal matters, developments in THOMAS, profiles of legal personae and Law Library staff, and legal history with a wide range of international perspectives.[80]

The Law Library is a natural and obvious provider of information by and about Congress. This service continued with the development of the Internet. In 1998, the Law Library launched A Century of Lawmaking for a New Nation: U.S. Congressional Documents and Debates, 1774–1873. This database is still operational today and provides access to U.S. laws, bills, regulations, treatises, debates, and journals of the first forty-three congresses.[81]

The Law Library of Congress is also known for its operation of THOMAS and now Congress.gov. THOMAS is a database of federal legislative information,[82] beginning with the 104th Congress (1995), with full texts of bills, resolutions, the *Congressional Record*, and Congressional reports.[83] Speaker of the House of Representatives Newt Gingrich and Librarian of Congress James H. Billington announced on January 5 the availability of THOMAS, a Congressional online public access information system named in honor of Thomas Jefferson. THOMAS was initiated by the leadership of the 104th Congress and is a bipartisan effort.[84]

On September 19, 2012, the Law Library of Congress introduced Congress.gov.[85] Congress.gov is the foundation for instituting all of the big changes the Law Library wanted to make in THOMAS over the years but could not because of the older, more fragile infrastructure inherent in the system. On Congress.gov, there is the ability to search all of the content in the system, refine results, obtain the status of a bill on a timeline, and view the new member pages with legislation sponsored and cosponsored. It is also designed to dynamically fit any size screen used, which includes monitors, tablets, and phones. The project will be ongoing, with additional content added to Congress.gov, with the *Congressional Record* up next in batches over time. The introduction of Congress.gov will also mean the eventual end of THOMAS.[86]

On January 18, 2012, the Law Library of Congress launched the Congressional Record App for the iPad. The goal of the app is to allow users to easily read the daily edition of the *Congressional Record* on iPads, as well as be able to browse editions of the *Congressional Record* by date.[87] On July 6, 2012, the app was updated to run on the iPhone and iPod Touch as well.[88]

NOTES

1. Christine Sellers is a research specialist at Nelson Mullins in Columbia, South Carolina. She was a legal reference specialist at the Law Library of Congress from 2009 to 2011. She would like to thank her former coworkers at the Law Library of Congress for all of their help in compiling information for this chapter, especially Jeanine Cali, Pam Craig, Robert Newlen, Andrew Weber, and Margaret Wood.

2. Library of Congress, *Law Library of Congress: A Brief History of the First Hundred and Fifty Years, 1832–1982* (Washington, DC: Library of Congress, 1982; reprint 1991), 1.

3. About Law Library of Congress, http://www.loc.gov/law/about/ and http://www.loc.gov/law/about/history.php.

4. About Law Library of Congress Organization, http://www.loc.gov/law/about/organization.php.

5. Library of Congress, *Law Library of Congress: A Brief History*, 1.

6. Ibid., 2.

7. Ibid.

8. Ibid.

9. Donald R. DeGlopper, "The Law Library and Collections," in *Encyclopedia of the Library of Congress: For Congress, the Nation, and the World*, ed. John Y. Cole and Jane Aikin (Washington, DC: Library of Congress, 2004), 23.

10. U.S. 4 Stat. 579.

11. DeGlopper, "The Law Library and Collections," 25.

12. Library of Congress, *Law Library of Congress: A Brief History*, 5.

13. Ibid.

14. Ibid.

15. Ibid., 7.

16. Ibid.

17. Ibid., 8.

18. 2 U.S.C. 138.

19. Library of Congress, *Law Library of Congress: A Brief History*, 11.

20. DeGlopper, "The Law Library and Collections," 25.

21. *Law Library of Congress: A Brief History of the First Hundred and Fifty Years, 1832-1982*, p. 13 (Reprint 1991).

22. DeGlopper, "The Law Library and Collections," 25.

23. Ibid.

24. Library of Congress, *Law Library of Congress: A Brief History*, 19.

25. Ibid.

26. Ibid.

27. Ibid., 22.

28. Ibid., 21.

29. Ibid., 25.

30. Ibid.

31. Ibid.

32. http://blogs.loc.gov/law/2011/02/the-big-move/

33. Library of Congress, *Law Library of Congress: A Brief History*, 27.

34. http://www.loc.gov/law/about/history.php

35. http://loc.gov/today/pr/2009/09-157.html

36. http://loc.gov/today/pr/2010/10-101.html

37. http://loc.gov/today/pr/2012/12-005.html

38. Library of Congress, *Law Library of Congress: Collection and Services* (pamphlet). (Washington, DC: Library of Congress, 2012).

39. DeGlopper, "The Law Library and Collections," 29.

40. Ibid.

41. Ibid., 30.

42. Library of Congress, *Law Library of Congress: Collection and Services* pamphlet.

43. DeGlopper, "The Law Library and Collections," 30.

44. Ibid.

45. Ibid.

46. Ibid., 31.

47. Ibid.

48. Library of Congress, *Law Library of Congress: Collection and Services* pamphlet.

49. DeGlopper, "The Law Library and Collections," 23.

50. Library of Congress, *Law Library of Congress: Collection and Services* pamphlet. More information about rare books can be found at http://www.loc.gov/law/find/rare-books.php.

51. http://catalog2.loc.gov/

52. More information about the reader registration card can be found at http://www.loc.gov/rr/readerregistration.html.

53. More information about the catalog can be found at http://catalog2.loc.gov/vwebv/ui/en_US/htdocs/help/index.html.

54. Law Library of Congress Organization, http://www.loc.gov/law/about/organization.php.

55. DeGlopper, "The Law Library and Collections," 26.

56. *Law Library of Congress: Collection and Services* pamphlet. (2012)

57. DeGlopper, "The Law Library and Collections," 26.

58. Ibid.

59. Ibid.

60. Law Library of Congress Organization, http://www.loc.gov/law/about/organization.php.

61. Library of Congress, *Law Library of Congress: Collection and Services* pamphlet. Ask-A-Librarian can be found at http://www.loc.gov/rr/askalib/ask-law.html.

62. 2 U.S.C. 138.

63. Library of Congress, *Law Library of Congress: Collection and Services* pamphlet.

64. Ibid. More information can be found at http://www.loc.gov/law/help/current-topics.php.

65. Library of Congress, *Law Library of Congress: Collection and Services* pamphlet. More information can be found at http://www.loc.gov/lawweb/servlet/Glic?home.

66. Library of Congress, *Law Library of Congress: Collection and Services* pamphlet. More information can be found at http://www.glin.gov/.

67. DeGlopper, "The Law Library and Collections," 28.

68. Library of Congress, *Law Library of Congress: Collection and Services* pamphlet. More information can be found at http://www.loc.gov/law/news/glm.php.

69. Library of Congress, *Law Library of Congress: Collection and Services* pamphlet. More information can be found at http://www.loc.gov/law/help/guide.php.

70. More information can be found at http://www.loc.gov/law/help/guide.php.

71. http://www.facebook.com/lawlibraryofCongress.

72. https://twitter.com/LawLibCongress.

73. http://blogs.loc.gov/loc/2009/10/now-tweeting-law-library-of-Congress/.

74. https://twitter.com/thomasdotgov.

75. http://blogs.loc.gov/law/2011/04/thomasdotgov/.

76. http://www.youtube.com/playlist?list=PL96401BE3402149B9.

77. https://itunes.apple.com/itunes-u/law-and-the-library/id386017780?mt=10#ls=1.

78. http://blogs.loc.gov/law/.

79. http://blogs.loc.gov/law/2010/08/in-custodia-legis/.

80. Library of Congress, *Law Library of Congress: Collection and Services* pamphlet.

81. Ibid. More information can be found at http://memory.loc.gov/ammem/amlaw/lawhome.html.

82. http://thomas.loc.gov/home/thomas.php.

83. Library of Congress, *Law Library of Congress: Collection and Services* pamphlet.

84. Library of Congress press release, January 5, 1995, http://loc.gov/today/pr/1995/95-002.html.

85. http://beta.CongressCongress.gov/.

86. Ibid. As of the launch, that included bill text, summary and status, and member profiles.

87. http://blogs.loc.gov/law/2012/01/now-theres-a-CongressCongressional-record-app-for-that/.

88. http://blogs.loc.gov/law/2012/07/CongressCongressional-record-app-updated-to-include-iphone/.

FOURTEEN

Library Consortia in the New Economy: Collaboration to Scale

Tracy L. Thompson-Przylucki

The way to get good ideas is to get lots of ideas, and throw the bad ones away.
—Linus Carl Pauling[1]

DEFINING CONSORTIUM

The quote by Pauling elegantly captures the highest calling of library consortia.[2] They strive to be the beneficiaries of lots of ideas and the implementers of the good ones. In the first edition of this book, I started with a definition of *consortium* that is still accurate and useful for purposes of this revision, so I repeat it here. The *Oxford English Dictionary*[3] defines consortium as a "Partnership, association. Now more specifically, an association of business, banking, or manufacturing organizations." Merriam-Webster OnLine comes closer to the character of library consortia with "an agreement, combination, or group (as of companies) formed to undertake an enterprise beyond the resources of any one member."[4] But to get even closer to the meaning of the word as it relates to libraries and educational institutions, we should consider some other words that may be used to describe the entity. *Network, alliance, coalition, collaborative,* and *association* are just some of the words that might be used to refer to the consortium relationship.

It might also be helpful to identify a few common characteristics of library consortia to further hone the definition and identify the enterprise. First, a consortium includes three or more institutions or libraries.[5]

267

Second, member institutions usually join together voluntarily to create a consortium, although the creation and maintenance of a consortium may, in some instances, be mandated by state law or required for the receipt of grant or government funding.[6] Third, library consortia typically are composed of institutional members, distinguishing them from professional associations, which are usually composed of individual members. The final, and probably most significant, attribute of library consortia is that they are as dissimilar as they are numerous. They have different organizational and governance structures, different membership requirements, different missions, and different funding models; provide different services; and aspire to different goals. As the joke goes, if you've seen one consortium, you've seen one consortium. But despite all these differences, consortia seek to be the proving grounds for good ideas.

A HISTORY OF COLLABORATION IN HIGHER EDUCATION

Collaboration among institutional entities such as colleges and universities or libraries is a predictable outgrowth of human nature. We thrive on collaboration and have long recognized the strength in numbers. Early humans realized that cooperative living—living in tribes, clans, or kinship groups—would be more likely to provide personal safety than living in isolation, and would be the most strategic route to a stable food supply. Collaboration led to survival.[7] Thankfully, the situation is not quite so dire for libraries in the twenty-first century. Nonetheless, since 2008, law libraries have been faced with increasingly grim economic realities. According to the 2011 AALL survey (see figure 14.1), law library acquisition budgets were lower in 2011 than they have been since before 2001. And our budgets are shrinking at a time when we have ready access to an enormous array of electronic resources and an increasingly tech-savvy population of users with high expectations regarding access to information. Collaboration may in fact be necessary for the survival of the library and of librarians as critical components in the education and research process, rather than quaint holdovers from an earlier era.

While libraries have been collaborating in some fashion for many years, the electronic information era has spurred consortium activity. A survey conducted by the author in 2010 shows that, of the forty-five library consortia from around the world that responded, twenty-six of them have been founded only in the last twenty years.[8] Of the nineteen founded before 1992, four were started in the '60s, seven in the '70s, and five in the '80s. The earliest library consortium among the survey respondents dates back only to 1949. While some of the impetus for library collaboration may be credited to Title II-C of the Higher Education Act of 1965,[9] the more recent growth of library consortia over the last two decades has it roots in collaboration on the educational institution level.

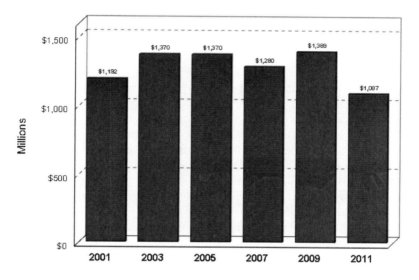

Figure 14.1. Total Information Budgets of All Members, 2001–2011

Colleges and universities in the United States began to explore the economic and developmental benefits of collaborative action as early as 1925,[10] with the founding of the Claremont Colleges in Sacramento, California. In 1923 James A. Blaisdell, then-president of Pomona College, articulated the dream:

> My own very deep hope is that instead of one great, undifferentiated university, we might have a group of institutions divided into small colleges—somewhat of an Oxford type—around a library and other utilities which they would use in common. In this way I should hope to preserve the inestimable personal values of the small college while securing the facilities of the great university.

Today, the thriving Claremont University Consortium (CUC) in Claremont, California, is one of the most innovative higher education collaborations.[11] CUC serves as a central coordinating and support organization, providing more than twenty-eight key services and programs to eight distinct colleges, and stands as a testament to Blaisdell's vision early in the twentieth century.

Writing in 1974 about the consortium movement among colleges and universities, Franklin Patterson, despite the successes of the CUC beginning nearly fifty years earlier, characterized that movement as relatively recent.[12] Patterson was seeing trends in collaboration among higher education institutions similar to what we see today among libraries. He noted that between 1925 and 1960, only nineteen consortia of higher education institutions had been established. Then, between 1960 and 1965, thirty-two more consortia emerged. By 1973, there were a total of eighty consortia listed in the *Consortium Directory; Voluntary Academic Cooperative Arrangements in Higher Education*.[13] (A 2009 list compiled by the National Association for Consortium Leadership [ACL] listed 119.[14]) Patterson's work provides a comprehensive history of the higher education consortium movement from its inception in 1925 through the mid-'70s.

That period in history, the post–World War II era, saw the greatest expansion of the American higher education system, with enrollment swelling from 1.5 million to 15 million students in a fifty-year period.[15] The G.I. Bill, combined with a growing social awareness of the importance of a college education to the future of the nation, created an environment in which greater attention was paid to the state of our system of higher education. The demands on the system were escalating, and it would become increasingly difficult to retain the status quo. "The old pattern of every college or university going it alone . . . would be eroded by the pressure of virtually unlimited needs on limited resources."[16] It made perfect sense for colleges and universities to pursue collaborative opportunities.

Collaboration during this period took many forms, including cross-registration, cooperative admissions programs, shared faculty, joint academic calendars, joint cultural programs, and cooperative faculty support. Of the fifty-five consortia upon which Patterson based his study, twenty-six had some shared library functions, including interlibrary loan, shared cataloguing, joint monograph purchasing, centralized journal deposits, and joint film libraries.[17] In fact, William Lanier, then director of one of the consortia that Patterson studied closely, the Greensboro Tri-College Consortium (GTC) in North Carolina, identified library cooperation as *the most successful program* carried out by his members.[18] It is following this period of dramatic expansion, growth, and cooperation at the higher education institutional level that we see the rise of the library consortium.

LIBRARY COLLABORATION TODAY

The history of collaboration in higher education suggests that before library consortia emerged as distinct organizations in their own right, they were likely to have had a tradition of collaboration as departments within their parent institutions. This gave libraries the benefit of having models to adopt or emulate in the development of their own consortia. Today, many library consortia operate as independent entities, responding to needs and interests distinct from those of the wider institution. This bifurcation of missions is especially clear from the existence of two distinct organizations, the National Association for Consortium Leadership

(ACL) and the International Coalition of Library Consortia (ICOLC), which each exist to meet the needs of one of these two types of consortia.

ACL, founded in 1975 as the Council of Interinstitutional Leadership, supports the work of higher education consortia in the United States. It is a membership organization that holds an annual meeting and a Summer Institute in Consortium Leadership,[19] provides networking and mentoring opportunities, and publishes important work in the field of educational cooperation.[20] The 2012 ACL Membership Directory lists seventy-two member consortia across the country.[21]

ICOLC is a more recent organization that has emerged to support the work of multiple types of library consortia. It is a less formally structured group,[22] launched in 1996 to address issues of concern to library consortia, librarians, and other information professionals engaged in collaborative work. ICOLC, while most heavily populated by and geared toward academic library consortia, includes consortia that serve special libraries, law libraries, school libraries, government libraries and public libraries. ICOLC is international in scope and provides support for library consortia through two meetings annually (one in the United States and one abroad); ad hoc, topical webinars; and a members-only electronic mailing list. ICOLC's goal is to help participating members stay informed about "new electronic information resources, pricing practices of electronic information providers and vendors, and other issues of importance to directors, governing boards, and libraries of consortia. From time to time ICOLC also issues statements regarding topics which affect libraries and library consortia."[23] ICOLC, essentially a consortium of consortia, lists more than 200 participating consortia.[24]

THE ROLE OF LIBRARY CONSORTIA

So now the entity has been defined and placed into its historical context. But what exactly do library consortia do? Why do they exist? The primary goals for library consortia today are to *reduce or eliminate redundancies* and *capitalize on efficiencies* for our member libraries. By focusing our efforts on these goals, we ultimately enable members to maximize their finite human and fiscal resources and avoid unnecessary costs.

Negotiating and Licensing Electronic Resources

Cost avoidance in the consortium environment can take many forms. One of the most common means is leveraging group purchasing power. A consortium may participate in group purchasing for a wide array of goods and services, including things like security systems, productivity tools, library furniture, and supplies, but saving on materials acquisitions, and particularly costly electronic resources, is a top priority for most libraries.

Over the first decade of this century, libraries have shown a dramatic increase in expenditures on electronic resources as a percentage of overall materials budgets. In 2001, ARL reported that on average, e-resources constituted about 19 percent of a library's materials budget. By 2010, e-resources consumed 62 percent of that budget.[25] Given this trend, participation in a consortium can lead to significant savings for libraries, as most library consortia play a key role in the acquisition of electronic resources for their member libraries.

Libraries and information providers/vendors/publishers alike recognize the value of working through consortia. The consortium serves a liaison role, providing vendors with a single point of access to multiple libraries. The consortium, having established a trust relationship with the members, will be able to gain their attention about a product on offer whereas a vendor may not. Librarians face a growing demand for their time and attention, and the consortium helps to filter that noise for their members.

The increasing importance of the library consortium as a point of access to the market for information vendors is best demonstrated by the emergence in 2011 of the Consortium Directory Online (CDO).[26] CDO, a subscription-based service marketed to the information vendor community, lists more than 400 library consortia in over 100 countries. CDO's stated aim is to help publishers gain the competitive intelligence they need to succeed in the library consortium market.

In a typical library consortium, many functions related to the acquisition of electronic resources are centralized and managed within the consortium, rather than duplicated at each of the member institutions. For example, a consortium may work with an information publisher/vendor to establish a trial of an electronic resource,[27] and to negotiate pricing of that resource for the entire consortium. Without the consortium, each library would work independently to set up trials and negotiate price, costing both the library and the information vendor significant investments of time.

When an electronic resource has been identified as one in which some or all members of the consortium have an interest,[28] the consortium may assume the task of negotiating a license agreement on behalf of the members. A license agreement sets forth the terms of use of an electronic resource and the rights and obligations of the parties to the agreement: the licensee (content purchaser) and licensor (content vendor). Licensing alone is a task that takes an enormous toll on personnel and administrative resources. Endless workshops, seminars, working groups, online courses, committees, professional development programs, and electronic mailing lists are devoted to the intricacies of licensing electronic resources. Many librarians, consortium staff members, information providers, and publishers participate in licensing listservs, such as the liblicense list.[29] Delegating licensing, a relatively demanding yet low-return task, to the consortium can provide significant savings to the member libraries and free up professional staff at the library level for high-return or high-visibility projects with more direct local impact.

Beyond Buying

After a resource has been successfully licensed for member libraries, the consortium may retain an ongoing role in the management of the resource as part of the service to its members. This can include things like billing and payments, renewals, troubleshooting, and even customer service. The goal is always to save the time and resources of both the member libraries and the information publisher/vendor.

Managing licensing at the consortium level also results in more *continuity* and *consistency* in the licensing process and in licensing terms and principles across the board, both on the library side and on the information provider side. ICOLC has made great strides in this regard. They have issued several best-practices statements and guidelines that have been widely endorsed by other consortia, individual libraries, and information providers, covering such licensing issues as pricing, access, fair use, archiving, privacy, and usage statistics. The current economic climate led to ICOLC's Statement on the Global Economic Crisis and Its Impact on Consortial Licenses (revised June 14, 2010).[30] These multiconsortium efforts are excellent tools that support the work of libraries and consortia.

Added to the work of ICOLC are the initiatives of library associations like the American Association of Law Libraries (AALL) and the American Library Association (ALA). In 1997, AALL and ALA, in cooperation with four other library associations,[31] drafted the Principles for Licensing Electronic Resources.[32] In 2004, that document was updated to reflect the changes in the licensing landscape in the intervening years,[33] and it was under revision again in 2012.[34] The evolution of the license agreement, and more importantly of licensing principles, has been on a steady course since the 1990s, thanks in large part to the efforts of these leading organizations.

While this is clearly not the only collaborative role of library consortia, it is one of the most tangible benefits of consortium membership and the one most often relied upon to justify membership.[35] Negotiating and licensing e-resources, and establishing norms and best practices in the process, will continue to be a significant role for consortia for the foreseeable future. In 2011, library consortia participating in ICOLC began taking the notion of cooperative acquisitions even one step further, pooling members across organizations to participate in interconsortial licensing (ICL) opportunities.[36] Lyrasis,[37] a consortium established in 2009 as the result of the merger of several regional library networks, has taken a lead role in ICL, and to date has negotiated a handful of such deals. ICL will need time to develop and take root, but it is hoped that new efficiencies will be gained by this expanded approach to group acquisitions.

The emergence of Lyrasis points to another recent trend in consortia: mergers. Joining one or more consortia into a single organization makes good sense when they are well aligned. Each consortium brings strengths and resources that, when combined, can provide added value to the member libraries while minimizing the costs of infrastructure. Other examples of recent mergers in the library consortium world include the Orbis Cascade Alliance,[38] the Midwest Collaborative for Library Services,[39] and Amigos Library Services.[40] This trend is likely to continue.

Consortia also tirelessly seek appropriate opportunities to collaborate with one another on programs and projects as another means of fully exploiting resources for members. Some examples of cross-consortium projects include a collaborative print journal archiving projects undertaken by the Association of Southeastern Research Libraries (ASERL)[41] and the Triangle Research Libraries Network (TRLN);[42] the California Digital Libraries' Western Regional Storage Trust project;[43] and the Preserving America's Legal Materials in Print (PALMPrint) Project,[44] undertaken by the Legal Information Preservation Alliance (LIPA)[45] and NELLCO, Inc.[46]

Consortia are engaged in a wide array of exciting and innovative activities and services that go beyond the purchasing and licensing of electronic resources. Consortia provide a forum for experimentation. They provide an opportunity for members to share both the costs and the risks associated with the implementation of new technologies or approaches to problems. Members may participate collaboratively in services, projects, and programs that they would be unwilling or unable to tackle independently. Such projects may include a shared integrated library system (ILS); discounts on print materials; customer service and troubleshooting for e-resources licensed through the consortium; courier service; equipment, hardware, and software purchases; technology management; shared digital or print repositories; digitization projects or services; reciprocal interlibrary loan or access agreements; shared offsite storage; collaborative virtual reference; educational programming; consulting services; networking opportunities; and shared meeting space. Each of these was identified by one or more survey respondents as services currently being offered to their members (see figure 14.2).[47]

Consortia also serve an important advocacy role. Libraries working together can have a significant impact on information providers and publishers. Project COUNTER[48] and the Shared Electronic Resource Understanding (SERU)[49] are perfect examples of the advocacy role reaping important results for libraries.

What types of services do you offer to members? (check all that apply)

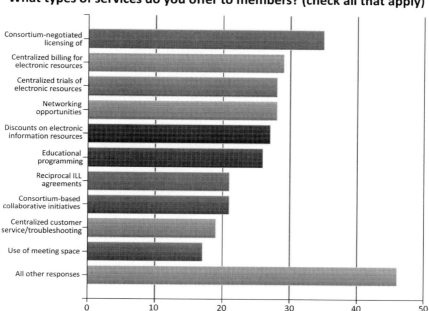

Figure 14.2.   What types of services do you offer to members? (check all that apply)

COUNTER is a single-purpose consortium, including among its members libraries, consortia, publishers, information providers, and associations. The focus of the UK-based group, since its inception in 2002, has been to develop a set of universally accepted standards for the recording and reporting of usage statistics for electronic resources. The project has been so successful that COUNTER compliancy has become an industry goal for publishers and information providers. Compliancy is monitored regularly, and a list of compliant vendors is maintained on the Project COUNTER site.[50]

SERU is a best-practice initiative of the National Information Standards Organization (NISO). Its goal is to replace the complex and time-consuming licensing process with a simpler set of commonly accepted terms. Libraries, consortia, and information vendors can implement SERU on a case-by-case basis under circumstances that each deems appropriate. NISO maintains registries of parties willing to consider SERU as a licensing alternative.

So despite the common and justifiable emphasis on the role of consortia as discount brokers and licensing professionals, there are many other less tangible but more enduring consortium activities that could lead to even greater cost avoidance for members in the long run.

ORGANIZATIONAL STRUCTURE AND GOVERNANCE IN LIBRARY CONSORTIA

Library consortia may be established for a *single specific purpose*, such as the creation of a shared library catalog, or simply to take advantage of *general opportunities for collaboration*.[51] Library consortia may be formally or informally organized.[52] Many begin as informal arrangements and evolve into formally recognized coalitions. The form an organization takes will depend on the forms available under their domestic law and the reasons for their existence.

In the United States many consortia are organized as nonprofit corporations as defined by Section 501(c)(3) of the Internal Revenue Code.[53] Meeting the Internal Revenue Code definition enables a consortium to enjoy tax-exempt status. Other forms include corporations, associations, government entities, and ministries, as well as committees, departments, or other subgroups of a formally organized parent institution. In addition to attending to its tax status, a consortium may be accountable to a variety of local, state, and federal regulatory bodies. Regardless of an organization's structure, a library consortium must remain compliant with all reporting requirements.

There are a number of common governance structures, and undoubtedly endless variations. The structure a group adopts will vary based on a number of characteristics, including the number of members, mission of the consortium, geographic boundaries, types of libraries included among the membership, and funding model. A good place to look for an organization's governance structure is in their bylaws or articles of incorporation. If a consortium is mandated by state or federal law, the governance structure may be set forth in administrative code or regulations.[54]

Many consortia have a board of directors, governing board, or council that provides direction and guidance, and has a fiduciary duty to the consortium. Members may be appointed or elected. Often, each member library has a seat on the board, which is commonly filled by the library director. Or, the board may be composed of regional representatives or representation by library type. In some cases, board responsibility rotates among the member libraries. The board has an obligation, sometimes statutory, to meet on a regular basis to ensure proper governance and establish the direction for the organization.[55]

An executive or steering committee may work more closely with the consortium staff to implement the plans set out and supported by the board. At this level, the members are often elected from among the full board and serve for a specified term of office.

Serving the consortium on the front lines, administering the programs and services of the consortia for the membership, is the consortium staff. Typically, a library consortium is led by an executive director, who may manage any number of staffers.[56] Not all consortia have paid staff; some have a rotating directorship or presidency from among the board or council. It can be exceedingly difficult to move a consortium forward without someone in a position of full-time leadership of the organization. If leadership falls to someone for whom the work of the consortium is just one task among many, a consortium can suffer from inertia.

The challenges of collaborative action are multiplied when no one is at the helm on a consistent basis. A crucial piece in the success of a consortium is regular, consistent, and reliable communication between the organization, the membership, and other key stakeholders. This is accomplished through an array of communication vehicles, including regular meetings, e-mail, social media, consortium Web sites, telephone calls, mailing lists, blogs, electronic and print newsletters, and videoconferences. Keeping the organization vibrant requires a continual evaluation of the effectiveness of the communication methods in use.

Communication to the membership is so vital because it takes many others, beyond the governing bodies and the administrative bodies, to carry out the collaborative work of the consortium. Standing committees, task forces, ad hoc working groups, interest groups, and other action groups realize the plans and goals set forth by the governing bodies. This is where much of the magic of library collaboration takes place. It is also a consequence of membership that is often named by members as the most valuable benefit. Library staff members get the opportunity to work with their colleagues from other institutions. They share experiences and begin to understand the challenges their colleagues face and the strengths that they bring to the mix. This leads to the professional growth and development of participating library staff members, creative thinking and problem solving, and building strong relationships between and among member libraries. All of the synergies created at this level of the consortium feed back into the organization to enhance its effectiveness.

Membership Requirements

Membership in a library consortium may be defined by statute or regulation, or defined within the organization's bylaws or articles of incorporation. Membership may be limited by library type, collection size, geographic region, user population, or some other criterion. Some consortia are even composed of distinct libraries within a single system or institution, such as across multiple campuses or across libraries by discipline.[57] A consortium may offer several categories of membership, such as full members, associate members, affiliate members, and cooperative

members.[58] Each category of membership will have distinct requirements, rights, and responsibilities.

Funding Models

As might be expected, the fiscal needs and resources of a consortium
vary widely depending upon the size, composition, reach, and mission of
the organization (see figure 14.3).

To fund their activities, consortia may rely on any number of sources
of income. Members typically pay some form of membership dues or
assessment.[59] Dues may be apportioned equally to all members in a giv-
en membership category, or they may be proportional based upon some
weighting factor, such as student or staff population measured by full-
time equivalents (FTE), library budget size or endowment, or some other
agreed-upon criteria. In addition to dues, consortia may rely on funding
from grants, fees for services, contributions, royalties, service charges,
administrative fees, government allocations, or funding from the budget
of a parent institution or Board of Regents. None of these funding sources
is necessarily exclusive, and consortia may rely on one or more of them as
need dictates.

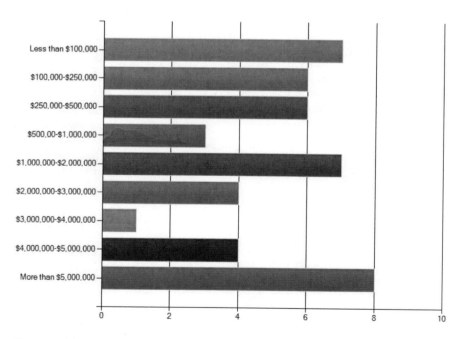

Figure 14.3. **Which of the following reflects your annual consortium budget? (in USD)**

THE FUTURE OF LIBRARY CONSORTIA

Consortia are, by their nature, nimble organizations that in many ways exist to manage change. With the current rate of change accelerating in the library and information technology industry, and in legal education, the need for law libraries to collaborate with one another, and with external stakeholders, is likely to intensify before it declines. Four significant change agents are currently affecting how library consortia will serve their members into the future: changes in the publishing industry, technological advancements, economic trends, and the changing role of the library professional.

Consortium professionals, when polled about the future of library consortia, reflected on these factors. They expect that expertise around negotiating and licensing will continue to be within the purview of consortia. However, the importance of the consortium as so much more than a buying club comes through loud and clear in their comments: "consortia will continue to play an important role in negotiating licenses. But consortia can do so much more"; "as well as cost avoidance, consortia can offer a united voice for member libraries and a responsive vehicle for developing new services"; "consortia need to support libraries as they make transitions into new service models"; "increasing digitizing . . . and preservation"; "continual engagement with our members is essential, and the ability to develop and retire services according to current needs"; "consortia may find themselves working more with print resources as libraries looks for ways to economize on their legacy print collections."[60]

All of the issues currently facing libraries and information providers, from open access, to digital archives, to the evolution of copyright, to the role of repositories, to the development of new authentication techniques are fertile ground for collaborative efforts. In order for consortia to continue to participate, it will be important for consortium members and their funding institutions to see beyond the immediate and tangible benefits of group discounts to the enduring value of collaboration in these complex and dynamic matters.

It is no secret that people working together can usually accomplish more than an individual working alone. The same can be said of libraries. We are in the process of building on our relatively recent history of institutional collaboration, and we will continue to leverage our strengths into the foreseeable future.

NOTES

1. Linus Pauling (1901–1994) was an American-born scientist who won the Nobel Prize in Chemistry in 1954 and the 1962 Nobel Peace Prize.
2. I will use the general term *library consortia/um* throughout this chapter to include law library consortia. I will use the specific term *law library consortia/um* when my

reference is to facts or statements that are unique to those entities, and may or may not be applicable to the broader consortium community.

3. *Oxford English Dictionary*, 2nd ed. (New York: Oxford University Press, 1989).

4. "Consortium." Merriam-Webster Online Dictionary. http://www.m-w.com/.

5. A consortium may consist of several libraries or several campuses under one institutional umbrella, as is true with the California Digital Library.

6. This is the case with consortia such as OhioLink (Ohio Rev. Code Ann. § 3333.04 [2005]) and Texshare (Tex. Government Code Ann. § 441.221-441.230 [2005]).

7. "Evolution, Human," in *The New Encyclopedia Britannica*, 15th ed.

8. Author's survey (developed, collected, and analyzed using SurveyMonkey) conducted via the International Coalition of Library Consortia (ICOLC) electronic mailing list. Over two hundred consortia are listed on the ICOLC Web site (http://icolc.net/about-icolc) as participating members; fifty responded to the survey. Complete results on file with author.

9. 20 U.S.C. § 1041 (1965). This act established the *Strengthening Research Library Resources Program*, which encouraged library cooperation through the provision of special-purpose grants.

10. In the United Kingdom, the Association of Commonwealth Universities (ACU), "the oldest inter-university association in the world," dates to 1913. John Kirkland, "Change and Continuity: The Case of the Association of Commonwealth Universities," in David Teather, ed., *Consortia: International Networking Alliances of Universities* (Victoria, Australia: Melbourne University Press, 2004), 49–68.

11. See http://www.cuc.claremont.edu/.

12. Franklin Patterson, *Colleges in Consort* (San Francisco: Jossey-Bass, 1974), 3.

13. Lewis D. Patterson, *Consortium Directory; Voluntary Academic Cooperative Arrangements in Higher Education*, 6th ed. (Kansas City, MO: Kansas City Regional Council for Higher Education, 1973).

14. Unpublished. On file with author.

15. Theodore J. Marchese, "U.S. Higher Education in the Postwar Era: Expansion and Growth," *Electronic Journal of the U.S. Information Agency* 2, no. 4 (December 1997), http://usinfo.state.gov/journals/itsv/1297/ijse/marchese.htm.

16. Patterson, *Colleges in Consort*, 2.

17. Ibid., 11.

18. Ibid., 87.

19. First offered in 2011, plans are now underway for the third institute in the summer of 2013. For more information, see http://www.national-acl.com/institute/abouttheinstitute.asp.

20. Two examples are Lawrence G. Dotolo and John B. Noftsinger, *Leveraging Resources Through Partnerships: New Directions for Higher Education* (San Francisco: Jossey-Bass, 2002), and Lawrence G. Dotolo and Jean T. Strandness, *Best Practices in Higher Education Consortia: How Institutions Can Work Together* (San Francisco: Jossey-Bass, 1999).

21. Association for Consortium Leadership 2012 Membership Directory at http://www.national-acl.com/resources/downloads/ACL_phone_dir.pdf .

22. To date, the ICOLC has not sought any official organizational structure. There are no membership dues, no governance structure, no institutional affiliation. ICOLC continues to function, with a great deal of success, as a grassroots undertaking.

23. From the ICOLC Web site at http://icolc.net/about-icolc/.

24. Complete list at http://icolc.net/consortia.

25. See Electronic Resources and Materials Expenditures in ARL University Libraries, 1992–2010, at http://www.arl.org/stats/annualsurveys/arlstats/arlstats10.shtml.

26. Published by Ringgold, which grew out of Oxford University Press. See http://www.ringgold.com/pages/cdo.html.

27. A trial provides for an extended period of free access to an electronic resource in order for a library to adequately evaluate the content, interface, and functionality of the resource for acquisition purposes.

28. Most library consortia offer electronic resources to their members on an opt-in basis, with members paying only for those resources they select. However, some consortia move in lockstep, licensing resources for the whole rather than for individual members. The former model is the predominant one, with twenty-nine of forty-three survey respondents reporting the opt-in model, and only six organized as strictly all-in collaboratives (see note 8).

29. For more information or to subscribe, please see http://liblicense.crl.edu/discussion-forum/introduction/.

30. The most recent of these are "ICOLC Response to the International Association of Scientific Technical and Medical (STM) Statement" (June 22, 2011); "Revised Statement on the Global Economic Crisis and Its Impact on Consortial Licenses" (June 14, 2010); "Statement on the Google Book Settlement" (December 13, 2009); "Statement on the Proposed OCLC Policy for Use and Transfer of WorldCat Records" (May 11, 2009); "Statement on the Global Economic Crisis and Its Impact on Consortial Licenses" (January 19, 2009), all of which can be found at http://icolc.net/statements.

31. The Association of Academic Health Sciences Libraries, the Association of Research Libraries, the Medical Library Association, and the Special Libraries Association.

32. See http://www.arl.org/sc/marketplace/license/licprinciples.shtml.

33. Available on the AALL Web site at http://www.aallnet.org/main-menu/Advocacy/recommendedguidelines/licensing-electronic-resources.html.

34. In 2011, AALL president Darcy Kirk appointed a Library Procurement Process Improvements Task Force, charged in part with revising the Licensing Principles. See http://www.aallnet.org/main-menu/Leadership-Governance/committee/activecmtes/library-procurementtf.html.

35. For a fuller treatment of the value proposition of library consortia, see Faye A. Chadwell, "Assessing the Value of Academic Library Consortia," *Journal of Library Administration* 51 (2011): 645–61.

36. At the 2012 Charleston Conference, Ann Okerson (Center for Research Libraries) and Tom Sanville (Lyrasis) led a "Lively Lunch" discussion on the current efforts in this area. http://2012charlestonconference.sched.org/event/2bcda9ca4a3a22e47dc3454451417ab3

37. See http://www.lyrasis.org/.

38. Formed by merger of Orbis and Cascade. See http://www.orbiscascade.org/index/history-as-an-unicorporated-association.

39. Formed by merger of the Michigan Library Consortium and INCOLSA, Inc., an Indiana consortium Counting Online Usage of Networked Electronic Resources. Their Web site is at http://www.projectcounter.org/.
See http://www.projectcounter.org/compliantvendors.html.
Of the forty-six survey respondents to this question (see note 8), thirty were established for general collaboration and sixteen for a specific purpose. See http://mlcnet.org/cms/sitem.cfm.

40. Formed by merger of Amigos and the Missouri Library Network Consortium. See http://www.amigos.org/.

41. See http://www.aserl.org/.

42. See http://www.trln.org/.

43. See http://www.cdlib.org/west/

44. See http://www.nellco.org/?page=palmprint.

45. See http://lipalliance.org/.

46. See http://www.nellco.org.

47. See note 8.

48. COUNTER is an acronym for Counting Online Usage of Networked Electronic Resources. Their Web site is at http://www.projectcounter.org/.

49. See http://www.niso.org/workrooms/seru/.

50. See http://www.projectcounter.org/compliantvendors.html.

51. Of the forty-six survey respondents to this question (see note 8), thirty were established for general collaboration and sixteen for a specific purpose.

52. Of the forty-six survey respondents to this question (see note 8), twenty-nine were formally organized, while seventeen were not.

53. 26 U.S.C. § 501 (2003).

54. This is the case with TexShare. Their statutory charge (Texas Government Code §441, Subchapter M) mandates that management of the consortium will fall to the Texas State Library and Archives Commission. See http://www.statutes.legis.state.tx.us/?link=pr.

55. Of the forty-three survey respondents to this question (see note 8), thirty-eight met face to face at least once a year with their members, and of those, fifteen met at least four times per year.

56. Of the forty-six survey respondents to this question (see note 8), five had no staff, twenty-five had one to five staff members, six had six to ten staff, two had eleven to twenty staff, two had twenty-one to thirty staff, one had thirty-one to forty, three had forty-one to fifty, and two had more than fifty staff members.

57. Of the forty-six survey respondents to this question (see note 8), twenty-four characterized their membership as being derived from a single system, network, or institution.

58. Of the forty-five survey respondents to this question (see note 8), twenty-two had a single membership category, eighteen had two to three categories, and five had four to five categories of membership.

59. Of the forty-six survey respondents to this question (see note 8), thirty-one assess their members a fee for consortium membership.

60. Excerpts from the responses to an open-ended question about the future of consortium, ten to twenty years out, posed in the survey (see note 8).

Appendix A

Core Competencies of Law Librarianship

Approved by the American Association of Law Libraries Executive Board, March 2001, Tab34A

The American Association of Law Libraries seeks to define the profession of law librarianship and its value to the legal field, today and in the future, by identifying, verifying, and actively promoting competencies of law librarianship. Competencies are the knowledge, skills, abilities, and personal characteristics that help distinguish superior performance.[1] These competencies may be acquired through higher education such as library and information science programs,[2] through continuing education, and through experience.

The first section, "Core Competencies," includes those that apply to all law librarians, and will be acquired early in one's career. The subsequent sections are related to specific areas of practice. Some law librarians (for example, solo librarians or librarians in smaller institutions) may have multiple responsibilities and need to be proficient in more than one of the "Specialized Competencies." Other law librarians may specialize in just one area or in a subset of one area.

Individual librarians may use the AALL Competencies for coordinating their continuing education as they identify areas for professional growth. Employers may use the Competencies to make hiring, evaluation and promotion decisions, and to make recommendations for professional development. The American Association of Law Libraries uses the Competencies as a framework within which to structure professional development programs. This framework provides guidance to ensure that the programs offered will assist law librarians in attaining and maintaining the skills or knowledge necessary for their current and future work.

1. Core Competencies

Core Competencies apply to all law librarians and will be acquired early in one's career.

- 1.1 Demonstrates a strong commitment to excellent client service.
- 1.2 Recognizes and addresses the diverse nature of the library's clients and community.
- 1.3 Understands and supports the culture and context of the library and its parent institution.
- 1.4 Demonstrates knowledge of the legal system and the legal profession.
- 1.5 Understands the social, political, and economic context in which the legal system exists.
- 1.6 Demonstrates knowledge of library and information science theory, information creation, organization, and delivery.
- 1.7 Adheres to the Ethical Principles of the American Association of Law Libraries and supports the shared values of librarianship. [3]
- 1.8 Exhibits leadership skills including critical thinking, risk taking, and creativity, regardless of position within the management structure.
- 1.9 Demonstrates commitment to working with others to achieve common goals.
- 1.10 Acts within the organization to implement the principles of knowledge management.
- 1.11 Exhibits an understanding of the importance of a multidisciplinary and cross-functional approach to programs and projects within the organization.
- 1.12 Shares knowledge and expertise with clients and colleagues.
- 1.13 Displays excellent communication skills and is able to promote the library and advocate for its needs.
- 1.14 Communicates effectively with publishers and other information providers to advance the interests of the library.
- 1.15 Recognizes the value of professional networking and actively participates in professional associations.
- 1.16 Actively pursues personal and professional growth through continuing education.

Specialized Competencies

Specialized Competencies relate to specific areas of practice. Some law librarians may have multiple responsibilities and need to be proficient in more than one of the Specialized Competencies. Other law librarians may specialize in just one area or subset of one area.

3. *Reference, Research, and Client Services*

- 3.1 Provides skilled and customized reference services on legal and relevant non-legal topics.
- 3.2 Evaluates the quality, authenticity, accuracy, and cost of traditional and electronic sources, and conveys the importance of these to the client.
- 3.3 Assists clients with legal research using both print and electronic resources.
- 3.4 Assists non-lawyers in accessing the law, within the guidelines provided by the American Bar Association's Model Code of Professional Conduct and other applicable codes.
- 3.5 Aggregates content from a variety of sources and synthesizes information to create customized products for clients.
- 3.6 Creates research and bibliographic tools (handouts, aids, pathfinders, bibliographies) on legal and related topics.
- 3.7 Monitors trends in specific areas of the law.

NOTES

1. Kenneth H. Pritchaerd, CCP. Society for Human Resource Management White Paper, August 1997, reviewed April 1999.
2. See "AALL Guidelines for Graduate Programs," November 1988; AALL Professional Development Policy, July 1996.
3. American Association of Law Libraries Ethical Principles, 1999.

Appendix B
Top-10 List for New Depository Staff

If you are a newly designated federal depository library coordinator, the U.S. Government Printing Office (GPO) welcomes you to the Federal Depository Library Program (FDLP). This guide is intended to help you learn about your library's depository and the responsibilities of being a depository coordinator.

1. Update contact information about your library's depository.

- Update the Federal Depository Library Directory.
  (http://www.fdlp.gov/administration/fdld)

  o Identify your library's depository library number through the FDL Directory, if not previously known. The number may include leading zeroes and a letter at the end.
  o Use the library's internal depository password to edit the directory. If needed, contact GPO to attain the password.

- Sign up for FDLP-L, the current official announcement service for the FDLP. (www.fdlp.gov; Home; FDLP News; Subscribe to FDLP-L)
- Notify your regional librarian.

  o Identify your regional librarian through the FDL Directory, if not already known.
  o Please note that some states are not served by a regional depository library.

2. Review basic publications of the FDLP to learn about the legal requirements, program regulations, and guidance for managing a federal depository library, as well as major resources with FDLP content. These include:

- Legal requirements and program regulations of the federal depository library program
  http://www.fdlp.gov/administration/fdlp-legal-requirements
- FDLP.gov (http://www.fdlp.gov/)
- FDLP Connection
  (http://www.fdlp.gov/home/fdlpnews/newletters)
- State Plan, if your state has one (check with your regional librarian)
- Catalog of U.S. Government Publications (CGP)
  (http://catalog.gpo.gov/F)
- Federal Digital System (FDsys) (http://www.gpo.gov/fdsys/)
- Federal Depository Library Handbook
  (http://www.fdlp.gov/administration/handbook)

3. Learn more about the depository collection at your library.

- Locate any relevant depository or library written policies and procedures, such as collection development or access policies.
- Identify all collection housing locations, including selective housing sites, if any.

  o Locate any selective housing site agreements.

- Determine how publications in all formats are identified and made accessible.

  o For any publications not cataloged, identify the inventory record (i.e., the piece level record).

- Determine how FDLP content within the Basic Collection, official content partnerships, subscription-based resources available free to depositories, the CGP, and FDsys is made accessible.

  o Contact GPO to attain needed passwords.

- Identify how your library promotes the federal depository library resources and services.

  o If you would like to increase visibility, you may order free FDLP promotional materials

(http://www.fdlp.gov/outreach/promotionalresources/promom
aterials).

- Identify library staff involved in the depository operation and what
their roles are.

4. Review your library's selection profile. Depositories choose materials
to receive by selecting item numbers.

- Learn about the *List of Classes* and the depository item number
system. (http://www.fdlp.gov/collections/selection)
- Learn how to amend the selection profile, if needed, through DSIMS
(Depository Selection Information Management System).

o Update based upon a current collection development policy or
community profile of depository users that documents the Federal
Government information needs of the community.

**5. Learn procedures for tangible collection management at your
library.** Review processes in place for:

- Timely processing of new shipments, including review of shipping
lists, claims when needed, and identifying materials as federal
property and with date information.
- Cataloging all receipts.
- Review of classification and catalog record changes.
- Weeding the collection, including supersession and official
substitution.

o Locate the regional depository's guidelines to determine the
processes to follow.

**6. Identify how online only publications as well as CDs and DVDs are
made accessible.**

- Determine the process in place to identify online federal depository
publications.
- Determine which online-only publications are cataloged.
- Review public computer workstations used for access to electronic
resources within the library.

7. Find out more about the history of the depository and how it currently fits into the library. With this knowledge, communicate regularly with your library's administration about the depository operation and services.

- Locate Biennial Survey of Depository Libraries submissions from your library and GPO Inspection, Self-Study, or Public Access Assessment reports about your library's depository. These provide useful historical information.
- Locate the library's mission, vision, goals, and strategic plans as well as annual reports or statistical records and review to determine how the depository fits into the overall library organization.
- Check library Web pages and literature for public access and depository information and ensure that a consistent message is delivered to all current and potential depository users.

8. Look for training opportunities and network within the FDLP.

- GPO offers several opportunities, including:

  o Interagency Depository Seminar, held annually for five days in Washington, D.C
  o Federal Depository Library Conference, currently held each fall in the Washington, D.C., area
  o Online learning activities
  o FDLP Community forum

- Identify and learn about your neighboring depositories.
- Contact your regional library and check library associations for additional training ideas and information about collaborative activities.

9. Ask questions. Federal depository libraries and GPO are partners in the FDLP. Take advantage of the network to help you gain knowledge.

- Contact GPO. If you have any questions about specific publications and their classification numbers or catalog records, changes at your library affecting the depository operation, educational opportunities, specific patron problems, or other issues, please feel free to contact GPO. We're here to help you make the most of your federal depository operation. Multiple contact options include:

o askGPO. (http://www.gpo.gov/askgpo/) Use this service to ask questions about depository management and services. By using the Category drop-down boxes, your question is routed to the appropriate subject specialists in GPO.

o Contact Us Form. (http://www.fdlp.gov/help/contact) This suite of forms is useful when you know which person or unit within GPO's Library Services and Content Management (LSCM) you wish to reach.

o Phone 202-512-1119 or email [FDLPOutreach@gpo.gov] for the Office of Education and Outreach. Librarians in this unit have a shared phone number and email address so you may always reach someone right away and consult about depository issues.

o Also, please take advantage of your contacts with your regional library and neighboring depository libraries. As no single depository library may serve all user needs, collaboration is key to successful service.

o Contact your regional librarian for information about any regional or other statewide communication mechanisms.

o Consider signing up to non-GPO listservs, such as GOVDOC-L or DocTech-L.

o Since GPO does not have a collection of publications, your regional library personnel serve as valuable contacts when you have questions about the contents of publications. If you're at a regional depository library, we encourage you to contact GPO to consult about your role within your state or region.

10. Review additional non-GPO resources about the FDLP.

Web Resources

• Documents Data Miner 2 (http://govdoc.wichita.edu/ddm2/gdoc-frames.asp)

• ALA GODORT Toolbox for Processing and Cataloging Federal Government Documents (http://www2.lib.udel.edu/godort/cataloging/toolbox.htm)

• ALA GODORT U.S. Federal Government Information Competencies for Beginning Government Information and General Reference Librarians (http://wikis.ala.org/godort/images/a/af/Federal_gov_competencies.pdf)

Books

Andriot, Donna, ed. *Guide to U.S. Government Publications.* Farmington Hills, MI: Gale Group, annual. Annually identifies agency series and SuDocs class stems and provides publication history.

Boyd, Anne M. *United States Government Publications*, 3rd ed. Rev. Rae E. Ripps. New York: H. W. Wilson, 1949, reprinted 1952. Guide to historical information about government printing and dissemination.

Forte, Eric, et al. *Fundamentals of Government Information: Mining, Finding, Evaluating, and Using Government Resources.* New York: Neal-Schuman Publishers, 2011. Describes current online and print government information resources. Also includes exercises.

Hernon, Peter, et al. *United States Government Information: Policies and Sources.* Westfield, CT: Libraries Unlimited, 2002. Scholarly approach combines reference sources with government policies.

Morehead, Joe. *Introduction to United States Government Information Sources*, 6th ed. Englewood, CO: Libraries Unlimited, 1999. First edition in 1975 supplanted Schmeckebier.

Morrison, Andrea, ed. *Managing Electronic Government Information in Libraries: Issues and Practices.* Chicago: American Library Association, 2008. Experienced FDL librarians write on all topics, from preservation to information literacy to cataloging and more. Management oriented, but still useful for new librarians.

Robinson, Judith Schiek. *Tapping the Government Grapevine: The User-Friendly Guide to U.S. Government Information Sources*, 3rd ed. Phoenix: Oryx Press, 1998. Readable and fun classic.

Schmeckebier, Laurence F., and Roy B. Eastin. *Government Publications and Their Use.* Washington, DC: Brookings Institution, 1969. Provides the history of documents, bibliographies, and catalogs.

Sears, Jean L., and Marilyn K. Moody. *Using Government Information Sources: Electronic and Print, 3rd ed.* Phoenix: Oryx Press, 2001. In-depth reference text for sources, emphasizing subject approach.

Bibliography

CASES

Federal

Hart v. Massanari, 266 F.3d 1155 (9th Cir. 2001).
Authors Guild v. Hathitrust, 2012 WL 4808939 (S.D.N.Y. 2012).

State

Cambridge v. Becker, 2012 WL 1835696 (N.D. GA 2012).

STATUTES

Federal

2 U.S.C. § 138 (2012).
17 U.S.C. §§107–112 (2006 & Supps.).
20 U.S.C. § 1041 (1965).
26 U.S.C. § 501 (2003).
42 U.S.C. §12101 (2006 & Supps.)

State

Cal. Bus. & Prof. §§ 6300 et seq., available at http://www.leginfo.ca.gov/cgi-bin/dis-playcode?section=bpc&group=06001-07000&file=6300-6307.
Md. Code Ann., Cts. & Jud. Proc. § 2-501 (2006).
Md. Code Ann., Cts. & Jud. Proc. § 13-501 (2006).
Md. Code Ann., Cts. & Jud. Proc. § 13-504 (LexisNexis 2006).
Md. Code Ann., Educ. § 23-301 (LexisNexis 2008).
Md. Code Ann., State Gov't § 10-616(e) (LexisNexis 2009 & Supp. 2012).
OhioLink, Ohio Rev. Code Ann. § 3333.04 (2005).
Texshare, Tex. Gov't Code Ann. § 441.221-441.230 (West 2005).

BOOKS

Abbate, Janet. *Inventing the Internet*. 2000.
Ahlers, Glen-Peter, Sr. *The History of Law School Libraries in the United States: Defining Moments*. 2011.
———. *The History of Law School Libraries in the United States: From Laboratory to Cyberspace*. 2002.
Barkan, Steven M., et al. *Fundamentals of Legal Research*. 9th ed. Foundation Press, 2009.
Matthew Battles, *Library: An Unquiet History*. Norton, 2003.

Berring, Robert C., Jr. "A Brief History of Law Librarianship." In *Law Librarianship in the Twenty-First Century*, edited by Roy Balleste et al. 2007.

Berring, Robert C., and Elizabeth A. Edinger. *Finding the Law*. 12th ed. 2005.

Boyd, Anne Morris, and Rae Elizabeth Rips. *United States Government Publications*. H. W. Wilson Company, 1949.

Bracey, Hyler, et al. *Managing from the Heart*. 1993.

Brown, Garrett E., Jr., Mark C. Cramer, and Mary Lee Carson. *Legislative Histories of the Laws Affecting the U.S. Government Printing Office as Codified in Title 44 of the U.S. Code*. 6 vols. Washington, DC: Government Printing Office, 1982.

Cahill, Thomas. *How the Irish Saved Civilization*. 1995.

Cain, Susan. *Quiet: The Power of Introverts in a World That Can't Stop Talking*. 2012.

Canadian Library Association. *Anglo-American Cataloging Rules*. 2nd ed. 2002.

Canfora, Luciano. *The Vanished Library*. 1987.

Chan, Lois Mai, and Theodora Hodges. *Cataloging and Classification: An Introduction*. 3rd ed. Lanham, MD: Scarecrow Press, 2007.

Chapman, Liz. *Managing Acquisitions in Library and Information Services*. Rev. ed. 2008.

Cohen, Morris L. *Bibliography of Early American Law*. 1998.

———. *How to Find the Law*. 1976.

Crews, Kenneth D. *Copyright Law for Librarians and Educators: Creative Strategies and Practical Solutions*. 3rd ed. 2011.

Danner, Richard A., and Jules Winterton, eds. *The IALL International Handbook of Legal Information Management*. 2011.

Deibert, Ronal, et al., eds. *Access Denied: The Practice and Policy of Global Internet Filtering*. 2008.

Dickens, Charles. *A Tale of Two Cities*. Penguin Classics, 1859.

Dotolo, Lawrence G., and Jean T. Strandness. *Best Practices in Higher Education Consortia: How Institutions Can Work Together*. 1999.

Dotolo, Lawrence G., and John B. Noftsinger. *Leveraging Resources through Partnerships: New Directions for Higher Education*. 2002.

Gaebler, Ralph, and Maria Smolka-Day, eds. *Sources of State Practice in International Law*. 2002.

Galitz, Wilbert O. *The Essential Guide to User Interface Design: an Introduction to GUI Design Principles and Techniques*. 2007.

Garner, Bryan. *The Elements of Legal Style*. 2nd ed. 2002.

———. *Garner's Dictionary of Legal Usage*. 3rd ed. 2011.

Garson, Marjorie A., et al., eds. *Reflections on Law Librarianship*. AALL Publication Series 29. Littleton, CO: Fred B. Rothman, 1988.

Gasaway, Laura N., and Michael G. Chiorazzi, eds. *Law Librarianship: Historical Perspective*. AALL Publication Series 52. Littleton, CO: Fred B. Rothman, 1996.

Government Printing Office. *100 GPO Years 1861–1961: A History of United States Public Printing*. Sesquicentennial ed. Washington, DC: GPO, 2010.

Gregory, Vicki L. *Collection Development and Management for 21st Century Library Collections: An Introduction*. 2011.

Harvard Law School Association. *The Centennial History of the Harvard Law School: 1817–1917*. 1918.

Heller, James S., et al. *The Librarian's Copyright Companion*. 2nd ed. 2012.

Hicks, Frederick Charles. *Men and Books Famous in the Law*. 1921.

Holden, Jesse. *Acquisitions in the New Information Universe*. 2010.

Houdek, Frank. *The First Century: One Hundred Years of AALL History, 1906–2005*. Buffalo, NY: William S. Hein, 2008.

Investment Laws of the World. 1973.

Jackson, Mary E. *Assessing ILL/DD Services: New Cost-Effective Alternatives*. Association of Research Libraries, 2004.

Johnson, George. *A Shortcut through Time: The Path to the Quantum Computer*. 2003.

Johnson, Peggy. *New Directions in Technical Services: Trends and Sources (1993–1995)*. Chicago: American Library Association, 1997.

Knowles, Elizabeth, ed. *Oxford Dictionary of Quotations.* 7th ed. 2009.

Kovacs, Diane K. *The Kovacs Guide to Electronic Library Collection Development: Essential Core Subject Collections, Selection Criteria, and Guidelines.* 2nd ed. 2009.

Krieger, Tillie, ed. *Subject Headings for the Literature of Law and International Law, and Index to LC K schedules: A Thesaurus on Law Subject Terms.* Littleton, CO: Rothman, 1996.

Lembke, Melody Busse, Rhonda K. Lawrence, and Peter Enyingi. *Cataloging Legal Literature: A Manual on AACR2R and Library of Congress Subject Headings for Legal Material.* Littleton, CO: Rothman, 1996.

Levit, Alexandra. *Blind Spots: The 10 Business Myths You Can't Afford to Believe on Your New Path to Success.* 2011.

Library of Congress. *Law Library of Congress: A Brief History of the First Hundred and Fifty Years, 1832–1982.* 1991.

———. *Library of Congress Subject Headings for Legal Materials.* 3rd ed. Littleton, CO: Rothman, 1996.

Matthews, Joseph R. *Strategic Planning and Management for Library Managers.* 2005.

Matthews, Richard J., et al., eds. *State-By-State Report on Permanent Public Access to Electronic Government Information.* Chicago: Government Relations Committee and Washington Affairs Office, American Association of Law Libraries, 2003.

Morehead, Joe. *Introduction to United States Government Information Sources.* 6th ed. Englewood, CO: Libraries Unlimited, 1999.

The New Encyclopedia Britannica. 15th ed. 2005.

Nimmer, Melville B., and David Nimmer. *Nimmer on Copyright: A Treatise on the Law of Literary, Musical and Artistic Property, and the Protection of Ideas.* New York: Matthew Bender, 1963–.

O'Hara, Frederic J., ed. *Reader in Government Documents.* Washington: NCR/Microcard Editions, 1973.

Oliver, Chris. *Introducing RDA: A Guide to the Basics.* 2010.

Palfrey, John, and Uris Gasser. *Born Digital: Understanding the First Generation of Digital Natives.* 2008.

Patterson, Franklin. *Colleges in Consort.* 1974.

Patterson, Lewis D. *Consortium Directory; Voluntary Academic Cooperative Arrangements in Higher Education.* 6th ed. 1973.

Price, Harry, and Miles O. Bitner. *Effective Legal Research.* 1953.

Prince, Mary Miles. *Prince's Bieber Dictionary of Legal Abbreviations: A Reference Guide for Attorneys, Legal Secretaries, Paralegals and Law Students.* 6th ed. 2009.

Ranganathan, S. R. *The Five Laws of Library Science.* Asia Pub. House, 1957.

Relyea, Harold C. *Public Printing Reform: Issues and Actions.* Washington, DC: Library of Congress Congressional Research Service, 2003.

Rubin, Richard E. *Foundations of Library and Information Science.* 2nd ed. 2000.

Rupp-Serrano, Karen, ed. *Licensing in Libraries: Practical and Ethical Aspects.* 2005. Also reprinted in *Journal of Library AdministrationLibrary* 42, nos. 3-4 (2005).

Schmeckebier, Laurence F. *The Government Printing Office: Its History, Activities and Organization.* 1st ed. Baltimore: The Johns Hopkins Press, 1925.

Schmeckebier, Laurence F., and Roy B. Eastin. *Government Publications and Their Use.* Washington, DC: Brookings, 1969.

Simpson, John Andrew, and Edmund S. C. Weiner, eds. *The Oxford English Dictionary.* 2nd ed. 1989.

Stallings, William. *Data and Computer Communications.* 8th ed. 2007.

Susskind, Richard. *The End of Lawyers? Rethinking the Nature of Legal Services.* 2008.

Tamanaha, Brian. *Failing Law Schools.* 2012.

Technical Services Law Librarian. Los Angeles: Technical Services Special Interest Section, American Association of Law Libraries, 1979.

Wilson, Patrick. *Second-Hand Knowledge: An Inquiry into Cognitive Authority.* 1983.

Wolfrum, Rüdiger, ed. *Max Planck Encyclopedia of Public International Law.* 2nd ed. 2012.

Chapters

Carr, Nicholas. "World Wide Computer." In *The Big Switch: Rewiring the World, From Edison to Google*. 2008.

DeGlopper, Donald R. "The Law Library and Collections." In *Encyclopedia of the Library of Congress: For Congress, the Nation, and the World*, edited by John Y. Cole & Jane Aikin. 2004.

Gilliland, Kris. "The Successful Law Library Manager: Training and Skills." In *How to Manage a Law School Library: Leading Librarians on Updating Resources, Managing Budgets, and Meeting Expectations*. 2008.

Hazelton, Penny A. "Law Library Director of the Twenty-First Century." In *How to Manage a Law School Library: Leading Librarians on Updating Resources, Managing Budgets, and Meeting Expectations*. 2008.

Heller, James S. "Collection Development, Licensing and Acquisitions." In *Law Librarianship in the Twenty-First Century*. Lanham, MD: Scarecrow Press, 2007.

Kirkland, John. "Change and Continuity: The Case of the Association of Commonwealth Universities." In *Consortia: International Networking Alliances of Universities*, edited by David Teather, 2004.

Knott, Christopher A. "Libraries as Service Institutions: Meeting Patron Needs in a Changing Environment." In *How to Manage a Law School Library: Leading Librarians on Updating Resources, Managing Budgets and Meeting Expectations*. 2008.

Knutt, Rebecca J. "China's Destruction of the Libraries of Tibet." In *Lost Libraries: The Destruction of Great Book Collections since Antiquity*, edited by James Raven. 2004.

Langdell, Christopher Columbus. Preface to *Selection of Cases on the Law of Contracts with References and Citations*. Little, Brown & Co., 1871. Reprinted in Glen-Peter Ahlers Sr., *The History of Law School Libraries in the United States: Defining Moments*. 2011.

Nichols, Sarah L. "Aligning Library Service Lines with Business Strategy." In *How to Manage a Law Firm Library: Leading Librarians on Providing Effective Services, Managing Costs, and Updating and Maintaining Resources*. 2008.

Pagel, Scott B. "Changing Libraries and Changing Relationships: Challenges for the Library Director." In *How to Manage a Law School Library: Leading Librarians on Updating Resources, Managing Budgets, and Meeting Expectations*. 2008.

Smith-Butler, Lisa. "Administration." In *Law Librarianship in the Twenty-First Century*. Lanham, MD: Scarecrow Press, 2007.

Whiteman, Michael. "Law Library Management in the Twenty-First Century." In *How to Manage a Law School Library: Leading Librarians on Updating Resources, Managing Budgets, and Meeting Expectations*. Aspatore Books, 2008.

ARTICLES

Acosta, Luis M., and Anna M. Cherry. "Reference Services in Courts and Governmental Settings." *Legal Reference Services Quarterly* 26, nos. 1–2 (2007): 113.

Adams, Jennifer. "Digital Divide: Tips for Developing a Digital Collection Development Policy." *AALL Spectrum* 15 (Sept./Oct. 2010): 36.

Agrawal, Neel Kant. "Training in FCIL Librarianship for Tomorrow's World." Available at http://works.bepress.com/aallcallforpapers/70.

Aiken, Julian, and Femi Cadmus. "Who Let the Dog Out? Implementing a Successful Therapy Dog Program in an Academic Law Library." *Yale L. Sch. Legal Scholarship Repository.* Available at http://digitalcommons.law.yale.edu/cgi/viewcontent.cgi?article=1008&context=ylss.

Aldrich, Duncan M., Gary Cornwell, and Daniel Barkley. "Changing Partnerships? Government Documents Departments at the Turn of the Millennium." *Government Information Quarterly* 17, no. 3 (2000): 273–90.

Alford, Duncan E. "The Law Librarian's Role in the Scholarly Enterprise." *Journal of Law & Education* 39 (2010): 351.

Anderson, Kristine J., et al. "Buy, Don't Borrow: Bibliographer's Analysis of Academic Library Collection Development through Interlibrary Loan Requests." *Collection Management* 27 (2002): 1.

Anzalone, Filippa Marullo. "Servant Leadership: A New Model for Law Library Leaders." *Law Library Journal* 99 (2007): 793.

Association of Research Librarians. "Principles for Licensing Electronic Resources." July 15, 1997. http://www.arl.org/sc/marketplace/license/licprinciples.shtml.

Baish, Mary Alice. "Washington Brief: GPO Plan to Reduce Print Distribution to Depository Libraries." *AALL Spectrum* 9, no. 6 (2005): 4.

Berring, Robert C. "Dyspeptic Ramblings of a Retiring Past President." *Law Library Journal* 79 (1987): 345.

Breakstone, Elizabeth R. "Now How Much of Your Print Collection Is Really Online? An Analysis of the Overlap of Print and Digital Holdings at the University of Oregon Law Library." *Legal Reference Services Quarterly* 29 (Oct.–Dec. 2010): 255.

Brigger, Patrick. "Managing from the Heart." *Washington Post*, January 20, 2012, http://www.washingtonpost.com/blogs/leadership-books/post/managing-from-the-heart/2011/03/07/gIQA3rWbDQ_blog.html .

Burchfield, Amy, and Kevin Garewal. "Meeting Evolving Research and Curriculum Needs: A Survey of Interlibrary Loan and OhioLINK Borrowing at an Academic Law Library." *Journal of Interlibrary Loan, Document Delivery and Electronic Reserve* 19 (2009): 137.

Calkins, Hugh. "Really Simple Syndication." *Maine B.J.* 21 (2006): 190.

Campbell, Leslie M., and Ellen Platt. "The ABA Reaccreditation Inspection Visit: Process and Preparation." Am. Ass'n. of L. Librs. 2000. Available at http://www.aallnet.org/sis/allsis/abavisit/aba.prog.bib.pdf.

Chadwell, Faye A. "Assessing the Value of Academic Library Consortia." *Journal of Library Administration* 51 (2011): 645.

Cheney, Kristin. "Is An Annual Report in Your Library's Future?" *Law Library Journal* 97 (2005): 493.

Cofield, Melanie, and Kasia Salon. "Making the Most of LibGuides in Law Libraries." *AALL Spectrum* 16 (2011): 17.

Cohen, Alan. "Law Librarian Survey." *The American Lawyer* 34, no. 8 (Aug. 1, 2012): 39.

Daniels, Bethany. "A Study in Light and Nature." *AALL Spectrum* 16, no. 7 (2012): 16. Available at http://www.aallnet.org/main-menu/Publications/spectrum/Archives/Vol-16/No-7/pacific-mcgeorge.pdf.

Dunn, Donald J. "From Librarian to Dean to Librarian, or to Hell and Back." *Law Library Journal* 93 (2001): 391.

———. "What to Expect When the ABA Site Evaluator Arrives—and Perhaps a Bit Before." Am. Ass'n. of L. Librs. 2000. Available at http://web.archive.org/web/20060225075835/http://www.aallnet.org/sis/allsis/abavisit/dunn.pdf.

Eschenfelder, Kristin R. "Behind the Website: An Inside Look at the Production of Web-based Textual Government Information." *Government Information Quarterly* 21, no. 3 (2004): 337–58.

Esposito, Joseph. "What if Wal-Mart Ran a Library?" *Journal of Electronic Publishing* 9, no. 1 (Winter 2006). Available at http://www.hti.umich.edu/cgi/t/text/text-idx?c=jep;view=text;rgn=main;idno=3336451.0009.104.

Farbenblum, Bassina. "Executive Deference in U.S. Refugee Law: Internationalist Paths through and beyond Chevron." *Duke Law Journal* 60 (2011): 1119.

Farrell, Elizabeth. "Renew, Reuse, Renovate!" *AALL Spectrum* 16, no. 7 (2012): 13. Available at http://www.aallnet.org/main-menu/Publications/spectrum/Archives/Vol-16/No-7/fsu.pdf.

Fitchett, Taylor, et al. "Law Library Budgets in Hard Times." *Law Library Journal* 103 (2011): 91.

Franklin, Jonathan A. "One Piece of the Collection Development Puzzle: Issues in Drafting Format Selection Guidelines." *Law Library Journal*Library 86 (1994): 753.

Gabriel, Raquel J. "Managing Conflict." *Law Library Journal* 103 (2011): 685.

Gerson, Kevin D. "Faculty Research Services at the UCLA Library." *Trends in Law Library Management and Technology* 18 (2008): 55.

Ginsberg, Deborah, et al. "I Want My Web 2.0." *AALL Spectrum* 13 (2009): 28.

Grossman, Andrew. "Towards Cooperation in Access to Foreign Primary Law." *International Journal of Legal Information* 30 (2002): 28.

Hale-Janeke, Amy, and Sharon Blackburn. "Law Librarians and the Self-Represented Litigant." *Legal Reference Services Quarterly* (2008): 65.

Harper's Index. Harper's Magazine February 2001.

Harrell, Merrilee. "Self-Help Legal Materials in the Law Library: Going a Step Further for the Public Patron." *Legal Reference Services Quarterly* 27 (2008): 283.

Healey, Paul D. "Pro Se Users, Reference Liability, and the Unauthorized Practice of Law: Twenty-Five Selected Readings." *Law Library Journal* 94 (Winter 2002): 133.

Heen, Heather. "Beyond the Shelves: Law Librarianship in the New Economic Climate." *Law Tech. News*, September 10, 2012. Available at http://www.law.com/jsp/lawtechnologynews/PubArticleLTN.jsp?id=1346617720885.

Heller, James S. "Collection Development and Weeding à la Versace: Fashioning a Policy for Your Library." *AALL Spectrum* 6 (Feb. 2002): 12.

Hernon, P., and H. Relyea. "Government Publishing: Past to Present." *Government Information Quarterly* 12, no. 3 (1995): 309–30.

Hirsch, Cindy. "The Rise and Fall of Academic Law Library Collection Standards." 58 Legal Reference Services Quarterly 58 (2012): 65.

Howard, Jennifer. "Publishers Settle Long-Running Lawsuit Over Google's Book Scanning Project." *The Chronicle*, October 4, 2012. Available at http://chronicle.com/article/Publishers-Settle-Long-Running/134854/.

Hudson, John. "This Laser Trick's a Quantum Leap." *Wired*, October 4, 2005. Available at http://www.wired.com/science/discoveries/news/2005/10/69033.

Ireland, Peter N. "A New Keynesian Perspective on the Great Recession." *Journal of Money, Credit and Banking* 43 (February 2011): 31.

Jackson, Mary E. "Measuring the Performance of Interlibrary Loan and Document Delivery Services." *ARL: A Bimonthly Newsletter of Research Library Issues and Actions* 195 (Dec. 1997). Available at http://www.arl.org/resources/pubs/br/index.shtml.

Jackson, Mary E., et al. *Assessing ILL/DD Services: New Cost-Effective Alternatives*, ARL 236 Bimonthly Rep., October 2004. Available at http://www.arl.org/bm~doc/ill-study.pdf.

Jacobs, James A., et al. "Government Information in the Digital Age: The Once and Future Federal Depository Library Program." *The Journal of Academic Librarianship* 31, no. 3 (2005): 205.

Jacobs, James A., James R. Jacobs, and Shinjoung Yeo. "Government Information in the Digital Age: The Once and Future Federal Depository Program." *Journal of Academic Librarianship* 31, no. 3 (May 2005): 198–208.

Johnson, Nancy P. "Best Practices: What a First Year Law Students Should Learn in a Legal Research Class." *Legal Reference Services Quarterly* 28(2009): 77.

Johnston, Janis L. "Managing the Boss." *Law Library Journal* 89 (1997): 21.

Justiss, Laura K. "A Survey of Electronic Research Alternatives to LexisNexis and Westlaw in Law Firms." *Law Library Journal*Library 103 (Winter 2011): 71. Available at http://www.aallnet.org/main-menu/Publications/llj/LLJ-Archives/Vol-103/2011-01/2011-04.pdf.

Kesselman, Martin A., and Sarah Barbara Watsein. "Creating Opportunities: Embedded Librarians." *Journal of Library Administration* 49 (2009): 383.

Knight, Lianne Forster. "What About RSS?" *Austrl. L. Library* 14 (2006): 7.

Kolonay, Brittany, and Gail Mathapo. "Experimenting with Embedding: A Law School Embeds Librarians in Clinics and Seminars." *AALL Spectrum* 16 (2012): 18.

Kolowich, Steve. "Publishers Fallback Position." *Inside Higher Ed*, http://www.insidehighered.com/news/2012/06/04/publishers-seek-injunction-e-reserve-case.

Krause, Margaret. "Westlaw and Lexis: The Graphical User Interface." *Trends in Law Library Management and Technology*Library 5 (1991–1993): 7.

Lambert, Greg. "A Westlaw Product at a Google Scholar Price." *Vermont B.J.* 37 (2011–2012): 47.

Lehman, Jeffrey. "International Law and the Legal Curriculum." *American Society of International Law Proceedings* 96 (2002): 55.

Leichter, Matt. "Tough Choices Ahead for Some High Ranked Law Schools." *The American Lawyer*, July 3, 2012. Available at http://www.americanlawyer.com/PubArticleTAL.jsp?id=1202561764452&slreturn=2012090113030.

Lin, Katherina R., and Erin Murphy. "Reflections on a JX Reclassification Project." *Law Library Journal* 90 (2000): 459.

Lines, Michael. "Are Legal Texts Grey Literature? Towards an Understanding of Grey Literature that Invites the Preservation of Authentic and Genuine Originals." January 2010. Available at https://dspace.library.uvic.ca:8443/bitstream/handle/1828/3221/2010-01-GL11Lines-AreLegalTexts.pdf?sequence=1.

Marchese, Theodore J. "U.S. Higher Education in the Postwar Era: Expansion and Growth." *Elec. J. of the U.S. Info. Agency* 2 (Dec. 1997): 4. Available at http://usinfo.state.gov/journals/itsv/1297/ijse/marchese.htm.

Martin, Kristin E. "Publishing Trends within State Government: The Situation in North Carolina." *Journal of Government Information* 30, nos. 5/6 (2004): 620–36.

Marzolla, Mary K. "Facing Reality: The Death of the Reference Desk? Quality Service and Accessibility Are Vital to Reference Services." *AALL Spectrum* 6 (Sept. 2001): 34.

Matasar, Richard A. "Viability of the Law Degree: Cost, Value and Intrinsic Worth." *Iowa Law Review* 96 (2010–2011): 1579.

McDonough, Molly. "In Google We Trust? Critics Question How Much Judges, Lawyers Should Rely on Internet Search Results." *ABA Journal* 90 (2004): 30.

McFadden, David. "Survey of FCIL Membership: Results." *FCIL Newsletter*, Feb. 1992, 17.

Matheson, S., and S. Davidson. "The Evolution of Providing Access to Information: Is the Online Catalog Nearing Extinction?" *Legal Reference Services Quarterly* 26, no. 1 (2007): 57.

Meyerowitz, Steven A. "The Changing Role of the Law Firm Librarian." *Penn. Law* 26 (May/June 2004): 28.

Murley, Diane. "Law Libraries in the Cloud." *Law Library Journal* 101 (2009): 249.

———. "The Power of RSS Feeds." *Law Library Journal* 101 (2009): 127.

Otani, Akane. "Watershed Ruling on Digital Lawsuit Advances Cornell's Digital Library Project." *Cornell Daily Sun*, October 15, 2012. Available at http://cornell-sun.com/section/news/content/2012/10/15/%E2%80%98watershed%E2%80%99-ruling-lawsuit-advances-cornells-digital-library-project.

Palfrey, John. "Cornerstones of Law Libraries for an Era of Digital-Plus." *Law Library Journal* 102 (Spring 2010): 171.

Perdue, Jennifer, and James A. Van Fleet. "Borrow or Buy? Cost-Effective Delivery of Monographs." *Journal of Interlibrary Loan, Document Delivery & Information Supply* 9 (1999): 19.

Peterson, Eric. "Concepts for Reform of Title 44." *Nat'l Comm'n on Librs. and Info. Sci.* Available at http://www.nclis.gov/govt/assess/assess.html.

Price, Derek J. de Solla. "An Ancient Greek Computer." *Scientific American* 200, no. 6 (June 1959): 60.

———. "Gears from the Greeks: The Antikythera Mechanism—A Calendar Computer from ca. 80 B.C." *Transactions of the American Philosophical Society* 64 (1974): 7. Available at http://www.jstor.org/discover/10.2307/1006146?uid=2&uid=4&sid=21101783948263.

"Principles for Licensing Electronic Resources." American Association of Law Libraries. November 2004. Available at http://www.aallnet.org/main-menu/Advocacy/recommendedguidelines/licensing-electronic-resources.html.

Raisch, Marylin J. Book Review. *International Journal of Legal Information* 30 (2002): 370.

Relyea, Harold C. "E-Gov: The Federal Overview." *The Journal of Academic Librarianship* 27, no. 2 (March 2001): 131–48.

Rhodes, Sarah. "Breaking Down Link Rot: The Chesapeake Project Legal Information Archive's Examination of URL Stability." *Law Library Journal* 102 (Fall 2010): 581.

Rhodes, Terrel L. "Making Learning Visible and Meaningful through Electronic Portfolios." *Change: The Magazine of Higher Education*, Jan.–Feb. 2011. Available at http://www.changemag.org/Archives/Back%20Issues/2011/January-February%202011/making-learning-visible-full.html.

Rumsey, Mary. "New Member Profile: Julie Horst." *Foreign, Comparative and International Law Special Interest Section Newsletter* 19, no. 2 (Feb. 2005): 17.

———. "Strangers in a Strange Land: How to Answer Foreign Law Research Questions." *AALL Spectrum* 8 (July 2004): 14.

Sahl, Silke. "Introduction." *International Journal of Legal Information* 31 (2003): 151.

Saricks, Joyce. "At Leisure: The Lessons of Weeding." *Booklist* 108 (2011): 43.

Shuler, John A. "Beyond the Depository Library Concept." *The Journal of American Librarianship* 27, no. 4 (July 2001): 299–301.

Silber, Karen. "Every Library Is Special and So Is Its Collection Development Policy." *AALL Spectrum* 4 (Dec. 1999): 10.

Slater, Robert. "Challenges and Changes: A Review of Issues Surrounding the Digital Migration of Government Information." *Science & Technology Libraries* 21, nos. 1/2 (2001): 153–62.

Small, A. J. "Reflections." *Law Library Journal* 24 (1931): 12.

Smith-Butler, Lisa. "Public Relations: Overcoming Your Aversion to the M Word." *AALL Spectrum* 14 (2010): 7. Also available at http://www.aallnet.org/main-menu/Publications/spectrum/Archives/Vol-14/pub_sp1003/pub-sp1003-pr.pdf (last visited October 19, 2012).

Smith, Robert H. "The Librarian's Risk of Irrelevance (In the Eyes of the Law School Dean)." *Law Library Journal* 95 (2003): 421.

Smith, Sallie, et al. "Database Ownership: Myth or Reality?" *Law Library Journal* 103 (2011): 233.

Soma, Amy K., and Lisa M. Sjoberg. "More than Just Low-Hanging Fruit: A Collaborative Approach to Weeding in Academic Libraries." *Collection Management* 36 (2011): 17.

Tice, Beatrice. "Academic Law Library in the 21st Century: Still the Heart of the Law School." *U.C. Irvine Law Review* 1 (2011): 157.

Wagner, Judith Welch. "Teaching Legal Research: Educating Lawyers: Carnegie Report Reveals New Challenges, Fresh Possibilities for Law Librarians." *AALL Spectrum* 13 (2009): 20.

Wang, Fang. "Building an Open Source Institutional Repository at a Small Law School Library: Is It Realistic or Unattainable?" *Info. Tech. and Librs.* 30 (2011): 81.

Watson, Carol, and James Donovan. "Institutional Repositories: A Plethora of Possibilities." *Trends in Law Library Management and Technology* 21 (2011): 19.

Wilkins, M. Lesley. "Harvard Law School Library Collections & Services Related to Law of the Islamic World." *International Journal of Legal Information* 31 (2003): 383.

Wu, Michelle M. "Why Print and Electronic Resources Are Essential to the Academic Law Library." *Law Library Journal* 97 (2005): 233.

Yirka, Carl. "The Yirka Question and the Yirka Answer: What Should Law Libraries Stop Doing in Order to Address Higher Priority Initiatives." *AALL Spectrum* 12 (2008): 28.

Zeilinger, Anton. "Quantum Teleportation." *Scientific American* 13, no. 1 (May 2003): 34.

SESSION LAWS

Printing Act of 1895, ch. 23, 28 Stat. 601-24.

Act of Aug. 26, 1852, ch. 91, 10 Stat. 30.

Act of Aug. 26, 1852, ch. 91, 10 Stat. 35.

Act of February 5, 1859, ch.22, 11 Stat. 379.

Act of July 14, 1832, ch. 221, 4 Stat. 579.

Act of March 20, 1922, Pub. L. No. 67-171, 42 Stat. 422.

Act of March 3, 1869, ch. 57, 15 Stat. 283.

An Act to Provide for the Safe-keeping of the Acts, Records and Seal of the United States, and for Other Purposes, 1 Stat. 68 (1789).

An Act providing for the Election of a Congressional Printer, ch. 59, 14 Stat. 398 (1867).

Government Printing Office Electronic Information Access Enhancement Act of 1993, Pub. L. No. 103-40, 107 Stat. 112 (1993).

J. Res. 1, 13th Cong., 3 Stat. 140 (1813).

J. Res. 25, 36th Cong., 12 Stat. 117 (1860).

No. 10, *A Resolution to authorize the Attorney General to contract for copies of a proposed edition of the Law and Treaties of the United States,* 5 Stat. 798 (1845).

No. 14, *A Resolution regulating the Printing of Congress, and establishing the Compensation of [for] the same,* 9 Stat. 112 (1846).

No. 16, *Joint Resolution directing the Manner of procuring the Printing for the Two Houses of Congress,* 9 Stat. 113 (1846).

Paperwork Reduction Act of 1980, Pub. L. No. 96-511, 94 Stat. 2812 (1980).

Pub. L. No. 90-620, 82 Stat. 1238 (1968).

Resolution directing the manner in which the printing of Congress shall be executed, fixing the prices thereof, and providing for the appointment of a printer or printers, 15th Cong., 3 Stat. 538 (1819).

LEGISLATION

Federal

An Act for the More General Promulgation of the Laws of the United States, ch. 50, 1 Stat. 443 (1795).

An Act in Addition to an Act Entitled "An Act for the More General Promulgation of the Laws of the United States," ch. 30, 1 Stat. 724 (1799).

An Act Legalizing and Making Appropriations for Such Necessary Objects as Have Been Usually Included in the General Appropriation Bills without Authority of Law, and to Fix and Provide for Certain Incidental Expenses of the Departments and Offices of the Government, and for other Purposes, ch. 202, 5 Stat. 523 (1842).

An Act making appropriations for the legislative, executive, and judicial expenses of the Government for the year ending June thirtieth, eighteen hundred and seventy-five, and for other purposes, ch. 328, 18 Stat. 85 (1874).

An Act to Amend the Act Entitled "An Act for the More General Promulgation of the Laws of the United States," ch. 1, 1 Stat. 496 (1796).

An Act to amend the act, entitled "An Act to Provide for the Publication of the Laws of the United States, and for other Purposes," ch. 92, 3 Stat. 576 (1820).

An Act to Authorize the Publication of the Laws of the United States within the Territories of the United States, ch. 6, 3 Stat. 145 (1814).

An Act to Provide for the Publication of the Laws of the United States, and for other Purposes, ch. 80, 3 Stat. 439 (1818).

An Act to Provide for the Safe-keeping of the Acts, Records and Seal of the United States, and for other Purposes, ch. 14, 1 Stat. 68 (1789).

Government Printing Reform Act of 1996, H.R. 4280, 140th Cong. (1996).

H.R. Res. 24, 104th Cong. (1995).
H.R. 1024, 104th Cong. (1995).
Wendell H. Ford Government Publications Reform Act of 1998, S. 2288, 105th Cong. (1998).

State

Assemb. 2648, 2002 Leg., Reg. Sess., (Cal. 2002), available at http://
    www.leginfo.ca.gov/pub/01-02/bill/asm/ab_2601-2650/
    ab_2648_cfa_20021008_165850_asm_floor.html.
H.R. 0113A, Engrossed 2, 2003 Leg., Spec. Sess. A (Fla. 2003), available at http://
    archive.flsenate.gov/data/session/2003A/House/bills/billtext/pdf/h0113Aer.pdf.

TREATIES

Convention on International Trade in Endangered Species of Wild Fauna and Flora, March 3,
    1973, 27 U.S.T. 1087, 993 U.N.T.S. 243.
Convention on the Prevention and Punishment of the Crime of Genocide, December 9, 1948,
    78 U.N.T.S. 277.

GUIDELINES, STANDARDS, AND RULES

American Bar Association. 2012–2013 Standards and Rules of Procedure for Approval
    of Law Schools, Standard No. 606. Available at http://www.americanbar.org/con-
    tent/dam/aba/publications/misc/legal_education/Standards/chap-
    ter_6_2012_2013_aba_standards_and_rules.authcheckdam.pdf.
American Association of Law Librariess. AALL Ethical Principles, April 5, 1999. Avail-
    able at http://www.aallnet.org/main-menu/Leadership-Governance/policies/Public-
    Policies/policy-ethics.html.
———. Standards for Appellate Court Libraries & State Law Libraries, March 2005.
    Available   at   http://www.aallnet.org/sis/sccll/docs/
    Sccll%20Appellate%20Standards%20Mar%202005.pdf.
American Library Association. Code of Ethics of the American Library Association
    (amended Jan. 22, 2008). Available at http://www.ala.org/advocacy/proethics/code-
    ofethics/codeethics.
Special Libraries Association. SLA Professional Ethics Guidelines. Available at http://
    www.sla.org/content/SLA/ethics_guidelines.cfm.
State Law Library Committee. Guidelines for E-Mail Reference Service at the Mary-
    land State Law Library. November 16, 2011. *Available at* http://
    www.lawlib.state.md.us/aboutus/policies/EmailReferenceGuidelinesMSLL.pdf.

ELECTRONIC DATABASES

Bloomberg Law: http://about.bloomberglaw.com/.
Casemaker: http://www.casemaker.com/.
Cornell's Legal Information Institute: http://www.law.cornell.edu/.
Fastcase: http://www.fastcase.com/.
Findlaw: http://www.findlaw.com.
Justicia: http://law.justia.com/.
Loislaw Connect: http://estore.loislaw.com/default.aspx.
THOMAS: http://thomas.loc.gov/home/thomas.php
Versuslaw: http://www.versuslaw.com/
Washlaw: http://washlaw.edu

WorldCat, OCLC: www.worldcat.org

INTERNET RESOURCES

2005 Essential Titles Survey Initial Analysis, FDLP Desktop, http://fdlp.gov/component/content/article/19-general/189-essentialtitles-survey2005.

2011 Syllabi and Course Materials Database, American Association of Law Libraries. FCIL-SIS, http://www.aallnet.org/sis/fcilsis/syllabi.html.

2012 Meeting Proceedings, FDLP Desktop, http://www.fdlp.gov/home/repository/cat_view/177-outreach/97-events/101-depository-library-council-dlc-meetings/357-2012-meeting-proceedings.

The 2012 Statistical Abstract, U.S. Department of Commerce, United States Census Bureau, http://www.census.gov/compendia/statab/.

About FDsys, U.S. Government Printing Office, http://www.gpo.gov/fdsysinfo/aboutfdsys.htm.

About GPO, U.S. Government Printing Office, http://www.gpo.gov/about/.

About Law Library of Congress, Library of Congress, http://www.loc.gov/law/about/.

About the AALL Computing Services SIS, AALL CS-SIS, http://cssis.org/about/about-cssis.

About the Institute on Collaboration in Higher Education, Association for Collaborative Leadership, http://www.national-acl.com/institute/abouttheinstitute.asp.

About the ICOLC, International Coalition of Library Consortia, http://icolc.net/about-icolc/.

About the LC Online Catalog, Library of Congress, http://catalog2.loc.gov/vwebv/ui/en_US/htdocs/help/index.html.

About the Liblicense-L Discussion Forum, LIBLICENSE: Licensing Digital Content, http://liblicense.crl.edu/discussion-forum/introduction/.

About the Organization, Library of Congress, http://www.loc.gov/law/about/history.php.

Michael Alexander, *Defining Excel Dashboards and Reports*, For Dummies http://www.dummies.com/how-to/content/defining-excel-dashboards-and-reports.html.

ALM Media, Law.com, http://www.law.com.

AALL Price Index for Legal Publications, American Association of Law Libraries. http://www.aallnet.org/main-menu/Publications/products/pub-price.

American Association of Law Libraries, *Library Procurement Process Improvements Task Force*, http://www.aallnet.org/main-menu/Advocacy/recommendedguidelines/licensing-electronic-resources.html.

U.S. Government Printing Office, *American Library Association (ALA) Update (Midwinter 2006)*, http://www.fdlp.gov/home/repository/doc_download/523-american-library-association-ala-update-midwinter-2006.

Amigos Library Services, http://www.amigos.org/.

Ask a Librarian, Law Library of Congress, Library of Congress, http://www.loc.gov/rr/askalib/ask-law.html.

Association of Southeastern Research Libraries, http://www.aserl.org/.

Authentication, U.S. Government Printing Office, http://www.gpo.gov/authentication/.

Backstage Library Works, http://www.bslw.com.

Basic Information, Frequently Asked Questions (FAQ), World Summit on the Information Society, http://www.itu.int/wsis/basic/faqs.asp.

Bloglines, http://www.bloglines.com/.

Bylaws and Executive Committee Regulations Pertaining to the Requirements of Membership, the Association of American Law Schools, http://www.aals.org/about_handbook_requirements.php.

Cali DVDs, the Center for Computer-Assisted Legal Instruction, http://www.cali.org/content/cali-dvds.

California Digital Library, http://www.cdlib.org/west/.

Cambridge Sound System, http://www.cambridgesoundmanagement.com/ ?gclid=COqU8u2CibMCFYuY4AodW0kA2g.

Cameron, James, *GPO's Living History: Adelaide R. Hasse*, FDLP Desktop, http:// www.access.gpo.gov/su_docs/fdlp/history/hasse.html.

Kurt Carroll, *Thirty Years Ago—The Big Move*, Law Library of Congress: In Custodia Legis: Law Librarians of Congress (February 2, 2011), http://blogs.loc.gov/law/2011/ 02/the-big-move/.

Cataloger's Desktop, Library of Congress, http://desktop.loc.gov.

A Century of Lawmaking For a New Nation: U.S. Congressional Documents and Debates 1774–1875, Library of Congress, http://memory.loc.gov/ammem/amlaw/la- whome.html.

Checkpoint, Thompson Reuters, http://checkpoint.riag.com.

The Chesapeake Digital Preservation Group, http://www.legalinfoarchive.org/.

Claremont University Consortium, http://www.cuc.claremont.edu/.

Classification Web: World Wide Web Access to Library of Congress Classification and Library of Congress Subject Headings, Library of Congress, http://classificationweb.net.

Congress.gov: United States Legislation Information, http://beta.congress.gov/.

The Congressional Record App, iTunes, https://itunes.apple.com/us/app/the-congression- al-record/id492077075.

Consortium Directory Online, http://www.ringgold.com/pages/cdo.html.

CONTU Guidelines on Photocopying under Interlibrary Loan Arrangements, Coalition for Networked Information, http://old.cni.org/docs/infopols/CONTU.html.

Counting Online Usage of Networked Electronic Resources, http:// www.projectcounter.org/about.html.

Current Awareness Services, University of Oxford, Bodleian Law Library, http:// www.bodleian.ox.ac.uk/law/e-resources/current-awareness-services-draft.

Current Index to Legal Periodicals, University of Washington School of Law, Gallagher Law Library, http://lib.law.washington.edu/cilp/cilp.html.

Current Legal Topics, Library of Congress, http://www.loc.gov/law/help/current-top- ics.php.

David S. Mao Appointed Deputy Law Librarian of Congress, Library of Congress (May 5, 2010), http://loc.gov/today/pr/2010/10-101.html.

David Mao Appointed Law Librarian of Congress, Library of Congress (January 4, 2012), http://loc.gov/today/pr/2012/12-005.html.

Depository Library Council: About, FDLP Desktop http://www.access.gpo.gov/su_docs/ fdlp/council/aboutdlc.html.

Deutsche Telekom, https://www.telekom.com/dtag/cms/content/dt/en/258604;jsessio- nid=DF766904E7BB81C67011E75D2DD5B444#.

Digital Commons, *Law School Institutional Repositories*, http://digitalcom- mons.bepress.com/institutional-repository-law/.

Dina, Yemisi, *UPDATE: Guide to Caribbean Law Research*, NYU Law Hauser Global Law School, Program, http://www.nyulawglobal.org/globalex/Caribbean1.htm.

Dulin, Kim, *Harvard Law Library Collection Development Policy and Collection Develop- ment Matrix*, Et Seq. The Harvard Law School Library Blog (February 4, 2010), http:/ /etseq.law.harvard.edu/2010/02/har- vard_law_library_collection_development_policy_and_collection_developmen/.

Dupont Circle Group, *The Future of the Federal Depository Library Program*, Association of Research Librarians, http://www.arl.org/info/frn/gov/dupont.html.

Index to Legal Periodicals, EBSCO, http://www.ebscohost.com/academic/index-to-legal- periodicals-books.

Echo 360, http://echo360.com/.

.edu Administration, EDUCAUSE, http://net.educause.edu/edudomain/.

Electronic Resource Guide, Am. Soc'y of Int'l. L., http://www.asil.org/erg.

Essential Titles for Public Use in Paper or Other Tangible Format, FDLP Desktop, http:// www.fdlp.gov/collections/collection-tools/essential-titles-list.

FDL Handbook, FDLP Desktop, http://www.fdlp.gov/administration/handbook.

FDLP Desktop, U.S. Government. Printing Office. http://www.access.gpo.gov/su_docs/ fdlp/.

Federal Depository Library Council, FDLP Desktop, http://fdlp.gov/component/docman/ cat_view/72-about-the-fdlp/77-federal-depository-library-council.

Finance Market Authority, http://www.fma.gv.at/.

Foreign Law Guide, Thomas A. Reynolds and Arturo Flores, http:// www.foreignlawguide.com.

Frequently Asked Questions, U.S. Government Printing Office, http://www.gpo.gov/ factsheet/index.html#4.

Gadgets that Circulate, Stanford Law School Robert Crown Law Library, http://li-blog.law.stanford.edu/gadgets/.

Getting the Deal Through, http://www.gettingthedealthrough.com.

Gheen, Tina, *Happy Birthday Science.gov!*, In Custodia Legis: Law Librarians of Congress, http://blogs.loc.gov/law/2012/12/happy-birthday-science-gov/.

Global Legal Information Catalog, Law Library of Congress, http://www.loc.gov/law-web/servlet/Glic?home.

Global Legal Information Network, http://www.glin.gov/.

Global Legal Monitor (GLM), Library of Congress, http://www.loc.gov/law/news/ glm.php.

Google Books Library Project, http://www.google.com/googlebooks/library/in-dex.html.

Google Reader, http://www.google.com/reader/.

Google Scholar, http://scholar.google.com/.

Gov Docs Online Tutorial, Module 3: The Superintendent Of Documents (Sudocs) Classifica-tion System, AALL Gov't Documents Special Interest Section, http:// www.aallnet.org/sis/gd/tutorial/mod3a.html.

Government Printing Office Adopts Internal XML System, Nextgov (September 12, 2012), http://www.nextgov.com/mobile/2012/09/government-printing-office-adopts-inter-nal-xml-system/58065/.

Government Printing Office. *Keeping America Informed: The U.S. Government Printing Office: 150 Years of Service to the Nation*. Washington, DC: GPO, 2011. Available online at http://purl.fdlp.gov/GPO/gpo8534 or http://www.gpo.gov/fdsys/pkg/ GPO-KEEPINGAMERICAINFORMED/pdf/GPO-KEEPINGAMERICAIN-FORMED.pdf.

———. Press Releases 2012 and Press Release Archives. Washington, DC: GPO, 2012. Available online at http://gpo.gov/newsroom-media/.

Government Revenue Collection Association, *Revision 7 of Article V out of Florida Legis-lation* (July 1, 2008), http://www.govcollect.org/files/ FL_Court_Article%20_V_Revision_7.pdf.

GPO and the LOCKSS Alliance—Pilot Project, FDLP Desktop, http://fdlp.gov/compo-nent/content/article/715-gpolockss?start=6.

GPO Mobile, U.S. Government Printing Office, http://www.gpo.gov/mobile/.

GreyNet: Grey Literature Network Service, http://www.greynet.org/greyne-thome.html.

Guide to Law Online, Library of Congress, http://www.loc.gov/law/help/guide.php.

HathiTrust Digital Library, http://www.hathitrust.org/.

Hines, N. William, *Empirical Scholarship: What Should We Study and How Should We Study It?*, Association of American Law Schools, http://www.aals.org/am2006/ theme.html

History of the Law Library, Library of Congress, http://www.loc.gov/law/about/histo-ry.php.

ICOLC Statements, http://icolc.net/statements.

IFLA Position on Internet Governance, IFLA, http://www.ifla.org/publications/ifla-po-sition-on-internet-governance.

In Custodia Legis, Law Librarians of Congress, http://blogs.loc.gov/law/.

Jurist, *Paper Chase*, http://jurist.org/paperchase/.

Law and the Library by Library of Congress, iTunes, https://itunes.apple.com/itunes-u/law-and-the-library/id386017780?mt=10#ls=1.

Law Library of Congress, Facebook, https://www.facebook.com/lawlibraryofcongress.

Law Library of Congress, Twitter, https://twitter.com/LawLibCongress.

Legal Information Preservation Alliance, http://www.aallnet.org/lipa/.

Legal Information Preservation Alliance, http://lipalliance.org/.

Library of Congress, Youtube, http://www.youtube.com/playlist?list=PL96401BE3402149B9.

Libcal, Springshare, http://www.springshare.com/libcal/.

Libguides, Springshare, http://springshare.com/libguides/.

Library of Congress Online Catalog, Library of Congress, http://catalog2.loc.gov/.

Library Resources for Administrative History: Congressional Serial Set, Archives Library Info. Center, http://www.archives.gov/research/alic/reference/admin-history/congressional-serial-set.html.

Library Techs, Inc., www.librarytech.com.

Lyrasis, http://www.lyrasis.org/.

MacGilvray, Daniel R. "A Short History of GPO." First printed in *New Typeline* (1986–1987), reprinted in *Administrative Notes* (1986–1987). FDLP Desktop. http://www.access.gpo.gov/su_docs/fdlp/history/macgilvray.html.

Marcive, Inc., www.marcive.com.

Maryland AskUsNow!, http://www.askusnow.info/.

Maryland State Law Library, *About the Maryland State Law Library*, http://www.lawlib.state.md.us/aboutus/aboutus.html.

Maryland State Law Library, *Digital Collections*, http://www.lawlib.state.md.us/collections/digitalcollections.html.

Maryland State Law Library, *Resources for Maryland Circuit Court Libraries*, http://www.lawlib.state.md.us/audiences/cclib/cclib.html.

McGarr, Sheila M., *Snapshots of the Federal Depository Library Program*, FDLP Desktop, http://www.access.gpo.gov/su_docs/fdlp/history/snapshot.html.

McKinney, Richard J., *An Overview of the U.S. Congressional Serial Set*, Law Librarians Society of Washington, D.C., http://www.llsdc.org/sourcebook/sch-v.htm#over.

———, *An Overview of the Congressional Record and Its Predecessor Publications*, Law Librarians Society of Washington, D.C., http://www.llsdc.org/cong-record/.

———, *A Research Guide to the Federal Register and the Code of Federal Regulations*, Law Librarians Society of Washington, D.C., http://www.llsdc.org/fed-reg-cfr/.

Merriam-Webster Online Dictionary, http://www.m-w.com/.

Miami Dade County Law Library, *News about the Law Library*, http://www.mdcll.org/html/News.htm.

National Center for Education Statistics, *IPEDS Data Center*, http://nces.ed.gov/ipeds/datacenter/.

National Information Standards Organization, *Shared Electronic Resource Understanding*, NISO, http://www.niso.org/workrooms/seru.

New England Law Library Consortium, *PALMprint*, http://www.nellco.org/?page=palmprint.

New England Law Library Consortium, http://www.nellco.org.

Newsgator, http://www.newsgator.com/?mkwid=s9pxuMAAO&pcrid=14557693059&gclid=CMTxuPWxl7MCFQWnnQodfEsA6w.

Northeast Document Conservation Center, dPlan™: The Online Disaster-Planning Tool for Cultural and Civic Institutions, http://www.dplan.org/.

O'Grady, Jean P., "eBooks: Why are Publishers Pouring Digital Content into 19th Century Wineskins?" Dewey B Strategic (Sept. 28, 2011), http://deweybstrategic.blogspot.com/2011/09/ebooks-why-are-publishers-pouring.html.

Orbis Cascade Alliance, http://www.orbiscascade.org/index/history-as-an-unicorporated-association.

Osler, Mark, *Unkind Cuts: Shrinking the Law School Budget*, Law school Innovation Blog (October 20, 2012), http://lsi.typepad.com/lsi/2012/10/unkind-cuts-shrinking-the-law-school-budget.html.

Overview of GPO's Authentication Program, U.S. Government Printing Office, http://www.gpo.gov/pdfs/authentication/authenticationoverview.pdf.

People's Law Library of Maryland, http://www.peoples-law.org/.

Pew Internet: Pew Internet & American Life Project, http://www.pewinternet.org/.

Phases of the GPO Access Shut-Down, U.S. Government. Printing Office, http://www.gpo.gov/pdfs/fdsys-info/ThePhases_GPOAccessShut.pdf.

Practical Law Co., http://us.practicallaw.com.

Professional Life, Roytennant.com, http://roytennant.com/professional.html.

Rare Book Collection, Library of Congress, http://www.loc.gov/law/find/rare-books.php.

Raymond, Matt, *Now Tweeting: Law Library of Congress*, Library of Congress Blog (October 22, 2009), http://blogs.loc.gov/loc/2009/10/now-tweeting-law-library-of-congress/.

Reader Registration and Access to Library of Congress Reading Rooms, Library of Congress, http://www.loc.gov/rr/readerregistration.html.

Roberta I. Shaffer Appointed Law Librarian of Congress, Library of Congress (Aug. 20, 2009), http://loc.gov/today/pr/2009/09-157.html.

Saunders, Virginia, *U.S. Congressional Serial Set: What It Is and Its History*, U.S. Government. Printing Office, http://www.access.gpo.gov/su_docs/fdlp/history/sset/index.html.

Serials Section, Acquisitions Committee, American Library Association, Association for Library Collections & Technical Services, *Acquisitions Glossary* (3rd ed. 2005), http://www.ala.org/alcts/sites/ala.org.alcts/files/content/resources/collect/serials/acqglossary/05seracq_glo.pdf.

Sonic Foundry's Media Site, http://www.sonicfoundry.com/mediasite-by-sonicfoundry.

Speaker of the House and Librarian of Congress Announce Online Public Access to Congressional Information, Library of Congress (January 5, 1995), http://loc.gov/today/pr/1995/95-002.html.

Strategic Plan for the Future of the FDLP, FDLP Desktop, http://fdlp.gov/home/about/237-strategicplan.

Superintendent of Documents (SuDocs) Classification Scheme, FDLP Desktop, http://www.fdlp.gov/cataloging/856-sudoc-classification-scheme.

Technical Services Law Librarian, American Association of Law Libraries, http://www.aallnet.org/sis/tssis/tsll/.

THOMASdotgov, Twitter, https://twitter.com/thomasdotgov.

Triangle Research Libraries Network, http://www.trln.org/.

U.S. & World Population Clocks, U.S. Dep't. of Commerce, United States Census Bureau, http://www.census.gov/main/www/popclock.html.

Update for ALA, U.S. Gov't. Printing Office, http://www.access.gpo.gov/su_docs/fdlp/events/ala_update06.pdf.

Visualize Excel salaries around world with these 66 Dashboards, http://chandoo.org/wp/excel-dashboards/ and http://chandoo.org/wp/2012/07/30/excel-salary-survey-contest-results/.

vLex, http://vlex.com.

Weber, Andrew, *@THOMASdotgov*, In Custodia Legis: Law Librarians of Congress (April 27, 2011), http://blogs.loc.gov/law/2011/04/thomasdotgov/.

———, *Congressional Record App Updated to Include iPhone*, In Custodia Legis: Law Librarians of Congress (July 6, 2012), http://blogs.loc.gov/law/2012/07/congressional-record-app-updated-to-include-iphone/.

———, *Now There's a Congressional Record App for That*, In Custodia Legis: Law Librarians of Congress (January 18, 2012), http://blogs.loc.gov/law/2012/01/now-theres-a-congressional-record-app-for-that/.

———, *What Exactly is In Custodia Legis?*, In Custodia Legis: Law Librarians of Congress (August 2, 2010), http://blogs.loc.gov/law/2010/08/in-custodia-legis/.
WGIG Background Report, WGIG.org, http://www.wgig.org/WGIG-Report.html
What We Have: Non-Book Items, Cornell University School of Law, Cornell Law Library, http://www.lawschool.cornell.edu/library/WhatWeHave/Non-Book-Items.cfm.
The World in 2011: ICT Facts and Figures, Int'l. Telecomms Union, http://www.itu.int/ITU-D/ict/facts/2011/index.html.
World Intellectual Property Organization, http://www.wipo.int/portal/index.html.en.
Whisner, Mary, *Choosing Law Librarianship: Thoughts for People Contemplating a Career Move*, LLRX.com, http://www.llrx.com.features/librarian.htm.
Wyman, Carolyn, *Hillary Clinton at Yale Law School*, Hillary Clinton Q., available at http://www.hillaryclintonquarterly.com/hillary_yale.htm.

REPORTS

Government Printing Office. *Government Printing Office: Actions to Strengthen and Sustain GPO's Transformation*. Report to Congressional Committees. GAO-04-830. Washington: United States General Accounting Office, June 2004. www.gao.gov/cgi-bin/getrpt?GAO-04-830.
———. *GPO Strategic Plan FY 2011–2015*. Washington, DC: GPO, 2011. Available online at http://www.gpo.gov/pdfs/about/2011_StrategicPlan.pdf.
———. *GPO Strategic Plan FY 2013–2017*. Washington, DC: GPO October 2012. Available online at http://www.gpo.gov/pdfs/about/2013-2017_StrategicPlan.pdf.
———. Strategic Vision for the 21st Century. Washington: United States Government Printing Office, December 2004. Available at http://www.gpo.gov/congressional/pdfs/04strategicplan.pdf.
———. Study of FDLP Selection Mechanisms. Available at http://fdlp.gov/component/content/article/184-gpoprojects/462-selection-mechanisms.
———. Study to Identify Measures Necessary for a Successful Transition to a More Electronic Federal Depository Program. U.S. GPO Pub. 500.11, June 1996.
House of Representatives, Committee on House Administration, Subcommittee on Oversight. *GPO—Issues and Challenges: How Will GPO Transition to the Future?* 112th Cong., 1st sess., May 11, 2011.
Thompson-Przylucki, Tracy L. Survey of Library Consortia, conducted via the International Coalition of Library Consortia. 2010.

VIDEOS

Charthouse Learning. *Fish!* Philosophy Video. Media Partners, 2012. Available at http://www.catchthefishphilosophy.com/fish_video.htm?atc=GOG&ctc=FSFV&gclid=CPzlicvK7bICFUui4AodgxEAoQ.
Field of Dreams. Gordon Company, 1989.

SPEECHES AND ADDRESSES

Humphries, LaJean, and Denise Pagh. "What Makes a Librarian Worth a Million Bucks? Valuing Staff, Resources and Services when Dollars are Scarce." Program J-4 from the 105th Annual Meeting and Conference of the American Association of Law Libraries, Boston, Massachusetts, July 21–24, 2012.
Internet Governance Forum. Chairman's Summary, Second Meeting of the Internet Governance Forum. Rio de Janeiro, November 12–15, 2007, available at http://

www.intgovforum.org/cms/Rio_Meeting/Chair-man%20Summary.FINAL.16.11.2007.pdf.

Pearson, Sarah, et al. "Seminoles and Gators: Can Shared Patron Driven Acquisitions of EBooks Overcome the Rivalry?" Presentation at the annual meeting of the Southeastern Chapter of the American Association of Law Libraries, Clearwater Beach, Florida, March 22–24, 2012.

Reischer, Bridget. Statement at FCIL-SIS Foreign Law Selectors Interest Group Meeting, American Association of Law Librarians Annual Meeting, July 22, 2012.

Smith-Butler, Lisa. *Does Your Building Reflect Your Law School?* Program presentation, American Bar Association, Bricks'NBytes: Continuous Renovations, San Diego, California, March 2012, available at http://www.slideshare.net/lsb32031/does-your-building-reflect-your-law-school-11980053.

———. *Throw It Out or Store It? The Digital Future and Unbound Collections.* Program presentation, South Eastern American Association of Law Libraries (SEAALL), Clearwater, Florida, March 2012.

Workshop for Deans and Law Librarians: Reconciling Core Values and the Bottom Line. Program presentation, Association of American Law Schools Annual Meeting, San Francisco, California, 2011.

JUDICIAL ORDERS

Court of Appeals of Maryland. *Administrative Order Creating the Conference of Maryland Court Law Library Directors,* February 21, 2008, http://www.mdcourts.gov/lawlib/audiences/cclib/conference/2008_order.pdf.

OTHER UNPUBLISHED MATERIALS

American Association of Law Libraries. *Gateways to Leadership: AALL Educational Program Handout Material.* 93rd Annual Meeting. 2000.

Association of American Publishers. Statement released by Google and the Association of American Publishers, October 4, 2012, available at http://www.publishers.org/press/85/.

Government Printing Office. *The Congressional Record,* May 9, 2011, available at http://www.gpo.gov/pdfs/news-media/press/11news24.pdf.

———. *Future Digital System (FDsys) Facts and Timeline,* available at http://gpo.gov/pdfs/news-media/press/FDsysFactSheet.pdf.

———. *GPO & Federal Judiciary Enhance Public Access to Federal Court Opinions,* May 4, 2011, available at http://gpo.gov/pdfs/news-media/press/11news23.pdf.

———. *GPO Achieves Two Milestones in Producing E-Passports,* May 23, 2007, available at http://gpo.gov/pdfs/news-media/press/07news15.pdf.

———. *GPO Advances Strategic Vision,* April 10, 2006, available at http://gpo.gov/pdfs/news-media/press/06news09.pdf.

———. *GPO and Cornell University Pilot open Government Initiative,* February 22, 2010, available at http://gpo.gov/pdfs/news-media/press/10news07.pdf.

———. *GPO and Library of Congress to Digitize Historic Documents,* February 16, 2011, available at http://gpo.gov/pdfs/news-media/press/11news13.pdf.

———. *GPO and National Archives Launch Federal Register 2.0,* July 16, 2010, available at http://gpo.gov/pdfs/news-media/press/10news26.pdf.

———. *GPO Announces Five-Year Strategic Plan,* October 22, 2012, available at http://gpo.gov/pdfs/news-media/press/12news46.pdf.

———. *GPO Begins 150-Year Anniversary Celebration,* June 23, 2010, available at http://gpo.gov/pdfs/news-media/press/10news22.pdf.

———. *GPO Celebrates 150 Years of Keeping America Informed,* March 3, 2011, available at http://gpo.gov/pdfs/news-media/press/11news14.pdf.

———. *GPO Creates its First Ever On-Line Guide to Members of Congress*, November 13, 2007, available at http://gpo.gov/pdfs/news-media/press/07news32.pdf.

———. *GPO Establishes First Preservation Librarian Position*, July 14, 2010, available at http://gpo.gov/pdfs/news-media/press/10news23.pdf.

———. *GPO Expands eBook Titles*, July 13, 2011, available at http://gpo.gov/pdfs/news-media/press/11news38.pdf.

———. *GPO Forges Ahead in Creation of Future Digital System*, April 4, 2006, available at http://gpo.gov/pdfs/news-media/press/06news08.pdf.

———. *GPO Introduces New eLearning Tool for Federal Depository Libraries*, May 15, 2012, available at http://gpo.gov/pdfs/news-media/press/12news25.pdf.

———. *GPO Joins Alliance for Digital Preservation*, June 14, 2010, available at http://gpo.gov/pdfs/news-media/press/10news19.pdf.

———. *GPO Launches Facebook Page*, February 7, 2011, available at http://gpo.gov/pdfs/news-media/press/11news09.pdf.

———. *GPO Makes Available the Federal Budget for the First Time as an App*, February 13, 2012, available at http://gpo.gov/pdfs/news-media/press/12news12.pdf.

———. *GPO Partners with Google to Offer Federal E-Books*, December 14, 2010, available at http://gpo.gov/pdfs/news-media/press/10news46.pdf.

———. *GPO Partners with Treasury Department on Public Access to Digital Collections*, October 17, 2012, available at http://www.gpo.gov/pdfs/news-media/press/12news44.pdf.

———. *GPO Produces Global Entry Card for Expedited Airport Travel*, July 27, 2011, available at http://gpo.gov/pdfs/news-media/press/11news41.pdf.

———. *GPO Produces One Million Trusted Traveler Program Cards*, May 17, 2011, available at http://gpo.gov/pdfs/news-media/press/11news28.pdf.

———. *GPO Produces 75 Million Electronic Passports*, April 24, 2012, available at http://gpo.gov/pdfs/news-media/press/12news21.pdf.

———. *GPO Receives Top Honors for Social Media Initiatives*, December 23, 2010, available at http://gpo.gov/pdfs/news-media/press/10news45.pdf.

———. *GPO Teams with Barnes & Noble to Sell Federal eBooks*, May 22, 2012, available at http://gpo.gov/pdfs/news-media/press/12news26.pdf.

———. *GPO to Authenticate by Digital Signature and Distribute Printed Copies of the Budget of the U.S. Government Fiscal Year 2009*, January 16, 2008, available at http://gpo.gov/pdfs/news-media/press/08news02.pdf.

———. *GPO's Federal Digital System (FDsys) Operational*, February 4, 2009, available at http://gpo.gov/pdfs/news-media/press/09news02.pdf.

———. *GPO's Federal Digital System Achieves Milestone*, June 5, 2012, available at http://gpo.gov/pdfs/news-media/press/12news27.pdf.

———. *GPO's Federal Digital System Achieves Record Number of Visits*, February 7, 2012, available at http://gpo.gov/pdfs/news-media/press/12news09.pdf.

———. *GSA Turns to GPO's Partnership with Google to Offer Free Government Publications Online*, April 5, 2011, available at http://gpo.gov/pdfs/news-media/press/11news17.pdf.

———. *Library Advocate Becomes Superintendent of Documents*, January 20, 2011, available at http://gpo.gov/pdfs/news-media/press/11news04.pdf.

———. *Public Printer Testifies at Congressional Hearings*, May 12, 2011, available at http://gpo.gov/pdfs/news-media/press/11news27.pdf.

———. *Public Printer Makes Historic Appointment*, December 20, 2011, available at http://gpo.gov/pdfs/news-media/press/11news74.pdf.

———. *Public Printer Makes Historic Appointment*, January 3, 2012, available at http://gpo.gov/pdfs/news-media/press/12news01.pdf.

———. *The White House, National Archives and Government Printing Office Achieve Open Government Milestone*, October 5, 2009, available at http://gpo.gov/pdfs/news-media/press/09news40.pdf.

Law Library of Congress. Collection and Services. 2012).

McCahill, M., et al. *Network Working Group, Request for Comments: 1436, The Internet Gopher Protocol* (a distributed document search and retrieval protocol). University of Minnesota, March 1993.

Memorandum of Understanding Between the U.S. Department of Commerce and the Internet Corporation for Assigned Names and Numbers, available at http://www.ntia.doc.gov/page/1998/memorandum-understanding-between-us-department-commerce-and-internet-corporation-assigned-. (1998).

Mockapetris, P. *Domain Names: Implementation and Specification, Network Working Group, Request for Comments.* November 1987.

Nova Southeastern University, Shepard Broad Law Center. *Faculty and Law Library Staff Publications,* 1974–2000, compiled by Lisa Smith-Butler; edited by Gail Levin Richmond, 2001.

Okerson, Ann, and Tom Sanville. *Inter-Consortial Licensing (ICL): Ramping up Cooperation for Win-Win Results,* November 9, 2012, available at http://2012charlestonconference.sched.org/event/2bcda9ca4a3a22e47dc3454451417ab3#.UUYpf46ZNLw.

Postel, Jon, and Zaw-Sing Su. *The Domain Naming Convention for Internet User Applications, Network Working Group, Request for Comments.* August 1982.

University of Florida, George A. Smathers Libraries. "Press Release: University of Florida and University of Miami Libraries Collaborate to Establish a Shared Collection," available at http://blogs.uflib.ufl.edu/news/2012/10/05/university-of-florida-and-the-university-of-miami-libraries-collaborate-to-establish-a-shared-collection/.

Index

AACR2 (Anglo-American Cataloging Rules), 183, 186, 190–191

AALL. *See also* American Association of Law Libraries (AALL)

AALS. *See also* Association of American Law Schools (AALS)

ABA. *See also* American Bar Association (ABA)

academic law libraries: changes in, 46–47; clientele, 15; collections, 16, 54–58, 74, 150; directors, 30, 47–50, 63; facilities, 50–54, 67; history, 5–8, 11; importance of, 45–46; job market, 17; mission and goal statements, 15, 134, 135; new roles, 82; public services, 72; reference services, 77; scope statements, 140; standards, 142, 143. *See also* faculty; students

accessibility and the digital divide, 236, 238

access points for wireless technology, 241

access to facilities, 52, 75–76

accounting departments, 121

ACL (National Association for Consortium Leadership), 270, 271

acquisitions: check-in process, 39, 93, 191; demand-driven, 137–138; ILL statistics and, 25; in Maryland State Law Library, 92; overview, 20–21, 183–185; placing orders in ILS, 185; technology and, 181

administration of Maryland State Law Library, 101

administrative offices, 52. *See also* directors of libraries

Admissions department, 48

advancement, 29–32

advocacy role of consortia, 274

after-hours reference services, 81

AI (artificial intelligence), 243

ALA. *See* American Library Association (ALA)

ALCTS (Association for Library Collections and Technical Services), 184

alerts, 59

all-in collaboratives, 281n28

American Association of Law Libraries (AALL): *AALL Reference Book*, 2; *Annual Price Index for Legal Publications*, 58; budget survey, 268; core competencies, 86; Ethical Principles, 120; FCIL and, 175; history, 2, 5, 11; membership, xv; minimum collection size, 6; national information policies, 12; Principles for Licensing Electronic Resources, 273; SISs, 11, 248; standards, 91, 144

American Bar Association (ABA): academic law library requirements, 16; accreditation requirements, 55, 56–57, 64; Law Library of Congress and, 257; management requirements, 30; minimum collection size, 6; standards, 58, 142, 143; statistical reports, 192–193

American Library Association (ALA): competencies, 283–285; Principles for Licensing Electronic Resources, 273; surveys, xvii

American Society of International Law, 148, 170

Anglo-American Cataloging Rules (AACR2), 183, 186, 190–191

Anne Arundel Community College, 101

annex collections, 153

Annual Price Index for Legal Publications (AALL), 58
Antikythera mechanism, 237, 243
Anzalone, Filippa, 49
Appellate Court Libraries and State Law Libraries Standards, 144
Archimedes, 237, 243
archives, 205
Ariel program, 41
artificial intelligence (AI), 243
Association for Library Collections and Technical Services (ALCTS), 184
Association of American Law Schools (AALS): director/dean workshops, 47; standards, 142, 142–143
audiovisual (AV) services, 17, 26, 55
authentication, 205
authority control, 186
automation, 23, 181. *See also* technology
AV (audiovisual) services, 17, 26, 55
Aztecs' historical records, 240

Balleste, Roy, 250
Beardsley, Arthur, 6
Bernardo, Anne, 114
bias, elimination of, 97
binding of serials, 191
Bitner, Harry, 6
Blaisdell, James A., 269
blanket book plans, 20
blogs, 60
BloombergBNA, 148–149
Bloomberg Law, 62, 82
book bindings, 94
book-on-the-shelf library, 57. *See also* print *vs.* digital resources
book reviews, 137
borrowing privileges, 98
Brandeis Brief, 4
Bricks'nBytes, 67
Bucknell University, 137
budgets and budgeting process: AALL survey, 268; advancement and, 32; collections and, 57–58, 185; declining law school enrollments and, 47; private law firm libraries, 120–123; technology and, 239
Bush, Jeb, 110

CALI (Center for Computer-Assisted Legal Instruction), 176, 249
California county law libraries, 109–110, 111–114
CALR (Computer Assisted Legal Research) tools, 46. *See also* Lexis; Westlaw
Career Services department, 48, 62
career tracks for librarians, 29–32
catalog: electronic resources in, 191; for government documents, 217, 219, 222; MARC records, 21; marketing, 60; in Maryland State Law Library, 93
cataloging process: AACR2, 183, 186, 190–191; classification of materials, 186; FCIL, 172–173; in Maryland State Law Library, 92–93; overview, 21–22, 186–189; in private law firm libraries, 120; RDA standards, 186
Catalog of Government Publications (CGP), 205
CCCLL (Council of California County Law Librarians), 111–114, 114–115
censorship, 246–247
Center for Computer-Assisted Legal Instruction (CALI), 176, 249
changes in law librarianship, xvi
check-in process, 93, 191
checklists for government documents, 217
Chesapeake Digital Preservation Group, 95
chronology of government printing: early years, 209–211; twentieth century, 211–213; twenty-first century, 214–217
CILP (Current Index to Legal Periodicals), 36, 59
circulation: atypical items for, 66; as central service point, 73; desks for, 50–51; overview, 22–24, 73–76; policies, 75; systems. *See* integrated library system (ILS)
claiming process, 19, 185
Claremont University Consortium (CUC), 269
Clarke, Arthur C., 235
classification of materials, 186

clerical work, 31, 39
client-development products, 37
Clio software, 41
Cohen, Morris, 6
collaborative collection development, 57
collection development: annex collections, 153; costs, 171–172; digitization projects, 160–161; FCIL, 171–172; gifts, 153–154; ILLs and, 84–85, 161–162; importance of, 162; individuality of, 133; intensity levels, 138–139; loose-leaf services, 149; lost materials, 155; newletters, 148–149; policy guidelines, 141; popular materials, 149–150, 163; scope statement, 140; selection criteria, 141–142; special collections, 154; standards, 142–144; tools for, 135–138; updating titles, 157–158. *See also* media format; weeding process
collections: in academic law libraries, 16, 54–58; in private law firm libraries, 74, 125–126; reference, 150; reflecting users' needs, 133–135; on reserve, 74, 150; size of, 6
Commerce Clearing House, 148–149
communication within consortia, 277
company information, 37
comparative law, 166. *See also* foreign, comparative, and international law (FCIL) librarianship
competencies, 283–285
Computer-Assisted Legal Instruction (CALI), 176, 249
Computer Assisted Legal Research (CALR) tools, 46. *See also* Lexis; Westlaw
computer labs, 242
computers. *See* digital resources; technology
Computing Services Special Interest Section (CS-SIS), 248
Conference of Maryland Court Law Library Directors, 100
confidentiality, 84, 160
conflict checking, 37
conflict management, 47, 49

Congress.gov, 263
Congressional Quarterly, 230
Congressional Record, 197
Congressional Record app, 263
Congressional Research Service (CRS), 257
connectivity (wireless technologies), 54, 241–242
conservation projects, 94–95, 206
consortia: collaboration within, 270–271; definitions, 267; future of, 279; history of, 268–270; ILL and, 84, 161–162; organization and governance, 276–278; role of, 271–275
Consortium Directory Online (CDO), 272
construction projects, 53–54
continuing access to resources, 146–147
continuity-of-operations plans, 95
contract negotiations, 126–127. *See also* vendors
CONTU (National Commission on New Technological Uses of Copyright Works), 161
cooperation among libraries, 84. *See also* consortia
copy-catalogers, 187
copyright law, 83, 127, 158–159. *See also* confidentiality; license agreements
core and specialized competencies, 283–285
corporate law libraries. *See* private law firm libraries
costs: of collection development, 171–172; of Congressional Quarterly, 230; consortia and, 271–272, 278, 279; of digital resources, 28, 55, 145, 160; of employees, 43; Florida's Revision 7 and, 108–109; of ILLs, 24–25, 41; of physical environment, 38; of print *vs.* electronic resources, 55
Council of California County Law Librarians (CCCLL), 111–114, 114–115
COUNTER (Counting Online Usage of Networked Electronic Resources), 275

Counting Online Usage of Networked Electronic Resources (COUNTER), 275
country research guides, 169
county law libraries: changes in, 106–109; comparison of Florida and California, 109–114; confusion surrounding, 105–106; mission and goal statements, 134, 135; today and in the future, 114–115. *See also* public law libraries
County Public Law Library Standards, 144
CQ.com, 220
CRS (Congressional Research Service), 257
CS-SIS (Computing Services Special Interest Section), 248
cube farms, 29
Current Awareness services, 59–60
Current Index to Legal Periodicals (CILP), 36, 59
customary law, 169
customer groups, 91. *See also* faculty; stakeholders; students

dashboards, 121–123
database maintenance, 188
data migration, 189
Davis, Gray, 110
DDA (demand-driven acquisition), 137–138
deaccessioning guidelines, 93
deans of law schools, 47–48
decision making and stakeholders, 47
definitions of law librarianship, 1–2
delegation of tasks, 31
demand-driven acquisition (DDA), 137–138
demographic changes, 108
Depository Library Council (DLC), 204
Depository Library Program, 198–199. *See also* Federal Depository Library Program (FDLP)
depository management/information tools, 221–223
design suggestions, 53–54
destruction of libraries, 237–238
Dialog databases, 37

Digital Commons, 61
digital divide, 236, 238
digital resources: accessibility, 76, 145–147; connectivity, 54; consortia's role in negotiating/licensing, 271–272, 279; costs, 28, 55, 145, 160; foreign law, 169; government documents, 199–200, 201–203, 220–221; issues, 144–147; levels of service with, 80; online databases, 239; preferences for, 56; preservation of, 95; in private law libraries, 74, 128; rise of, 106; serials/continuations, 190; technical services and, 191. *See also* copyright law; digitization projects; Lexis; license agreements; print *vs.* digital resources; Westlaw
digital signatures, 205
digitization projects, 56, 160–161, 218
Dina, Yemisi, 169
directional assistance, 42
directors of libraries, 30, 47–50, 63
disabled users/employees, 85
disaster preparedness documents, 95, 126
discontented employees, 50
DLC (Depository Library Council), 204
document delivery, 33, 98
do-it-yourself research aids, 35
donations from patrons, 153–154
dual degrees of librarians: FCIL, 174; not needed, 118; as requirement, 7, 17, 29, 30

e-book collections, 145–146. *See also* digital resources
Education. *See* training of librarians; training of users
Einstein, Albert, 240
electronic communication, 77
electronic data interchange (EDI), 40, 185
Electronic Resource Guide (American Society of International Law), 170
electronic resource-management tools (ERMs) for licenses, 128
electronic services librarian (ESL), 26–28, 247–249

E-mail reference services, 97
employee tours, 18
employment prospects, 17, 173–174.
    See also advancement
English-language publications for
    FCIL librarians, 172
entanglement, 243–244
ephemeral information, 37
*Essential Titles for Public Use in Paper
    Format*, 206
ethical issues, 97
Excel dashboards, 121
experimentation in consortia, 274

face-to-face discussions, 77
faculty: information services, 60;
    relationships with, 48; research
    services, 61; technology and, 59, 61
Failing Law Schools (Tamanaha), 57
fair-use doctrine, 159
FCIL. *See* foreign, comparative, and
    international law (FCIL)
    librarianship
FDsys (Federal Digital System), 205,
    208, 220
Federal Depository Library Manual, 206
Federal Depository Library Program
    (FDLP), 202, 206–207, 222, 287–292
Federal Digital System (FDsys), 205,
    208, 220
federal document finding aids:
    bibilographic tools, 217–219;
    depository management/
    information tools, 221–223;
    electronic databases, 220–221;
    secondary sources, 223–224
film collections, 150, 163
Finley, Elizabeth, 6
firm law libraries. *See* private law firm
    libraries
first-sale doctrine, 146, 159
Fish (video), 49
Flores, Arturo, 168
Florida county law libraries, 108–109,
    110–113, 115
Florida State, Court & County Law
    Libraries (FSCCLL), 111
Florida State University, 138
flowcharts in research, 130

food in libraries, 52
foreign, comparative, and international
    law (FCIL) librarianship: about,
    165–166; attractions of, 173–174;
    number of positions, 179;
    qualifications, 174–176;
    responsibilities, 167–173; sample
    day in the life, 176–178
foreign and international law (FIL)
    collections, 151
foreign language skills, 78
foreign law, 165–166, 256–258, 259, 260,
    260–261
Foreign Law Guide (Reynolds and
    Flores), 168
foreign legal systems, 167–169
foreign publishers, 21
formal training of users, 99
Frost, Robert, 249
furnishings in libraries, 52, 53
future of law librarianship, xvi–xviii,
    11–12
future of librarianship, 208

Gallagher, Marian Gould, 6
general principles of law, 170
geographic information, 37
Giegengac, Augustus E., 199
gifts, 153–154
Global Legal Information Catalog
    (GLIC), 262
Global Legal Information Network
    (GLIN), 258, 262
goal statements, 134–135
Google Books Project, 56
government documents: beginnings,
    195–198; bibilographic tools for
    federal documents, 217–219; current
    digital and print options, 207–208;
    depository management/
    information tools for federal
    documents, 221–223; electronic
    databases for federal documents,
    220–221; future of, 208; growth and
    downsizing in twentieth century,
    198–203; recent initiatives, 205–207;
    secondary sources for federal
    documents, 223–224; strategic
    planning in twenty-first century,

203–204. *See also* chronology of government printing

government law libraries. *See* county law libraries; Maryland State Law Library; public law libraries

Government Printing Office Electronic Information Access Enhancement Act, 201

Government Printing Office (GPO). *See* Federal Depository Library Program (FDLP); government documents

graphical user interface (GUI), 242

grey literature, 125

Guide to Caribbean Law Research (Dina), 169

GUI (graphical user interface), 242

Harvard Law Library, 171, 172

Harvard Law School, 3–4, 5

Hasse, Adelaide, 198

HathiTrust, 56, 218

Hazelton, Penny, 6

HeinOnline, 28, 42, 220

Heisenberg, Werner, 244

help desk, 51

Hicks, Frederick, 6

history: AALL, 2, 5, 11

history of law librarianship: academic libraries, 5–8, 11; classic era, 3–4; digital revolution in, 10–11; private sector age, 8–9; questions about the future, 11–12. *See also* chronology of government printing; government documents

horse analogy, 31

Houdek, Frank, 2

IALL (International Association of Law Librarians), 175

ICL (interconsortial licensing) opportunities, 273

ICOLC (International Coalition of Library Consortia), 270, 271, 273

IFLA (International Federation of Library Associations and Institutions), 246

IIC: International Review of Intellectual Property and Competition Law, 177

ILL process. *See* interlibrary loan (ILL) process

ILS. *See* integrated library system (ILS)

incarcerated clients, 36

indexes to government documents, 217, 218, 219

Index to Foreign Legal Periodicals, 178

Index to Legal Periodicals (ILP), 59

information sharing, 235–236. *See also* consortia

information society, defined, 251n21

Information Technology (IT), 27

Innovative Interfaces, 238

institutional support of libraries, 101

Instructions to Depository Libraries, 206

integrated library system (ILS): about, 73–74; acquisitions and, 20–21; check-ins, 39; government documents and, 205; grey literature and, 125; in Maryland State Law Library, 93; placing orders in, 185; in private law firm libraries, 120; serials/continuations and, 191; statistics from, 192–193; systems librarian for, 189

integrating resource, 190

interconsortial licensing (ICL) opportunities, 273

interlibrary loan (ILL) process: collection development and, 161–162; consortium involvement, 84, 84–85; costs, 24–25, 41; DDA and, 137; overview, 24–25, 83, 84–85; SEFLIN, 41

International Association of Law Librarians (IALL), 175

International Coalition of Library Consortia (ICOLC), 270, 271, 273

International Federation of Library Associations and Institutions (IFLA), 246

international law, 166, 169–170. *See also* foreign, comparative, and international law (FCIL) librarianship

Internet: accessibility to, 236, 238; archives on, 219; GUI, 242; information sharing, 235–236; search engines, 219; Web page

hyperlinks, 27
Internet Corporation for Assigned Names and Numbers (ICANN), 246–247
Internet governance, 245–247
Internet Protocol (IP) addresses, 27, 42, 245
invoice coding, 121
IP (Internet Protocol) addresses, 27, 42, 245
IT (Information Technology), 27

Jacobs, James A., 204
Jacobs, James R., 204
Jacobstein, Mike, 6
Jefferson, Thomas, 255, 256
jobbers, 19–20, 40, 184
job markets, 17, 173–174
Joint Resolution in Relation to the Public Printing, 197
journals, 41, 147. *See also* digital resources; magazines; serials/continuations
JSTOR, 147
judicial decisions, 3, 5
Jurist's Paper Chase, 59

Kaufman, Billie Jo, 250
Kirby, Michael, xviii

ladder of authority, 170
Langdell, Christopher Columbus, 5, 45
language skills, 174–175
law degree. *See* dual degrees of librarians
law firm libraries. *See* private law firm libraries
law librarianship: defining, 1–2; effects of society on, xvi; in transition, 250
Law Librarians' Society of Washington, D. C., 220
Law Library Journal (LLJ), 2, 7
Law Library of Congress: collection, 259–260; FCIL training, 175; history, 255–258; overview, 255; Reading Rooms, 257–258, 261; services and products, 260–263
laws of library science, 133
legal bibliographies, 6

Legal Information Preservation Alliance (LIPA), 56
legal secretaries, 8–9
legislative advocates for county law libraries, 111
Lexis: about, 42; costs, 28; ownership of, 11; as pioneer, 10; rise of, 106; specialized services, 37; training students in, 62; watches, 43, 148
LibGuides, 61
librarians of influence, 6
librarians (terminology), 11
library facility. *See* physical environment
library hours, 52, 75–76
Library of Alexandria, 237
Library of Congress: authority records based on, 186; classification system, 74, 172–173, 187, 258; subject headings, 187
library users: differences in, 15–16; prisoner clients, 36; privacy of, 77, 160; problem patrons, 86; *pro se* patrons, 35, 43, 79. *See also* faculty; students
license agreements, 83, 127–128, 146, 158–160, 273, 279. *See also* copyright law
LIPA (Legal Information Preservation Alliance), 56
listservs, 35, 44, 176
LLJ (Law Library Journal), 2, 7
LOCKSS Pilot Project, 206
loose-leaf services, 40, 149
lost materials, 155
lunch schedules, 34
Lyrasis, 273–274

machine-readable cataloging (MARC) records, 21
magazines, 149. *See also* digital resources; journals; serials/continuations
mail receiving/processing, 19–20
maintenance of facilities, 52
management, 30–32, 119. *See also* academic law libraries; directors of libraries; private law firm libraries; public law libraries

Managing from the Heart, 49
MARC records, 21
Marke, Julius, 6
Maryland Access to Justice
    Commission, 100
Maryland State Law Library:
    administration, 101; collections,
    90–95; instructional programs,
    98–101; mission, 90; reference
    services, 96–98
masters in library information science
    (MLIS), 118–119, 174
material selection policies. *See*
    collection development
*Max Planck Encyclopedia of Public
    International Law*, 170, 177
media format, 91, 125; digital resource
    issues, 144–147; microfilm, 147–148;
    selection options, 184
membership in consortia, 277
mergers of consortia, 274
Mersky, Roy, 6
Miami-Dade County Law Library, 113,
    115
microfilm format, 26, 147–148, 191
Microform Project Initiative, 199
missent items, 19
misshelved items, 23
mission of libraries, 90, 134
MLIS (masters in library information
    science), 118–119, 174
mobile applications, 128, 145–146
modular furniture, 52, 53
monographs, 190
Muller v. Oregon, 4
multistakeholder process, 246
Murphy, William, 6

National Association for Consortium
    Leadership (ACL), 270, 271
National Commission on New
    Technological Uses of Copyright
    Works (CONTU), 161
National Information Standards
    Organization (NISO), 275
National Printing Office, 196
negotiation of contracts, 126–127
newletters, 148–149
newspapers, 149

NISO (National Information Standards
    Organization), 275
nonlegal reference, 42

Oakley, Robert, 12
OCLC (Online Computer Library
    Center): Clio software, 41; ILL
    system, 24–25; management tools,
    238; services, 21, 188; WorldCat,
    183, 188
off-hours reference services, 81
Office of Technology Assessment
    (OTA), 200–201
office raids, 34
off-site storage of materials, 57
Olmecs, 240
online resources. *See* digital resources
opt-in collaboratives, 281n28
OTA (Office of Technology
    Assessment), 200–201
outreach education, 100–101
outsourcing of services, 189, 191

paper format of serials, 26
Parma, Rosamond, 6
patron-driven acquisition. *See*
    demand-driven acquisition (DDA)
Patterson, Franklin, 269–270
Pauling, Linus Carl, 267
people finders, 37
people information, 37
People's Law Library of Maryland
    Web site, 99–100
perpetual access to digital resources,
    146–147
personal interactions, 31
Pew Internet Project, 238
photons, 243, 245
physical environment: allocation for
    collections, 93; costs of, 38;
    deterioration of, 108; furnishings in
    libraries, 52, 53; office spaces, 29;
    shaping and reflecting usage, 85;
    stress of construction, 67. *See also*
    shelves; stacks
policies: gift, 153–154; ILL, 85;
    newsletters, 149
political climate, 111
popular materials, 149–150, 163

Portico, 147
practice materials, 16
practice of law, 79, 97
preorder searching, 182–183
prepayment for materials, 40
preservation projects, 94–95, 206
Price, Derek J. de Solla, 237
Price, Miles, 6
primary authority, 3. *See also* judicial
    decisions
primary sources, 92
Principles for Licensing Electronic
    Resources, 273
Printing Act, 197
print *vs.* digital resources: balancing,
    91, 95, 156–157; costs, 55; decreases
    in tangible items, 200; need for both,
    240
prisoner clients, 36
privacy of library users, 77, 160
private law firm libraries: budgets,
    120–123; circulation services, 75;
    clientele, 15; collection
    development, 16, 158; collections,
    74, 125–126; copyright law and, 127;
    daily activities, 33–35; dual degrees
    of librarians in, 17; education
    requirements, 118–119; future of,
    129; history, 8–9, 11; job markets, 17;
    mission and goal statements, 134,
    134–135, 135; new roles, 81;
    newsletter policy, 149; professional
    development, 119–120; public
    services, 72; reference services, 77,
    81; scope statements, 140; strategic
    planning, 123–124; uniqueness of,
    117–118; vendors, 126–127
Private Law Librarians SIS, 11
private sector age, 8–9
private subscription libraries, 3
problem patrons, 86
professional catalogers, 187
professional development:
    organizations for, 44; for private
    law librarians, 119–120. *See also*
    advancement
profiles: for outsourcing, 189; for
    vendors, 136
project management, 123–124

Project MUSE, 147
ProQuest, 37, 220–221
pro se patrons, 35, 43, 79
proxy servers, 27
public law libraries: about, 35–36;
    clientele, 15; collection
    development, 16; dual degrees, 17;
    job markets, 17; new roles, 82;
    public services, 72; reference
    services, 77; scope statements, 140.
    See also county law libraries;
    Maryland State Law Library
public printing. *See* government
    documents
public services: background
    requirements, 71; core
    competencies, 86; definition of, 87;
    overview, 22–24; physical
    environment for, 85; problem
    patrons, 86; requirements, 73; role
    of, 71; scope of, 72. *See also*
    circulation; interlibrary loan (ILL)
    process; reference services
publishers: acquisitions dealing with,
    21; catalogs of, 136; consolidation of,
    11; definitions, 184; jobbers and, 40;
    Law Library of Congress, 262;
    stamping materials from, 43
purchase orders, 185
purchases. *See* acquisitions
Purdue University, 137

quantum computers, 243–245
qubit, 243
questions on reference desk, 96
Quiet, 49

Ranganathan, S. R., 133
rare book collections, 260
RDA (Resource Description and
    Access) standards, 186
Reed, Elsevier, 11. *See also* Lexis
reference desk, 51
reference offices, 52
reference services: collections, 150;
    directional assistance, 42; of FCIL
    librarians, 167–170; Maryland State
    Law Library, 96–98; new roles,
    81–82; nonlegal reference, 42;

overview, 28–29; policies, 82; practice of law and, 79; reference interviews, 76–77, 96–97; role of, 76; service levels, 80; specialized competencies, 285; specialized knowledge, 78–79; technology, 81
regional research guides, 169
Reischer, Bridget, 171
relationships: in academic law libraries, 47–50
remote collections, 153
research instruction, 80
reserve collection, 74, 150
reshelving function, 23
Resource Description and Access (RDA) standards, 186
Reynolds, Thomas A., 168
Roalfe, William, 6
RSS feeds, 44, 60
Russo, Antoinette (Babe), 6

salary caps, 29
San Diego county law libraries, 109–110, 111–114
SCC-SIS (State Court and County Special Interest Section), 144
scope statements, 140
search engines, 219
searches in databases, 144–145
secondary sources, 91, 92, 223–224
Second Life, 128
SEFLIN, 41
selection of materials, 141–142, 183, 185. *See also* acquisitions; collection development
self-discipline, 32
self-help Web sites, 99–100
self-represented groups, 107
self-starters, 32
Serials Acquisitions Glossary (ALCTS), 184
serials/continuations: costs, 28; DDA and, 138; definitions, 183, 190–191; department for, 188; formats, 26–28, 38; overview, 190–191; routing among faculty, 59. *See also* Lexis; Westlaw
Serial Sets, 195
series definition, 183

SERU, 275
Servant Leadership, 49
shareholder value, 119, 120–121, 124, 129
shelf reading, 23, 31
shelf-ready materials, 184, 187
shelves: cleaning, 24; open space on, 32; planning for, 53. *See also* stacks
Shuler, John A., 204
SISs (Special Interest Sections), 11, 144, 248
SkyRiver Technology Solutions, 21, 40
slips program, 20
Small, A. J., 5
social activities, 65, 66
social influence of law librarianship, xvi
social media, 62, 128, 206, 262
South East Florida Library and Information Network (SEFLIN), 41
special collections, 74, 154
Special Interest Sections (SISs), 11, 144, 248
specialized competencies, 284–285
specialized knowledge of reference staff, 78–79
specialized services, 36–37
Special Library Association, 11
stacks: designing, 53; maintenance of, 23–24, 39, 74. *See also* shelves
staff and director relationships, 49–50
staff directories, 60
stakeholders, 47, 246
standards: AALL, 91, 144; AALS, 142, 142–143; ABA, 58, 142, 143; academic law libraries, 142, 143; collection development, 142–144; NISO, 275; RDA, 186
Standards for Appellate Court Libraries & State Law Libraries (AALL), 91
State Court and County Special Interest Section (SCC-SIS), 144
state government: document finding aids, 224–225; law libraries, 102; online resources, 225–226. *See also* Maryland State Law Library; public law libraries
state practice, 170
Statistical Abstract, 231

statistics, 25, 192–193
strategic planning, 123–124
"Strategic Vision for the 21st Century", 203
stress of construction, 67
students: directors' relationships with, 50; "hiding" library materials, 39; services for, 61–62; Student Services department, 48; supervision of, 31
study rooms, 54
subject bibliographies, 61
SuDocs (Superintendent of Documents) classification system, 92, 198, 218
suggestion of five, 161
superceded materials, 156
Superintendent of Documents (SuDocs) classification system, 92, 198, 218
systems librarians, 189

Tamanaha, Brian, 57
tangible items, 207. *See also* print *vs.* digital resources
teaching duties, 171
technical services: about, 19–22; as heart of library, 182; location of, 52; overview of functions, 181; processing mail, 19–20; sorting/distributing mail, 19; statistics, 192–193; technology changing, 181–182. *See also* acquisitions; cataloging process
technology: changes in, 238–240; digital revolution history, 10–11; for faculty, 59, 61; help desk, 51; importance of information and, 237; maximizing future innovations, 249–250; reference services and, 81; shifting role of librarians in, 72; technical services and, 181–182; trends, 248; Wi-Fi technologies, 54, 241–242. *See also* digital resources; electronic services librarian (ESL); Internet
teleportation, 244
Tennant, Roy, 249–250
termination of employees, 50
THOMAS.gov, 221, 263

Thomson Publishing, 11. *See also* West Publishing Company
Title 44, 201–202
top-level domain (TLD), 245
training of librarians: FCIL, 174, 175–176; in ILS use, 189; in law firm libraries, 118–119
training of users: in digital resources, 62; instructional programs, 98–99; in Maryland State Law Library, 98–99; outreach, 100–101; via Web sites, 99–100
training rooms, 54
Transition Plan for move to electronic formats, 202–203
translations of foreign law, 175
treaties, 169, 170
trends: in the law, 78; in technical services, 182; in technology, 248
Trotter, Victoria, xvii

UCFF (Uniform Civil Filing Fee plan), 113
unauthorized practice of law, 43
uniform cataloging, 21
Uniform Civil Filing Fee plan (UCFF), 113
United Nations, 169, 236
University of Florida, 138
U.S. Congressional Serial Sets, 195
U.S. Department of Commerce, 246–247
U.S. Government Printing Office. *See* Federal Depository Library Program (FDLP)
user authentication, 27

vendors: collection profiles, 136; consortium role as liaison, 272, 279; definitions, 184; placing orders, 185; private law firm libraries and, 126–127; selecting, 184. *See also* license agreements
virtual libraries, 191. *See also* digital resources
virtual private network (VPN), 27
virtual reference desk (VRD), 248
vLex, 172
VPN (virtual private network), 27

VRD (virtual reference desk), 248

Web page hyperlinks, 27
weeding process, 43, 155–157
Wendell H. Ford Government
    Publications Reform Act, 202
Westlaw: about, 42; costs, 28; as
    pioneer, 10; reference librarians'
    role in, 82; specialized services, 37;
    training students in, 62; watches, 43,
148
West Publishing Company, 8, 11
wireless (Wi-Fi) technologies, 54,
    241–242
WorldCat, 15, 183, 188
World Wide Web, 242. *See also* Internet

Yeo, Shinjoung, 204

zones of libraries, 52

About the Contributors

Steve Anderson is the director of the Maryland State Law Library, a position he has held since 2005. Prior to that, he served as director of research services for the Baltimore law firm of Gordon Feinblatt Rothman Hoffberger & Hollander, LLC. From 1995 to 1998, he was an associate librarian at the Baltimore County Circuit Court Library. He holds a BA from the University of California, Berkeley, a JD from the University of Maryland School of Law, and an MA in library science from the University of Arizona. He has been active in professional activities throughout his career, and in December 2011, was elected vice president/president-elect of the American Association of Law Libraries. He is a member of the Maryland Access to Justice Commission and the Conference of Maryland Court Law Library Directors.

James E. Andrews is the director and associate professor of the University of South Florida (USF) School of Information. The school offers an ALA-accredited master's degree in library and information science, in which students can choose to focus their studies on law librarianship, and also offers a bachelor of science in information studies. Dr. Andrews earned both his master's in library and information science and PhD in information science from the University of Missouri–Columbia School of Information Science and Learning Technologies. His doctoral work was funded by Predoctoral Medical Informatics Fellowship through the National Institutes of Health, National Library of Medicine, as part of the Health Informatics Training Program Grant at the University of Missouri School of Medicine. Prior to coming to USF, Dr. Andrews was a graduate faculty member in the College of Communication and Information Studies, University of Kentucky. There, his work focused on health communication and health informatics. Dr. Andrews is active professionally at the state, national, and international levels, and he has served on the editorial boards for the *Journal of the Medical Library Association*, and *Mousaion*, the international journal of the University of South Africa, Department of Information Science (where he is also a research fellow). Currently, Dr. Andrews's research has been in cancer genetics–related information behaviors, and clinical research informatics, and he has developed strong collaborative ties with colleagues at USF Health. He has coauthored/authored numerous journal articles, conference presentations at all levels, and the first edited book on clinical research informatics.

Roy Balleste, J.S.D., is Law Library Director and Professor of Law at St. Thomas University, in Miami Gardens, Florida. Professor Balleste has concentrated his scholarship in the areas of internet governance, human rights and the relationship between information, technology, and people. He teaches internet governance at the School of Law. In November 2007, he participated in the Second UN Internet Governance Forum in Rio de Janeiro. He also participated in the Fifth UN Internet Governance Forum in Vilnius, Lithuania, September 2010. Professor Balleste is a member of the Global Internet Governance Academic Network (GigaNet), and a member of ICANN's Noncommercial Users Stakeholder Group (NCSG-NCUC). Professor Balleste served one tour in the US. Navy and one tour in the U.S. Army. He is a life member of the Disabled American Veterans.

Robert C. Berring Jr. is a professor of law at Boalt Hall Law School, Berkeley. He is a past president of the American Association of Law Libraries, and former dean of the School of Library and Information Studies at Berkeley. He has also served as interim dean of Boalt Hall Law School. Berring worked at the law libraries of the University of Illinois, the University of Texas, Harvard University, and the University of Washington before coming to Boalt as a professor of law and director of the Law Library in 1982. He holds a BA (cum laude) from Harvard College (1971); a JD from Boalt Hall Law School (1974); and an MLIS, University of California, Berkeley (1974). He has published widely on the topic of legal research and legal information.

Frederick W. Dingledy is a reference librarian at the College of William & Mary Law School. Dingledy has a BS from the Pennsylvania State University, a JD (cum laude) from the University of Minnesota Law School, and a MALIS from the University of Wisconsin–Madison. He has served as president of the Virginia Association of Law Libraries.

Karl T. Gruben is the associate dean for library and information services, director of the Legal Research Center, and professor of law at the University of San Diego School of Law. Karl was formerly with the St. Thomas University's School of Law Library in Miami Gardens, Florida. He has also worked in law firm libraries, as well as in a court law library. He holds a BA and an MLS from the University of Texas at Austin, and a JD from the South Texas College of Law in Houston, Texas. He has served as president of the Houston Area Law Librarians and on the executive committee of the American Association of Law Libraries' Private Law Libraries SIS. He has also served as an officer, the secretary, and board member on the executive board of the American Association of Law Libraries. Among his publications are *A Reference Guide to Texas Law and Legal History* and contributions to *Law Library Journal*.

Benjamin J. Keele is a reference librarian at the College of William & Mary Law School. He earned a BA from the University of Nebraska–Lincoln and a JD and MLS from Indiana University–Bloomington.

Anne Klinefelter is director of the Law Library and associate professor of law at the University of North Carolina at Chapel Hill. She teaches privacy law courses and writes and speaks on information policy and law topics, including privacy and confidentiality law, the First Amendment, copyright law, and licensing, particularly as these areas apply to libraries. Professor Klinefelter has taught law librarianship and legal research courses to law and library school students and is active in law library associations and consortia. Prior to her work at the University of North Carolina, Anne Klinefelter served in a number of public services positions and as acting director of the Law Library at the University of Miami. She also has experience as a reference librarian in the law libraries at Boston University and the University of Alabama and as a reference librarian at the Gorgas Main Library at the University of Alabama.

Sonia Luna-Lamas is the associate director and head of technical services at St. Thomas University School of Law, in Miami Gardens, Florida. Her previous positions include foreign and comparative law cataloger and serials librarian at the University of Miami School of Law Library. She holds a BA from the University of Miami and an MLS from the University of South Florida. She has held various positions in county, state, and regional library associations, as well as chaired various SIS and technical services–related network groups, and organized and helped present various workshops and institutes in the library field.

Roy M. Mersky is deceased. Before his death, he was a member of the University of Texas law school faculty and the director of its law library since 1965. Professor Mersky held the Harry M. Reasoner Regents Chair in Law and the Hyder Centennial Faculty Fellowship in Law. He was also a professor in the university's graduate School of Information, where he taught courses and was involved in the development of the legal information/law librarianship program.

Professor Mersky was a pioneer in law librarianship. Under his leadership, the Jamail Center for Legal Research became one of the most important legal research institutes in the United States. He was known for his innovative approaches to library management and services and his strong commitment to improving library resources, services, and facilities. He received the American Association of Law Library's 2005 Marian Gallagher Distinguished Service Award.

Professor Mersky was widely published and a frequent lecturer, particularly in the areas of legal research, language and law, and the history of the United States Supreme Court. He coauthored *Fundamentals of Legal Research*, which is the recognized authority on legal research and the standard textbook used in first-year legal research courses across the United States. He completed *The First 108 Justices* with Bill Bader (W. S. Hein & Co., 2004), which examines and evaluates the character, intellect, and statesmanship of current and former U.S. Supreme Court justices; and *Landmark Supreme Court Cases: The Most Influential Decisions of the Supreme Court of the United States*, with Gary Hartman and Cindy Tate Slavinski (Facts on File, 2004). He also coedited a multivolume series, The Supreme Court of the United States: Hearings and Reports on Successful and Unsuccessful Justices by the Senate Judicial Committee, and collaborates on the Documentary History of the Legal Aspects of Abortion in the United States, with the most recent volume in that series published in 2003.

Professor Mersky made significant contributions to the field of law, active in national law and library organizations. Professor Mersky is a member of the state bars of Wisconsin, Texas, and New York, and has been admitted to practice before the Supreme Court of the United States. He routinely served as a consultant to many academic institutions and law firms, as well as private corporations seeking to establish or organize collections of law-related materials. Active in both state and civic organizations, Professor Mersky was an executive board member of the Wisconsin Non-Resident Lawyers Division, past president of the Texas Humanities Alliance, and an executive board member and treasurer of the Texas Supreme Court Historical Society.

Professor Mersky received his BS in 1948, a JD in 1952, and a master's degree in library science in 1953 from the University of Wisconsin–Madison.

Jennifer Bryan Morgan has been the documents librarian at the Maurer School of Law at Indiana University since 2001. She earned her BA from Saint Mary-of-the-Woods College in 1990 and her MLS from Indiana University–Bloomington in 1995. As documents librarian, Morgan is responsible for providing specialized reference service in the use of U.S. government documents and directing the law library's U.S. government depository program. She teaches legal research in the Legal Research and Writing Program and provides guest lectures on specialized legal research in other law school classes. She is also an affiliated faculty member at Indiana University's School of Library and Information Science. Serving on local and national committees, she is a member of the Indiana University Librarians Association; the American Association of Law Libraries, and its Government Documents Special Interest Section; INDIGO (Indiana Networking for Documents Information and Organizations); and the Ohio Regional Association of Law Libraries. Morgan's research interests are in the areas of legislative history and electronic access to state and local government information.

Lisa Smith-Butler is the associate dean and director and a professor of law at the Charleston School of Law, Sol Blatt Jr. Law Library, where she has been since 2009. She received her BA (magna cum laude) from Hastings College, her JD from Creighton University (cum laude), and her MLS from Clark Atlanta University. Before entering the field of librarianship, she practiced law in Georgia. In the librarianship field, she worked as reference/operations librarian for the Atlanta firm of Powell, Goldstein, Frazier, & Murphy. She then moved to Georgia State University, where she headed public services. Before joining the Charleston School of Law, she was the associate director and later assistant dean at Nova Southeastern University, Shepard Broad Law Center, Law Library and Technology Center. She was president of the South Florida Association of Law Libraries (SFALL). At Charleston, she teaches advanced legal research and children and the law.

Robert E. Riger is director of research for pushDC.com and author of the blog techbytes4lawyers. He formerly served as director of libraries at the San Diego County Law Library and executive director at the Miami Dade County Law Library. Prior to that, he managed private law firm libraries in New York. Riger holds a BA in history from Pace University and an MS in library and information science from Pratt Institute. He has served as president of the South Florida chapter of the American Association of Law Libraries and vice president of the California Council of County Law Libraries. Riger is a recipient of the American Association of Law Libraries Presidential Certificate of Appreciation for his leadership and advocacy on behalf of restoring funding for Florida's county law libraries.

Abigail F. Ellsworth Ross is the library manager at the law firm of Keller and Heckman LLP in Washington, D.C., and has worked in law firm libraries for fifteen years. As head of the library department, she is responsible for managing the print and electronic resources for all the offices of the firm. She is also an adjunct faculty member at the Catholic University of America, teaching law librarianship. Ross has served in many volunteer and elected positions with AALL and SLA and has spoken many times at both associations' annual conferences. She holds a BSLA from Georgetown University and an MLS from the University of Maryland.

Mary Rumsey is foreign, comparative, and international law librarian at the University of Minnesota Law Library. She holds a BA from the University of Wisconsin, a JD from the University of Chicago, and an MLIS from Dominican University. Among her publications are contributions to

Law Library Journal, Legal References Services Quarterly, the EISIL project of the American Society of International Law, and other periodicals. With Marci Hoffman, she wrote *International and Foreign Legal Research: A Coursebook* (2nd ed. Brill, 2012).

Sara Sampson is deputy director of the library and clinical assistant professor of law at the University of North Carolina at Chapel Hill. Before arriving at UNC, she worked at Georgetown University as head of reference and at Ohio State University College of Law as a reference librarian. Sampson has taught legal research and writing courses to law school, library school, and paralegal students. Actively engaged in professional associations, she speaks regularly at library and legal writing conferences, has chaired AALL's Research and Publication Committee, and served as the secretary/treasurer of the Academic Law Libraries Special Interest Section of AALL. Her publications reflect her interest in political law, reference services, and teaching legal research.

Jennifer E. Sekula is the head of access services/foreign and international law specialist at the College of William & Mary Law School library. She has a BS from the College of William & Mary, a JD and a master of studies in environmental law from Vermont Law School, and an MSLS from the Catholic University of America.

Christine Sellers is a research specialist at Nelson Mullins in Columbia, South Carolina. She previously served as a legal reference librarian in the Law Library of Congress in Washington, D.C., created the Law Librarians of Leisure blog, and was a senior research librarian at Haynsworth Sinkler Boyd in South Carolina. Christine holds a bachelor's degree in art history and English from Wellesley College, as well as a JD and a master's of library and information science from the University of South Carolina. She is an active member of the American Association of Law Libraries and the Southeastern Chapter of the American Association of Law Libraries.

Tracy L. Thompson-Przylucki serves as the executive director of the New England Law Library Consortium (NELLCO), in Albany, New York. NELLCO is an international consortium of law libraries. Prior to assuming that post in 2001, Thompson-Przylucki served as international reference librarian at the Lillian Goldman Law Library at Yale Law School. She is an active member of the American Association of Law Libraries, having served on numerous committees, most recently as chair of the Copyright Committee and cochair of the Task Force on Library Procurement Process Improvements. She also serves on the board of the Association for Consortium Leadership (ACL) and is an active member of the American Society of Association Executives (ASAE). Thompson-Przylucki is a graduate of the University of South Florida and the Yale Law School.